VOID
Library of
Davidson College

NEW DIRECTIONS IN
FEDERAL TAX POLICY
FOR THE 1980s

NEW DIRECTIONS IN FEDERAL TAX POLICY FOR THE 1980s

Edited by
CHARLS E. WALKER
and
MARK A. BLOOMFIELD

The American Council for Capital Formation:
Center for Policy Research

BALLINGER PUBLISHING COMPANY
Cambridge, Massachusetts
A Subsidiary of Harper & Row, Publishers, Inc.

Copyright © 1983 by Ballinger Publishing Company, with the exception of Chapter 3—Fiscal Policy for the 1980s, copyright © by Martin Feldstein. All rights reserved. No part of this publication may be reproduced, stored in a retrieval system, or transmitted in any form or by any means, electronic, mechanical, photocopy, recording or otherwise, without the prior written consent of the publisher.

International Standard Book Number: 0-88410-638-1

Library of Congress Catalog Card Number: 83-17242

Printed in the United States of America

Library of Congress Cataloging in Publication Data

Main entry under title:

New directions in federal tax policy for the 1980s.

   "American Council for Capital Formation: Center for Policy Research."
   Includes index.
   1. Taxation—United States—Addresses, essays, lectures.
I. Walker, Charles E. (Charls Edward), 1923-   .
II. Bloomfield, Mark A. (Mark Andrew), 1949-
HJ2381.N47   1983   353.0072'4   83-17242
ISBN 0-88410-638-1

Contents

List of Figures	xi
List of Tables	xiii
Preface	xv
Overview—*Charls E. Walker and Mark A. Bloomfield*	xvii

PART I THE POLITICAL AND ECONOMIC CHALLENGE FOR TAX REFORM

Chapter 1
The Political Environment
—*Horace W. Busby*   3

Chapter 2
The Challenge for Tax Reform
—*John B. Connally*   13

Chapter 3
Fiscal Policy for the 1980s
—*Martin Feldstein*   23

Chapter 4
Monetary Policy for the 1980s
—*Paul A. Volcker*   35

PART II SOLUTIONS TO THE PROBLEM WITH THE TAX SYSTEM: REFORM OF THE FEDERAL INCOME TAX

**Chapter 5
The Accelerated Cost Recovery System:
An Evaluation of the 1981 and 1982 Cost
Recovery Provisions**
—*Norman B. Ture* 47

Discussants:

Does ACRS Foster Efficient Capital Allocation?
—*Alan J. Auerbach* 77
The Effects of ERTA and TEFRA on the Cost of Capital
—*George N. Hatsopoulos* 79
Changes in Capital Cost Recovery Policies: Costs and Benefits
—*Frederic W. Hickman* 89

**Chapter 6
Saving Incentives: The Role of Tax Policy**
—*Michael J. Boskin* 93

Discussants:

Expanding Saving Incentives: Practical and Political Problems
—*Edwin S. Cohen* 112
The Effect of Government Absorption of Savings on Capital Formation
—*William Fellner* 116
The Congressional Outlook for Increased Saving Incentives
—*W. Henson Moore* 119

**Chapter 7
Capital Gains: An Evaluation of the 1978
and 1981 Tax Cuts**
—*Gerald E. Auten* 121

Discussants:

The Option of a Tax Deferred Rollover on Capital Gains
—*Alan Cranston* 149
Lower Capital Gains Tax Rates and the Stock Market
—*Steven R. Resnick* 150

Proposals to Index Capital Gains
—*James W. Wetzler* 154
Was the 1978 Capital Gains Tax Cut Successful?
—*Ed Zschau* 157

Chapter 8
The State of the Corporate Income Tax: Who Pays It? Should It Be Repealed?
—*Arnold C. Harberger* 161

Discussants:

Is Repeal of the Corporate Income Tax Possible?
—*Robert F. Dee* 171
The Energy Industry and Federal Tax Policy
—*Tor Meloe* 172
Another View of the Corporate Income Tax
—*Joseph A. Pechman* 177
Political Reality and the Corporate Income Tax
—*Steven D. Symms* 180

PART III   SOLUTIONS TO THE PROBLEM WITH THE TAX SYSTEM: RESTRUCTURING THE FEDERAL TAX SYSTEM

Chapter 9
Value Added Tax: Has the Time Come?
—*Charles E. McLure, Jr.* 185

Discussants:

The Value Added Tax: A Triumph of Form over Substance
—*Henry Aaron* 214
A Retailer's Perspective on the Value Added Tax
—*Donald V. Seibert* 218
Why Congress Will Not Accept the Value Added Tax
—*James M. Shannon* 222
The Potential of the Value Added Tax
—*Al Ullman* 225

Chapter 10
The Choice Between Income and Consumption Taxes
—*David F. Bradford* 229

Discussants:

Policies, Problems, and Politics of the Consumption Based Tax
—*David L. Boren* 253
An Equity Case for Consumption Taxation
—*Lawrence H. Summers* 257
The Consumption Based Tax: Prospects for Reform
—*Perry D. Quick* 261

Chapter 11
The Comprehensive Income Tax: Advantages and Disadvantages
—*Richard Goode* 265

Discussants:

The Achilles' Heel of the Comprehensive Income Tax
—*William D. Andrews* 278
The Political Problems of Implementing a Comprehensive Income Tax
—*Barber B. Conable, Jr.* 285
Broadening the Tax Base through a Comprehensive Income Tax
—*Emil M. Sunley* 289

Chapter 12
The Flat Rate Tax: A Proposal for Tax Simplification
—*Robert E. Hall and Alvin Rabushka* 297

Discussants:

A Framework for Evaluating a Flat Rate Tax
—*J. Gregory Ballentine* 311
The Flat Rate Tax and the Fiscal Appetite
—*James M. Buchanan* 314
Prospects for Enactment of a Flat Rate Tax
—*James R. Jones* 316
Costs and Benefits of Adopting a Flat Rate Tax
—*John S. Nolan* 319
An Opportunity for Tax Reform
—*Bob Packwood* 323

Chapter 13
International Tax Issues: Aspects of Basic Income Tax Reform
—*Thomas Horst and Gary Hufbauer* 325

Discussants:

The Outlook for International Trade
— *William E. Brock*   344
Tax Policy and International Capital Flows
— *C. E. Hussey II and Stuart M. Berkson*   346
Political and Economic Complexity in International Tax Issues
— *Daniel Patrick Moynihan*   353
Priorities for the Reform of International Tax Policy
— *John G. Wilkins*   357

Index   361

About the Editors   371

List of Participants   373

List of Figures

7-1	Marginal Tax Rates on Long-Term Capital Gains, Taxpayer in the 70 Percent Bracket, 1976-78	128
8-1	Adjusted After-Tax Profits of U.S. Corporations (1972 dollars)	174
8-2	U.S. Petroleum Industry Capital and Exploration Expenditures (billions of dollars)	174
12-1	Hall-Rabushka Simplified Flat Rate Tax Form (Business Tax)	301
12-2	Hall-Rabushka Simplified Flat Rate Tax Form (Individual Compensation Tax)	304

List of Tables

5-1	Investment Tax Credit (ITC) Required to Provide the Equivalent of True Expensing at Alternative Rates of Other Taxes against Which Accelerated Cost Recovery System (ACRS) and ITC Are Not Allowed, at Various Rates of Discount	68
5-2	Average Distribution of Business Capital for U.S. Nonfinancial Corporations, 1979-81 (percentage)	80
5-3	Effects of Tax Legislation on Cost of Capital Services (percentage)	81
5-4	Net Assets of Nonfinancial Corporations for 1981	87
6-1	Average Annual Increase in Labor Productivity, Private Business Sector, Postwar Period, between Cycle Peaks	98
6-2	Quinquennial Averages of Investment Rates	101
6-3	Real Before-Tax Return Required to Yield a 4 Percent Real After-Tax Return in 1986 (assumes 5 percent inflation)	104
7-1	Nominal and Real Long-Term Capital Gains, 1971-75	132
7-2	The Bunching of Capital Gains, 1971-75	134
7-3	Simulation of the Effects of the 1978 and 1981 Tax Cuts on Capital Gains	137

7-4	Equations of the Capital Gains Model	142
7-5	Employment, Capital Spending, and Sales are Linked	151
7-6	Capital Gains and Losses on Returns with Tax Liability (billions of dollars)	154
8-1	Method of Phasing in Expensing and Eliminating the Investment Tax Credit	169
9-1	Estimated Base of Consumption-Type Value Added Tax with Limited and Liberal Exemption at 1981 Levels of Consumption (billions of dollars)	192
9-2	Three-Stage Example of 10 Percent Value Added Tax	202
9-3	Illustration of Exemption and Zero-Rating of Retailer under Credit-Method Value Added Tax	204
9-4	Illustration of Exemption and Zero-Rating of Wholesaler under Credit-Method Value Added Tax	204
10-1	Illustration of the Effect of Inflation on the Price (via Borrowing or Lending) of a Dollar of Purchasing Power Thirty Years Hence	239
10-2	Information on Tax Returns for Illustrative Comprehensive Income and Cash Flow Taxes	244
10-3	Tax Revenue Estimates	263
11-1	Personal Income Tax Revenue in Relation to Total Tax Revenue and Gross Domestic Product, Selected OECD Countries, 1978-80	266
11-2	Employer Contributions for Major Employee Benefits, 1970 and 1981	292
12-1	Income Flows and Tax Yields (from U.S. National Income and Product Accounts for 1981)	307
12-2	Computation of Flat Tax Yield over 1981-85 Period	308
13-1	Essential Features of Taxation of Foreign Income by the United States, Canada, the United Kingdom, West Germany, France, and Japan	331
13-2	Comparison of Present U.S. Tax System with Income Tax Systems Based Solely on Residence of Individual, Location of Production, or Location of Consumption	334
13-3	Estimates of Foreign Income of U.S. Residents, U.S. Income of Foreign Residents, and Income of U.S. Citizens Who Are Foreign Residents, by Type of Income, 1981	341

Preface

The papers presented in this volume were prepared for a conference on New Directions in Federal Tax Policy for the 1980s, sponsored by the American Council for Capital Formation: Center for Policy Research. Held in Washington, D.C., in January 1983, the conference brought together economic policymakers from Congress and the Administration, corporate leaders, and members of the economic media for a comprehensive and fruitful discussion of the most pressing federal tax policy questions facing the nation for the remainder of the decade.

Funding for the conference was provided by grants from the following organizations: *patron*: American Business Conference; *sponsors*: American Petroleum Institute; The Beloit Foundation, Inc.; Citibank, N.A.; General Electric Company; IBM Corporation; Robert H. Krieble; Merrill Lynch & Co. Inc.; Mobil Corporation; Reliance Group Holdings, Inc.; Mr. and Mrs. John P. Renshaw; SmithKline Beckman Corporation; Sun Company, Inc.; United States Fidelity & Guaranty Company; Union Pacific Corporation; Weyerhaeuser Company; *contributors*: American Association of Equipment Lessors; Arthur Andersen & Co.; The Heritage Foundation; Institute for Research on the Economics of Taxation; McDermott, Will & Emery; National Association of Small Business Investment Companies; National Association of Wholesaler-Distributors; Panhandle Eastern Corporation; and Roosevelt Center for American Policy Studies.

The conference and this volume represent the work of many individuals. Certainly, as coeditors, our job would not have been possible without the ongoing support of our contributors, the staff of the American Council for Capital Formation: Center for Policy Research, and our publisher. Special thanks go to Carol Simpson, CPR Conference Publications Manager; Margo Thorning, CPR Conference Director; Ernestine Johnson, CPR Assistant Conference Director; Mari Lee Dunn, CPR Vice President; and Carol Franco, Senior Editor, Ballinger Publishing Company. Our thanks also go to CPR staff members Claire Sym Gisselbeck, Doreen Kreger, and Deborah Alexander, without whose efforts neither the conference nor this book would have become realities.

Washington, D.C.

Charls E. Walker
Mark A. Bloomfield

Overview

Charls E. Walker and
Mark A. Bloomfield

Each participant in the conference on New Directions in Federal Tax Policy for the 1980s came away with different ideas and different conclusions, but there is no question that a solid consensus emerged from the sessions. Our own conclusions follow.

The first conclusion we reached after listening to the conference discussions was that the Tax Equity and Fiscal Responsibility Act of 1982 (TEFRA) did not represent a repudiation of the American voter's support for capital formation. We know, of course, that the tax increases in TEFRA were directed substantially toward business. Calculations made by the American Council for Capital Formation: Center for Policy Research showed that by 1987 TEFRA will take back 46 percent of the accelerated cost recovery provisions enacted in the Economic Recovery Tax Act of 1981 (ERTA). Some participants said that TEFRA was a U-turn in the road and that the public no longer supported capital formation.

In 1978 and 1981 the terms of the debate on tax reform were jobs, growth, and productivity. By 1982 the terms of the debate had shifted to the concept of tax equity in a very narrow sense and toward the closing of loopholes (and not in the broad sense that dominated the debate in 1978 and 1981 and characterized our discussions at the conference). We are convinced that TEFRA, not the Revenue Act of 1978 and ERTA, was an aberration—that both the inability to cut spending and the very high interest rates were the real driving forces in moving the Congress through the budget process and

TEFRA last year. The Congressional procedure that bypassed the Ways and Means Committee in 1982 is not likely to happen again.

Capital formation appears to be an idea whose time has come. By 1978 the American people were dissatisfied with our economic progress, with stagflation, with a lack of productivity growth, and with the then-current policy prescription. That dissatisfaction came across even more strongly in 1981 with the passage of ERTA. As the Members of Congress who participated in the conference indicated, the 1982 experience was not a permanent reversal in the fundamental trend toward tax reform that encourages capital formation and economic growth.

The second conclusion we drew from the conference is that the passage of a Congressional budget resolution that forces the Congress to look for revenue from a large variety of places in the tax Code—the "cat and dog" approach to tax policy used so effectively in 1982—is less likely today than it was in 1982. All the Members of Congress who attended the conference, from liberals to conservatives, stressed that the government must have more revenue—that the size and obdurateness of the budget deficit is driving us to an examination of some version of a consumption tax. As Senator Bob Packwood told us, there is just not enough revenue in the "cat and dog" approach to solve our deficit situation. That does not mean, however, that Congress will refrain from addressing specific tax provisions. A TEFRA-2 does not seem likely; a TEFRA-1½ is still a danger.

The third conclusion we reached is that real, fundamental pro-capital formation tax reform is not just something to talk about. It can be achieved. At the start of this conference, John Connally presented a comprehensive plan to shift taxes from saving and investment and toward consumption. He called for a dialogue, and during the course of this conference, that dialogue was launched. Horace Busby is optimistic that government can become more bipartisan than it has been in recent years. Members of Congress believe that U.S. revenue needs may produce a shift away from the taxation of saving and investment and toward the taxation of consumption. These speakers represent a very broad spectrum of political opinion and when you have a spectrum like that, you are almost saying that there may be a consensus emerging.

Our fourth conclusion addresses the nature of this kind of tax reform. In contrast to twenty years ago, when preferences and so-called loopholes were in the spotlight, current reform focuses on a sharp cut in marginal rates that would move this country substantially in the direction of a flat tax. Conference panel members also discussed reductions in the corporate tax and implementation of some sort of consumption-based tax. Further discussion of the specifics is needed, but the direction is clear.

The fifth conclusion we reached grew in part out of Horace Busby's remarks about the President's Commission on Social Security Reform. He said, "I see a role in the future for commissions on these tough problems." This could be one way to achieve the bipartisanship on tax reform that currently is so difficult to achieve in the Congress.

To sum up, the capital formation locomotive is still on track. The chances of a divisive "cat and dog" approach to tax policy seem lessened. We now have a wide spectrum of opinion supporting tax reform in the basic sense and not merely in the loophole-closing sense. As our conference has shown, there are ways to be explored that might make this fundamental, pro-capital formation tax reform succeed.

PART I

THE POLITICAL AND ECONOMIC CHALLENGE FOR TAX REFORM

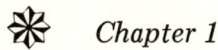 Chapter 1

The Political Environment
Horace W. Busby

I must tell you that several months ago I returned to my office after lunch and found waiting a message to call Charls (without-an-"e") Walker. I was flattered, as any young man would be, to be the object of the attentions of the second most powerful man in Washington. When I got through to him, he told me that the American Council for Capital Formation: Center for Policy Research was planning this meeting and that he was getting together some corporate clout, distinguished members of the tax bar, and a few freelancing economic ideologues to study taxes. He asked if I would consent to keynote the conference. Well, becoming incautious at this exciting prospect, I accepted without asking any questions. Then he dropped the other shoe. He said, "Oh, by the way, the other keynoter" (I didn't know you could have two keynoters) "is going to be His Worship, John Connally."

Well, I felt at that moment about Charls Walker somewhat as I feel at this moment. If I just could find that missing "e," I would take great pleasure in reinserting it—but not necessarily between the "l" and the "s." Only a sadist would ask a fellow who paddles an oratorical canoe to follow this close in the wake of the QE II of the American public platform. John and I were trained in the same school of politics, but at the University of Texas we somehow got different speech teachers.

I

This conference has been convened for an important and urgent purpose: to begin a national effort to secure action on creating the next tax system of the United States. This effort is urgent because the existing tax system is a failed system. Its levies are not equitable. Its revenues are not adequate. Its effect is to penalize savings, punish investment, and imprison productivity. It is a system that no longer deserves respect and no longer receives it. On the present course, the tax system promises to become for the 1980s what Prohibition was for the 1920s.

The effort begun at this conference—to start the dialogue and make the issue move—is crucial because, if left unchanged, the existing tax system assures that the government of the United States will never again conclude a fiscal year without a deficit. Further, if the existing tax system is left unchanged, in some not too distant decade the land of the free and the home of the brave may be forced to abandon pride and dignity and to join the banana republics in relying on public lotteries, bingo games, and dog races for revenues.

If this effort is to succeed, of course, its success must be achieved in the political arena. In this nation born of tax revolt, taxes are, first and last, politics, the central politics of every level of government. My part in these proceedings is to consider with you the political environment of the 1980s, the environment in which the effort to reach this decision will either succeed or fail. Appropriately, as this conference is called New Directions in Federal Tax Policy for the 1980s, my remarks are devoted to New Directions in Federal Politics for the 1980s.

II

In considering the politics of taxation, the first question to be faced is one of credibility. The old lore of American politics teaches that the single most difficult task for the political process is that of trying to move a county seat from one town to another. It is so difficult that it has not been tried in a great many years. That same lore also teaches that the second most difficult task in our politics is that of installing, at any level of government, a new form of taxation. You can raise rates and have new rates on old bases (which, as we learned last year, can be done in the dead of night by crafty politicians), but a new form of taxation is unimaginably difficult to achieve. And here lies the matter of credibility.

Our national politics has rarely been so weak as it is now. An anti-Washington government has now been succeeded by an antigovernment government. Over the last four fiscal years, neither one of them has been able to get a budget or, for that matter, much else that governing requires. Is it really credible to begin this effort to accomplish the second most difficult feat in politics when our politics is in such a state that it has trouble accomplishing what has long been the easiest of political tasks—that is, legislative pay raises?

In its present state, no. Our politics cannot accomplish the magnitude of change. It cannot even address the matter of change in our tax system, at least not of the magnitude that this conference anticipates.

All is not lost, however. Our politics is beginning a historic era of root-and-branch change that may result in a very different political environment, an environment in which change in the tax system will not only be possible but virtually mandatory. But change is very rare in American politics. That is by the design of the Founding Fathers, who created a system expressly intended to frustrate what they so feared: change resulting from the spirit of faction, as they liked to write in *The Federalist Papers*, or from the caprice of momentary passions.

That system has succeeded. Over the last 194 years (we have had a country 200 years, but we have had a government for only 194 years) the forms of our government are, as political scientists like to observe, the least changed of any nation on earth.

III

Nonetheless, a process of change is under way in this decade that will significantly change the realities and possibly even some of the forms of our government. Through both of the American centuries, our politics has been immature, naive, unsophisticated, and very often aimless. Today, a maturing nation appears ready to evolve a mature politics.

Since the memorable evening around the turn of the century when William McKinley stayed up all night at the White House praying for divine guidance in foreign affairs, our politics has had a strong messianic tendency. On that occasion, President McKinley revealed to the country that the Lord had disclosed to him that it was the "manifest destiny" of the United States to make Christians out of Filipinos, even if it meant sending a fleet into Manila Bay with all guns blazing. Domestically, as well as internationally, our political goals, and some of our political styles, have often been in the messiah mode. Great passions throbbed through our system. Americans were bent on accomplishing through politics what no other people had ever achieved. These goals have long characterized our politics.

In the 1960s the last of those great passions was requited with the enactment of the civil rights legislation. The messianic era had exhausted its agenda: building of a middle class, bringing peace to the relations between labor and management, assuring the well-being of the elderly, and flooring the income of the poor. It also had exhausted the consent of the governed in respect to foreign involvements.

At that point, though, the imperatives of our politics changed. The nation no longer needed political messiahs. It needed, as it still desperately needs, political managers. That is the direction in which we are moving: from a messianic era in politics to a managerial era in politics. Yesterday's passions are yielding to tomorrow's pragmatism.

IV

How can one be sanguine, even optimistic, about the future of our politics when it is in the middle of making an epochal mess of national affairs? First, it is a well-kept secret of the political press that historic changes are taking place in American politics in the 1980s. Just this year our politics is beginning to run on a very different track than ever before. That will have important consequences as we proceed. Second, the mess, as it were, in our affairs actually serves a constructive purpose in that it is a forcing agent. It has to be addressed. It has to be overcome. It will be a forcing agent on presidents and on parties. In other words, things are reversed. Instead of presidents and parties setting the course, the course itself is going to chart the way for presidents and parties, and they will have few options but to follow that course.

The thing that must be understood, however, is how this national agenda came about. What confronts us now in Washington in the political process is not the legacy of forty years, as is often heard said, but an accumulation from a specific period in which the politics of the nation simply could not function.

Go back to the year 1972. That year is etched in irony. In that year the American people came together politically as never before. When the electoral college met in December of 1972, this nation was as close to unanimous in the results as it ever had been, far closer than it ever had been or is likely ever to be again. Forty-nine states voted to install in office a conservative president.

It is ironic that in the very year that the American people came together, American politics began coming apart. It was in that year, of course, that two things happened. The results of the 1972 elections gave Democrats cause to wonder if they had lost their party. At the same time, the 1972 break-in at the Watergate was soon to give Republicans cause for that same worry about their party.

That worry reflects very clearly in the budgets. Impeachment was hanging over Washington all 1974. In that climate a distracted executive and an even more distracted Congress put together a fiscal 1975 budget. The deficit stands out among all postwar deficits because in fiscal 1975 the deficit was $45 billion. That was ten times greater than the deficit for the preceding year. We were off to the races without knowing it.

The last five deficits of the 1970s were cumulatively almost 200 percent greater than the cumulative deficit of the preceding twenty-five years. Seventy-one percent of the entire post–World War II run-up in the national debt accumulated in the fiscal years 1972 through 1982.

These deficits occurred not as a function of political philosophy but as a function of political panic. Parties and politicians had lost continuity and their bases and without those things present simply could not function. Indeed, it is in this period that all the items now on our national agenda acquired their presently menacing size and much of their difficulty. This is true of the budget, of social security, of infrastructure (at least of the federal portion of the infrastructure), of the crisis in productivity, of the crisis in agriculture, of the crisis in the tax system. (It is well to remember that Governor Connally and Dr. Walker shared the experience, at the beginning of the period I am talking about, of seeing the very first effort that was going to be made to change the tax system and install a value added tax go down in flames because of Watergate.) So we experienced a ten-year discontinuity in our system.

V

Why does this rather sad history encourage optimism for the future? At this point in time our politics is escaping its history, something that is essential if it is to be reformed and begin working effectively for us.

American politics in the twentieth century was organized by the outcome of the Civil War. Both major parties and, to an extent, their dominant philosophies or interests have derived from that event. On January 3 of this year, however, both parties began new histories. When the Ninety-eighth Congress convened, control of the House of Representatives was, for the first time since 1862, *not* in the states that won the Civil War. The 1980 reapportionment served to stand our politics on a new base.

That new base is in the Sun Belt, a phenomenon that, for political purposes, runs from the Delmarva Peninsula northeast of Washington to the Arizona–California state line and then includes the states west of the Mississippi Valley. That is the new base of American politics, a fact that has been neglected by the political commentators of this period.

Well, we are all Americans. What is the difference? The difference is in the political perspective, outlook, and product of these newly powerful regions. First of all, there is a strong pay-as-you-go tradition in these states. There is an antipathy to debt and borrowing that is far greater than that of people schooled in the politics of, say, the Northeast. There is even an antipathy to welfare, or, at least, to high welfare costs.

This political base now includes all of the right-to-work states, based on the transfer of Congressional seats. The states from which seats were taken in the 1980 reapportionment averaged 30 percent of the unionized work force. The states into which those seats transferred average 12.5 percent of the work force with union cards. Those figures are significant.

VI

The elections of 1980 and the elections of 1982 together reveal much of the future. Since 1858, when the two major parties we now know began their present competition, voters have used those parties for different purposes. Parties do not like to acknowledge this.

From 1860 through 1984, the White House has been occupied 61 percent of the time by the Republican party. It has been the presidential party of the American people to that substantial extent. Over the same span the Democrats have controlled the House of Representatives, in fifty-eight different Congresses, 60 percent of the time. These percentages show that the American people want different things from different parties.

The elections of 1980 and 1982 prepared the way for more of the same. The presidency has always, since the two major parties began, been under a lock, one party or the other. The Lincoln lock lasted seventy-two years, the Roosevelt lock, twenty years. We are now under the Eisenhower lock, which has stood for thirty years.

When I first presented this explanation of the Republican lock, *The Washington Post* called it "the most provocative theory in years." It is not a theory; it is just history. At the time, I said that the lock indicated that Jimmy Carter could very likely be the last Democratic president of the century. When you have friends who are Republicans (and I have many of them) you have to get accustomed to something that is genetic in Republicans: Republicans transmit to their children a gene that makes them paranoid. They are always looking for ways to lose the White House, and quite often they do come up with them. So my phone has been ringing a great deal lately, and rather weak-voiced Republicans have been saying, "Are you sure that lock still holds?"

The "lock" does not attach to a party name. Before it is Republican, that lock is conservative. There are twenty-nine states that in the last eight presidential elections have voted at least 75 percent of the time for the Republican choice. It assures a majority to the party perceived as offering an acceptable conservative or moderate candidate, a type that is just currently in short supply among Democrats.

VII

One of the most significant elections in recent times was the 1982 election because it changed the dynamics and the nature of both our parties. The reapportionment based on the 1980 census took seventeen House seats out of the industrial states of the North and East, one from Massachusetts, and one from South Dakota. It transferred those seats: four seats to the Pacific Basin, three seats to the Mountain States above Arizona, and ten seats into the Sun Belt.

In the states from which these seventeen seats were taken the Republicans came out with eighteen fewer seats in this Congress than they had won in the 1980 election. In other words, they were not able to preserve any of those seats. That is clearly a message to the Republican party, as all its leaders outside the White House say, that it must change, that it must have a broader appeal.

But even worse for Republicans is what happened in the Sun Belt. Over the last twenty-five years Republicans have gradually gained ground in the Sun Belt. Of the ten new seats transferred into the Sun Belt, Republicans won two in Florida. The other eight went Democratic. In addition to that, from Virginia to Arizona, there suddenly was a total of eighteen new Democratic seats. The election wiped out the gains of the last twenty-five years.

What this says, of course, is that the South, again as a function of the Civil War, has a Democratic base for its politics. The last Congress, the Ninety-seventh Congress, suddenly brought the flowering of something that has not appeared there in a long time: Congressmen from the Sun Belt could be conservative Democrats. With a rather amazing performance, the Sun Belt went back to its home party—the Democratic party. That is ominous for Republicans, who have no history and no base in many of the Sun Belt states.

It has changed the Democratic party, though, in the following way. In this Congress, as has not been true before, the Democratic party finds that its strongest regional base is the Sun Belt and that in the Sun Belt it holds 71 percent of all the seats.

Now, if the purpose of the Democratic party is to remain credible as a national party, it must devote itself to holding the House. Presidential candidates, presidential platforms, pursuits in Congress are now hostage to the Sun Belt. If Democrats want to start losing seats again, if they want to lose Congress in a hurry, then they should offend the Sun Belt. That is not going to occur.

VIII

We are on a new track. Politics has escaped a history that did not serve it well. Here is where the magnitude of the national agenda begins to have its effect. First of all, from now on, anything that comes through the system by way of Washington must be done on a bipartisan basis. Furthermore, the parties are placed in a position of standing together or falling together. Now both parties have to succeed. There is no longer any place for an obstructionist role on the part of either party. It also means that there must be action. The agenda is so heavy and affects so many people that it is no longer acceptable just to pass things off.

We have already seen bipartisanship in effect in relation to social security. Nobody could agree on that issue a few months ago, and now everybody agrees. Many of us have worried about the magnitude and complexity of this new agenda, as to whether the process itself could handle it without collapsing. Any one of the issues I mentioned is of once-in-a-generation, if not once-in-a-lifetime, magnitude.

When the American political system really gets under pressure, as it last did in the 1930s, it creates a new form of governance. The late Speaker Sam Rayburn used to say that the Constitution did not create the presidency; Congress invented it to save its rear end. There is a great deal of truth in that perspective. We are likely to see (as we saw last year on the tax bill) a new form of government appear since we just winked at the Constitution and said that the Constitution does not mean it when it says that tax bills have to originate in the House. But the process worked.

What has happened on social security is something that I expect to see rather frequently, including on tax issues. That was the appointment of the Greenspan Commission, and, finally, everybody lets it do the work. It becomes in the interest of the political forces both in the White House and on the Hill to let a commission do this, a commission of expert, informed, and reasonable private citizens. We probably will see a great deal more of that sort of thing in the future.

Another important thing that the agenda does is to wipe out ideologies. It wipes out little philosophical excursions. You just have to stay with the agenda until it is cleared. That is healthy for our politics.

The first steps have been taken toward a gradual improvement in our politics. But when all the other items that are now pressing for resolution have been addressed, the last one to be dealt with, and the hardest, will be the matter that brings you together here today: changing the tax system of the United States.

 *Chapter 2*

The Challenge for Tax Reform

John B. Connally

The task of a keynoter is to keynote, and I would like to make my keynote as clear as possible: The only real problem with the federal tax system is that we rely far too heavily on a set of individual and business income taxes that are unfair, complex, and obstructive to sustained economic growth. It is time that we quit talking about alleged tax reform in which we fiddle around with so-called tax loopholes, and engage in true tax reform instead. That reform would involve a sharp scaling back and simplification of both the individual and corporate income tax, along with introduction of a value added tax to sustain federal revenues.

This keynote thrust is, to be sure, a different and, to some, a radical statement. But the American Council for Capital Formation: Center for Policy Research has, in effect, asked us to consider all sorts of alternatives by titling this conference New Directions in Federal Tax Policy for the 1980s. If my keynote statement is indeed strong, then so are my reasons for making it.

I

What do we want from our tax system? In a democracy, the first requisite is that it be both fair in fact and fair in taxpayer perception. The tax burden should be roughly the same for individuals in similar circumstances; this might be referred to as "horizontal equity," or treating equals equally. At the same time, "vertical equity," or treating unequals fairly, can be fully as important.

Most of the other things we want from our tax system can, I think, be summed up under "efficiency." We want to minimize the cost to taxpayers of keeping records and filing returns, along with the costs of collection and, of great importance, the costs associated with invasion of privacy.

Surely the overriding efficiency criterion for our tax system has to do with the economy—the impact of taxation on output, employment, and price stability. For those of Keynesian persuasion, the key relationships might be between taxes and the level of overall demand for goods and services. So-called supply-siders would emphasize the impact of taxation on decisions to work, innovate, save, and invest. Although this conference should be interested in both the demand and supply side of the equation, it is the latter that has received insufficient emphasis during the past half century. Indeed, one of the primary reasons for the problem with today's tax system is that important questions of supply have, until recently, been all but ignored.

II

How well does our federal system meet these criteria? Very poorly, indeed. Far from being simple, the complexity of our federal income tax system borders on national disgrace. Millions of taxpayers find it too difficult or too troublesome to prepare their own returns. The business of tax preparation has flourished. Tax lawyers and accountants are in constantly growing demand.

The individual income tax system also fails to provide a desirable degree of horizontal equity—treating equals equally—but its shortcomings in this respect are not nearly so great as either the self-styled tax reformers or editorial writers would have us believe. Many of the so-called loopholes for individuals are provisions relating to such widely acclaimed American values as home ownership, health care, and saving for retirement. Moreover, the tax shelter business has fallen on relatively bad days as top marginal rates have been reduced from above 90 percent two decades ago to 50 percent today.

It is the individual income tax system's treatment of people at different income levels that is most unfair and in need of true reform. The problem is excessive progressivity. Although tax burdens that rise with income are almost universally viewed by Americans as fair and equitable, the progressivity of the existing system goes too far; it could be justified only as a socially oriented goal of income redistribution. It borders on deliberate flagellation of the American middle class.

Consider, if you will, how our individual income tax system treats two middle-income families—one at the lower end of the range, with an annual income of $15,000, and one at the higher end, with an annual income of $60,000. After July 1, 1983, when the final installment of the 25 percent individual tax reduction enacted in 1981 is fully effective, the annual tax bills of these two families will be $952 and $9,706, respectively. With four times the income, the higher earning middle-income family will pay ten times the taxes of the lower earning family. That is manifestly unfair.

Look at this excessive progressivity in another way, in terms of marginal rates. As of next July, the individual income tax rate will be 11 percent on the first $5,500 of taxable income, but then it will rise rapidly to 22 percent on income above $20,200, 33 percent above $35,200, and 42 percent above $60,000. The top marginal rate of 50 percent locks in when income exceeds $162,400.

The steeply rising marginal rates should warn us that the "bracket creep" which enraged middle class Americans in the 1970s and early 1980s is not necessarily a thing of the past. Return to high inflation could well restore it as a major social, political, and economic problem.

The economic aspect of the problem is of overriding importance. I am not an economist, but I do know enough about human nature to understand that economists are right when they emphasize the importance of decisions "at the margin." If you want a fellow to work more, or think more, or save and invest more, it is what he gets at the margin that is important—that extra dollar for that extra effort.

That is why steeply progressive marginal tax rates can be so damaging economically. When the breadwinner in a family with $46,000 in taxable income (and that is not all that high an income today) ponders the wisdom of extra effort to earn more, he or she must recognize the fact that Uncle Sam will grab thirty-three cents out of each extra dollar earned. That's a lot better than it was two years ago, before the passage of the Economic Recovery Tax Act of 1981 (ERTA), but it is still not good enough. It is not fair, and it does not make economic sense.

Steeply progressive marginal tax rates are especially damaging to the cause of personal saving and investment—and therefore capital formation—*because an income tax is inherently biased against saving.* It taxes saving twice: first, when earned as income; and second, as the income from the investment that the saving generates comes in. Look at it this way: If that $15,000 lower middle-income family saves $150 and puts it in the savings and loan, the $150 is taxed once as part of the family's original income and again when the interest earned on the deposit is taxed. That is not fair, either. Even worse, in this time of capital shortage and lagging productivity, it is not smart.

It is high time that we performed radical surgery on an individual income tax system that is both unfair and obstructive to realization of our economic goals. Nothing short of fundamental reform will serve the true needs of this nation in the 1980s, 1990s, and on into the twenty-first century.

III

Some variation of the flat tax proposals that have recently caught the fancy of the public and the press could do the required job of lowering individual tax rates and also eliminating excessive progressivity from the individual income tax. The feasibility of shifting to a flat tax would be greatly increased if it were phased in over time. The task would also be eased if the total revenue raised by the individual income tax were cut sharply—in other words, if introduction of a flat rate system were accompanied by a substantial cut in the income tax take.

How much of a revenue reduction would be desirable? Perhaps as much as one-third to one-half—cutting the total proceeds from the individual income tax from the current $300 billion annually to $150 to $200 billion. That can be done, of course, only if the revenue is made up with either a new tax or by increasing an existing tax. My solution to this problem, which I shall come back to shortly, is to phase in a consumption based value added tax at the same time the individual income tax is phased down.

Would these reforms simplify payments of the individual income tax? Only if the transition to a flat tax system carried with it significant reduction in the credits and deductions that now make the individual tax so complicated. Such reduction might be desirable, but I am not one who favors complete elimination of income tax credits and reductions and replacement with a flat tax.

The reason? Many of the credits and deductions are in the law for good reasons. In addition, any attempt to eliminate them would result in a wave of political opposition that could jeopardize the basic reform that I favor—that is, drastic reductions in income tax rates on individuals and businesses. In addition, we should be very careful about establishing any broad-based tax with a single flat rate. Such an arrangement could make it all too easy for legislators to fund ever higher spending with relatively small increases in the tax rate.

IV

The individual income tax can and should be reformed; it has good as well as bad points. The same cannot be said of the corporate income tax. It is a bad tax from almost every standpoint. To understand the perversity of the corporate income tax, we have to start with one fundamental truth: The tax is *not* paid by the corporation; it is paid by people—the people who buy the company's products, the people who work for it, the people who provide the capital. A corporation is nothing more and nothing less than a legal arrangement under which *individuals* do business—and, judging by this country's unparalleled record of economic progress, an excellent arrangement at that. Since no corporation really pays the tax, the corporation is, in effect, only a surrogate tax collector for the Internal Revenue Service.

Who does pay the tax? No one knows precisely. When Congress raises corporate taxes, the legislators really do not know who they are going to tax. They are legislating in the dark. That fact alone should be sufficiently damning for press and public to relegate the corporate income tax to the economic dump heap. When the possibilities as to the true impact of the corporate income tax are described, however, its egregious shortcomings stand out even more starkly.

The tax must be passed either forward to the consumers or backwards to the factors of production—there are no other alternatives. To the extent it is passed on to consumers, the corporate income tax is doubtless regressive in impact; this is because people with low incomes spend more of those incomes on the products of American corporations than do people with high incomes, who save more. Such regressivity should be anathema to those of liberal persuasion.

The regressive feature of the corporate tax can be seen most clearly with respect to public utilities; all but the most poverty stricken consumers have to buy their products, and ratemaking procedures allow for recovery of taxes in the selling price. Other industries are another matter. If the market for a corporation's product is weak—as with steel and automobiles today—the tax must be passed backward, to the factors of production. Corporate employees in effect "pay the tax" through wage cuts, shorter workweeks, even loss of jobs. If dividends are cut back, stockholders, many of whom are not well off, bear the burden.

The general impact of the corporate tax is, therefore, clear. In varying degrees it raises consumer prices and, in this respect, is regressive in impact; or it cuts jobs and earnings, thus hurting workers;

or it reduces the return to the people who provide the capital, and thus hampers capital formation and productivity. Since this is the full range of possibilities, and none of the events is today viewed as desirable, the corporate tax itself should be labeled Fiscal Enemy Number One.

The fact that the corporate tax exists leads to its increasing misuse. Politicians are tempted to take the easy way out when revenues have to be increased. With the press as a prime and essential accomplice, politicians have correctly assumed that they could avoid political heat in raising revenues by avoiding direct taxes on individuals, who vote, and hitting corporations, who do not vote. The corporate tax has been, in essence, the politically "painless" approach to raising federal revenues. Indeed, when a general tax increase has seemed necessary, politicians and the press, ignoring the facts, have even argued that it would be unfair to individuals not to make corporations "pay their fair share." What nonsense!

How long will a press that prides itself on deflating the claims of politicians be party to this indecent and economically damaging deception? Will we ever see headlines taking politicians to task for piously stating that a corporate tax increase is fair because it does not hit people? When shall we see headlines that Congress, under the guise of a corporate tax increase, is about to raise taxes on consumers, workers, and savers?

Speaking of journalistic treatment of tax policy, I am curious about how the press will treat proposals to sharply scale or even eliminate the corporate income tax. Will the headlines trumpet "Unjust Enrichment of Corporate Fat Cats"? Will they complain about "Red Meat for Business," while individuals are left with "Mother Hubbard's Cupboard"?

Or will journalists instead note that any reductions in the corporate tax will, in turn, enhance corporate cash flows—extra money that is going to be used in much the same way that corporations now use their cash? Most goes to pay labor. A lighter federal tax burden would make it easier to meet corporate payrolls, and this should be good news for workers in the hard-pressed basic industries, now in a half-century low point. Stockholders are likely to receive a little more; this would reward saving and promote badly needed capital formation. Over the longer pull, the most likely use for the extra money would be for corporate investment in plant and equipment, for the simple reason that any reduction in the corporate tax rate increases the attractiveness of such investment by raising its after-tax rate of return. More money for labor, more money for stockholders, more money for investment—that is where the extra corporate money would go if Fiscal Enemy Number One, the corporate income tax, were scaled back.

How much should the corporate tax be cut back? Perhaps someday we can completely eliminate this unfair and economically destructive tax that is all the worse because politicians use it as a cop-out in order to avoid the wrath of voters. I am too realistic to propose so drastic an action today, even though it would be eminently sensible. Instead, a percentage cut in the corporate income tax about equal to the cut in the individual income tax would constitute solid tax reform and also be perceived by press and public as fair. This cut in the corporate tax should be phased in over the same period as the shift to a flat tax for individuals and the creation of a Value Added Tax (VAT)—perhaps in a period of five to eight years.

V

Governments must have revenue; that is especially true of our government today. If we are to scale back sharply the individual and corporate income tax, as we should, how can we make up the loss in revenue and do so in a way that meets the criteria of equity and efficiency in taxation? The answer lies in shifting our system strongly toward a VAT, the most neutral tax yet devised in its impact on economic activity. VAT is such a good idea that the real question is not whether we should move toward it, but why we have waited so long.

Those who would substitute a consumption-based VAT for other taxes—and I have been in the group for a number of years—claim that such a step would foster capital formation, reduce the trade deficit, and help stabilize federal revenues over the business cycle. We are convinced that VAT would be self-policing and easy to administer, that it would foster greater efficiency in business and, since people seem more willing to pay their taxes a day-at-a-time than in larger lumps, that taxpayer revolts would be less likely.

The opponents of VAT believe otherwise. Some liberals argue that VAT is nothing more nor less than a national sales tax and would thus be very regressive. Others assert that its introduction would result in a sharp increase in the cost of living, or that, as a hidden tax, VAT is undemocratic. Conservatives are uneasy with VAT because they are convinced that it is a powerful and relatively painless revenue raiser that would feed the big spenders in Congress.

All of these objections can be met. If a VAT does, as many people believe, put a disproportionate burden on low-income individuals, that burden can be neatly offset by granting a refundable income tax credit per family member, an approach used in some states to offset the regressivity of state sales taxes. For example, if a 15 percent VAT would result in a four-member family paying $1,000 per year on the purchase of $7,000 in necessities, an income tax credit of $250 per family member would counter the regressivity.

The charge that VAT is undemocratic because it is hidden can be easily dealt with. *Don't* hide it; show the total tax take on each product that is sold. In fact, put that figure in red ink, so that it stands out to the purchaser. Anything that brings home to taxpayers and consumers the true cost of government is, in my view, a good thing. A clearly identified VAT would stand in sharp contrast to the corporate income tax, which is now a hidden tax in every sense of the term.

Is VAT inflationary? To be sure, introduction of VAT might result in some one-time increases in the most commonly accepted measure of inflation, the consumer price index. But those increases would result from a statistical procedure: Excise taxes, such as VAT, are included in the computation of the index; income taxes are not. It is just as likely, however, that a VAT combined with reduced corporate and individual income taxes would enable producers and retailers to keep prices unchanged.

To the extent VAT is not used to raise net revenue, but only to offset a reduction of the individual and corporate income tax, the total tax burden on people is not increased. The consumer price index might go up, but so would take-home pay and other forms of purchasing power, as VAT is substituted for the individual income tax. It is a wash.

I number myself among those conservatives who fear that a VAT, once adopted, would be gradually increased by the Congressional big spenders who want to see the federal government grow and grow and grow. The answer to this is to cap any VAT through a Constitutional amendment. Such an amendment might authorize an increase in VAT above a stated level of, say, 15 percent, only on the approval of three-fourths of the votes of the Constitutional membership of each House of Congress.

VI

The fundamental question is whether the ideas I have advanced make sense. If our existing tax system is as unfair and economically perverse as I think it is, then reasonable people will be willing to talk about fundamental reform. What is needed, and what has been sadly lacking up to now, is a meaningful dialogue on the issue. That dialogue, of course, must be conducted by people who are both concerned and informed and whom other people respect—people such as those whom the American Council for Capital Formation: Center for Policy Research has so wisely brought together for these two and one-half days.

The role of the press in this dialogue cannot be overstated. If I have raised questions concerning press treatment of tax policy here today, it is only because I am convinced that the real story, for whatever reason, has not yet been told, but must be told, if we are to enjoy true rather than phony tax reform. Working reporters need not take sides; I am not asking journalists to become advocates for my proposal or any other proposal. All I ask is a thorough ventilation of tax policy issues, so that the American people can at long last understand those issues and their gravity. If a substantive, sustained dialogue is launched among the public, in government, and all points in between, then I am perfectly satisfied to let events take their course. I have enough faith in the American people to believe that the right answers will ultimately be reached.

Will those answers be precisely what I have proposed today? I am neither vain enough nor foolish enough to think so. It is "new directions" in tax policy that we are talking about. I have tried to lay out my thoughts on some of those new directions, perhaps with a little more specificity than the sponsors of this conference expected. Such specificity is appropriate. While it runs the risk of generating attacks on details that may or may not be important, it is far superior to vague abstraction.

Think back over the histories of other radical ideas whose times have come. Think of the crucial role of academicians, businessmen, politicians, and the press in bringing those ideas to legislative fruition. If we truly want fundamental tax reform, we can make it happen. But I repeat: The first order of business is a meaningful dialogue.

I want to express my personal thanks to the American Council for Capital Formation: Center for Policy Research for organizing—and letting me participate in—what may well turn out to be a truly seminal event.

 *Chapter 3*

Fiscal Policy for the 1980s
Martin Feldstein

I have admired the work that the American Council for Capital Formation: Center for Policy Research has done during the past several years in bringing the problem of capital formation to the attention of the Congress and of the public. I am convinced that this work has had an important effect on the tax legislation of the past several years.

Although the progress in this area has been considerable, much more remains to be done. This paper discusses the low rates of saving and investment in the United States and the progress that has been made during the past two years in enacting tax legislation that will increase the long-run rate of capital formation. It also investigates the consumption tax approach to tax reform that is now being considered within this Administration. Finally, it comments on the relationship between budget deficits and capital formation and on the Administration's commitment to decreased budget deficits in future years.

THE LOW RATE OF SAVING

Increasing the rate of capital accumulation must remain one of the central and continuing long-run goals of economic policy. A higher rate of capital formation is the most dependable way to increase productivity and to raise our nation's rate of economic growth.

We see around the world that countries devoting a higher share of their national income to investment enjoy a faster rate of growth of

Copyright © 1983 by Martin Feldstein.

productivity. During the 1970s, gross fixed investment in the United States averaged 18.4 percent of our Gross National Product (GNP). About two-thirds of this investment was needed just to replace the capital that was wearing out or becoming obsolete. As a result, we spent only 6.6 percent of GNP on net fixed investment. Output per employee hour in manufacturing increased at an annual rate of 2.6 percent.

During the same period, the British devoted slightly more of GNP to net fixed investment (8.1 percent) and enjoyed a slightly higher rate of real productivity growth (2.9 percent). But the French and German investment rates were about twice ours (11.8 percent of GNP in Germany and 12.2 percent in France), and their growth rates were also about twice as high as ours (4.8 percent in France and 4.9 percent in Germany). As we all know, Japan had the highest rates of both investment and growth; the Japanese devoted 19.5 percent of GNP to net fixed investment (almost three times the U.S. share) and enjoyed a rate of productivity increase that was also nearly three times as fast (7.4 percent a year instead of 2.6 percent). At those growth rates, output per man hour would double in Japan in a decade while in the United States it would take more than a quarter of a century.

The lesson in this experience and in the experience of other time periods as well is very clear: We must achieve and maintain a high rate of investment if we want to maintain a high rate of growth in productivity and real incomes.

The low rate of net national investment in the United States reflects a correspondingly low rate of net saving by our nation's households, businesses, and governments. For the past three decades as a whole, this net national saving rate has averaged only 6.7 percent of GNP, essentially the same share of GNP that has been devoted to net domestic investment. With a net saving rate that is only about half of the average among the other major industrial countries of the world, it is not surprising that our investment rate is also only about half of that in the other industrial countries. Although in principle we might augment our domestic savings by borrowing from other countries and by attracting net investment from other countries, the experience of the past several decades indicates that over the years our businesses and individuals want to invest just about as much abroad as foreigners want to invest in the United States. The next few years are likely to be an exception to this pattern, with a substantial inflow of foreign capital offsetting, in part, the sharp reduction in net savings that will be caused by large budget deficits. But this is not a satisfactory situation for the longer term, and we will return to a situation where investment in the United States is largely determined by our nation's rate of saving.

Our low rate of capital formation means that we as a nation are passing up the opportunity to earn a high rate of return and to raise our future standard of living. Additions to the stock of plant and equipment earn a real rate of return (before tax but after adjusting for inflation and real depreciation) of about 11 percent. This rate of return is probably at least as high and possibly higher than the return earned by the other industrial countries that devote so much more of their national income to net investment in plant and equipment.

Why, then, have we had such a low rate of saving and investment? Our low rate of capital formation during the past several decades reflects a whole range of government policies—from tax rules that penalized saving and discouraged business investment to credit market rules that encouraged large mortgages while limiting the rate of return to the small saver. The antisaving government policies were not an accident of history but can be traced back to the Keynesian fear of saving that permeated much of economic thinking and economic policy for the past forty years. As you may recall, Keynes argued that the depression of the 1930s was due to inadequate spending or, equivalently, to excessive saving. The implication of his theory was therefore clear: Develop explicit policies to discourage saving and encourage consumer spending. This theory, designed for the British depression of the 1930s, came to have a powerful and inappropriate effect on the economic policies of the United States and Britain in the 1950s, 1960s and 1970s.

In this way, the United States and Britain were very different from the other major industrial nations of Europe and from Japan. In those countries, Keynes' intellectual and professional influence was much weaker. The possibility of a new depression caused by inadequate spending seemed to be a far less serious problem than the urgent need to rebuild and replace the capital stock that had been so severely damaged during the war. As a result, those countries developed policies that were designed to encourage saving while the United States and Britain developed policies to discourage saving.

The impact of this whole array of policies has been more powerful than a simple sum of the separate effects of the individual policies taken alone. By its combination of antisaving policies and pronouncements, the actions of the American government during much of the postwar period contributed to an antisaving attitude among the present generation of Americans. In effect, while the French, German, and Japanese governments have been telling their citizens in both words and incentives that more saving would create the capital for better jobs and a higher standard of living, our government was induced by the Keynesian fear of saving to tell the American public that saving less and spending more on American-made consumer goods was the key to jobs and prosperity. Unfortunately, this combination of adverse incentives and misguided cajoling were so influential that the United States and Britain have had the lowest saving rates in the industrial world during the past two decades.

RECENT TAX CHANGES

All that began to change a few years ago. The Reagan Administration and many leading Members of Congress in both parties have come to recognize that a permanently higher saving rate would be a good thing for the American economy. The 1981 tax legislation was clear evidence of such a change in thinking and of the strong bipartisan support that now exists for policies to encourage savings and capital formation.

Indeed, there were no fewer than six substantial changes in the personal tax rules aimed at encouraging individuals to save more. Of particular significance was the feature that permits the forty million employees who already participate in company pension plans to make additional tax deductible contributions of up to $2,000 a year to Individual Retirement Accounts (IRAs). This change has established the principle that individuals should not pay tax on a portion of their income that is not spent and that the interest and dividends on that saving should also accumulate tax free until the entire amount is withdrawn to be spent.

I believe that the new IRA accounts will gradually increase the rate of saving in the economy. I do not agree with the critics who claim that the expanded IRA provision and other rules will simply induce individuals to transfer assets from one type of account to another to claim the tax advantage. In a study that I did before joining the government, I found that the majority of families have enough financial assets on hand to take advantage of the new Individual Retirement Account (IRA) option for less than two years; they then would have to save more to get any tax benefit.

Of course, there are some individuals who would save at least $2,000 a year even without the IRA account. For them, the IRA provides no additional incentive to save. The 1981 tax law therefore provided a further saving incentive for savings that are not part of an IRA, a Keogh plan, or a corporate pension plan. Beginning in 1985, a taxpayer will be able to exclude from taxable income 15 percent of all interest receipts up to $6,000. Although this exclusion is only very partial and also subject to a dollar limit, it does increase the overall incentive to save and reinforces the tax principle that savings or capital income deserves special treatment.

Before 1981 all forms of personal investment income were subject to tax rates of up to 70 percent. The reduction in the maximum tax rate from 70 percent to 50 percent implies a substantial increase in the after-tax rates of return; for someone who pays the maximum tax rate, the net yield associated with a 10 percent interest rate nearly doubled, rising from 3 percent to 5 percent.

An indirect but very important source of reductions in the effective tax rate on income from savings has been the decline in inflation. Because our tax law bases tax liability on nominal interest income and nominal capital gains, a lower rate of inflation can mean a substantial reduction in the effective rate of tax. An individual in the 30 percent tax bracket who earned a 15 percent interest rate when the inflation rate was 10 percent had an after-tax yield of 10.5 percent and an after-tax *real* yield of only 0.5 percent. By contrast, if that individual earns a 10 percent interest rate when the inflation rate is 5 percent, the after-tax yield is 7 percent and the real after-tax yield is 2 percent. The effective tax rate on the same real interest income falls from 90 percent when inflation is 10 percent to 60 percent when inflation is 5 percent. In emphasizing that the tax reduction caused by lower inflation is substantial, it is important not to minimize the remaining tax distortion that even a 5 percent rate of inflation can cause.

The interaction of inflation and the existing tax accounting methods for depreciation and inventories also caused the effective tax rate on the income from corporate capital to rise sharply in the 1970s. In the mid-1960s, nonfinancial corporations, their shareholders, and their creditors paid taxes to federal, state, and local governments equal to 55 percent of their real capital income, including both equity and debt. By the second half of the 1970s, the tax share had jumped to 68 percent—back to where it had been in the early 1950s before accelerated depreciation and before the Investment Tax Credit. With the tax bite rising from 55 percent to 68 percent, the share left for the providers of capital fell from 45 percent to 32 percent, a decline of nearly one-third. The real after-tax rate of return to those who provide the debt and equity capital was only 3.1 percent by the late 1970s, not enough to provide an adequate incentive for saving and risk-taking.

I want to emphasize that this substantial increase in the effective tax rate occurred despite occasional reductions in the statutory corporate tax rate and liberalization of the statutory depreciation rules.

The effective tax rate rose because the increasing rate of inflation caused a rise in the value of artificial tax accounting profits relative to real profits. The primary source of this was due to the reduced value of real depreciation of plant and equipment.

The great significance of this is that the sharp reduction in the rate of inflation that has been achieved since 1980 automatically implies a substantial reduction in the effective rate of tax on the income from corporate capital. In addition, the Administration proposed and Congress enacted in 1981 a major change in tax depreciation rules that provides for substantially faster and therefore more valuable depreciation than had previously existed. Although the 1982 tax act modified the 1981 improvements, the net effect of the two tax changes and the lower rate of inflation represented a significant improvement for all types of depreciable investment.

A useful way to measure the effect of the changes in tax rules and in inflation is by the resulting change in the present value of the depreciation allowances and the Investment Tax Credit. To be specific, consider a company that discounts the tax value of depreciation at a *real* discount rate of 7 percent; when inflation is 8 percent, the corresponding nominal discount rate is 15 percent. Under the pre-1981 tax rules, a piece of equipment with a 9.5 year tax life would have depreciation tax savings and an Investment Tax Credit that together had a present value of forty cents per dollar of investment. The Economic Recovery Tax Act of 1981 (ERTA) provision increased that value to forty-five cents. The Tax Equity and Fiscal Responsibility Act of 1982 (TEFRA) provisions cut it back to forty-three cents. But reducing the expected inflation rate from 8 percent to 6 percent increases the value back from forty-three cents to forty-four cents, and bringing inflation down to 4 percent can raise the value of depreciation and the ITC back to the forty-five cent level of the original ERTA tax rule.

These rather technical details have two very important implications. First, the combination of a low inflation rate and the tax changes that the Administration successfully sponsored in 1981 can bring the overall effective tax rate on the income from corporate capital down substantially and back below even the 55 percent effective tax rate of the mid-1960s. Although this effective tax rate would still be higher than many of us would like to see, it would be at its lowest level in the entire postwar period. The result would be a substantial improvement in the incentive to invest in corporate capital. Second, the present value of depreciation and the effective tax rate on corporate investment still depends a great deal on the rate of inflation. A return of the rate of inflation to 10 percent would offset more than half of the gain that has been made in improving the value of depreciation allowances.

There are, of course, those who point to the current low level of investment in plant and equipment as evidence that the increased investment incentives have failed and are unlikely to improve investment in the future. It is indeed true that real business investment in new plant and equipment was about 5 percent lower in 1982 than in 1981 and is expected to decline another 5 percent between 1982 and 1983. But this should not be interpreted as evidence that the improved tax climate for business investment has failed. The fall in investment indicates that the short-run business cycle conditions have outweighed the long-run improvement in potential after-tax profitability. With capacity utilization below 70 percent and real corporate profits about one-third lower than they were in 1979, it is not at all surprising that investment has declined substantially. Investment continues at its current rate only because firms look at their longer-run needs for capacity and at the opportunities for cost-saving investments in modernizing existing plants. Without the favorable tax changes, the investment rate might have been significantly lower than it is today. I am convinced that as the recovery begins and capacity utilization increases, the new tax rules will mean a higher level of capital formation in business plant and equipment than would otherwise have occurred.

Although the recent changes in the tax treatment of saving and investment represent a major improvement over the earlier tax rules, there is no reason for complacency. More can be done and should be done to strengthen the incentives to save and to invest in business plant and equipment. It would be inappropriate for me in my current position to suggest any specific changes that I might favor. However, I want to assure you that this is a subject that will continue to receive careful attention in the Administration. I am personally very interested in this subject and would welcome your comments and suggestions on possible future tax changes that could strengthen and improve the process of capital formation without imposing unacceptable strains on the budget deficit.

A CONSUMPTION TAX

Many of you already have heard that the Administration is considering a major tax reform initiative and that one of the approaches being discussed is moving from the existing income tax to a tax on consumption or, "consumed income," as some prefer to say. Let me emphasize, however, that this very attractive approach to tax reform is merely being considered at this time and that no specific or final decisions have been made.

Just what is a consumption tax? The fundamental feature of a consumption tax is that individuals pay tax on the amount that they spend on personal consumption. More precisely, each individual adds all of his cash receipts for the year and then substracts all of his savings, including additions to bank accounts, purchases of stocks or other assets, and repayments of loans. This difference between total receipts and total savings-investment outlays is the amount on which the individual paid tax.

There are some important things to note about this procedure. For example, the entire proceeds from the sale of stock or other investments would be included in the individual's cash receipts. At the same time, however, the individual could subtract any amount that is reinvested in new stocks and bonds or added to his bank balance. Capital gains as such are not taxed. Instead, the individual pays tax on the entire value of the sale if those funds are used to finance consumption but pays no tax at all if those funds were reinvested. (This implies that a *process* of transition from the current law to a consumption tax would have to be devised to avoid taxing individuals on the sale of assets that they previously purchased with after-tax income.)

Another noteworthy difference is in the treatment of loans. With a consumption tax, funds obtained by borrowing are included in total receipts subject to taxation. To the extent that such funds are used for investment in financial or real assets, however, those outlays are subtracted from the taxable amount. Thus, only borrowing used to finance consumption is subject to tax.

As these examples make very clear, the consumption tax is not a value added tax or a national sales tax. Instead, like the current income tax, it is collected from each individual based on an individual tax return and a schedule of tax rates. The progressivity of that rate schedule is an issue separate from the question of the appropriateness or desirability of basing individual tax liabilities on a measure of consumption rather than a measure of income received or accrued. The schedule of rates can be set to maintain the current degree of progressivity; taxpayers in each adjusted gross income class can pay the same total tax under the consumption tax that they would pay under the current income tax. Of course, within each adjusted gross income class, those individuals who saved a larger than average proportion of their income would pay less tax than those who saved a smaller than average proportion of their income. Alternatively, the degree of progressivity can be defined in terms of consumption rather than adjusted gross income: The current degree of progressivity can be maintained by setting tax rates so that the taxpayers in each consumed income class pay the same total tax as they would under current income tax rules. Of course, although the current degree of progressivity could be maintained in either of these senses, it need not be. As mentioned above, the progressivity of the tax schedule is a separate issue; consumption tax rates can be designed to achieve any distribution of tax burdens that the electorate wants.

The consumption tax approach appeals to many tax experts as a way of broadening the tax base and lowering tax rates—that is, as an approach to what some have called a flat tax or, perhaps more accurately, a flatter tax. Although a consumption tax does provide a framework for broadening the tax base and lowering rates in this way, many of the same questions about the appropriateness of particular deductions and exclusions that arise in discussions of broad-based income taxes remain in defining the appropriate base of the tax on consumed income.

Some examples will illustrate the nature of these choices. Consider the deduction for state and local taxes. This deduction might be continued under a consumption tax on the grounds that money paid in taxes is clearly not consumed and should be subtracted in calculating net receipts. Similarly, charitable contributions might be deducted in calculating taxable consumption on the basis that a charitable contribution is not itself consumption but transfers the power to consume to the charity. The value of stolen property and casualty losses might be subtracted in calculating total receipts on the grounds that such losses reduce the ability to consume. Personal spending on health care could be treated like other forms of consumption or could be excluded on the theory that health care spending offsets personal losses in a way that is analogous to losses of property. Similarly, employer payments for health insurance premiums might be taxable or excluded depending on the view that is taken about the nature of health care.

As with the income tax, the more that is included to broaden the base, the lower the schedule of tax rates can be to collect any given level of revenue. For each aspect of income or spending, the tax policy decision must reflect the logic of tax fairness, the effects of a specific economic incentive, and the general effect on economic incentives that results from lower overall tax rates.

The consumption tax approach is appealing in a number of ways. The most obvious advantage is the increased incentive to save. Levying the tax on consumption removes the distortion in the present law that favors current consumption and discourages saving.

Many people regard a tax on consumption as inherently fairer than a tax on income. With a consumption tax, two individuals with the same standard of consumption pay the same tax. Some say that the consumption tax is fairer because individuals are taxed on what they consume rather than on what they produce, on "what they take out of the pot instead of on what they put into the pot." Still others think the consumption tax is fairer because it eliminates the opportunity to use tax shelters that reduce tax liabilities by altering measured income.

A consumption tax would significantly simplify personal tax reporting by emphasizing cash receipts and outlays instead of complex accounting definitions. For example, the record keeping and calculations associated with capital gains taxation are eliminated, and only current sales receipts and reinvestment amounts are reported. Calculations of depreciation and amortization are unnecessary since all investment expenses are deducted immediately instead of being stretched out over a number of years.

The experience of the last decade has shown us how inflation distorts the taxation of personal investment income. By taxing nominal capital gains and nominal interest income, current law overstates real income and artificially raises tax liabilities. A consumption tax avoids all such problems since it bypasses the measurement of income and focuses exclusively on taxing consumption.

Of course, any shift from our current system of taxation to a system based on consumption would have to be gradual. Investments made under existing law must be protected from the losses that might result from a capricious change in tax rules. Moreover, individuals who have accumulated savings out of after-tax income should not be subject to a new round of taxes when those savings are consumed.

I have described the consumption tax and discussed some of its advantages and problems because I know there is great curiosity about this approach. I must emphasize, however, that we in the Administration are just beginning to discuss this idea and that no decisions have been made. Many of us do think that taxing consumed income is a promising approach to tax reform—an approach that could guide decisions of a full-scale redesign of our tax system or of more modest piecemeal reform.

BUDGET DEFICITS

This paper has focused on the relationship between tax rules and capital formation. For the long run, an appropriate tax structure can play a central role in achieving a favorable rate of capital formation. During the next several years, however, an equally critical issue is the size of the government's budget deficit.

The primary effect of budget deficits is to reduce capital formation. Government deficits reduce private investment because government borrowing absorbs private saving that would otherwise absorb private investment. If nothing were done to change the spending and tax receipts implied by existing law, the budget deficit could reach 5 or 6 percent of GNP several years from now as the economy approaches full employment. Peacetime deficits of that magnitude are unknown in the United States.

The adverse impact of such deficits far outweigh the favorable effects of tax incentives for greater saving and investment. Since total net private saving has averaged only some 7 percent of GNP for the past several years, budget deficits of 5 or 6 percent of GNP would absorb virtually all net private saving. The long-term consequence of such deficits would clearly be an unacceptably low rate of net investment. Moreover, in the near term the low rate of investment would significantly weaken the recovery in the key industries that are associated with capital formation, including the construction industry, the makers of machinery and equipment, the steel industry, and others. A further effect of large budget deficits is to strengthen the dollar relative to foreign currencies and therefore to encourage imports and weaken the competitive position of U.S. exports in the world economy.

We in the Administration recognize the danger of continuing budget deficits in future years and are committed to reducing the deficits as fast as is possible. The Administration's economic forecast for the period from now through 1988 implies that we have realistically assessed the likely future deficits and that we are not avoiding the possibility of such deficits by assuming improbably rapid growth.

1983 is a critical year for economic policy. The rate of inflation has been dramatically reduced. The economy should soon begin a sustained recovery in which both unemployment and inflation can decline. The tax laws have been modified to encourage saving and investment. High marginal tax rates have been significantly reduced, and tax indexing will soon stop inflation from pushing incomes into higher tax brackets in the future.

One critical problem remains if we are to have a healthy recovery and a future of satisfactory economic growth. The large budget deficits implied by existing law must be reduced sharply. I am confident that the Administration's new budget will in fact propose changes that can lead to rapidly declining deficits in future years. I fervently hope that Congress will share these goals and will work with the Administration to enact this budget.

Chapter 4

Monetary Policy for the 1980s
Paul A. Volcker

We are deluged these days—and we have been for some time—with learned, and not so learned, analyses about the budgetary problem. There has been a lot of plain confusion about the facts and the outlook—and the reality is that any budgetary projection cannot approach the mathematical precision we associate with neat computer printouts. Much of the discussion is overlaid and often confused by differing social, security, or other priorities, which impact the budget. And there are differences in economic analysis as well.

All of this has made it harder to reach a consensus, and to take action in an area where action is inherently difficult. That is one reason why I welcome the effort the American Council for Capital Formation: Center for Policy Research has been making to clarify the issues. I believe it is realistic to suggest that out of discussions like this, a large measure of agreement *is* emerging about the nature of the problem, if not yet agreement about just how to go about dealing with it.

My contribution may fall more in the former category than the latter, which does raise issues outside the purview of my own responsibilities. But, on the assumption that the interaction of fiscal with monetary policies is of critical importance to economic developments, I will not apologize for reviewing some familiar ground.

We don't yet have the benefit of the Administration's budget plan or updated projections from the Congressional Budget Office. But the general magnitudes involved are familiar enough. The deficit for the current fiscal year—and it's probably too late to do much about it, even if there were a consensus that action were desirable—is generally estimated at $175 to $200 billion. And, as I will amplify later, the outcome will remain in that range, or higher, as far ahead as one can see, given present programs and assuming healthy and prolonged economic growth. Indeed, the figures have been cited so often that any sense of alarm may be dissipated by the very familiarity with the numbers. The burden of my comments today is that the hazard is real; that the deficits around 20-25 percent of expenditures and 5 percent or more of the GNP are unacceptably large in a growing economy; and that absence of timely action to reduce those deficits as the economy grows raises a most serious question as to whether the economic expansion we want could, in fact, be sustained for long.

Obviously, we are negotiating a most difficult period in our nation's economic history. But I also believe we can lay—we are in the process of laying—the base for more vigorous and lasting growth. There are now signs that recessionary pressures in some key sectors have abated. Certainly, considerable progress has been made in reversing the inflationary trend of the previous decade. Thus, the stage is set for an economic recovery that can combine the increase in job opportunities and real income that we all desire with greater price stability and more stable, accommodating financial markets. The relevance of action on the deficit is that it is needed to help reconcile those objectives; without such a reconciliation, we risk losing them all.

As you know, consumer prices rose less than 5 percent last year, the slowest rate of increase in a decade and a remarkable improvement from other recent years. We need to recognize that part of the improvement reflected unusually favorable food and energy price developments, low commodity prices generally, and more intense price competition from abroad because of exchange rate considerations. We can't count on those factors continuing indefinitely. Moreover, we must also recognize that we are still far short of price stability; in fact, inflation is really only back to the pace of 1971, which was judged so intolerable at that time that wage and price controls were imposed.

Unlike 1971, however—in fact unlike the entire 1970s—trends of underlying costs and inflation expectations are now moving lower; and those trends should be sustainable as the economy recovers its upward momentum in 1983 and beyond. In that connection, the recent behavior of productivity is encouraging. After declining throughout much of the late 1970s and into the early 1980s, labor productivity turned up appreciably last year. The data are always hard to interpret in the midst of recession, but there is now quite a lot of evidence that potentially lasting improvements in efficiency by both workers and management are underway. Combined with continuing moderation in growth of nominal wage and salary payments, the result should bring long-lasting reductions in cost pressures and expansion of real incomes.

I am acutely aware that these gains against inflation have been achieved in a context of serious economic hardship. Millions of workers are unemployed, many businesses are hard-pressed to maintain profitability, and business bankruptcies are at a postwar high. In my view, those hardships could not have been escaped by simply letting inflation proceed and accelerate, with all the damage that would imply to the basic productive capability of the economy and the social fabric. But it certainly does emphasize the need to carry through—not simply to start a recovery, but to put policies in place that can sustain an expansion of output and employment over the years ahead.

It is in that context—the need to realize the longer-run promise in our current situation—that our ability to bring the ballooning federal deficits under control is critical.

A few figures suggest the perspective. During the 1970s, the federal deficit averaged around 2 percent of GNP, rising to a peak of 4 percent in fiscal year 1976 in the middle of the deepest recession of the postwar period. We thought those figures were high, and in historical perspective they were. In contrast, the deficit in the current fiscal year could reach about 6 percent of GNP.

While hardly comforting, that figure is still not the crux of the problem. The current deficit reflects the effects of unsatisfactory economic performance and high unemployment. In that sense, well over half—perhaps two-thirds—reflects cyclical factors. The heart of the difficulty is that there is, as things stand, no reasonable prospect that we can grow out of the deficit. Even if the economy expands at or beyond most projections, over the next few years and with satisfactory price performance, the deficit is not likely to fall below 4-5 percent of GNP over the rest of the decade, assuming no change in current policies. Even those estimates may be a bit low.

It has become fashionable (and useful) to talk in terms of "cyclical" and "structural" deficits. These often are not well-understood concepts, and it would be useful to review them briefly.

The cyclical portion reflects the effect of current business conditions on the deficit. In a recession, the deficit is temporarily enlarged as slack activity and high unemployment cut into revenues and raise outlays for certain programs, most notably—but not exclusively—

unemployment benefits. When activity is depressed these cyclical deficits can help support spendable incomes and reduce the fluctuations in activity. Today, that explains a large portion of the deficit, and it can be reasonably agreed at least that portion is benign, supporting income during recession.

In contrast, calculation of the structural deficit attempts to abstract from the cyclical stage of the economy. It reflects the imbalance that would remain even if the economy were operating at a fairly high level.

The reason the total deficit will not recede significantly as business recovers, and could even grow larger, is that the structural portion threatens to grow at least as fast as recovery reduces the cyclical component.

It is tempting to suggest that the budget problem is a statistical artifact related to "pessimistic" economic forecasts and can be eliminated by stronger economic growth than is expected by most forecasters. But that is wishful thinking; under any reasonable forecast for sustained growth and without further policy adjustment, the deficits will remain historically huge unless we make the unacceptable assumption that we will also revert to an historically high inflation rate. I would point out that deficits of the size projected would feed on themselves because, in those circumstances, interest payments on the debt will remain a rapidly growing budget category, even in an environment of reasonably declining interest rates.

Ironically, the budget difficulties over the medium term are compounded by our success in bringing down inflation. Although there is little doubt of the longer-run benefits to the economy (and eventually the budget) of lower inflation, the transition to lower inflation for a while widens the deficit. In terms of revenues, the adjustment to reduced inflation largely is contemporaneous, as receipts quickly reflect the slower expansion of nominal income. On the spending side, however, the response is considerably slower and possibly smaller.

Outlays in indexed programs—which comprise about a third of the budget—respond automatically to inflation, but with a lag. At the same time, a large share of the budget is set in nominal, not real, terms. In logic, appropriations should be cut to reflect a lower rate of price increase; in practice, that response to disinflation is likely to be imperfect. Specific action must be taken to pare outlays to reflect the lower prices, and inertia works against the process. One example of this problem has recently received attention in the press: how to "spend" the dividend of lower inflation for defense programs.

In this connection, I would note that price performance last year was far better than expected by many forecasters. While that has had short-run budgetary consequences, we are still obviously some distance from price performance that could be called "reasonable stability." Realistically, it seems to me, we can and should look to further declines in the inflation rate, and take account of that in our budgetary planning.

As I suggested earlier, we can all try to refine estimates, looking at different growth and inflation rates, as well as more technical considerations. But what stands out in the present situation is that, whatever those particular assumptions, we now have a federal budget situation in which current spending plans for years ahead outrun the revenue base by a wide margin. The problem will not go away as the economy recovers from the recession.

Left unattended, that situation poses a strong potential for a clash between the need to finance the deficit and the rising financial requirements for housing and the business investment that is crucial to healthy and sustained recovery. In the end, all those needs have to be met out of saving, and all our experience suggests there isn't likely to be enough to go around.

Savings—net of depreciation—has typically run at 10 percent or less of the GNP. The prospective *structural* deficits later in the decade could well absorb as much as one-half of that amount. Gross savings—that is, including capital consumption—are roughly twice the net. But the prospective deficits would still preempt as much as a quarter of the total. Looked at either way, the diversion of savings would be without peacetime precedent for relatively prosperous years.

Of course, the government will be financed. It will be financed in the market, and the unavoidable implication is that interest rates will in real terms be bid higher than otherwise. The higher interest rates will dampen private investment and housing. They may also attract funds from abroad, supplementing our domestic savings. But a net transfer of savings from abroad implies a current account deficit—in other words, relatively weak exports and high imports, hardly a happy prospect. The long-run implication is both a weak investment and a weak balance of payments structure, with a lower level of output over time.

That, essentially, is the "text book" analysis. In the real world of today, the adverse consequences are likely to be exacerbated.

After years of inflation, sharp fluctuations in interest rates, and unsatisfactory economic performance, an atmosphere of exceptional caution and uncertainty about future planning by business is understandable. I don't think there is much doubt that the prospect of huge budget deficits contributes to that mood in a way that cannot be precisely measured—lingering concerns about a sharp rebound in interest rates from already relatively high levels, continuing strong pressures on monetary policy, or a reversion to inflationary policies "forced" by the deficits.

The point is reinforced by the sense of uncertainty in financial markets and institutional strains domestically and internationally, strains that are aggravated to the extent that the basic level of interest rates is higher than otherwise necessary. We fortunately have a strong and effective governmental apparatus undergirding the stability of the financial structure. But we work at cross purposes to encouraging recovery to the extent that anticipation of future excessive budgetary deficits adds to market pressures.

In that respect, let me emphasize again that my concern is much more about the growing structural deficit than the present cyclical deficit.

In the fiscal policy environment we became accustomed to in the postwar era, the expansion of federal budget deficits in periods of economic slack certainly did not prevent interest rate declines in recession, and interest rates have, of course, declined in 1982 despite a larger deficit. In circumstances like those, private credit demands drop, helping to offset the impact of the deficit. Moreover, in the past the reasonable expectation that large deficits would recede as business activity turned up sustained confidence about the stabilizing role of the federal budget.

The current atmosphere is quite different in that respect. To be sure, it can be said that most of the recent and current budget deficits are recession-induced, replacing rather than competing with private credit demands. But we cannot now look forward to a return to balance or low deficits as the economy expands.

That is one reason, despite the large recent declines, interest rates remain high by historical standards. Moreover, concern is expressed that interest rates have neared their cyclical lows and could rise again as economic activity recovers, even though they remain well above current inflation rates.

The question naturally arises, if all that is true, whether monetary policy shouldn't do something about it in the interests of speeding lower interest rates and recovery. In approaching that question, I must first emphasize that monetary policy cannot itself create real savings and correct a structural deficit. The basic savings-investment balance—with all its implications for future real interest rates—is simply beyond our influence.

We can, indeed, influence the growth of the money supply and other liquid assets and the degree of current pressure on bank reserve positions. In fact, growth in the monetary aggregates has been relatively high in recent months, and exceeded the targets set early in 1982. Reserve pressures have been minimal. Under all the circumstances, that result has seemed appropriate, given the evident desire to hold more liquidity, and fully consistent with the needs of the economy *and* progress against inflation.

But there are limits to the process of credit and money creation. Beyond a certain point, the result would be to create further doubt about the prospects for further disinflation and lower interest rates, aggravating the uncertainties in those respects related to the budget deficit. In the end, excessive monetary growth would put us back in the same unsatisfactory situation of more deeply ingrained inflation expectations and greater skepticism about the ability of our nation to manage its economic affairs. The effects on interest rates—particularly long-term interest rates—and on prospects for sustained recovery would thus be perverse.

There was a time when the American public felt confident about the ability of government to maintain stability and improve its economic situation. The events of the past decade and more undermined that sense of conviction, and we must restore it. In some ways—notably in the progress against inflation—we are making progress. But fears that excessive budget deficits will undermine financial discipline work in the opposite direction, and those fears would only be compounded by excessive monetary expansion.

Let me put the point another way. We are exposed to fears of "out-of-control" structural deficits, and the result is upward pressure on interest rates, particularly at the longer end of the maturity spectrum, for reasons beyond measurable economic effects. The budget is a plan: as such, it is a powerful symbol of the government's resolve to follow a disciplined non-inflationary course. To the extent the budget deficit appears to be intractable, the burden placed on monetary policy to demonstrate the government's resolve to restore stability is increased, and our flexibility in responding to current developments is reduced, not enhanced. The converse is equally true—meaningful action to demonstrate the government's economic discipline on the fiscal side would reduce concern about future inflation and future interest rates. In the process, it would reinforce confidence that monetary policy over the years ahead can do its job in maintaining a course consistent with price stability without intolerable market pressures.

The focus on monetary policy—together with the understandable urge to seek a relatively simple, comprehensible and desirable measure for "policy" in the interest of maintaining confidence—has spawned a number of proposals for a fixed rule, whether a pre-set monetary target for years ahead, a fixed price for gold or other commodities, or keeping interest rates, real or nominal, short or long, within some band. I can understand and sympathize with the desire. But I am skeptical, to say the least, that in so complex and changing an economy as ours, the policy problem or the policy objective can be reduced to so simple and unvarying a measure. The recent distortions in the monetary aggregates relating to purely institutional change—the introduction of new high-interest deposit instruments on the border of "money" and "savings"—reflect one kind of difficulty that arises from time to time. More significant over time may be shifts in established relationships in trends in the "target" and the real world of economic activity and inflation. We can all appreciate the desirability of laying out policy intentions as clearly and simply as possible. But I doubt that we can, in effect, ever put policy on "automatic pilot," and that any simple rule for monetary policy can effectively substitute for a coherent overall policy approach, of which the budget is inevitably an important part.

I also don't want to suggest there is a simple "tradeoff," as sometimes suggested, between future budget policy and current monetary policy. Reducing the threat of those large structural deficits stretching out to the end of the decade, in and of itself, should have favorable effects on current interest rates and in damping concerns about future increases. In this setting, the old maxim about virtue providing its own reward should be measurable in a tangible way. And there can be broader benefits. The lower the structural deficit the greater the confidence, not just of the financial markets but of the community at large—labor and management, storekeeper and shopper, at home and abroad—in the government's will to follow a disciplined course. This should reinforce the disinflation process, even as recovery proceeds. It will support moderation in wage bargaining, caution in pricing policies, confidence in financial markets—and, of course, lower real interest rates.

None of that would justify monetary policy moving in a contrary direction—abandoning our continuing and necessary concern with restoring reasonable price stability. That point remains central. At the same time, a better fiscal outlook—with all it implies—would certainly provide a better environment for the conduct of monetary policy, relieving concern about the longer-term implications of every twist and turn in the monetary aggregates or short-term policy actions. As things stand, fear of growing deficits clouds the future and contributes to market pressures and inflationary uncertainties, adding to the burdens on monetary policy.

I am conscious that I have taken too long to identify a problem with which you are broadly familiar. The need is to resolve the problem. We have time, in the sense that we are talking about changes that should only begin to take effect in 1984, with full impact in 1985, in 1986, and the years beyond; an abrupt change in 1983 is neither feasible, nor in the midst of recession and with the structural portion of the deficit still limited, desirable. But it is also true that if those future deficits are to be controlled, the process must start now and with energy and force. Basic budget trends take time to change, and the knowledge that they will be changed is what will affect markets now.

The amounts involved are large, but certainly not beyond our capacity. The necessary changes can be phased in over a two or three year period. Our capacity to save and to finance is large enough so that some residual deficit can be managed.

It is obviously beyond my competence, or the province of the Federal Reserve, to deal with all the particular priorities that must be balanced—national and social security, entitlements and taxes. The sheer arithmetic of the Budget does suggest that some changes will be necessary in all the major budget components, and we are all aware that initiatives have already been proposed in a number of areas.

I do not for a moment underestimate the task before the Administration and the Congress in reconciling the competing claims, and achieving the necessary legislation. But I also believe the problem is now well recognized, and that the bleak budgetary picture I have described earlier will not, in fact, be permitted to materialize. We have come a long way toward laying the groundwork for lasting expansion, and we can and will deal with this challenge.

PART II

**SOLUTIONS TO THE PROBLEM
WITH THE TAX SYSTEM
Reform of the Federal Income Tax**

 Chapter 5

The Accelerated Cost Recovery System: An Evaluation of the 1981 and 1982 Cost Recovery Provisions

Norman B. Ture

INTRODUCTION: THE CHANGING FOCUS OF TAX POLICY REGARDING DEPRECIATION

For a capital intensive country like the United States, the income tax treatment of capital recovery has weighty effects on the nation's economic efficiency and progress. In the twentieth century history of the U.S. income tax, these effects have occasionally, but not always, been a major policy concern. From today's vantage point, it is fair to say that although tax policy in this respect has been uneven, faltering, often misguided and poorly informed, its long-term trend has been in the direction of achieving greater neutrality in the income tax treatment of durable, exhaustible capital instruments. As this discussion will show, tax neutrality in this regard requires "true expensing" of costs incurred to acquire and use such capital. Tax policy progress in this area, therefore, is to be measured in terms of how close the law and regulations have taken tax practice to true expensing.

This progress has been uneven because policy has focused on concerns other than those dictated by the requirements of neutrality. Policymakers have at times looked to equity considerations in shaping tax rules pertaining to depreciation. At other times, there has been a thrust toward making depreciation for tax purposes more "realistic": this greater realism has been variously perceived, sometimes in the sense of conforming the number of taxable years over which particular types of assets might be written off for tax purposes with actual business practice, and sometimes in the sense of seeking to conform the depreciation charges allowed for tax purposes with "true economic" depreciation. At yet other times, changes in capital recovery provisions have been perceived as potentially effective means for altering incentives for private capital formation and for promoting economic growth. On several occasions, capital recovery provisions have been revised to increase federal tax revenues, and a frequently addressed criterion in depreciation policymaking has been standards of accounting for book purposes.

Only in very recent times has a concern about tax neutrality—more particularly about reducing the income tax bias against saving and capital formation—figured significantly in policymaking with respect to capital recovery provisions. Ironically, this concern was the rationale for those provisions in the Tax Equity and Fiscal Responsibility Act of 1982 (TEFRA) that repealed the scheduled acceleration of the Accelerated Cost Recovery System (ACRS) allowances in 1985 and 1986. It was alleged that, combined with the Investment Tax Credit (ITC), the fully accelerated ACRS provisions would be "better than expensing." As is shown later in this discussion, this assertion is mistaken; these TEFRA provisions should be seen as a move away from, rather than toward, neutrality. As a result of the TEFRA provisions, there is renewed urgency in efforts to achieve neutrality in the tax treatment of saving committed to additions to the stock of durable but exhaustible capital.

This is not to say that the other concerns are necessarily inconsequential or uninteresting, but the very essence of policymaking is discrimination among alternative considerations and the selection of priorities. Too often the policymaking process has faltered because it has been inadequately advised; policymakers have stumbled into decisionmaking instead of carefully and deliberately choosing their objectives and devising effective means for their attainment. Conferences such as this can contribute bountifully to good policymaking by sharpening perceptions of the issues at stake and the bases for setting priorities among the goals of policy.

This discussion urges that neutrality is the appropriate central goal of tax policy with respect to the design of capital recovery provisions and examines the conditions required for attaining this neutrality within the framework of income taxation. Several of the other policymaking considerations in this area are critically reviewed to show their inadequacies as guides to depreciation for tax purposes.

Finally, the discussion turns to the Accelerated Cost Recovery System (ACRS) enacted in the Economic Recovery Tax Act of 1981 (ERTA), to the major retreat from ERTA in the Tax Equity and Fiscal Responsibility Act of 1982, (TEFRA), and to some of the requirements for renewed progress in this policy area.

EQUITY AS A CRITERION FOR DEPRECIATION POLICY

At times, efforts to revise the statutory provisions or regulations on depreciation in the interests of greater tax neutrality have been criticized, if not indeed frustrated, on grounds of equity. If all businesses were sole proprietorships, some concept of equity might be an appropriate constraint on depreciation practice for tax purposes. It is difficult, if not impossible, however, to perceive the relevance of an equity criterion applied to depreciation for purposes of determining the taxable income of a corporate business or partnership.

The issue here, of course, far transcends depreciation; it addresses the basic questions raised by a separate corporate income tax. The often repeated—and more often in practice, ignored—truism that corporations do not pay taxes means that there is no rational basis for applying equity criteria to elements of the corporation income tax. At least until the tax shifting process begins, corporation income tax liabilities are, in fact, assumed by individual corporate shareholders. Tax law provisions that systematically or haphazardly differentiate tax liabilities among corporations imply nothing with respect to meeting or violating either horizontal or vertical equity standards, unless one assumes perfect homogeneity of the shareholder population. The fact that the tax liabilities of "similarly situated" corporations differ does not necessarily result in differing tax liabilities for those of their shareholders who are "similarly situated." By the same token, insisting on equal tax liabilities for "similarly situated" corporations does not guarantee that their shareholders' tax liabilities will meet the equity tests. The same observations apply in the case of partnerships.

ACCOUNTING STANDARDS AND DEPRECIATION FOR TAX PURPOSES

In the discipline of accountancy, the concept and measurement of depreciation are ancient concerns, long predating the contemporary income tax. In the accountant's view, the acquisition and use by a firm of durable but exhaustible assets requires some systematic time allocation of the acquisition cost against the firm's revenues, in order to measure the firm's net income. In the ordinary case, the time path of the costs the firm incurs in acquiring such assets, installing them, and readying them for use does not coincide to any significant extent with the time path of the revenues to which the use of the assets contributes. In the extreme case, all of those costs may be incurred before the assets are put in use; the costs are prepaid and, if charged against the revenues of the year(s) in which they are incurred, would misrepresent the net income results of that year's (or those years') operations and those of the subsequent years in which the assets are used, as well. In this setting, depreciation is a system for allocating over time, in a defined and definite way, these prepaid costs as charges against the revenues that they helped to produce.

As an accounting device for allocating prepaid costs, depreciation will only accidentally result in an accurate measure of net income in any given operating period. By the same token, it will only accidentally result in accurate valuation of the assets being depreciated. It would result in accurate measurement of income and of asset values only if it provided a correct measure of the change from the beginning to the end of the operating period in the present value of the gross income still to be produced by use of the assets. As is shown later in this discussion, providing such a measure is a virtual impossibility, even when the depreciation system deliberately seeks to do so. When the depreciation system seeks, instead, to allocate prepaid costs over time, there is virtually no likelihood that its use will result in accurate measures of income or asset worth.

In a world without income taxation, any inelegance in the delineation or measurement of depreciation would impose costs for the firm's owners and managers by misinforming them about both the assets' valuation and the most efficient way of using them. If such costs were systematic rather than random, they would contribute to misallocation of resources, with respect to both the aggregate level and the composition of saving and capital formation. In efficient capital markets, however, any such distortions resulting from mistakes in measuring depreciation would tend to be self-correcting. In a world with income taxes, on the other hand, incorrect determinations of depreciation impose not only the costs of transitory misallocation resulting from misinformation but also much longer lasting costs of misallocation resulting from differences in the present value of the tax liabilities incurred over the "life" of the assets. In this tax-burdened world, even if efficient capital markets were to cast up information to show the nature and extent of the mistake in depreciation, the distortive effects of the mistaken depreciation practice would continue until the law or regulations dictating that practice were changed.

Whatever their merits for purposes of reporting company results and conditions, the accounting concept and measure of depreciation do not offer useful guides for depreciation policy for tax purposes. From time to time, tax policymakers and commentators have criticized the tax treatment of depreciation on the grounds that it differed in form and/or in results from the accounting treatment. It has sometimes been proposed that business taxpayers be allowed substantial latitude in depreciation practice for tax purposes provided they "booked" the depreciation claimed on their tax returns. In some part, proposals of this sort have reflected the view that taxpayers would be prevented from claiming excessive depreciation for tax purposes if they were required to report such changes to their shareholders and to the investing public at large. Conformity, in this case, has been seen as a means for permitting more liberal and more flexible tax treatment without fear of tax avoidance. In some part, such proposals have reflected the view that if depreciation for tax purposes conformed with depreciation for book purposes, one could safely assume that the tax depreciation was "realistic," hence not excessive.

These views reflect a long-standing but ill-founded belief that the depreciation system appropriate for an income tax requires the correct measure of the actual depreciation sustained on the particular assets used by each particular taxpayer during a particular operating period. Over most of the U.S. income tax history of depreciation rules, this particularization of depreciation has been a dominant criterion, although, to be sure, it has seldom been rigorously observed in practice. While particularization might very well be a desirable goal for accountants to pursue in a world free of income taxes, given the marvelous variety of business experience, its pursuit in depreciation for tax purposes works against neutrality and erroneously assigns tax liabilities among business taxpayers. In this light, conformity might well constrain business taxpayers' depreciation practice for tax purposes but only at the expense of distortion of relative valuation of assets from business to business.

ECONOMIC DEPRECIATION AND TAX NEUTRALITY

While many economists would agree that there is no relevant equity case for implementing economic depreciation in the tax law, there is very likely a broadly based consensus that economic depreciation is required in the interests of tax neutrality. The latter consensus, if it does indeed exist, is mistaken; implementing economic depreciation, were it feasible to do so, would preclude tax neutrality.

The neutrality issue has two dimensions. The primary neutrality issue is how to treat saving so as to insure that the income tax does not increase the cost of saving disproportionately with the cost of current consumption. The secondary dimension of neutrality concerns how to treat outlays for capital to insure that the tax does not differentially change the value of diverse units of capital. Neutrality, in short, requires that the tax does not alter either the cost of saving (= investment) relative to that of consumption or of one type of saving or capital relative to that of another.

The Primary Neutrality Question

A simple and rigorous way of assessing the effect of an income tax on the cost of acquiring or holding capital (the source of future income) relative to the cost of consumption is to compare the percentage reduction in consumption with the percentage reduction in future income that can be acquired with a dollar of pretax income after an income tax is levied. For example, suppose that absent a tax, one can obtain a perpetual income stream of 10 cents if $1.00 of current income is used to buy a unit of capital instead of $1.00 of consumption goods. Now, impose an income tax at a rate of, say, 50 percent. With the tax, $1.00 of income now buys either 50 cents of consumption goods or a perpetual income stream of 2.5 cents: The $1.00 of pretax income is reduced to 50 cents by the tax; invested in the same asset at the same yield, it provides 5 cents of pretax income, which is in turn taxed, leaving 2.5 cents as the available income. The tax reduces the amount of future income obtainable with $1.00 of pretax income twice as much as it reduces the amount of current consumption. Equivalently, the tax doubles the cost (the required amount of current pretax income) of consumption but quadruples the cost of any given amount of available future income. Hence, the tax doubles the cost of future income compared with that of current consumption.

A formal proof is afforded by setting the cost (P) of a source of future income, absent the income tax, equal to the present value of the stream of gross returns (quasi rents) that the source will provide.

$$P = \sum_{i=1}^{N} Y_i^* , \qquad (5.1)$$

The Accelerated Cost Recovery System 53

where

Y_i^* = the present value of the quasi rent in year i, and
N = the number of years during which the capital will be held.

Clearly, P is the amount of current consumption foregone to acquire the future income.

With an income tax at rate t, obtaining the same stream of quasi rents (assuming no change in the real yield of the capital) requires having $\frac{P}{(1-t)}$ of pretax income. But these quasi rents are also taxed under an income tax of the present configuration. Hence,

$$\frac{P}{1-t} \rightarrow \sum_{i=1}^{N} Y_i^*(1-t) \ . \tag{5.2}$$

Equivalently, P dollars will buy an after-tax stream of future income $= \sum_{i=1}^{N} Y_i^*(1-t)^2$, and to have $\sum_{i=1}^{N} Y_i^*$ requires $\frac{P}{(1-t)^2}$ of pretax income. On the other hand, to have P dollars of current consumption requires $\frac{P}{1-t}$ dollars of pretax income. The income tax increases the cost of saving relative to the cost of consumption by $\frac{P}{(1-t)^2} / \frac{P}{(1-t)}$, i.e., by $\frac{1}{(1-t)}$.

Where the future income is provided by depreciable capital, the availability of depreciation allowances for tax purposes ameliorates this income tax bias against saving in varying degree, depending on how rapidly the amount invested may be written off. The bias remains in some degree, however, so long as the present value of depreciation and any other capital recovery allowance is less than the amount invested.

Notationally, under the present tax law,

$$\frac{P}{1-t} \rightarrow \sum_{i=1}^{N} Y_i^*(1-t) + \sum_{i=1}^{M} tD_i^* \ , \tag{5.3}$$

or

$$\frac{P}{(1-t)^2} - \frac{\sum_{i=1}^{M} tD_i^*}{(1-t)} = \sum_{i=1}^{N} Y_i^* \ , \tag{5.3A}$$

where

M = the number of years over which depreciation deductions must be allocated for tax purposes, and

D_i^* = the present value of the depreciation deduction in year i.

If $\Sigma D = P$ and $M > 0$, then $\sum_{i=1}^{M} D_i^* < P$, and the tax increases the cost of saving relative to consumption.

In the general case, neutrality may be achieved either by expensing, that is, by excluding the amount invested from current taxable income while taxing the gross quasi rents (including the proceeds from any ultimate disposition of the capital) or by including the amount saved and invested in current taxable income but fully excluding from tax all of the quasi rents. These are perfectly equivalent in terms of their effects on the cost of saving, given a constant rate of tax over the "life" of the asset. With expensing, the current income used to acquire the capital escapes the income tax by virtue of the deduction of the capital outlay, but all of the gross returns—rather than the gross returns after depreciation—are taxed as they accrue, that is,

$$P \to \sum_{i=1}^{N} Y_i^* (1-t) \ . \tag{5.4}$$

In the alternative, the current income used to purchase the asset is subject to tax, but no tax applies to the gross returns; the current income needed to buy the asset must be enough so that after tax, an amount equal to the cost of the asset remains, that is,

$$\frac{P}{1-t} \to \sum_{i=1}^{N} Y_i^* \ . \tag{5.5}$$

It is obvious that (5.5) may be obtained simply by dividing both sides of (5.4) by $(1-t)$.

Either approach results in the tax's having the same effect on the cost of saving as on the cost of consumption. As shown, in order to have P dollars of current consumption with the tax, one needs $\frac{P}{1-t}$ dollars of pretax current income. In order to have $\sum_{i=1}^{N} Y_i^*$ of future income with the tax under neutral tax treatment, one needs $\frac{P}{1-t}$ of current income. The income tax with neutral tax treatment of saving does not alter the cost of saving relative to that of consumption.

In contrast, the use of economic depreciation—indeed, of any depreciation method that spreads depreciation deductions over time—locks in the income tax bias against saving and in favor of current consumption. With respect to this primary income tax nonneutrality, the considerations advanced for using economic depreciation for tax purposes are irrelevant. Unless immediate expensing of saving (i.e., capital outlays) is allowed, the only valid generalization is that the more rapid the depreciation (i.e., the greater the proportion of the saving or investment that may be charged against income in the early years of the capital unit's "life"), the less the tax bias against saving.

The standard objection to this position is that, in effect, it calls for replacing the income tax with an expenditure tax. The objection, however, is more a matter of nomenclature than of substance. Nothing in the concept of income for income tax purposes requires including in the tax base both the annual return generated by capital and the capitalized amount of those returns. Expensing of saving is one route toward assuring neutral *income* tax treatment of consumption and saving uses of income.

The Secondary Neutrality Question

The secondary neutrality question pertains to the tax treatment of differing types of capital required to assure that the tax reduces the value of diverse capital units in the same proportion.

Those who believe that economic depreciation is required to provide this assurance maintain that any deviation of measured depreciation from economic depreciation results in understatement or overstatement of taxable income to an extent that is likely to vary from firm to firm and therefore result in imposing differing real tax rates among them. Moreover, it is maintained that these differences are likely to be associated with diverse types of capital and their "useful lives," resulting in a tax bias with respect to particular kinds of capital and distorting the allocation of saving among capital alternatives.

This view is challenged at two levels. At one level, the practical possibility of measuring conceptually correct depreciation is seriously questioned. This question is examined subsequently. The more basic challenge pertains to whether any depreciation system can provide tax neutrality in the sense that the tax alters the value of different types of capital in the same proportion.

The view that economic depreciation assures income tax neutrality is based on the implicit and unreal assumption of perfectly homogeneous capital. In fact, given any differences in the physical attributes and uses of capital such that there are differences in the time paths of the quasi rents different units of capital produce, the use of economic depreciation assures *non*neutrality of the income tax among types of capital. That is to say, the application of a tax to net income, defined as quasi rents less economic depreciation, differentially alters the present value of the stream of after-tax quasi rents of different kinds of capital compared with the relative prices of these capital types in the absence of the tax. A cursory glance at the simplest notational statement of the present value of the quasi rent stream shows why this is so.

Absent any income tax, the value (V) of the asset at any point in time is the present value of the expected remaining quasi rents, equal to P in equation (5.1) above. With an income tax imposed at rate t, the value of the asset at any point in time is the present value of the expected remaining quasi rents less the tax on each such quasi rent plus the tax value of any capital recovery or depreciation deduction allowed for tax purposes. This relationship is expressed as

$$V_t = \sum_{i=1}^{N} \left[Y_i^*(1-t) + tD_i^* \right], \qquad (5.6)$$

where D_i^* = the present value of the economic depreciation expected in year i.[1] The difference in the value of the asset with and without tax is equal to the tax rate times the difference between the present value of the stream of depreciation deductions and the present value of the quasi rents, that is,

$$V_t - V = t \left[\sum_{i=1}^{N} (D_i^* - Y_i^*) \right]. \qquad (5.7)$$

The percentage change in the value of the capital resulting from the imposition of the tax is

$$\frac{V_t - V}{V} = t \left[\frac{\sum_{i=1}^{N} D_i^*}{\sum_{i=1}^{N} Y_i^*} - 1 \right] \times 100. \qquad (5.8)$$

Consider any two units of capital with the same value at a given point in time, absent income taxation but with differing time paths of expected quasi rents. Since the amount of economic depreciation in any year is a function of the time path of the remaining quasi rents, differences between the capital units in the time paths of their quasi rents means differences in the time paths of the economic depreciation. Since the *un*discounted sum of the economic depreciation amounts of each asset is equal to the present value of its quasi rents, hence is the same for both units, the differences in their time paths means that the present values of the depreciation streams of the two units must differ. With the application of the income tax, the percentage changes in the values of the two units of capital must differ. Hence, the use of economic depreciation means that the tax will affect the value of differing units of capital in differing proportions, that is, the use of economic depreciation insures that the tax will not be neutral.[2]

The view that economic depreciation must be used in the determination of taxable income in order to assure income tax neutrality among types and units of capital is analytically mistaken. It cannot, therefore, serve as a basis for evaluating the rightness or wrongness of any depreciation method actually used for tax purposes.

True expensing of amounts saved and invested assures income tax neutrality among diverse capital units. With expensing, there is an immediate reduction in the amount of pretax income required to obtain the given amount of future income, so that, as in (5.4) above,

$$P \to \sum_{i=1}^{N} Y_i^* (1-t) = V_{t_x} .$$

The percentage change in the value of any asset resulting from the tax with expensing, then, is

$$\frac{V_{t_x} - V}{V} = \frac{\sum_{i=1}^{N} Y_i^* (1-t) - \sum_{i=1}^{N} Y_i^*}{\sum_{i=1}^{N} Y_i^*} \qquad (5.9)$$

$$= -t.$$

Expensing reduces the present value of any and every capital unit in the same percentage as the income tax rate. It affords neutrality, therefore, both in the primary and secondary terms, (i.e., with respect to the relative costs of saving and consumption and with respect to the reduction in the values of diverse capital units). Insofar as neutrality is deemed to be an important criterion, therefore, durable but exhaustible capital should be expensed, not depreciated, for tax purposes. Economic depreciation does not conform with the requirements of the relevant neutrality concepts.

The Feasibility of Economic Depreciation

If economic depreciation were to be adopted for tax purposes despite the violence it would do to neutrality, severe problems of administration and compliance would be posed. The only purpose to be served by the use of economic depreciation is to particularize depreciation deductions to each firm and to the capital it holds. This purpose is not served by any convention regarding depreciation. Accordingly, averages of useful lives of various broad classes of property held by more than one taxpayer or patterns of depreciation deemed to be common to various classes of property are not relevant or useful. If economic depreciation were to be used in order to measure the actual net income generated by the particular capital put to particular use by particular taxpayers, it would have to be determined on a taxpayer-by-taxpayer, capital-by-capital basis. If any conventional system were to be applied—whether or not guided by findings of investigations of average useful lives or typical depreciation patterns—there would be no occasion for concern with economic depreciation. Any write-off convention is as good as any other; the choice among such conventions is a matter of the overall tax rate to be applied to income produced by depreciable capital.

The determination of economic depreciation sustained on particular assets in particular uses by particular taxpayers poses enormous difficulties. These difficulties derive from the very concept of economic depreciation, that is, the loss between two points in time in the present value of the remaining stream of quasi rents produced by the asset. Consider what must be known to determine the amount of economic depreciation expected to be sustained in any given period of time:[3] (1) the amount of the quasi rent expected to be produced in each ensuing year the asset is held by the taxpayer; (2) the salvage value or proceeds from disposition of the asset; (3) the number of remaining years the asset will be held; (4) the tax rate and any and all other tax provisions that bear on the amount of tax payable on each of the remaining year's quasi rents; and (5) the rate at which future receipts and outlays are to be discounted to find their present values. Without accurate measures of each of these variables, economic depreciation for any period cannot be accurately determined. But less than precise measurement of economic depreciation negates the very reason for using it rather than any depreciation convention.

Information requirements argue that economic depreciation is not practicable. The determinants of the change in the value of a capital unit are so varied from firm to firm, capital to capital, and time to time as to preclude ready and confident calculation by any firm.

Whatever its utility in abstract economic analysis, economic depreciation has no corresponding virtues as part of an income tax. Rather than providing neutrality among diverse types of capital, economic depreciation would insure that the income tax would differentially affect their values. It would, moreover, also insure the income tax bias against saving and capital formation and in favor of consumption. Even if these objectives were disregarded, economic depreciation could not, as a practical matter, be implemented.

DEPRECIATION AND INCENTIVES FOR GROWTH

One of the major issues in tax depreciation policy is whether depreciation provisions should be addressed to promoting greater amounts of capital formation and faster economic growth than would otherwise occur. The issue has been addressed from various perspectives, including (1) the extent to which capital formation responds to changes in depreciation provisions and (2) the contribution that additions to the stock of capital make to expanding real output. If capital formation were inert with respect to structural tax provisions, and if the pace of economic progress were substantially independent of the amount of capital, the issue might be deemed moot.

To argue that capital formation is unaffected by depreciation provisions in the tax Code is to assert that the cost of capital does not enter into saving and investment decisions, which in turn implies some very peculiar and unreasonable things about individuals' utility functions. Both heuristic and empirical analysis argue the contrary view, that both the aggregate amount and the composition of additions to the stock of durable but exhaustible capital are significantly responsive to capital recovery allowances in the tax laws or changes therein.

Similarly, to argue that the rate of investment is of little or no significance with respect to the rate of increase in total output is to maintain superabundance—or very nearly so—in the amount of capital relative to other production inputs. The ratio of capital to other production inputs differs among economies and through time, but this ratio has never become so high that use of an additional capital unit adds zero to total output. To be sure, as this ratio rises so does the amount of current consumption that must be foregone to acquire any given amount of future income from capital instruments—that is, the greater the cost of capital and the smaller the share of total output and income that will be devoted to capital additions. By the same token, the higher this ratio, the more difficult it will be to devise public policies to accelerate capital formation and productivity gains for other production inputs. In a capital-rich country like the United States, accordingly, the cost of capital is relatively high, the equilibrium share of output allocated to capital additions is relatively low, and the change in public policies required to elicit any significant increase in the pace of capital formation relative to the growth of other production inputs is relatively drastic. This does not mean, however, that the marginal product of capital is zero.

These are interesting questions for both heuristic and empirical research, but they are not the fundamental issue. What is really at issue is whether depreciation policy should aim at accelerating economic growth. The answer, if top priority is given to neutrality as a policy criterion, is that influencing the growth rate of the stock of capital and of the economy is not, itself, an appropriate concern. Instead, the concern is to assure that tax provisions do not distort the market measure of the cost of capital. This would result in a less than optimum division of income and production capability between saving and capital formation, on the one hand, and consumption, on the other, or in an inefficient allocation of production capability to the production of differing capital instruments.

Implementing the neutrality criterion, in other words, has no specific implication for the rate of expansion of the stock of capital or total output. Neutrality and high growth rates are not identical policy objectives, although they have often been so cast. Recognizing that they are not the same, there should be little question that neutrality is the policy desideratum and that the "right" growth rate results from the operation of efficient markets—that is, markets operating in the most nearly neutral public policy environment that can be contrived.

It must be obvious that capital recovery tax provisions that conform with the neutrality conditions will be consonant with a larger stock of depreciable capital, both absolutely and compared with the amounts of other capital, than the U.S. economy has enjoyed for many years past. If that neutral capital recovery system were implemented in the tax law, the transitional response would surely be a faster expansion of the stock—a higher capital formation rate—and more rapid growth in total output than would otherwise occur. In time, however, a new higher equilibrium growth path would be achieved, the slope of which would be much the same as that in the face of a capital recovery system like the present one, which retains a considerable bias against durable, exhaustible capital.

Whatever that new, long-term growth rate would be, it is difficult to identify relevant policy criterion arguing for a faster rate. For most of us, there is no cardinal growth target, only an ordinal one—faster. But faster growth is not achieved at zero cost. Assuming the most nearly neutral public policy environment prevails, one must ask on what basis a free society would wish public policymakers to override market measures of opportunity costs and rewards and set nonmarket determined targets for economic expansion.

ACRS, TEFRA, AND WHAT REMAINS TO BE DONE

ACRS, the Accelerated Cost Recovery System enacted in 1981's Economic Recovery Tax Act (ERTA), ostensibly had its origins in the so-called 10-5-3 proposal of the late 1970s. In fact, its antecedents are considerably earlier; they are the recommendations made by President Nixon's Task Force on Business Tax Policy whose report was released in 1970.

The task force concluded that the focus of then-existing depreciation practice on particularizing depreciation allowances to the particular circumstances of each taxpayer in his use of his particular assets was the source of unreasonable and unnecessary complexity in both compliance and administrative procedures and of continuing disputes between taxpayers and the Internal Revenue Service. Just as important, the task force found that prevailing depreciation practices for tax purposes in the United States were significantly less generous than in many other industrial economies and concluded that this was an important factor in the slower pace of economic growth in the United States than in most of those other economies.

It recommended, therefore, that the then-existing depreciation provisions in the Internal Revenue Code and the regulations be replaced by a conventionalized capital cost recovery system. Under this proposal, the concept of "useful life" of depreciable property, which presumably set the standard for determining tax "lives" of various classes of property used in different industries, was to be entirely eliminated. In its place would be designated capital cost recovery periods, which the task force recommended should be set at 40 percent less than the so-called guideline lives then authorized for facilities other than real property. Along with this recommendation, the task force also urged the elimination of the so-called reserve ratio task, which sought to require each taxpayer to conform the replacement cycles for the various types of facilities be owned and used to the guideline lives he assigned to each class of such facilities. "Useful life" was deemed to be neither realistic nor useful as a tax concept. The reserve ratio test, it was found, imposed substantial pressure on taxpayers to replace facilities earlier than would otherwise be economical; that is, the task force concluded that the loss of tax benefits from having to use longer guideline lives as a result of the reserve ratio test was greater than the after-tax quasi rents foregone by disposing of facilities earlier than they would have in the absence of the test. To the extent that taxpayers responded to those pressures, the result would be a smaller stock of production facilities at any time than would otherwise be the case.

The task force's recommendations were embodied, in part, in the Asset Depreciation Range (ADR) system adopted in 1971 (the 1971 legislation also reenacted the Investment Tax Credit [ITC] that had been repealed by the Tax Reform Act of 1969). The ADR system, however, fell short of the capital cost recovery system the task force had proposed; it provided a range of 20 percent in the write-off periods around the class lives of the specified classes of property (these class lives were essentially the same as had been provided in 1962), instead of the 40 percent shorter write-off periods the task force had urged; more important, it retained the useful life concept.

Both the task force's report and the subsequent ADR provisions should be seen as advances in tax policy. In neither case, however, was the concept of tax neutrality or the conditions required for achievement of neutrality adduced as the basic concern or goal of the recommendations or legislation. As the 10-5-3 proposal was developed, on the other hand, it was increasingly recognized that for many types of facilities, the proposed write-off methods and recovery periods, combined with a 10 percent Investment Tax Credit, would represent an important step toward providing expensing of capital outlays against the federal income tax. Indeed, this was very much the perception of at least one of the Congressional sponsors of 10-5-3 who identified expensing as the ultimately correct tax treatment but said that it could not be achieved in a single legislative enactment and that 10-5-3 would be a major step toward that goal. As the 1981 legislation proceeded toward enactment, increasing credence was given to (1) expensing as meeting the requirements of tax neutrality and (2) ACRS, a modified 10-5-3, as an approximation of expensing.

To be sure, the ACRS proposal that was ultimately enacted in ERTA was not explicitly or precisely designed as a form of expensing. A major impetus was a much recognized need to moderate inflation's erosion of real capital recovery allowances, which was perceived as accentuating the basic income tax bias against saving and capital formation, particularly depreciable capital. While an indexing system might have been contrived to this end, the policymaking consensus was that indexing presented serious conceptual, compliance, and administrative complexities. Moreover, the objective was not merely to moderate the hidden increase in real tax rates on returns to depreciable capital resulting from inflation but also to make substantial progress toward reducing the anticapital tax bias. An important collateral objective was to provide a set of statutory rules that would greatly simplify compliance and administration, eliminating capital recovery deductions as a subject of dispute or negotiation between taxpayers and the Internal Revenue Service.

ACRS, as enacted, contained several provisions that created new complexities. It was, in some respects, a less dramatic step toward reducing the antisaving tax bias than had been contemplated in the initial proposal by the Administration. Nevertheless, it represented a dramatic and basic improvement in the income tax treatment of durable, exhaustible capital. Moreover, it laid the groundwork for further tax legislative advance toward true expensing.

One of the most important aspects of ACRS is that it replaces depreciation with capital recovery. The concept of useful life is virtually eliminated and replaced by predetermined recovery periods. In lieu of the large number of property classes under prior law, ACRS groups all personal property into four classes: Three-year property consists principally of autos, light-duty trucks, research and development (R&D) equipment, and certain other personal property that had an Asset Depreciation Range (ADR) midpoint life of four years or less; five-year property consists of most other machinery and equipment other than long-lived public utility property; ten-year property consists principally of public utility property with ADR midpoint lives of more than eighteen but less than twenty-five years; and fifteen-year property is public utility property with an ADR midpoint life of more than twenty-five years. For each of these property classes, longer recovery periods are specified as options which the taxpayer may elect. Real property is assigned a fifteen-year recovery period, with an option for specified extended recovery periods.

For personal property, taxpayers had the option, under ERTA, to use the straight-line method for computing the ACRS deduction or a prescribed accelerated schedule. For property placed in service in the years 1981 through 1984, the prescribed schedules were based on 150 percent declining balance, changing to straight-line; for property put in service in 1985, the schedule was derived from 175 percent declining balance, shifting to sum-of-the-years' digits (SYD); and for property placed in service in 1986 and subsequent years, the method was 200 percent declining balance, shifting to SYD.

Real property other than low-income housing may be written off using the 175 percent declining balance method, shifting to straight line. Low-income housing may use the 200 percent declining balance method, shifting to straight line. The straight-line option is also available.

Accompanying the ACRS was an increase in the Investment Tax Credit. For three-year property, the credit rate became 6 percent. For all other personal property, the rate was set at 10 percent.

It was generally recognized that the ACRS system, as enacted in ERTA, was not the ultimate advance and that it might be seen as a way station on the road toward expensing. Unfortunately, a year after ERTA was enacted, TEFRA laid violent hands on ACRS and reversed its forward momentum.

TEFRA made two major changes in the capital recovery provisions in the income tax. One of these repeals the increases in the ACRS allowances scheduled under ERTA to take effect for property acquired in 1985 and 1986. As originally proposed in 1981, the ACRS allowances were to be computed on the basis of a schedule embodying 200 percent declining balance, shifting to sum-of-the-years' digits (SYD) (using a half-year convention). In an effort to accommodate the revenue losses from the numerous additional provisions added to the original ERTA proposals, the Treasury proposed to cut the ACRS schedules back to 150 percent declining balance, shifting to SYD. The compromise achieved in ERTA was to provide 150 percent declining balance straight-line allowances for property placed in service through the taxable year 1984, stepping up to 175 percent declining balance-SYD for property put in service in 1985 and to the full 200 percent declining balance-SYD for property put in service in 1986 and thereafter. The TEFRA provision eliminated the scheduled step-up to 175 percent declining balance for 1985 property and to 200 percent declining balance for 1986 and subsequent years.

The second major change requires a reduction in the recoverable basis of property to which the Investment Tax Credit (ITC) applies in an amount equal to one-half the amount of ITC. (Alternatively, the taxpayer may elect to claim ITC at a lower rate without having to adjust the basis of the property for ACRS purposes). TEFRA also imposed a limit of 85 percent, rather than the 90 percent under prior law, on the amount of tax liability that may be offset by ITC.

These TEFRA provisions were based, ostensibly, on the view that ACRS, when fully accelerated in 1986 and later years, combined with the enriched ITC afforded by ERTA, would provide more generous tax benefits than expensing, that is, writing off the full cost of the investment in the year in which the investment is made. Since expensing of capital outlays presumably results in a zero tax on the returns to the capital, the (fully accelerated) ACRS-ITC combination would result in a negative tax on eligible capital. "Zero" tax does not literally mean that no tax is paid on these returns nor does "negative" tax mean that the government pays the taxpayer. Instead, zero tax means that the cost of the eligible capital is the same as it would be in the absence of taxes, and negative tax means that the cost of capital is less than it would be absent taxes. "Cost of capital" is defined as the amount of the pretax gross returns the property must produce so that the present or discounted value of these returns after tax equals the present value of the acquisition costs of the property. The charge against the (fully accelerated) ACRS-ITC combination was that it would reduce the amount of the pretax returns that satisfy this condition below the amount of these returns in the absence of taxes.

Contrary to the argument sketched above, true expensing does not result in a zero tax (as defined above). The required pretax gross return with expensing is not the same, but instead exceeds the gross return in the absence of taxes. If the present value of the acquisition cost of the property were the same with expensing as in the absence of the tax, that is, P_o, the present value of the pretax gross returns would have to exceed that in the absence of taxes by the amount $\frac{t}{1-t} \times \sum_{i=1}^{N} Y_{0_i}^*$:

With no taxes,

$$P_o = \sum_{i=1}^{N} Y_{0_i}^* . \tag{5.1}$$

With expensing,

$$\frac{P_o - tP_o}{1-t} = \sum_{i=1}^{N} Y_{1_i}^* (1-t)$$

or

$$P_o = \sum_{i=1}^{N} Y_{1_i}^* (1-t) . \tag{5.10}$$

Then

$$\sum_{i=1}^{N} Y_{1_i}^* (1-t) = \sum_{i=1}^{N} Y_{0_i}^* , \tag{5.11}$$

and

$$\sum_{i=1}^{N} Y_{1i}^* - \sum_{i=1}^{N} Y_{0i}^* = \frac{\sum_{i=1}^{N} Y_{0i}^*}{1-t} - \sum_{i=1}^{N} Y_{0i}^*$$

$$= \frac{t}{1-t} \times \sum_{i=1}^{N} Y_{0i}^* . \quad (5.12)$$

If the ACRS-ITC combination were precisely the equivalent of expensing, the same result would be obtained, that is, the cost of capital would exceed that in the absence of taxes by the amount $\frac{t}{1-t} \times \sum_{i=1}^{N} Y_{0i}^*$. This is not a zero, but a positive tax. If the ACRS-ITC combination were indeed "better than expensing," it would not necessarily or even likely mean that the cost of capital would be less than that prevailing in the absence of taxes but merely that it would exceed the no-tax cost of capital by less than the amount shown above.

In any event, the comparison of the ACRS-ITC combination with expensing would be meaningful only if the expensing used as the standard in the comparison were "true" expensing. True expensing is obtained if the present value of the capital recovery deductions just equals the present value of the costs incurred in the acquisition of the property, including all the costs required to ready it for actual participation in the production process. The ACRS-ITC combination, accordingly, would be the equivalent of true expensing, provided three conditions are met:

- The time at which the cost recovery under expensing applies in determining tax liability is the same as the time at which the cost of acquiring the facility is incurred;
- The cost recovery afforded by expensing is allowed against *all* taxes that apply to the facilities or the returns thereto; and
- The cost recovery deductions are not wasted, that is, are fully effective in reducing tax liabilities in the taxable years in which the deductions and the credit may first be claimed.

In reality, none of these conditions is usually fully satisfied. The ACRS deductions are allowed against income only beginning in the taxable year in which the property is placed in service; the ITC is not allowed before that first year. Except in the case of short delivery time assets—that is, capital goods that, in effect, can be "bought off the shelf," the capital recovery deductions are claimed at a later date, possibly several years later, than the time at which the costs of acquisition begin to be incurred.

Even were the timing condition met, however, the ACRS deductions and the ITC do not generally apply against all of the taxes applicable to the returns the property produces. For example, if the property is owned by a corporation, the ACRS and ITC are allowed only in computing the corporation income tax liability; they do not enter into determination of the individual shareholders' income tax liability with respect to the dividends paid out of the returns to the property nor with respect to the capital gains tax liability shareholders accrue with respect to the undistributed earnings produced by the property. Although ACRS may be allowed against income for state income tax purposes where the state's tax provisions are the same as tne federal, no capital recovery allowances are provided in the case of local property taxes that are the equivalent of an income tax levied at a significant tax rate.

Disregarding both of these conditions for equivalence of ACRS-ITC with true expensing, there remain shortfalls in many cases, resulting from the inadequacy of the taxpayer's gross returns to absorb fully the ACRS deductions and the ITC when they may first be claimed. To the extent these must be carried forward, their present value is less than it would be if the third condition were met.

When any one of the specified conditions is not satisfied, expensing for purposes of the federal income tax fails to eliminate the tax bias against saving and capital formation. Asserting that the combination of ACRS and ITC is better than expensing, therefore, does not necessarily imply that these tax provisions result in a bias in favor of saving and capital formation or, in the context of the argument advanced in support of the TEFRA provisions, in a negative tax.

Indeed, under realistic (but conservative) assumptions about the amount of tax liability on the returns on the property against which ACRS and ITC are *not* allowed, a substantial credit is required to produce the result that would be obtained if the true expensing conditions were met.

Table 5-1 shows the ITC rates required to achieve the equivalent of true expensing for properties with three-, five- and ten-year ACRS recovery periods, using discount rates of 5, 8 and 10 percent to find present values, at various effective marginal rates of other taxes imposed on the returns to the property. **Even with a discount** rate as low as 5 percent and with an effective combined marginal rate of all

Table 5-1. Investment Tax Credit (ITC) Required to Provide the Equivalent of True Expensing at Alternative Rates of Other Taxes against Which Accelerated Cost Recovery System (ACRS) and ITC Are Not Allowed, at Various Rates of Discount.

Rate of Other Taxes	Discount Rates								
	5 Percent			8 Percent			10 Percent		
	3-Year Property	5-Year Property	10-Year Property	3-Year Property	5-Year Property	10-Year Property	3-Year Property	5-Year Property	10-Year Property
1	4.1%	5.5%	8.7%	5.8%	8.0%	12.6%	6.9%	9.5%	14.9%
4	7.2	8.6	11.8	8.9	11.1	15.7	10.1	12.7	18.0
5	8.2	9.6	12.8	10.0	12.1	16.7	11.2	13.7	19.1
6	9.2	10.7	13.9	11.0	13.2	17.8	12.2	14.8	20.1
7	10.2	11.7	14.9	12.1	14.2	18.8	13.2	15.8	21.2
8	11.3	12.7	15.9	13.1	15.3	19.9	14.3	16.9	22.2
9	12.3	13.7	16.9	14.1	16.3	20.9	15.3	17.9	23.3
10	13.3	14.8	18.0	15.2	17.4	21.9	16.4	19.0	24.3

other taxes imposed on the property's returns as low as 5 percent, the equivalent of true expensing would require an 8.2 percent ITC for three-year property, a 9.6 percent credit for five-year property, and a 12.8 percent credit for ten-year property.[4] At an 8 percent discount rate, the required ITC rates are 10 percent, 12 percent and almost 17 percent respectively.

In fact, there is no theoretical justification for the violence done by TEFRA to ACRS and ITC. The ACRS and ITC enacted by ERTA provided capital recovery that fell significantly shy of true expensing for most property even at discount rates one can only wish were appropriate.

The shortfall from true expensing—which results because acquisition costs generally precede capital recovery or because gross returns are inadequate fully to absorb ACRS deductions and the ITC on a timely basis—should not be minimized. In fact, this timing differential was one of the principal reasons for ERTA's safe-harbor leasing provisions. Once it is granted that true expensing or its equivalent is the correct capital recovery treatment, the taxpayer should not be denied this treatment because of delay in the realization of income from use of the property. The safe-harbor leasing provisions in ERTA assured the availability of ACRS and ITC on a much more nearly timely basis. As such, the safe-harbor leasing provisions provided a major improvement in the taxation of business income. The alleged abuses were inconsequential and afforded no valid basis for TEFRA's punitive modification in 1983 and repeal thereafter of ERTA's safe-harbor leasing provisions.

The combined effect on the cost of business capital of TEFRA's ACRS and ITC modifications, along with the abrupt sun-setting of safe-harbor leasing, is difficult to determine precisely. It is obvious, however, that these TEFRA provisions eliminate a substantial amount of the reduction in the cost of capital afforded by the ACRS, ITC, and safe-harbor leasing provisions enacted in ERTA for facilities placed in service in 1986 and subsequent years. It is likely that virtually all of the cost of capital reduction afforded by ERTA for property in the ACRS three-year class is canceled. For property in the ACRS five-year class, TEFRA took back a larger portion of the cost of capital reduction the shorter the former ADR life. For example, for assets that had had a five-year ADR life and were included in the five-year ACRS class, TEFRA removed all of the ERTA cut in the cost of capital. Substantial losses of ERTA-afforded gains were also imposed by TEFRA on property with longer ADR lives. Without knowing how much of each type of property would have been added had the ERTA provision remained intact, one cannot precisely determine the overall weighted increase in cost of capital from the level that would have prevailed under ERTA. It seems a safe estimate, however, that at least four-fifths of the ERTA reduction in cost of capital for personal property was rescinded by TEFRA.

THE CHALLENGE THAT LIES AHEAD FOR CAPITAL RECOVERY

As punitive as TEFRA is and as much of a setback for good tax policy as it represents, things might have been worse. It did leave in place the basic elements of the ACRS system upon which it might be possible to build for the future. More importantly, it established expensing as the correct criterion for evaluating a capital recovery system.

A major objective for some future time when progress toward tax neutrality can be resumed should be full implementation of true expensing of capital outlays. True expensing calls for (1) write-offs for tax purposes concurrent with incurring costs of acquiring and installing capital items; (2) capital recovery against all taxes bearing on capital and the returns thereto; and, finally, (3) assurance that capital cost recovery will not be wasted. The first and last of these conditions can be precisely satisfied for federal income tax purposes. Unless federal, state, and local tax systems were completely identical—not a desideratum in a truly federalist system—satisfying these conditions beyond the purview of the federal tax could not be assured. By the same token, there is no feasible way, in a truly federalist system, to assure that the capital recovery is fully effective against all taxes bearing on the capital.

There is no significant impediment to allowing costs to be written off as they are incurred instead of deferring their write-off until the facilities are placed in service, as under present law. "Placed in service" constraints are best seen as a vestige of depreciation for book purposes—the effort to allocate the prepaid cost through time in step with the flow of income produced by the capital facility. Once expensing is accepted as appropriate, "placed in service" becomes irrelevant. Indeed, this was recognized in an early version of ACRS that allowed write-offs of certain progress payments, a feature that was dropped from the ACRS in its legislative development. If progress toward a truly neutral cost recovery system is to be resumed, an important feature of the system should be to allow costs to be expensed as they are incurred.

To assure that expensing is truly effective rather than merely a statutory provision, the cost recovery deductions should be freely marketable. The objection to the safe-harbor leasing provision, which approached free marketability, was that it could and did permit some companies to eliminate substantially all of their corporate tax liabilities. This alleged abuse could properly be a source of concern only if some equity criterion and rules appropriate to corporations as taxpayers could be devised. In a tax analytic that properly identifies the corporation income tax as an excise on the returns to corporate equity capital—and by its very nature haphazardly distributed among the ultimate individual owners of that equity—there is no meaningful rule of equity for the corporate tax *per se*. The objection to free marketability of capital cost recovery allowances on the grounds of equity, therefore, is without substance.

A weightier problem is the one of trying to make the capital recovery allowances fully effective with respect to all taxes bearing on the capital. In this regard, some lack of precision in the device addressed to this problem is probably unavoidable; any such imprecision, however, is not likely to be of such consequence as to result in a serious shortfall from true expensing. As suggested above, the Investment Tax Credit should be seen as a useful and available device to offset taxes other than the corporate income tax on capital returns. The rate of the credit to serve this purpose should depend on empirical determination of the overall average of the rates of other taxes on the returns to the capital to be expensed for federal income tax purposes. True expensing does not require elimination of the ITC unless some other tax device is deemed to be more precise as a means for extending expensing against other taxes.

The short-term prospects for renewed progress toward true expensing do not appear bright, given the official projections of enormous federal deficits and the obvious proclivity for reducing them by raising taxes. Poor as these prospects now seem to be, they should not deter the developmental work that will be needed to translate the fundamental requirements of true expensing into a workable statutory proposal. It should be recalled that the prospects for 10-5-3 did not appear overly bright when the work on it first began. The dedication and determination of those who invested their energy and experience in its development have been rewarded much sooner than expected, even if not as fully as warranted. Equal dedication and determination to designing a workable true expensing system is likely to be more fully rewarded, even if not as soon as one would like.

APPENDIX
THE AMBIGUITIES OF ECONOMIC DEPRECIATION

Determination of economic depreciation in any period requires the quantification of several variables. The first of these—the expected amount of quasi rents over the remaining life of the asset—depends on a number of factors, including the production function governing the use of the asset; the conditions of demand for the output to the production of which the asset contributes; the conditions of supply, hence the prices, of the other production inputs with which the asset is combined in the production process; certain physical attributes built into the asset that influence its production efficiency; and the extent and character of maintenance and repair of the asset. The quasi rents in any year that different units of a given capital of the same vintage are expected to produce are likely to differ, often widely, depending on the use to which the units are put. As a corollary, with the same type of capital used in differing production functions, changes in supply prices of the other production inputs with which the capital units are used will result in changes in the ratios of capital to the other inputs, hence in changes in the marginal value products (quasi rents) of the differing units of capital. Differing changes in production technology will also differentially affect the quasi rents produced by diverse units of the capital. Even more obvious, changes in the conditions of demand of the output of the capital in its diverse uses are also likely to differ widely, resulting in substantially different changes in the quasi rents expected to be produced by different units of a given type of capital in its diverse uses.

All of these factors are likely to exert differing influences on the quasi rents of like capital not only from one taxpayer to another but also for any one taxpayer from one period of time to another. The past experience of any given taxpayer with any given type of capital is likely, therefore, to provide only the flimsiest sort of guide as to future quasi rents expected to be afforded by the same sort of capital. The experience of other taxpayers with such capital is likely to be still less useful as a basis for expectations about future quasi rents.

Apart from these factors, variations in the physical properties of the diverse units of a given kind of capital are also certain to contribute to variance in the quasi rents the differing units produce even in identical uses. Few production processes result in perfectly identical units of output; the physical characteristics of differing units of a given kind of capital instrument are likely to vary at least in some degree. So, too, is their physical productivity likely to differ.

Another source of variance in the quasi rents afforded by a given type of capital is the difference in repair and maintenance policies among taxpayers and at varying times for any one taxpayer. In general, the less the maintenance and repair, the more rapid and substantial will be the decrease in an asset's productivity and hence in the quasi rents it produces. Since repair and maintenance require the firm to use up some of its resources, however, there is a trade-off between the cost of repair and maintenance and loss of capital value. No maintenance and repair practice is uniquely associated, therefore, with any particular asset. These practices are likely to vary from firm to firm and, within the firm, among assets and from time to time. If for no other reason, the time path of quasi rents produced by any given type of capital is likely to be variable; economic depreciation, by the same token, is likely to vary for any firm with respect to any given type of capital from time to time and from firm to firm at any given time.

Determination of salvage value or proceeds from disposition of the capital unit is appropriately regarded as a problem of determining the capital's quasi rent in its terminal income period. The problem is a particularly difficult one because its solution requires the present owner of the capital to determine not only (1) how his expected use of it, including his repair and maintenance practices, will affect its productivity year by year from the present point in time, but also (2) how the conditions of demand for the capital's output in all of its varied uses and the differing supply conditions for other production inputs with which it is combined in the differing production functions in its other uses will affect its value to other firms. The variance in salvage value of a given type of capital, accordingly, is likely to be substantial. The consequences of this substantial variance for the precision with which economic depreciation for any year may be computed are obvious.

The conventional analysis of depreciation assumes known annual quasi rents and a determinant "useful life" of given types of capital. In fact, as shown, annual quasi rents are likely to vary substantially from unit to unit, owner to owner, and time to time. Equally variable is the number of periods over which it will pay to keep the capital unit in use; useful life, in fact, is an endogenous variable in the depreciation function.

It will pay the firm to keep a unit of capital in use so long as the quasi rent it is expected to produce—less the reduction in the present value of the expected remaining quasi rents—exceeds the quasi rent that might be obtained by disposing of the unit through sale or by scrapping and by investing the proceeds in some other capital. Useful life, accordingly, is not an attribute that inheres in any unit of capital. On the contrary, it is a function of the time distribution of the expected quasi rents obtainable from the unit of capital as used by the firm compared with the quasi rents that might be obtained from alternative capital units. Useful life, therefore, depends on all of the factors so far discussed that period by period affect this present value of the quasi rents afforded by the capital unit.

Where an income tax is imposed, economic depreciation is the change in the capitalized amount of *after-tax* quasi rents. Accordingly, economic depreciation cannot be determined independently of the provisions of the tax system that determine the amount of tax liability on the quasi rents. The applicability of these provisions, moreover, is likely to be significantly differentiated by specific taxpayer attributes. It follows, therefore, that the tax system itself is an important source of variability among taxpayers in the economic depreciation that would be sustained on any unit of capital. Since the tax system changes significantly over time, it is itself a major source of variance in economic depreciation from period to period, as well as from taxpayer to taxpayer.

Finally, the discount rate to be used in capitalizing after-tax quasi rent streams is variable and, accordingly, a source of variation in economic depreciation from time to time and among firms. The discount rate the firm should use in capitalizing nominal, after-tax quasi rents is a measure of its real opportunity cost plus a premium for any inflation it anticipates. Assuming efficient capital markets, the firm's real opportunity cost will closely approximate the weighted mean marginal value product of capital less the weighted mean income tax liability on this marginal return, plus the expected inflation rate. Although a substantial degree of stability may be properly attributed to the first of these factors, no realistic assessment of the economy would support the view of a stable rate of increase in the price level or of a stable marginal tax rate. If for no other reason, then, economic depreciation is likely to be highly variable through time and among firms by reason of the instability of the appropriate discount rate to be used in determining the present value of after-tax quasi rents.

The difficulties in determining economic depreciation in this part of the discussion ostensibly could be circumvented if the measure employed were based on the market prices of capital units rather than on the firm's valuation of expected after-tax quasi rents. There are, however, major reservations about this approach.

One problem, of a purely practical nature, is to establish reliable samples of homogeneous capital units in substantially homogeneous markets in order to determine how market prices of given capital units change through time. As already indicated, units of a given type of capital are not likely to be homogeneous in relevant respects—that is, the production processes and functions in which they are used are not likely to be substantially identical, nor are the factor proportions, the outputs, or the conditions of demand for these outputs. Similarly, the markets in which the capital units are exchanged are not likely to be substantially identical but are more likely to reflect substantial variations in fundamental economic circumstances. Real property markets, to take an obvious example, differ widely from California to Maine. If no other problems were confronted, the heterogeneity of the capital units and of the market place are sufficient to preclude any ready generalization about the pattern of value loss of various types of capital.

Even were this consideration ignored, the depreciation formulae that would emerge from analysis of market prices would have no necessary bearing on the experience of any specific taxpayer with the particular capital in the particular uses of the taxpayer. In other words, depreciation so derived would be conventionalized rather than particularized depreciation; as such, it would not serve the purposes for which economic depreciation is advocated.

A more fundamental objection is that market prices almost certainly must afford biased measures of changes in capitalized amounts of expected after-tax quasi rents. For the most part, the sale of "used" physical capital entails not only significant transaction costs but also substantial costs of removal, transportation, installment, and start-up. Clearly, the present owner of any given unit of capital will not sell it if the present value to him of its expected after-tax quasi rents exceeds the after-tax sale proceeds net of any part of these transactions and other costs he must bear. By the same token, any buyer must expect to obtain from use of the capital after-tax quasi rents the present value of which must at least equal the price plus any fraction of the transaction and associated costs he must assume. Given these costs, it follows that the expected remaining after-tax quasi rents of the capital in the hands of the present owner must be less than those in the hands of the potential buyer. Sale prices, accordingly, must exceed the present value of the after-tax quasi rents in the hands of the present owner. By the same token, the period-to-period loss in the present value of the after-tax quasi rents of the capital in the hands of the owner must be greater than that measured by the differences in market prices. Market prices, therefore, must understate the depreciation expected with respect to capital units that are retained by their existing owners.

76 Reform of the Federal Income Tax

Moreover, since transactions in used capital units must occur between nonhomogeneous taxpayers, the market prices at which the transactions take place cannot measure the changes in value of the capital for present owners. Whatever other purposes this market price information may serve, it cannot afford the basis for computing economic depreciation particularized to specific taxpayers and their specific uses of specific units of capital. Since economic depreciation can be justified only insofar as it affords this particularization, market price data cannot be used for this purpose.

NOTES TO CHAPTER 5

1. Economic depreciation in any year i may be stated as

$$D_i = \sum_{i=i}^{N} Y_i^* - \sum_{i=i+1}^{N} Y_i^* .$$

2. The conclusion that economic depreciation assures nonneutrality of the income tax with respect to different units of capital derives from the measure of economic depreciation that would occur in the absence of the tax. The same conclusion is reached using economic depreciation determined with respect to after-tax quasi rents. An easy way of seeing this is to advert to the notational exposition above and read D_i^* as the present value of depreciation in period i where D_i^* is derived from capitalization of after-tax quasi rents. The rest of the proof is as before.

There is a major impediment to the calculation of economic depreciation so determined. The value of a unit of capital at any time when an income tax applies is the capitalized amount of the remaining after-tax quasi rents. The amount of the depreciation for any given period, therefore, depends on the amount of tax to be paid on the pretax quasi rents in each period, but the amount of the tax depends in part on the amount of the depreciation. While a simultaneous or recursive solution can be obtained, either procedure would pose an impossible problem for taxpayers, particularly in connection with long-lived property (remember that the economic depreciation for any given year requires determination of the after-tax quasi rent, hence depreciation, for each of the remaining years). As a practical matter, the requirement that depreciation for tax purposes be economic depreciation based on after-tax quasi rents would confront the taxpayer with a dilemma he could not readily resolve.

3. Each of these requirements is examined briefly in the Appendix to this discussion.

4. Values in the table were computed assuming the property is acquired and put in service at midyear and that the 200 percent declining balance-SYD write-off method provided in ERTA for properties acquired in 1986 or later years is used to compute ACRS deductions. The computation also assumes that the costs of acquiring the property are incurred at the time the property is acquired and put in service and that there is no waste of the ACRS deductions and ITC.

Discussants:

DOES ACRS FOSTER EFFICIENT CAPITAL ALLOCATION?

Alan J. Auerbach

Are tax incentives for investment the right way to promote economic growth? In general, I believe that they are. Some recent and sobering statistics, however, indicate that between the third quarters of 1981 and 1982, according to the National Income Accounts, nonresidential fixed investment expressed in 1972 dollars fell by over 6.8 percent. This decline exceeded not only the overall decline in GNP over the same period of just over 2 percent but also the well-publicized decline in *residential* investment. This severe drop in business fixed investment came in spite of the incentives offered by the Economic Recovery Tax Act of 1981 (ERTA). I say "in spite of" because I believe the Accelerated Cost Recovery System (ACRS) provisions, taken by themselves, would have stimulated more investment. However, a combination of postwar highs in real interest rates and postwar lows in capacity utilization have been the main force behind recent investment patterns.

George Hatsopoulos describes quite accurately in his paper how a small rise in real interest rates can offset the impact of tax incentives. This should not be seen as a suggestion that the ACRS provisions did not go far enough, but rather that general macroeconomic conditions are more important in the short run. (As Norman Ture has reminded us, many assets actually enjoyed *negative* tax rates under the ACRS provisions, prior to the changes introduced by the 1982 legislation.) For example, suppose that a firm must earn a real return of 4 percent after-tax and that to do so a 5 percent before-tax return is required, as would be the case under a 20 percent tax on real income. A cut in the effective tax rate to zero would be entirely offset by an increase of one percentage point in the required after-tax return: The business would still have to earn 5 percent before tax. Thus, the fact that ACRS had the equivalent effect of a 0.75 percent decrease in the cost of funds does not mean it was a small tax cut. Growth, however, is something we should be concerned with over the longer run; it is important that the tax system faced by business investors should be structured to foster efficient capital allocation.

Dr. Ture argues that the current system of depreciation allowances and investment tax credits should be replaced by a system of immediate expensing, under which all investments would face a new effective tax rate. I agree with him that this should be a nondistortionary tax system. I do not agree that the tax system under ACRS resembles such a system. Though average effective tax rates may now be (or at least may have been between the 1981 and 1982 tax acts) close to zero, the variation in rates across different investments is substantial and very distortionary. This serious problem with ACRS was well-documented before the enactment of the Economic Recovery Tax Act of 1981 (ERTA). It is only slightly less serious since the passage of the Tax Equity and Fiscal Responsibility Act of 1982 (TEFRA).

I also hope that, in conjunction with his proposal for consumption-tax type treatment of physical investments, Dr. Ture intends a symmetric treatment for financial investments—namely, inclusion in the tax base of net borrowing. Together, these provisions would convert the corporate tax into a cash flow tax analogous to a consumption tax at the personal level, with the salient feature that all saving and dissaving would be undistorted by taxation. Without a provision for debt, Dr. Ture's system of expensing would not lead to zero effective tax rates on capital income, but to substantially negative ones.

Dr. Ture's statements on the distortions caused by a system of economic depreciation are confusing, at least to an economist. It is well-known that capital income taxation distorts saving behavior. With this I fully agree. It is also true that, *given* such a distortion, economic depreciation allowances lead to an efficient allocation of the existing capital stock, a desirable property in itself. Dr. Ture fails to make this distinction. I interpret his remarks in this vein as simply reiterating that non-zero taxes on capital income are distortionary.

Finally, let me agree with Dr. Ture on an important point. The asymmetric treatment of gains and losses under the tax system is hard to defend. Some mechanism is desirable for allowing all businesses to take advantage of the recently enacted investment incentives. ERTA's "safe harbor" leasing was an imperfect and devious method for doing this, but its repeal by TEFRA simply made things worse. It behooves Congress to deal with this sensitive political problem more openly than it has done in the past.

THE EFFECTS OF ERTA AND TEFRA ON THE COST OF CAPITAL

George N. Hatsopoulos

Introduction

The purpose of this study is to assess quantitatively the effect of the 1981 Economic Recovery Tax Act (ERTA) as modified by the 1982 Tax Equity and Fiscal Responsibility Act (TEFRA) on the marginal pretax cost of capital services employed by U.S. nonfinancial corporations.

The passage of ERTA was heralded as a major breakthrough in reducing the cost of capital services for U.S. corporations. Many of its benefits, however, were not scheduled to go into effect until 1985 and 1986. The passage of TEFRA in 1982 not only canceled the depreciation schedules planned for 1985 and 1986 but also reduced the benefits that went into effect in 1981. This study reveals that the after-tax cost of capital is now about 1 percent lower than it was prior to the passage of ERTA in 1981. TEFRA's modifications to the Accelerated Cost Recovery System (ACRS) provisions of ERTA reduced the already modest benefits provided by the 1981 act.

Real Cost of Capital Services

U.S. corporations increase their net capital with funds obtained from two sources: equity and debt. Equity is more expensive than debt for two reasons. More risk is associated with equity than with debt, and the returns on equity (dividends) are paid out of after-tax corporate income, whereas returns on debt (interests) are paid out of before-tax corporate income. Nevertheless, corporations generally rely upon equity rather than less costly debt for their principal source of financing. The reason behind this preference for equity financing is the need to maintain the risk level considered prudent by both corporate managers and lenders.

The cost of business funds at the margin may be obtained by combining the costs of equity and debt in their most advantageous fractions, limited by prudent restrictions on leverage, that is, debt to equity ratio.

Corporate funds are invested in fixed assets (equipment, structures, and land) and in operating capital (inventories and net accounts receivable). Appendix B analyzes the distribution of corporate funds for 1981. For 1979 through 1981, the average amount of each asset as a percentage of the net capital employed is listed in Table 5-2. These percentages have varied little over the past ten years.

Table 5-2. Average Distribution of Business Capital for U.S. Nonfinancial Corporations in 1979 to 1981 (*percentage*).

Net Equipment	31.59
Net Structures	30.07
Land	10.34
Inventories	22.82
Net Receivables	5.19

For a given cost of funds, each application of funds incurs a different cost because of different effects of inflation, taxation, and other factors. In general, the real cost of a capital service is composed of four parts: the cost of funds, the benefit of tax credits and capital consumption allowances, the benefit of any increases in residual value due to inflation, and the cost of asset decay (depreciation). A general expression for the cost of a capital service is derived in Appendix A. The cost is based on the concept of yearly constant dollar payments that would have to be made by a corporation to a hypothetical independent leasing unit. The approach is similar to that employed by Hall and Jorgenson,[1] except for the adjustment of costs to reflect capital gains resulting from inflation and the use of an annual rather than a continuous time model.

For the real cost of using land, the expression reduces to the difference of the cost of funds after taxes, minus the inflation rate, divided by unity, minus the effective tax rate. For inventories, we assumed no obsolescence[2] and no taxes on inventory appreciation.[3] Accordingly, the real cost of holding inventories is the same as that for land. The real cost of holding net receivables is simply equal to the cost of funds. Receivables are the most susceptible to increases in the cost of funds because they accrue no benefits from either tax deductions or inflation.

Empirical Results

The values of the parameters that determine the cost of capital services are discussed in Appendix B. Results of the analyses are summarized in Table 5-3.

The first and second rows of Table 5-3, respectively, show the real costs of each capital service under the Asset Depreciation Range (ADR) tax rates prevailing at the beginning of 1981 and under the Accelerated Cost Recovery System (ACRS) rates that became effective that year. Changes in cost due to ACRS rules are given in Row 3. Since the ACRS changes affect only equipment and structures, they provide the greatest total benefit to those industries having large fixed assets. Many fast growth (e.g., high technology) industries, by

Table 5-3. Effects of Tax Legislation on Cost of Capital Services (percentage).

	Equipment	Structures	Land	Inventory	Net Receivables	Total (weighted average)
(1) Real Cost in 1981 under ADR[a]	25.4%	22.2%	11.4%	11.4%	30.4%	20.2%
(2) Real Cost in 1981 under ACRS[b]	23.5	20.2	11.4	11.4	30.4	19.0
(3) Change in 1981 from ADR to ACRS	-1.9	-2.0	0	0	0	-1.2
(4) Increase in the after-tax cost of funds by 1 pp at constant inflation	+1.4	+1.7	+1.6	+1.6	+1.8	+1.6
(5) Change in ACRS due to TEFRA[c]	+0.5	0	0	0	0	+0.2

[a] ADR denotes Asset Depreciation Range.
[b] ACRS denotes Accelerated Cost Recovery System (1981).
[c] TEFRA denotes Tax Equity and Fiscal Responsibility Act of 1982.

contrast, employ a greater fraction of their total assets in working capital. Hence, they realize less total benefit from ACRS.

Overall, the effect of ACRS is seen to be fairly modest[4] —a drop of 1.2 percentage points in the total cost of capital services for corporations. In fact, a rise of only one percentage point in the after-tax cost of funds, other factors held constant, will more than offset the entire benefit of ACRS (see Row 4). The increase in cost due to higher cost of funds (Row 4) is fairly neutral to the various categories of capital services.

The benefits of ACRS were eroded somewhat in 1982 with the passage of TEFRA. As shown in Row 5, TEFRA raised the cost of equipment services by 0.5 percentage point through a cutback in tax credit/depreciation allowances. Overall, the rise in the cost of capital services was only 0.2 percentage point because TEFRA did not impact assets other than equipment.

Appendix A
Determining the Cost of Capital Services

Hall and Jorgenson[1] have derived an expression for the cost of asset services using instantaneous rates and excluding effects of inflation. In the derivation that follows, effects of inflation are taken into account. Moreover, an annual rather than a continuous time model is used.

The real cost of asset services before taxes is defined as a constant fraction of the constant dollar replacement value of the asset throughout its useful life. This cost is calculated by considering an asset whose replacement value in constant dollars decays at a constant annual rate. To specify exactly all costs that contribute to the value of the asset, we theorize a tripartite, zero-gain arrangement between a lender, a leasing company, and a user of the asset services.

The lender provides funds at the after-tax cost of funds of the user and receives an annual payment from the leasing company. The leasing company borrows funds from the lender, purchases the asset, and leases it to the user. Annually, the leasing company receives a payment from the user, pays taxes adjusted for tax credits and depreciation allowances related to the ownership of the asset, and returns to the lender the difference between user payment and taxes. Thus, the leasing company has a zero annual cash flow. The user leases the asset and pays the leasing company an annual installment, which is a fixed fraction of the replacement value of the asset in constant dollars.

The following definitions apply:

C = cost of fixed asset services before taxes
D_n = tax depreciation during year n
ITC = investment tax credit
L_n = lease payment before taxes for year n in current dollars
L_n^* = lease payment before taxes for year n in constant dollars
P_a = annual after tax cost of funds per year
q_n = replacement value of the asset at beginning of year n in current dollars
q_n^* = replacement value of the asset at beginning of year n in constant dollars
α = fraction of investment not subject to depreciation
Δ = decay rate of asset per year
Π = expected annual inflation rate per year
τ_1 = marginal tax rate
τ = effective tax rate

The value of an asset is equal to the discounted value of all its future stream of benefits and costs. Here, the yearly benefits are the lease payments and the investment tax credit, and the costs the taxes on the lease payments adjusted for depreciation. The discount rate, P_a, is the after-tax cost of funds. Thus, the value of the asset upon purchase, q_1, is given by the relation

$$q_1 = \sum_{n=1}^{\infty} \frac{L_n}{(1+P_a)^n} + \frac{q_1 \times ITC}{(1+P_a)^\nu} - \tau_1 \sum_{n=1}^{\infty} \frac{L_n - D_n q_1 (1-\alpha)}{(1+P_a)^{n+\nu}}$$

(A.1)

where ν is a fraction of a year that accounts for the difference between the mean time at which tax benefits accrue and the mean time at which investments are made during a particular year.[5]

The lease payment before taxes in current dollars, L_n, is related to the corresponding lease payment, L_n^*, in constant dollars and to the expected annual inflation rate, Π, by the expression

$$L_n = L_n^* \times (1+\Pi)^{n-1} .$$ (A.2)

Similarly, the replacement value of the asset at the beginning of year n in constant dollars, q_n^*, is related to the investment value, q_1, and the decay rate, Δ, by the expression

$$q_n^* = q_1 \times (1 - \Delta)^{n-1} . \tag{A.3}$$

By definition, the real cost of asset services, C, is

$$C \equiv \frac{L_n^*}{q_n^*} = \frac{L_n}{q_1 \times (1 - \Delta)^{n-1} \times (1 + \Pi)^{n-1}} . \tag{A.4}$$

Thus

$$L_n = C \times q_1 \times (1 - \Delta)^{n-1} \times (1 + \Pi)^{n-1} . \tag{A.5}$$

Substituting (A.5) in (A.1), and using the expressions

$$z = \sum_{n=1}^{\infty} \frac{D_n}{(1 + P_a)^n} \quad \text{and} \quad \tau = \frac{\tau_1}{(1 + P_a)^{\nu}} , \tag{A.6}$$

we find

$$q_1 = C q_1 (1 - \tau) \sum_{n=1}^{\infty} \frac{(1 - \Delta)^{n-1} (1 + \Pi)^{n-1}}{(1 + P_a)^n}$$

$$+ \tau q_1 z (1 - \alpha) + \frac{q_1 \times ITC}{(1 + P_a)^{\nu}}$$

$$= C q_1 \frac{(1 - \tau)}{P_a + \Delta - \Pi (1 - \Delta)} + \tau q_1 z (1 - \alpha) + \frac{q_1 \times ITC}{(1 + P_a)^{\nu}} . \tag{A.7}$$

Upon solving (A.7) for C, we obtain the expression

$$C = \frac{\left[P_a + \Delta - \Pi (1 - \Delta) \right] \left[1 - \frac{ITC}{(1 + P_a)^{\nu}} - \tau z (1 - \alpha) \right]}{(1 - \tau)} . \tag{A.8}$$

Appendix B
Parameters for 1981

The parameters needed to evaluate the cost of equipment services analyzed in Appendix A are: the rate of decay for equipment and structures, the Investment Tax Credit (ITC), the schedule of depreciation allowances for equipment and structures, the corporate income tax rate at the margin, the distribution of capital employed by type of assets, the projected inflation rate, and the after tax cost of funds.

Decay Rates. The average decay rates for equipment and structures were obtained from the Bureau of Economic Analysis.[6] The ratio of depreciation to net stocks for both equipment and structures was found to be fairly constant over the years 1960 to 1981, averaging about 13.6 percent and 6.5 percent for equipment and structures, respectively.

Investment Tax Credit. The Investment Tax Credit for equipment in 1981 was 10 percent, and none of it reduced the tax basis of the investment. The 1982 Tax Equity and Fiscal Responsibility Act specified that half of the Investment Tax Credit, namely 5 percent of the value of the equipment, would reduce the tax basis of the investment. Alternatively, TEFRA allows the full depreciation base but reduces ITC from 10 percent to 8 percent.

Depreciation Allowances. At the beginning of 1981 the prevailing Asset Depreciation Range (ADR) system allowed 200 percent declining balance, sum-of-the-years' digits, or straight-line depreciation at any time during the taxable life of equipment. Structures were restricted to 150 percent declining balance. In the above analysis, we assumed the most favorable schedule allowed by law. Average tax lives were assumed to be ten years for equipment and thirty years for structures. In accordance with the 1971 ADR guidelines, these lives are slightly lower than the average service lives of thirteen years and thirty-one years assumed in note 6.

The Economic Recovery Tax Act of 1981 specifies prescribed depreciation schedules under the Accelerated Cost Recovery System (ACRS) for equipment classified under three-year, five-year, and ten-year categories. In the ACRS analysis for 1981, we assume, on average, the five-year schedules for equipment and the specified depreciation rates applicable for property placed in service the sixth month of the year for structures.

Corporate Income Taxes at the Margin. In 1981 the statutory federal and state tax rates on corporate income were 46 and 8 percent, respectively. The state figure was derived by averaging the statutory corporate tax rates in 38 of the major industrialized states[7] and weighing each tax rate by the value added in manufacturing for that state.[8] An overall statutory corporate income tax rate of 50.3 percent was computed by combining the federal and state income tax rates, taking into account that state taxes are deductible against federal taxes.

Historically, the effective corporate tax rates have been much lower than statutory tax rates. In 1979, for instance, the combined federal and state statutory corporate tax rate was 50.3 percent, but the effective rate (calculated as flow-of-funds tax accruals divided by before-tax book profits) was 36 percent. Some of this difference can be accounted for by a variety of tax credits. The largest of these, for domestic earnings, is the Investment Tax Credit (ITC). In 1979 the total ITC claimed by all corporations was $14.6 billion.

Even taking the ITC into consideration, however, statutory and effective corporate tax rates are still very far apart. There are several reasons for this difference. First, several deductions are counted in the Internal Revenue Service (IRS) definition of income but not in the flow-of-funds, two of the largest being loss carryforward and earnings of Domestic International Sales Corporations (DISC). In addition, dividends and capital gains are treated differently by the flow-of-funds and the IRS, resulting in further divergences between effective and statutory tax rates calculated from NIPA[9] data.

Analysis revealed that, after taking account of the Investment Tax Credit, effective rates averaged about six percentage points below statutory rates. While, in principle, the marginal dollar of corporate income is taxed at the peak statutory corporate rate, in practice, there are special deductions and credits that imply a much lower tax rate to be used in marginal calculations by the typical manager. Accordingly, we assumed the effective corporate income tax rate at the margin to be six percentage points below the overall statutory rate.

Distribution of Capital Employed by Type of Assets. The 1981 balance sheet for nonfinancial corporations, shown in Table 5-4, was constructed from data obtained from notes 6 and 10.

Projected Inflation Rate. One method for determining the expected inflation rate is to construct some type of weighted average

Table 5-4. Net Assets of Nonfinancial Corporations for 1981.

Net Equipment		1,017
Net Structures	+	947
Land	+	308
Net Fixed Assets	=	2,272
Inventories		699 +
Trade Credit		496
Insurance Receivables	+	47
Consumer Credit	+	32
Trade Debt	−	366
Consumer Credit	−	10
Net Receivables	=	199 +
NET CAPITAL EMPLOYED		3,170 =

of actual inflation rates in the preceding years. This, of course, fails to account for any other inflation indicators that could be influencing investor expectations.

Another approach is to assume that the real rate of return demanded by lenders is constant with time, about two to three percentage points. The assumption here is that all indicators of expected future inflation are considered by lenders in arriving at the market interest rate for long-term debt. A major problem with this method is that real interest rates may vary significantly, due to changes either in the supply and demand of credit, or in perceived risks, or both. Real interest rates may vary, for example, in response to a combination of tight monetary policy and high government deficits.

In this study, we estimate the expected inflation rate by weighing equally (1) a retrospective projection of future inflation that is based on past inflation rates and (2) a prospective estimate of future inflation that is based on a real Aaa bond rate equal to 2.5 percent.

The actual inflation rate, measured as the rate of change of the average deflator for personal consumption expenditures from the preceding year, was 8.6 percent,[9] the average interest rate for Aaa corporate bonds 14.17 percent, and the expected inflation rate 9.9 percent.

Cost of Funds. The 1981 after-tax cost of funds assumed in this analysis is 17 percent. This figure was derived in a separate study[11] by combining the cost of equity and the cost of debt in the proportions 75 and 25 percent, respectively. Since the present study is concerned only with variations in the cost of capital services, rather than their absolute value, a precise determination of the cost of funds is not required.

Notes

1. R.E. Hall and D.W. Jorgenson, "Tax Policy and Investment Behavior," *American Economic Review* 57 (June 1967), pp. 391-414.
2. Data on inventory obsolescence is difficult to interpret. Case study evidence suggests a shrinkage and obsolescence cost of about 4 percent (see T.W. Hall, "Inventory Carrying Costs: A Case Study," *Management Accounting* [January 1974], pp. 37-39). However, our review of National Income Account Data suggested a somewhat smaller effect. The subject of obsolescence will be treated more fully in a future study.
3. Many corporations pay taxes on inventory appreciation. However, if a firm is on LIFO (last in, first out) accounting and its inventories are growing steadily, it will pay no taxes on inventory appreciation. Accordingly, in evaluating marginal costs associated with growth, capital gains on inventories were assumed to be not taxable.
4. The changes contemplated by ERTA for 1985 and 1986 would have had more pronounced benefits.
5. For example, approximately 20 percent of total expected investment tax credit is received in each of the five quarters following the beginning of the fiscal year at which the investment is made. If we assume that the investments are distributed approximately equally over the four quarters, v equals about 0.25.
6. Bureau of Economic Analysis, U.S. Department of Commerce, *Fixed Reproducible Tangible Wealth in the United States* (Washington, D.C.: Government Printing Office, March 1982, October 1982).
7. The Council of State Governments, *The Book of the States* (Lexington, Ky.: The Council of State Governments, 1962-1982).
8. Bureau of the Census, U.S. Department of Commerce, *Annual Survey of Manufacturers, 1978: Statistics for States, Standard Metropolitan Statistical Areas, Large Industrial Counties, and Selected Cities* (Washington, D.C.: Government Printing Office, 1978).
9. Bureau of Economic Analysis, Department of Commerce, "Revised Estimates of the National Income and Product Accounts," *Survey of Current Business* 62, no. 7 (July 1982), p. 31.
10. Board of Governors of the Federal Reserve System, "Balance Sheets for the U.S. Economy, 1945-1981," *Balance Sheets, Flow of Funds* (October 1982), Tables 705 and 725; "Flow of Funds Accounts," *Sector Statements of Saving and Investment, Nonfinancial Corporate Businesses* (Washington, D.C.: Board of Governors of the Federal Reserve System, September 1982).
11. G.N. Hatsopoulos, "High Cost of Capital: Handicap of American Industry," Thermo Electron Corporation (April 26, 1983); "America Cannot Afford Its Cost of Capital," *The Economist* 287, no. 7287 (April 30, 1983), pp. 118-119.

CHANGES IN CAPITAL COST RECOVERY POLICIES: COSTS AND BENEFITS

Frederic W. Hickman

Dr. Ture's analysis asserts that the income tax system is nonneutral with respect to income from capital and that it is even less neutral in periods of inflation. His solution is, in effect, to abolish the income tax insofar as it applies to capital investment. He approves of the Accelerated Cost Recovery System (ACRS) because it moves a long way toward neutrality but deplores the 1982 legislation because it retreats from neutrality. He is encouraged, however, because the Congress is at least discussing neutrality, which he thinks is the proper criterion. How one feels about that depends, I think, on how one's mother raised him or her.

I am sympathetic to much of what Dr. Ture says, but I am less sanguine than he is about long-run prospects in the legislative arena. I suspect that Congress made the changes he prefers not because its Members were suddenly struck with truth and light, but rather in a passing fit of political euphoria. I fear that the Congress may spend the next decade undoing those changes, as they, in fact, began doing in 1982. The temptation to make political hay out of large businesses' being ostensibly subject to an income tax but paying little or no tax is likely to be irresistible. Nor is the general public likely to understand such a system, as it inevitably appears to involve tax avoidance or evasion. A formal, candid elimination of the tax on capital income, if that is what is desired, would be more politically stable than a system that purports to impose a tax but does not.

I am more concerned than Dr. Ture, I think, about the differences in the treatment of different kinds of investment. It is true that an income tax does intrinsically discriminate against some kinds of investment. In general, the discrimination is on a spectrum: discrimination is least toward shorter-lived assets and greatest toward longer-lived assets, while in between, different time paths of economic depreciation give different results. The present system, however, has accommodated to that, and the bias generally works in a systematic way. When we make very rapid and drastic changes, as in the 1981 legislation, we upset existing relationships between different kinds of investments in different industries. We produce windfall gains and losses, and we find that those, in turn, create unemployment, plant closings, obsolescence, and so forth, as particular companies dealing in certain kinds of assets or having particular tax pictures of their own find that they can or cannot take advantage of the changes. If the changes were to move us clearly and uniformly toward a neutral tax system, those dislocations would be an appropriate price to pay, though perhaps the price could be minimized by careful transition rules. The kinds of changes that we have been making, however, have moved us erratically, at best, toward an overall neutral system, creating serious new inequalities between particular enterprises and particular mixes of business. Why should companies with heavy investments in depreciable assets, for example, be treated much more favorably than companies with heavy investments in nondepreciables, such as inventories? Why should companies that have an investment mix that produces large amounts of taxable income from existing assets be accorded tax benefits from new investments that are, in effect, denied to other companies making the same new investments? That is the kind of problem at which safe-harbor leasing was directed. It did not entirely solve the problem and, of course, does not solve it now that the measure has been repealed.

Dr. Ture argues for expensing, i.e., for immediate deductions for capital outlays. Before expensing can work, the enterprise must have other income from prior investments from which to deduct the expenses. Many companies do not have that. This is particularly the case in the so-called capital-intensive industries, which are often referred to as the "basic" industries. Thus, we are left with the paradox that the companies for which expensing is most necessary in order to produce a neutral tax would, in fact, not get the value of expensing if it were enacted tomorrow. The proponents of expensing (including Dr. Ture, I think) universally acknowledge the necessity of having taxable income from existing assets in order to make expensing for new assets produce neutrality. Most of them do not dwell on the issue, or dismiss it by proposing that expensing be "refundable," i.e., that the value of the expense deduction be remitted to taxpayers that do not have other taxable income against which to use the expense deduction. However, we do not now have a system of refundable deductions and credits, nor does one seem imminent. In the meanwhile, if we make capital investment expensable, it means that particular enterprises will be discriminated against, producing nonmodernization, plant closings and major dislocations for those companies, not because they are less efficient but because of the new nonneutralities in the tax law.

In sum, constant change and new discriminations are, in themselves, costly. For companies that can not take advantage of ACRS and the Investment Tax Credit, the 1982 changes that cut back the 1981 provisions were in many cases (and this is always shocking to some) a help rather than a hindrance. There are companies that are substantially better off because Congress went backwards, because of the kind of distortion I have described. I think we need to give greater attention to the implications of that fact.

 *Chapter 6*

Saving Incentives: The Role of Tax Policy

Michael J. Boskin

INTRODUCTION

It is tempting to describe the recent performance of the economy of the United States by paraphrasing Winston Churchill's description of Russia. Our economy is in a severe, sustained recession while undergoing enormous structural changes against the backdrop of a frightening, long-term growth slowdown. It is difficult to understand any of these three enormous economic events in isolation; they interact in many important ways. However, this paper will be confined primarily to a discussion of long-term issues of tax policy, saving, and economic growth and will abstract from short-term cyclical considerations.

While it is clear that much is at stake in the short-term performance of the economy, our long-term growth is equally, if not more, important. To put this notion in stark relief, consider the fact that even small differences in annual percentage growth rates compounded over relatively modest periods of time can drastically alter the nature of an economy and a society. For example, the United Kingdom, growing at about one percentage point less than did the United States, France, and Germany, managed to transform itself from the wealthiest society on earth toward the end of the nineteenth century to a relatively poor member of the Common Market today. While short-run cyclical issues correctly demand some attention, we must not lose sight of the enormous stake we all have in restoring our overall long-term rate of growth to something like its historic rate of 2 percent per year.

With this focus on long-term growth, what role does saving have to play in promoting or retarding long-term growth? What role does tax policy have in promoting or retarding saving? Are saving and tax policies sensible concerns for those wishing to do something to reverse our long-term growth slowdown? Or should we focus our attention on monetary policy, investment, overall fiscal policy, and so forth?

While there are undoubtedly a variety of influences on saving behavior, both as to its level and its composition, this paper argues that tax policy is likely to play an important, but hardly exclusive, role in determining our saving rate; that changes in our saving rate may well be necessary for long-term permanent changes in our rate of investment; that this, in turn, may well be necessary to increase our long-term growth rate via a variety of potential links between our rate of investment and our rate of technological progress. It also argues that our notion of saving should be defined quite broadly to include business and government saving or dissaving, as well as personal saving, in evaluating the first order effects of fiscal and other policies.

Further, there is substantial reason to believe that we have been and continue to be saving a substantially smaller fraction of our national income than is socially desirable. Once out of the recession, on average over cycles, our saving rate should be increased substantially. This is important both for efficiency considerations in the intertemporal allocation of consumption and, possibly, also for increasing our growth rate itself.

Tax incentives or disincentives to save or to borrow and consume, or to allocate saving for noneconomic reasons among different potential types of assets by risk class and duration, have an important role to play in the generation and allocation of capital in our society. While they are the focus of this paper, it is important to note (and I will allude to this point on occasion throughout the paper) that tax policy interacts with monetary policy, with the overall level of government saving or dissaving (a properly measured inflation and cyclically adjusted current services deficit), and with the uses of those government funds for investment and research and development, as opposed to government consumption, in affecting capital formation. Recent tax policy changes have substantially reduced tax disincentives to save in a variety of forms (and are also likely to cause increases in the real rate of interest, which in turn will affect saving positively) through the substantial changes in capital cost recovery and other business investment incentives.

It is important to note that the traditional bifurcation of saving incentives in the personal and investment incentives in the business tax is a less than useful division. Corporations are a veil; ultimately, their retained earnings reflect the shareholders' desire that saving be done on their behalf by the corporation. There is, therefore, a substantial interaction between personal and corporate saving. Further, during times of relatively normal employment and output, there is an important relation between saving and investment—namely, an equilibrium rate or structure of interest rates that allocates the supply of new capital to new investment. Thus, policies designed to increase investment will succeed in increasing investment only to the extent that there is some responsiveness of saving to this higher investment demand and increase in interest rate. If saving were totally insensitive to interest rates, an increased investment demand would merely drive up gross interest rates until the new tax incentives were negated with no more saving or investment than was forthcoming prior to the incentive. Simply put, the efficacy of business investment incentives or of personal saving incentives depends crucially on the elasticities with respect to the rate of return of *both* saving and investment in our economy.

We have made progress in removing some of the more extreme distortions that plagued our tax system both directly and also through its rather insidious interaction with inflation in the course of the 1970s. This paper suggests interim goals of neutrality, simplicity, and integration—that is, that we ought to integrate the corporate and personal tax, remove all saving (or reinvestment) from the tax base, and greatly simplify the tax Code and business decisions. These goals suggest a need to progress toward a comprehensive, integrated personal and corporate tax on consumption. All saving and investment—whether in plant and equipment, human beings, or quasipublic goods privately provided through charitable contributions—would be deductible from a comprehensive measure of income and the remaining direct consumption would be the proper tax base. We already have moved in this direction; it remains to be seen how this goal will be achieved and what might be accomplished if we can continue moving toward it over the course of the decade. Finally, this discussion concludes with a summary of all these suggestions and a presentation of various open questions for research.

THINKING ABOUT OPTIMAL NATIONAL SAVING AND INVESTMENT

There are a variety of both common sense and technical ways to explain why we may be under-saving in the United States.[1] The two lines of reasoning that follow raise a variety of potentially important issues. Note that I am taking a longer-term perspective. In this context, the opportunity cost of a little more saving is roughly measured by the inflation adjusted after-tax return to savers. While this has increased somewhat in the last two years, historically this number was on the order of 2 percent at most.

From society's point of view, the potential return from foregoing a little consumption, generating a little extra saving, and investing it is the before-tax rate of return at the margin on investment. Numerous studies have attempted to estimate this number; my own suggest that it is about 7 to 8 percent averaged over long periods of time. If the corporate sector alone were under consideration, the number would be slightly higher because of the extra tax wedge due to the separate corporate tax. Thus, the wedge driven between the net return to savers and the gross return to society from investment by taxes on capital income is a measure of the incremental value to society of a small increment in saving and investment. This wedge is large; and any modest response of saving and investment to rates of return suggests that the misallocation of resources has a substantial cost (Boskin 1978; Feldstein 1978; Summers 1981).

With perfect capital markets and the absence of taxes, consumers save to the point where their subjective time discount rate (ρ) equals the rate of interest (i), which, in turn, equals the marginal product of capital. Taxes on capital income reduce the net return to savers well below the marginal product of capital. Both the deadweight loss and the shortfall below the optimal saving rate are increasing functions of the interest elasticities of saving and investment and the size of the tax wedge. At the margin, the deadweight loss of additional revenue is proportional to the tax rate. For the U.S. economy, if investment demand were quite elastic, even a modest interest elasticity of private saving of 0.3 or 0.4 would imply that our saving rate is only half of its optimal level!

I have elsewhere detailed a more rigorous approach to the issue of optimal saving (Boskin 1981). While the analysis is somewhat more technical than can be presented here, the optimal saving rate at any given time (s_t) depends on the difference between the gross return to capital and the net rate of return in the steady state. It also depends upon the rate at which the marginal utility of income declines, the rate of technological progress and population growth, and various characteristics of production technology. My estimate, which suggests the net saving rate in the United States runs about 7 percent, implies that for various reasonable estimates of the relevant parameters, the optimal saving rate is considerably above this level—perhaps twice our current net national saving rate. We would either have to believe in an enormous pure rate of time preference or a rapidly declining marginal utility of income to render our current rate of capital formation socially optimal. Why is our rate of saving so low? There are a variety of possible answers to the question, but my own rough judgment suggests that the heavy taxation of capital income played a role, as has government dissaving in a variety of forms; finally, social insurance programs may have had some impact.

Beyond the simple deadweight loss kinds of calculations, there can be substantial first-order income effects from a depressed saving rate. Consider, for example, a closed economy or an open economy that must rely in the *long run* for the bulk of its supply of capital from internal sources; that is, short-run variations in domestically generated saving may merely be offset in international capital markets, but this is not a stable and dependable long-term source of investment finance or of life cycle resource reallocation. Thus, the investment rate will depend upon the rate of domestically generated saving. While many people think of growth rates in terms of a few months or quarters, we have in mind models of economies as they develop over much longer periods of time and their steady state potential growth rates. In an economy with no interaction between technological change and investment, increases in saving might increase the investment rate and therefore the capital/labor ratio on a once-and-for-all basis. The economy might transit to a higher growth path, but ultimately the growth *rate* would converge to its natural rate (in per capita terms, the rate of technological change).

However, technological change and investment may have important interactions. First, the rate at which society invests in technological change, perhaps as measured very grossly by research and development (R&D) expenditures, is likely to be positively related to the rate of new product and process innovation. Second, there may be a substantial amount of learning by doing. As new investment occurs, new techniques of production become apparent that would not have been discovered otherwise. This suggests that the rate of technological change will increase at higher rates of investment. Finally, there may be a substantial amount of embodiment. The embodiment hypothesis suggests that it is either impossible—or at least extremely costly and therefore uneconomic—to embed new technology in old capital. The rate of investment will affect the rate at which new technology is embodied and diffused throughout the capital stock and, therefore, the rate of technological change. These are the three potential avenues by which an increased saving rate (if it is a necessary prerequisite, as I believe it is, to an increased investment rate) may well also increase our rate of technological progress, that is, our potential long-term growth rate. Averaged over cycles, our actual rate of productivity growth declined markedly even prior to the early 1980s, as Table 6-1 reports.

Undoubtedly, there are a variety of other potential influences on technological progress that have much to do with culture, attitudes, and so forth. Moreover, we are only beginning to understand the changing role of the international capital market in our economy and others. However, an increase in our rate of saving is necessary for a substantial increase in our rate of investment over long periods of time. If we do not increase our saving rate domestically, either we will generate high interest rates rather than expand investment or we will have to import a progressively larger fraction of foreign capital in order to finance that investment.

To stimulate investment, the single most important thing we can do is to provide more capital to capital markets. In the short-run, this certainly cannot be done by increasing the private saving rate dramatically by any major tax change. The only way to supply more capital quickly to capital markets is to decrease government dissaving—that is, to decrease our deficit. I have written elsewhere about why the current measures of our deficits are substantially inadequate in measuring their impact on saving and dissaving in our society.[2] Concisely put, we need a separate, inflation-adjusted, cyclically adjusted, capital and current account with more attention paid to contingent liabilities and assets, which are marked to market continuously.

We are a long way from this, but it is reasonable to suggest that near-term deficits will substantially exceed any inflation correction or other adjustment of this sort and, therefore, that we face substantial government dissaving for the next several years. However, as noted above, we need not only to stimulate our rate of capital formation over the next few years but also to devote a much higher

Table 6-1. Average Annual Increase in Labor Productivity, Private Business Sector, Postwar Period, between Cycle Peaks.

Period	Increase in Productivity (percentage)
1948-53	3.6%
1953-57	2.4
1957-60	2.4
1960-69	3.1
1969-73	2.3
1973-79	0.6

fraction of our potential output to capital formation during normal times or averaged over economic fluctuations. This requires a restructuring of incentives to borrow in order to finance consumption. We need to consume slightly less (once we come out of the recession) for many years in order to increase our rate of capital formation for many years. Only then will we see enormous long-term benefits. Among the most important avenues for reducing consumption is to make substantive changes in our tax laws and overall fiscal policy.

TAX INCENTIVES OR DISINCENTIVES? WHAT HAS RECENT TAX POLICY WROUGHT?

In its most general form tax neutrality means that the tax system does not distort either the incentive to save or invest versus spend or the allocation of investment among asset types. In the best-of-all-possible worlds—with no other distortions, with sufficient revenue raised by taxes on commodities, and with factor supply that did not respond to these taxes and hence did not incur any deadweight loss—neutrality would be achieved. Unfortunately, other distortions do occur, and it is not possible to raise substantial amounts of tax revenues without distorting some incentives. The question then becomes: In this second-best world, which are the least distorting systems of taxes sufficient to raise the revenue necessary to provide the optimal level of public goods and transfer payments? For example, it is often argued that a pure consumption tax would be neutral with respect to intertemporal consumption decisions (i.e., the consumption/saving choice). Unfortunately, a pure consumption tax would have slightly higher rates than a corresponding income tax and, hence, might well distort the labor/leisure or work-in-the-market-versus-work-in-the-home decision. Various analyses of these second-best problems now exist, on both an analytical and empirical or simulation basis.[3] The general conclusion seems to be that, even with modest interest elasticities of saving, a consumption tax is likely to be more efficient than an income tax, even accounting for the slight increase in the labor supply distortion. Often the discussion of tax incentives or disincentives for saving (and, hence, neutrality) are couched in income versus expenditure tax terms.

It is extremely important to realize two fundamental points. First, the desirable base against which to levy taxes is not conceptually independent of the structure of rates and the unit and time period of account used (Boskin 1980). Second, while our current tax system is a hybrid of an income and consumption tax, the possible set of optimal tax rates would not necessarily be confined to a range of capital income taxation and labor income taxation that left us somewhere between a consumption and income tax. Conceptually, the optimal tax rates could imply capital income subsidies or heavier taxation of capital income than of labor income, as well as anything in between. The outcome depends on the behavioral responses of consumption and labor supply over the life cycle to changes in net rates of return and net wage rates (Atkinson and Stiglitz 1972; Feldstein 1978; Boskin and Shoven 1980).

Another important point concerns the differential risk characteristics or durability of different assets and the tax incentives that may affect these heterogeneous types of capital. In general, we should be leery of being driven from a benchmark of equal treatment of all capital, but conceptually cases can be made for differential tax treatment. In our attempt to tax capital income, we have created an enormous range of effective marginal tax rates on different types of assets in an unanticipated manner; we have not carefully thought out an occasional deviation from equal tax treatment that seems to be justified for externality or other reasons.

As an approximation, a second-best optimal tax system would be a general consumption tax. We have been hopscotching toward a consumption tax and away from an income tax in our personal tax system through a variety of changes in the tax base and rates. If the saving rate in an economy is suboptimal, changing the tax structure is not the only instrument available for dealing with this problem. The first-order effects of a suboptimal saving rate can be dealt with by running government surpluses, changing monetary policy, and so forth. It would still be important, however, to remove the wedge between the return to savers and the gross return to investors—that is, to remove the second-order efficiency distortion.

While it is not the major purpose of this paper to survey the empirical literature on econometric estimates of the responsiveness of saving and investment to after-tax real net rates of return, a few comments are in order. There is a substantial division among professional economists concerning the interest elasticity of the saving rate. A variety of studies, only some of which are my own (Boskin 1978; Boskin and Lau 1978; Hall 1981; Summers 1981), present a compelling case for at least a modest intertemporal substitution elasticity that is sufficient to render substantial the inefficiency of taxing many forms of saving twice at the margin. For a number of reasons, most other studies produce estimates that are biased toward low estimates of the interest elasticity of saving. The technical, statistical reasons for this conclusion are beyond the scope of this paper. Preliminary results of further research on this subject continue to suggest a modest interest elasticity of saving. Further, if our capital markets are open beyond the very short-run or if a nontrivial portion of saving at the margin is done for bequests, the conclusion of some elasticity of the saving function is further strengthened.

Most econometric studies of investment conclude that it is somewhat more elastic than is saving (Hall and Jorgensen 1967; Hall 1981), but these studies, as well as those on saving behavior, present a variety of problems. Thus, our conclusions about the interest elasticities of saving and investment are tentative and subject to revision as new data and improved analytical and estimation techniques are developed. It is likely that these elasticities, *over a span of time*, are substantial. There is enough evidence to suggest that they are substantial, and the nature of this evidence is sufficient to suggest that tax policies that affect the marginal returns to saving and investment can influence these decisions substantially, if not instantly.

With this in mind, it is interesting to note both the decline in the effective real net rate of investment (see Table 6-2) and also the sharp increase in effective marginal tax rates on capital income that occurred in the inflationary 1970s. While such simple correlations are hazardous at best, a variety of studies have suggested a nontrivial causal relation. A large number of empirical issues must be decided in assessing the impact of the structure of capital income taxation on saving and investment. Again, studies of Feldstein (1978), Feldstein and Summers (1978), and others discussed the impact of inflation in the corporate tax due to historic cost depreciation, taxation of nominal interest and so forth, which led to a rise in effective marginal tax rates. We should, of course, net out the deductibility of nominal interest as well.

Further, the relative size of the government versus the private sector, both in the short and long-run, are potentially important determinants of the national saving rate. This occurs for a variety of reasons. The larger the government sector, the higher (given a par-

Table 6-2. Quinquennial Averages of Investment Rates.

Period	Share of Net Productive Investment in GNP[a] (percentage)
1965-69	4.1%
1970-74	3.1
1975-79	2.2

[a]Subtracting direct pollution control expenditures from investment.
Source: Summers, L.H., "Taxation and Capital Investment: A *q*-Theory Approach," *Brookings Papers on Economic Activity* 1 (1981).

ticular tax base) tax rates will have to be to raise the revenue to finance it. If the revenue is not sufficient, deficits will ensue; and this government dissaving will offset, in general, the available private capital pool, although the nominal reported official budget deficit may be a very poor measure of the appropriate concept (Boskin 1981).

Next, the structure of the tax system can be important if across taxpayers there is a substantial difference in the marginal propensity to consume due to observable characteristics such as income or merely to "tastes"—that is, subjective rates of discount. Thus, the same tax revenue raised with the same tax base but generated with a different set of rates can have different impacts on private saving.

The government also invests some fraction of its revenue, although this fraction has declined substantially in recent years. When we talked about optimal national saving in the early part of this paper, we were summing personal, business, and government saving. This would be appropriate in the absence of distortions, assuming the government were doing its cost/benefit analyses properly, so that at the margin, government investment were as productive as private investment. In the absence of this (i.e., if there are a variety of distortions that create differential productivity of government and private investment), we would have to take some weighted average of these saving rates. Better yet, we would have to remove the distortions and equalize the productivity of investment, regardless of sector.

Therefore, evaluating the net impact of the Economic Recovery Tax Act of 1981 (ERTA) and the Tax Equity and Fiscal Responsibility Act of 1982 (TEFRA) can be quite complicated. It is too early to use contemporaneously generated data, especially since these would have to be separated from the effects due to general economic conditions. Also, the level and course of real interest rates have reflected an erratic and generally tight monetary policy that may well not prevail in the future. Any contemporaneous evidence would have to be rendered conditional on other policies and states of the economy prevailing or that economic agents expected them to prevail, a dubious proposition. The sharp reduction in inflation, if it persists, dramatically reduces some of the more insidious interactions of inflation and the tax system that drove up effective marginal tax rates. With all this in mind, let us briefly discuss several of the most important aspects of our last two sets of tax changes in terms of their potential impacts on investment and saving, with an eye toward where we ought to be going from here in structural tax policy.

RECENT TAX POLICY CHANGES

The most important structural features of ERTA and TEFRA were the following:[4]

1. The phased-in reduction of marginal personal rates;
2. The immediate reduction in the top-bracket rate of 70 to 50 percent on investment income;
3. The adoption of the Accelerated Cost Recovery System (ACRS);
4. The amendment of ACRS in the "out years" in TEFRA;
5. The adoption of universal Individual Retirement Accounts (IRAs);
6. The stopgap reform of the 1959 Life Insurance Company Income Tax, under which effective marginal rates were approaching 100 percent.
7. The net fiscal deficits, properly measured, created by the course of the economy, by these two acts, and by the government spending decisions accompanying them, which partly reflect 1 through 5 and partly reflect other tax provisions that we will not focus on here.

There was universal agreement that the rate of accelerated depreciation was decelerating due to the interaction of inflation and the corporate tax prior to 1981. There was also general consternation concerning the large number of asset classes and the complicated structure of depreciation guidelines. Many economists, myself included, felt that, even if we stayed within a separate corporate tax for a while, the case for moving to immediate expensing was overwhelming. While this could have been phased in through a variety of ways to prevent too much of a short-term revenue loss, it would have greatly simplified the tax system and created a much more neutral system of tax incentives than had existed previously. With ACRS the set of tax rates was simplified and certainly generally reduced. Unfortunately, ACRS still generated effective marginal tax rates under alternative hypothetical inflation scenarios and adjustment of gross interest rates to inflation, which varied markedly from asset type to asset type. Indeed, as Table 6-3, taken from the *1982 Economic Report of the President* shows, under certain scenarios, our investment policy was actually to subsidize investment. The before-tax return required to yield any after-tax return was lower than that after-tax return, potentially creating a situation where "uneconomic" investment as defined above would occur. Partly to redress this, as well as to reduce the staggering size of projected future deficits, TEFRA lopped off the phase-in of the last parts of

Table 6-3. Real Before-tax Return Required to Yield a 4 Percent Real After-tax Return in 1986 (*assumes 5 percent inflation*).

Type of Capital	Rate (percentage)
Construction machinery	2.3%
General industrial equipment	2.7
Trucks, buses, trailers	2.5
Industrial buildings	6.4
Commercial buildings	6.1

Source: *1982 Economic Report of the President.*

ACRS. This substantially decreased the effective reduction in marginal tax rates on investment income, although the full extent to which it will do so depends heavily on rates of inflation as well as other parameters. On balance, ACRS was well-founded in its attempts to simplify the tax system, accommodate the reality of inflation, and so forth.

It is my own view that it will never be possible to run a properly indexed corporate tax. It is too difficult to measure capital gains and losses, inventory profits, inflation premiums in interest payments and deductions, and such. For this practical reason (as well as for the efficiency reasons outlined above and some equity reasons to be discussed below), I personally favor scrapping the separate corporate tax, integrating it with the personal tax, and expensing all investment. Compared to this goal of neutrality, ACRS looks much worse than when compared to the horror story of the increase and variegation of effective marginal tax rates in the 1970s. TEFRA was designed to limit the combination of investment credits, depreciation, and so forth, in order to be no more generous than expensing. It still leaves us with substantially variegated effective marginal rates by asset type, and—given the different nature of production processes and possibilities in different sectors of the economy—substantially different effective marginal tax rates are likely to ensue by industry as well. These aspects of the tax system are dominated by a policy of expensing, and we ought to move toward this goal in the context of overall tax reform that I discuss below. In any event, the combination of ERTA and TEFRA, *ceteris paribus*, certainly increased the demand for new capital. Unfortunately, unless there is a corresponding increase in the supply available, it is likely that this will merely drive up gross interest rates. While higher real rates will call forth some additional saving, the enormous government dissaving that is going on more than compensates for the extra personal and business saving that could be expected from these tax incentives.

The general rate reductions, partly since they are partially offset by bracket-creep, should have some modest effect on saving in three separate ways. First, the lower effective marginal tax rates for the general population will increase the after-tax rate of return on taxable assets and therefore increase saving by these people. The sharp reduction in the top rate from 70 to 50 percent is probably the closest thing we have to generating a big bang for the buck. While some might object to this on equity grounds, this is the group with the highest propensity to save, and a large reduction in their effective marginal tax rate (which was observed more in the breech than in the observance) should generate some additional saving from these higher income individuals. However, it would be ridiculous to state that there are enough of these high income individuals or enough saving done by them to cause a substantial increase in our national saving rate.

Second, these rate of return effects will be buttressed by the universality of Individual Retirement Accounts and by a more reasonable taxation of life insurance companies. I have elsewhere (Boskin 1981) presented an estimate of what universal IRA accounts may do in the long-run and feel that a nontrivial amount of incremental saving will occur. Of course, this will be partly enmeshed with substantial tax arbitrage, since individuals who have wealth in taxable forms or who are able to borrow for other purposes will shift assets into IRA accounts rather than generate additional saving. This suggests a general principle: It is extremely difficult to eliminate such possibilities of tax arbitrage when one is trying to open up the "qualified accounts" approach to a consumption tax; much attention must be paid to this in a transition to a consumption tax. Generally, these saving incentives would be likely to increase the saving rate somewhat. However, since the federal government's nominal deficit is a huge fraction of the total privately generated new capital, it would be ridiculous to suggest that these incentives could create such a large increase in private saving as to offset this magnitude of government dissaving. However, interest rates probably would have gone up still further had these particular saving incentives not accompanied the investment incentives in our last two rounds of tax reform. The limits developed in TEFRA for the basis adjustment and the depreciation adjustments in 1985 and 1986 will weaken the incentives that were created in 1981; however, these can be more than overcome by a more sensible general fiscal policy that gets government spending under control and government revenue in closer line with government expenditure.

I do not wish to be too harsh on these policy changes. The inflationary environment of the 1970s, the rising effective marginal tax rates on capital income that occurred, the decline in the real net rate of investment, and our abysmal growth performance are ample cause for substantial structural changes in tax policy. A more consistent and neutral tax policy is available, however. While passing the provisions of ERTA was preferable to having done nothing, and while many of the act's features are quite sensible, the time is now at hand (in the context of some overall fiscal responsibility on the spending side) to exert pressure to move to a more sensible general tax reform: a comprehensive, integrated personal and corporate consumption tax (CIPCCT).

AN INTERIM GOAL: A COMPREHENSIVE, INTEGRATED PERSONAL AND CORPORATE CONSUMPTION TAX (CIPCCT) BY 1990

As mentioned above, there are a variety of reasons to prefer to tax consumption rather than income. The former is less distorting of the consumption/saving choice; it probably is much easier to administer since it would remove a large part of the difficulty in measuring capital income; and it actually may be more equitable. Let me begin by addressing this point, since there is much misunderstanding of the alleged regressivity of the consumption tax.

At any point in time, it is true that as one moves up the current income scale, the ratio of saving to income increases and consumption to income decreases. In this very simplistic static sense, a tax that was levied on consumption, as opposed to all income, would be regressive as measured against current income. But there are a variety of fallacies in this interpretation. First, current income is a very poor measure of general economic well-being. Income fluctuates from year to year and also has typical life cycle patterns. Our imperfect averaging procedures compound the problem substantially. In fact, many economists, myself included, believe that for the bulk of the population consumption is a better measure of "permanent" income than is current income. That is, people tend to smooth their consumption and react differently to transitory and permanent changes in their potential lifetime income. Therefore, if one really wanted to tax a comprehensive measure of economic income (while working within the context of an annual tax with imperfect averaging over time), consumption might be a better measure than current income. More importantly, an income and a consumption tax eventually reach the same end (with a proviso that I will mention below) over the long run. What will you consume over your lifetime? A family's consumption over its lifetime is the present value of its income. Therefore, ignoring bequests for the moment, an annual consumption tax over an individual's or family's lifetime will tax its lifetime resources, as will an annual income tax. The difference is that an annual consumption tax will be neutral with respect to when during its lifetime that individual or family consumed its wealth, whereas an income tax would not be neutral, penalizing those who wanted to save for future consumption late in life (for example, during retirement).

Many of those who oppose a consumption tax on equity grounds also ignore the possibility of a personal progressive consumption tax. While it is not my purpose here to discuss the appropriate degree of vertical equity in the tax system or ethical considerations concerning the distribution of economic well-being, it is important to note that a value added tax or a national sales tax are just particular potential vehicles at getting at a consumption tax base. Equally feasible and in some ways preferable is a tax system that developed a comprehensive income measure and allowed people to deduct their full net saving. This could be done on a tax form that looked similar to the one used today; in fact, it could be substantially simplified. The difference between income and saving equals, by definition, consumption. We could then use whatever rate structure and other devices that were deemed desirable in such a tax system. Therefore, arguments about equity and income distribution would more appropriately be placed on the structure of the new tax rather than the concept itself.

There are many problems of transition from our current tax system to such a consumption tax (see, for example, U.S. Treasury's *Blueprints for Basic Tax Reform* 1977; Mieszkowski 1980). However, none of these seem insurmountable relative to other changes we have made in the past. The important thing is that an abrupt shift would create substantial windfall gains and losses and that a gradual move, perhaps phased in in sequences over a decade or so, would be quite desirable.

It is important to note that we have begun to move toward a consumption tax goal, although only on one side of the balance sheet. For example, pensions, Individual Retirement Accounts, and so forth, are all deductible, and interest accrues tax free "inside." They are therefore treated as they would be under a consumption tax—an immediate deduction is available and the accumulation of interest income is taxed only when it is withdrawn for consumption. I, therefore, favor continuing this move in the "qualified" accounts manner toward a consumption tax. However, allowing interest deductions on borrowing to finance such tax-free saving vehicles is inconsistent with a pure consumption tax norm. Only if we believe that we ought to be subsidizing investment—rather than removing the disincentives to invest and restoring neutrality in the investment/consumption choice—is this appropriate. With the currently available evidence, this may well be going too far, and we need to include an orderly phased-in procedure for changing the deductibility of nominal interest.

It is also important not to tax corporate source income, or other types of personal saving, twice. Therefore, it is important to integrate the corporate and personal income tax. In the context of a consumption tax approach, this makes enormous sense, since retained earnings are saving on behalf of the shareholders and should not be taxed in the first place. Dividends that were used for consumption would be taxed at the personal level, but those that were reinvested or rolled-over would be exempt from taxation until withdrawn for consumption purposes. The same would be true of realized capital gains.

Such a tax system would obviously be more simple than our current tax system. No need for large numbers of combinations of investment credits, "tax lives," recovery schedules, and so forth. No need to worry about many of the reasons to generate income averaging and measurement problems in an inflationary economy. This tax would not be without difficulties, but it would be much more efficient and equitable than our current tax system.

The thorny issue of bequests remains. Should they be treated as consumption when made? Or only when the proceeds are used for consumption by the following generation? Should we have a separate estate and inheritance tax at all? These issues revolve around a variety of problems that are not the central focus of this paper. The choice between an income and consumption tax, however—or rather between our current tax system and the general structure of the one I have outlined above—does not hinge on the treatment of bequests. It is dubious that estate and inheritance taxes will generate anything other than a trivial fraction of government revenue. The concern that some people have about extreme concentrations of wealth that may carry some power above and beyond the power to consume economic goods and services can be dealt with in a variety of ways in the structure of any taxes on intergenerational transfers.

To return to my basic argument: If we have as a goal moving toward a comprehensive, integrated personal and corporate consumption tax by 1990, we will need over the course of the next several years to lay out a series of steps in doing so. These include: extending the nature and level of, and reducing the restrictions on, IRA accounts; rethinking interest deductibility; solving a myriad of accounting problems (some of which have been discussed in *Blueprints* and elsewhere); and exploring how this tax system relates to the spending process, fiscal federalism, and a myriad of other fiscal devices that now exist in the United States. For example, will transfer payment income be included in the comprehensive measure of income from which net saving is deducted? What is the time period to be used in phasing in the changes? Shall we start a consumption tax and gradually phase out the existing tax, allowing people, especially the elderly, to decide which tax they would prefer through a once-and-for-all election?

The tax changes I (and many others) favor would not substitute for careful control of the spending process. Nor would they alleviate the need for other tax devices, unless either the rates were raised or the base made much more comprehensive than our current tax system in attempts to get at "measured income." We can lower the rates with a more comprehensive tax base and preserve the amount of revenue, but there is strong opposition to virtually any conceivable major base broadening measure. Further, many of these base broadening measures, while desirable tax policy, may merely call forth additional spending (for example, taxing social security benefits). While a gradually phased-in CIPCCT promises us a more equitable and efficient tax system, it does not guarantee that the spending decisions will be made more cost conscious and target effective, or that spending and taxes will automatically fall into line when each is properly measured. Additional measures are needed for these purposes. Relative to our current tax system, however, such a tax system is likely to increase saving somewhat, although we have come a substantial fraction of the way through the tax deductibility of employer prepaid pensions, universal IRAs, and so forth. Further, a sharply progressive rate structure, even with a fairly comprehensive measure of consumption, might produce somewhat less saving than a flat rate or a value added tax. However, the differential marginal propensity to save by income classes is not so large that these effects are likely to dominate those concerning the general size of the public sector and, hence, level of the rates and the exclusion of net saving from the tax base.

CONCLUSION

This paper has traced a large number of considerations concerning tax policy, saving, and economic growth. Our long-term growth slowdown is an immense economic and societal problem. Further, an increased rate of capital formation and innovation is a prerequisite to restoring a healthy long-term growth rate, and an increase in the domestically generated supply of capital may well be necessary to assist in doing so. More sensible tax policy is one important vehicle for doing so. Quite apart from our growth doldrums and recession, our tax system is still replete with substantial inefficiency in the consumption/saving choice and the forms that saving and investment take. A simpler and more neutral tax system is available, and this tax system could, in principle, be at least as equitable as our current tax system. While the structural tax reform I advocate—moving toward a comprehensive, integrated personal and corporate consumption tax— is an important avenue to follow, it must be supplemented by sensible monetary policy, by sound overall fiscal policy that does not create enormous government dissaving over long periods of time, and by sensible spending decisions based on appropriately implemented cost/benefit analyses and target- and cost-effective transfer payment programs. Changing the tax system is not a panacea in and of itself. It is an important component in the overall change in economic policy that is underway as we attempt to change our society from one that borrows in order to consume to one that saves in order to promote its future well-being.

NOTES TO CHAPTER 6

1. For example, see Boskin (1981) or Boskin and Shoven (1980). Of course, many others have come to the same conclusion.
2. See Boskin (1982) for a discussion of conceptual and measurement problems in the unadjusted deficit figures.
3. For example, Feldstein (1978) and Shoven, Fullerton, and Whalley (1983) evaluate these second-best issues.
4. Many other provisions of these two tax acts are worthy of discussion in a longer paper (for example, safe-harbor leasing, the estate tax changes, and the net effect on risk-taking due to reductions in effective capital gains tax rates), but I do not believe these items would alter the qualitative conclusions drawn here.

BIBLIOGRAPHY

Atkinson, A.B., and J. Stiglitz. "The Structure of Indirect Taxation and Economic Efficiency." *Journal of Public Economics* 1 (1972): pp. 97-119.

Boskin, M. "Taxation, Saving and the Rate of Interest." *Journal of Political Economy* 86 (1978): pp. 53-527.

_____. "Federal Government Deficits: Myths and Realities." *American Economic Review* 72 (May 1972): pp. 296-303.

_____. "Some Issues in Supply-Side Economics." Carnegie-Rochester Conference Series, 1981.

_____. "Factor Supply and the Relationships among the Choice of Tax Base, the Tax Rates and the Unit of Account in the Design of an Optimal Tax System." In H. Aaron and M. Boskin, eds., *The Economics of Taxation*, pp. 147-157. Washington, D.C.: The Brookings Institution, 1980.

Boskin, M., and L. Lau. "Taxation and Aggregate Factor Supply." Compendium of Tax Research, U.S. Treasury, 1978.

Boskin, M., and J. Shoven. "Issues in the Taxation of Capital Income." *American Economic Review* 70 (May 1980): pp. 164-170.

Feldstein, M. "The Welfare Cost of Capital Income Taxation." *Journal of Political Economy* 86 (1978): pp. S29-S51.

Feldstein, M., and L. Summers. "Inflation, Tax Rules and the Long-Term Interest Rate." *Brookings Papers on Economic Activity*, 1978.

Hall, R. "Intertemporal Substitution in Consumption." NBER Working Paper #720, July 1981.

Hall, R., and D. Jorgensen. "Tax Policy and Investment Behavior." *American Economic Review* LVII (1967): pp. 391-414.

Mieszkowski, P. "The Advisability and Feasibility of An Expenditure Tax System." In H. Aaron and M. Boskin, eds., *The Economics of Taxation*, pp. 179-202. Washington, D.C.: The Brookings Institution, 1980.

Shoven, J.B.; D. Fullerton; and J. Whalley. "Replacing the U.S. Income Tax with a Progressive Consumption Tax: A Sequenced General Equilibrium Approach." *Journal of Public Economics* 20 (1983): pp. 3-24.

Summers, L. "Capital Taxation and Accumulation in a Life Cycle Growth Model." *American Economic Review* 71, no. 4 (September 1981): pp. 533-544.

U.S. Treasury. *Blueprints for Basic Tax Reform*. Washington, D.C.: U.S. Government Printing Office, 1977.

Discussants:

EXPANDING SAVING INCENTIVES: PRACTICAL AND POLITICAL PROBLEMS

Edwin S. Cohen

Michael Boskin presents a strong and cogent argument for elimination, or at least major amelioration, of the federal income tax as it applies to income that is saved and not consumed. Along with other noted economists, he points to our reduced savings rates in recent years and to the harmful effects this has on investment and technological innovation. While the extent of the adverse effect of our present income tax depends on the assumed interest elasticity of savings, he concludes that even on a modest elasticity assumption, the effect is substantial and serious.

As his preferred remedy, Dr. Boskin recommends adoption of a comprehensive, integrated personal and corporate consumption tax (CIPCCT), with a gradual shift from the present income tax to be completed by 1990. Every innovative proposal for basic changes in our complex tax structures presents practical and political difficulties, and we should bear in mind some of those that may stand in the path of the CIPCCT.

1. Integration. In the mid-1970s considerable work was done on various means of integrating the corporate and individual income tax, but the effort came to nought. Disagreements arose about specific matters, such as the treatment of overseas corporate income that is taxed abroad and the treatment of the investment credit and municipal bond interest. Surprisingly, the business community itself was not united in support. Moreover, while there are several ways of dealing with corporate earnings that are distributed to shareholders, it is far more difficult to achieve integration with respect to retained earnings.

Dr. Boskin would solve these problems by eliminating the corporate income tax entirely and taxing to the shareholder only distributed earnings that are used in consumption. He would relieve from tax all retained corporate earnings on the ground that they are saved and not consumed. This would be a radical political departure, however strong the economic foundation, and would require considerable public education and persuasion. Among other problems, complete elimination of the corporate tax would involve a revenue loss that would force upward the rates involved in the proposed tax on consumption.

2. **Comprehensiveness.** Dr. Boskin acknowledges the practical and political difficulties involved in broadening the income tax base to include such items as transfer payments and state and local government bond interest in order to fulfill his goal of achieving a comprehensive tax. Broadening the income tax base would seem especially crucial in a consumption type tax because the proposed deduction for savings should not be allowed if the savings represent investment of substantial amounts of untaxed income accretions. A major broadening of the income base, however, requires traversing a political mine field. Moreover, eliminating deductions for charitable contributions, home mortgage interest, automobile purchase interest, medical expenses, and so forth might make the Tax Equity and Fiscal Responsibility Act of 1982 (TEFRA) seem like a Sunday School picnic.

3. **Borrowing for Consumption.** Dr. Boskin cautions that in a comprehensive consumption tax there should be no deduction for interest on indebtedness incurred for consumption purposes. But even disallowance of the interest deduction may not be sufficient to prevent use of borrowed funds for consumption purposes, since borrowing the funds would postpone payment of tax on income until income is applied to repay the indebtedness. Eventually this effect would even out, but a tax deferred is a tax reduced.

4. **Gifts and Bequests.** From the standpoint of both donor and donee, the treatment of gifts and bequests is of major significance in a fair consumption tax. It would be wrong to permit a person to save his income, thus paying no tax, while consuming his inheritance over many years. Either gifts and bequests would have to be income to the recipient or represent consumption at the time when they are made, or some other solution would be required. Progressiveness of the rate structure and the annual nature of the tax would exacerbate this problem.

5. **The Rate Structure.** Of course, the lower the rate of consumption tax and the flatter the rate, the easier many of the solutions

would be. Unfortunately, the converse is also true, and Dr. Boskin calls attention to the need for base broadening to hold down the rate.

6. Transition. Because of windfall gains and losses that would result from the shift to a consumption tax, Dr. Boskin suggests that the change be made gradually until 1990. Lawyers instinctively shudder at the problem of two tax systems running side by side for a number of years and at the grandfather clauses that would be sought. Consider, for example, the problem of outstanding long-term tax-exempt bonds or the effect of a gradual disappearance of the deduction for contributions to charities.

7. Favoritism. Dr. Boskin acknowledges that a challenge will be made to using consumption as the tax base on the ground that it would favor the wealthy, who have a greater capacity for saving than lower income groups. I shall not attempt to repeat his counterarguments but only note that if all the other problems can be solved, this seems to be the major political issue involved in allowing a deduction for saving.

Dr. Boskin's proposal involves a major restructuring of current law over a substantial phase-in period. Several years ago I was asked to develop a proposal that would tend to promote savings and that would be sufficiently modest in scope to be likely of early enactment. After reviewing provisions in foreign laws and various possible changes in our own Code, I concluded that the most feasible approach was to build on the existing Individual Retirement Account provision (or IRAs) that had been adopted in the Employee Retirement Income Security Act of 1974 (ERISA). Economic analyses were provided by Dr. Boskin, to whom I turned for his sage advice and support. Sponsored by Congressman Henson Moore, and later by Congressman Gibbons, Senator Chafee, and others, much of the proposal was enacted as a part of the Economic Recovery Tax Act of 1981 (ERTA) and became effective in 1982. The amendments have stimulated savings through the following changes, among others:

1. IRAs were made available to all individuals under age 70.5 years, whether or not they are employed by employers that maintain pension or profit-sharing plans. This step extended the IRA program to government employees, to members of the armed forces, and to many employees in the private sector and eliminated a series of technical questions relating to eligibility.

2. ERTA raised the dollar ceiling on annual contributions from $1,500 to $2,000 ($2,250 in certain cases for married couples).
3. It eliminated the contribution ceiling of 15 percent of earned income, thus permitting a part-time worker earning $2,000 for the year to contribute the entire amount to an IRA and deduct the entire contribution. This should prove of value to housewives who work part-time.

Reports from financial institutions, such as insurance companies, mutual funds, savings and loan associations, commercial banks, and savings banks, indicate a major response to the enlargement of IRAs in the first half of 1982. It is too early, however, to make an informed judgment until data is available for contributions to IRAs at least through December 31, 1982 or April 15, 1983.

One provision that was included but not enacted in the 1981 proposal would have permitted a matching amount of nondeductible contributions to be made to IRAs. Thus, if a deductible contribution of $2,000 were made, another contribution of $2,000 could be made that would be nondeductible. The subsequent income in the IRA account on the entire $4,000 would be free of tax until withdrawn from the account, presumably for consumption. In addition, a further nondeductible contribution in an amount up to $10,000 over the lifetime of the taxpayer would be allowed, chiefly to permit the size of the account to be sufficiently large to absorb the expense of maintaining and advertising the accounts. Nondeductible contributions are permitted for H.R. 10 (National Development Investment Act) plans and qualified plans, and the same procedures for administering the deductible and nondeductible portions could be used. The deferment of tax on the income from the savings, both deductible and nondeductible, in the IRA account would accomplish many of the objectives that Dr. Boskin's more thorough revision would seek.

Of course, the mere enlargement of IRAs would not achieve some of Dr. Boskin's long-range objectives, such as an integration of the corporate and shareholder tax, a comprehensive income base, and an unlimited deduction for amounts committed to saving. Because the IRA enlargement is not a complete revision, it is necessary as a practical matter to impose dollar ceilings on the permitted contributions. But gradual expansion of the IRA provisions may be a realistic way to attain eventually many of the desirable economic goals toward which his scholarship is directing us.

THE EFFECT OF GOVERNMENT ABSORPTION OF SAVINGS ON CAPITAL FORMATION

William Fellner

Professor Michael Boskin has made valuable contributions to current policy debates, as well as to their underlying theories, by developing a line of argument favoring measures intended to promote saving, investment, and productivity growth. Since our inclinations are similar in many respects, this paper will discuss those points that I emphasize differently than Dr. Boskin does and then provide some reasons for supporting one of his main conclusions.

Boskin tends to overemphasize the technical, neo-Paretan approach when explaining the reasons why we should remedy the recent weakening of our productivity trends. Saving and productivity have more to do with the basic characteristics of the type of civilization that has developed in industrially advanced countries. Entrepreneurial activity and expanding market economies are essential characteristics of that type of civilization. This is how Schumpeter would have seen it and rightly so.

In other words, in all types of civilization, attitudes and value judgments come in a package. It is highly improbable that a population unwilling to moderate its time preference sufficiently to achieve major increases in the standard of living from generation to generation would in other essential respects want to live by the standards of a society that has raised living standards significantly by creating a favorable climate for entrepreneurial activity. This favorable climate is an essential ingredient in the blend; remove it, and the basic characteristics of contemporary Western-type civilization will change in hard-to-predict ways. For example, the political institutions of the stationary state would prove quite different from those of a progressive society in which private incentives play a crucial role. One may or may not want to experiment with this kind of change; neither Professor Boskin nor I have an inclination to do so. Moreover, there are a good many manifestations—though as yet somewhat unreliable manifestations—that large numbers of people in various countries are *refusing* to continue experimenting with such radical reorientation of general attitudes. *This* is the heart of the matter: The question cannot be decided by technical considerations ranking one kind of nonneutrality of the tax system higher or lower than another kind of nonneutrality (i.e., by ranking on technical grounds one kind of

Pareto inefficiency higher or lower than another kind). The emphasis must be placed on the general social, political, and cultural characteristics of the societies facing these choices.

Be that as it may, Boskin and I do agree on the desirability of raising the saving rate. We also agree that raising the saving rate would very likely have a larger effect on trends in labor productivity than is suggested by models postulating independence of technological progress of the rate of capital formation. These two sources of labor-productivity growth are practically certain to be interrelated, although this interrelation probably cannot be quantified with any reasonable degree of generality.

Boskin's and my views concur concerning the strategic significance of budget deficits. Any economist who stresses the adverse effect of deficits on private intestment and attributes much importance to attempts to reduce the prospective deficits along our growth path is explicitly or implicitly denying that three qualifying considerations (discussed below) have much significance. (These qualifying considerations should not be allowed to weaken the main thrust of the argument, which is that large deficits do reduce capital formation significantly.)

One qualifying consideration suggests that, though the public's acquisition of government securities is included in savings as these are conventionally measured (they are included in "after-tax income minus consumption"), rational savers should know that deficits are dissavings creating future tax liabilities. When the government engages in deficit financing, awareness of these future flows of tax liabilities should induce the public to increase its conventionally measured savings correspondingly.

This reasoning leads to the conclusion that tax financing and deficit financing are equivalent because, in the event of deficit financing, the equivalent present value of a future stream of tax payments is regarded as the present cost of the fiscal expenditures. This argument depends on assumptions explained by David Ricardo but considered unrealistic by him; the underlying assumptions have weaknesses even *beyond* those that Ricardo recognized.

Another qualification of the argument that continued deficits along the growth path go at the expense of private investment deserves more attention, though even this qualification does not seem to be of great quantitative importance. If deficits develop in an economy in which the general price level is rising, part of the interest payment comes rightly to be interpreted as a compensation for rising prices. Savers who presumably wish to raise their *real* net worth through abstention from consumption need to raise their conventionally measured savings by the equivalent of what they regard as the inflation component of the interest payments.

This is a qualification that should not be brushed aside. What is at stake here is the savings-increasing effect of a loss in the real value of the savers' assets and the savings-reducing effect of a gain in the real value of assets. The data do suggest the existence of weak effects of this type.

A third qualification relates to the likelihood that part of the channeling away of domestic savings from investment shows not in a reduction of domestic investment but in an increase in the foreign financing of domestic capital formation that results from capital inflows attracted by rising interest rates. That is a valid proposition, particularly when applied to a small country, but to a much smaller extent even when applied to the United States. The new capital will be foreign-owned, however, and investment from abroad is therefore less desirable than the formation of capital from domestic savings. What remains true, nevertheless, is that even the formation of foreign-owned capital has certain secondary advantages for the country in which the investment takes place, mainly because of the complementary relationship between capital and labor. In a country as large as the United States, the channeling away of large amounts of domestic savings from the financing of private investment to that of deficits is unlikely to be offset to any very major extent by capital inflows, even in the sense in which such inflows can be regarded as offsets.

Despite the qualifications that I have mentioned, large deficits do divert savings from private investment on a major scale (and in the United States the investment of practically all enterprise falls into the category of private investment). It follows that we should make an effort to reduce significantly our prospective deficits for years located normally or better in our future cyclical sequences. Since the objective is to prevent a deficit-induced shift of the consumption-investment mix away from investment, it is essential to keep in mind that deficit-reducing budgetary measures, considered jointly with our monetary policy, should raise investment relative to consumption at any level of nominal demand.

THE CONGRESSIONAL OUTLOOK FOR INCREASED SAVING INCENTIVES

W. Henson Moore

I completely agree with Michael Boskin in his basic thesis that we must boost saving in order to stimulate investment and productivity. That is the idea we are trying to sell in the Congress. I think the idea of shifting from an income tax to a consumption tax is something that most conservatives will buy, at least in theory. The idea of taxing an income on a graduated basis is something we think is counterproductive. Going to a consumption tax is something, in theory, we think we would like to work toward.

We have a real problem, though, in the political dynamics of an idea like this. Its time has not yet come. Nobody has ever accused the Congress of being brilliant, or of being dramatic, or of being exceptionally fast. Congressmen and Senators do not like to be surprised. They like to know all about an idea; they want to know where all the political skeletons are and what the people are going to think well in advance, even several Congresses in advance, of the anticipated action. Therefore, an enormous economic education effort must take place before the American people, and then the Congress of the United States, will be ready to accept a comprehensive, integrated personal and corporate consumption tax. The Congress does not create ideas, and it does not implement them early. Congress reacts to ideas.

To look at the problem philosophically for a moment, I think there are two problems with a consumption tax. There are many people who believe in a graduated income tax. They think that a graduated income tax, where the tax burden goes up the scale of income, is preferable to a consumption tax, which is regressive and goes down the scale of income in terms of burden. Regressivity is something that Dr. Boskin's paper addresses, and he convinces me. We have a long way to go, however, before we can convince the average American, the labor unions, the liberals, the Democrats, the Congressional Budget Office (CBO), and others that a consumption tax would not be regressive.

The second problem we have is with the conservatives. They view a Value Added Tax or a consumption tax as an addition to the income tax, not as a substitute for it. Most conservatives do not believe we will ever get away from the income tax. They fear a consumption tax means that we would simply have two taxes instead of one.

Finally, let me comment briefly on the idea of expanded Individual Retirement Accounts (IRAs). We intend to take and enlarge upon Dr. Boskin's suggestions to move to further expand the Individual Retirement Account as a step toward a consumption tax. We hope to expand the IRA concept to allow the nondeductible contribution. I emphasize that expansion of IRAs is possible, even in a year like this, because it does not cost the Treasury any money. We are talking about after-tax dollars being put in, instead of before-tax dollars. We would only be sheltering the income on investment thereon.

Other methods of stimulating savings have large revenue losses in the short run. With the large deficit projections over the next several years, I am not hopeful that proposals to stimulate saving, such as the outright exempt interest income, can be enacted in the near future.

In conclusion, I think Dr. Boskin's proposal for a comprehensive, integrated personal and corporate consumption tax (CIPCCT) is a direction in which we might want to move. Unfortunately, between now and 1990, I fear the political dynamics will not let it happen.

 Chapter 7

Capital Gains: An Evaluation of the 1978 and 1981 Tax Cuts
Gerald E. Auten

I. INTRODUCTION

Since the introduction of the modern income tax in 1918, one of the most controversial issues of tax policy has been the debate about whether and to what extent preferential treatment should be accorded to capital gains income. Underlying this controversy are a number of distinct and unresolved (perhaps unresolvable) questions: the economic effects of capital gains taxes, the relevance of these effects for tax policy, and the appropriate objectives of tax policy for capital gains. As a result of the ongoing debate, the tax rules that apply to capital gains are some of the most complex and most frequently changed of the entire income tax Code.

Following a review of the goals of taxation and of some historical aspects of capital gains taxation, Part II of this paper examines some of the most important economic effects of capital gains taxes. Economic effects discussed in Part II include effects on saving and risk-taking, the lock-in effect and how it affects tax revenues, and how the bunching of gains and inflation influences effective tax rates. Part III of the paper evaluates the effects of the recent reductions in capital gains tax rates in 1978 and 1981. The paper concludes with some comments on capital gains taxes within the frameworks of several recent proposals for changing the tax system.

Goals of Taxation Relevant for Capital Gains

Since this conference is intended, in part, to focus on the goals of taxation as they apply to different forms of taxation, this section considers the application of such goals to capital gains. One point should be noted at the beginning: Goals of taxation are not mutually consistent; therefore, tradeoffs between various goals are frequently required.

The first goal of a desirable tax system is to achieve horizontal and vertical equity. Horizontal equity requires that those with the same income or command over economic resources should pay the same effective tax rates. Horizontal equity implies that no income should be exempt from taxation and that income should not be taxed more than once. While horizontal equity might seem to require full taxation of capital gains, this is not necessarily so in the cases of inflation and/or double taxation of income. These issues are considered more fully later in the paper. Vertical equity relates to the progressivity or regressivity of the tax system. There is general agreement that the tax system should not be regressive. While it is also generally agreed that the rich should pay more, there is little agreement about determining an optimal amount of progressivity.

The second goal of a desirable tax system is that the welfare loss associated with the collection of tax revenues should be minimized. When taxes distort relative prices or relative returns from the supply of factor services, they induce people to alter their economic activity by, for example, working less or saving less. These distortions produce an extra cost, which economists call excess burden or deadweight loss, above the cost of the taxes actually collected. A longstanding principle of welfare economics is that this deadweight loss can be minimized by taxing more heavily those economic activities that are least affected by changes in relative prices and taxing lightly those activities that are most sensitive to changes in relative prices. Since the square of tax rates enters the calculation of excess burden, high marginal tax rates are generally to be avoided. Due to the ability of taxpayers to time or delay capital gains realizations, capital gains can be expected to be particularly sensitive to high marginal tax rates.

The third goal of a desirable tax system is that the tax Code should be as clear and concise as possible. The tax Code and regulations that apply to capital gains add considerably to the complexity for the tax system.

The fourth goal is that the form of tax unit organization should not affect the amount of tax paid. The separate tax on corporate income violates this principle, since dividends and capital gains are also taxed at the individual level. On the other hand, capital gains taxes can be avoided altogether in cases where the transaction can be structured as a business reorganization. Finally, the tax Code should promote, rather than hinder, the growth and stability of the economic system.

Historical Context: Changes in Capital Gains Taxes

Because the goals of taxation as they apply to capital gains not only conflict with each other but also change in relative importance over time, Congressional views on capital gains have changed frequently. Congress has made significant changes in the tax treatment of short-term or long-term capital gains and losses on at least fifteen separate occasions since 1913, and has made minor changes on innumerable occasions. Long-term capital gains have been accorded preferential treatment since 1921, when Congress provided for an alternative tax of 12.5 percent on gains on assets held at least two years. At various times the alternative tax rate on long-term capital gains, which generally established the maximum rate, was set at 12.5, 15, 16.5, 20, 22, 25, and 26 percent. The holding period required for the reduced tax rates accorded to long-term gains has been variously set at six months, nine months, one year, eighteen months, and two years. The percentage of long-term gains taxed as ordinary income has been 40, 50, 66.66, and 100 percent. From 1934 to 1937, the percentage of long-term gains included in taxable income varied with the holding period of the asset. The longer the asset had been held, the smaller the included percentage of the gain. On assets held at least ten years, only 30 percent of the gain was included.

From 1970 through 1978 several rate-increasing tax reforms were enacted. The alternative tax was limited to $50,000 of gains. The excluded portion of long-term capital gains was subjected to a minimum tax. The benefits of the maximum tax on earned income were reduced in proportion to the excluded portion of long-term gains. From 1976 through 1978 it was possible to have tax rates as high as 49.125 percent on long-term gains.[1] This rate is not the highest historical rate, however; the highest rates were 77 percent in 1918, 73 percent from 1919 to 1921, and 63.2 percent on assets held between one and two years in 1936 and 1937.

Marginal tax rates on capital gains have been reduced substantially in the last few years. The Revenue Act of 1978 reduced the percentage of long-term capital gains taxed as ordinary income from 50 to 40 percent and eliminated the minimum tax on the excluded portion of capital gains. This provision reduced the maximum tax rate on capital gains from 49.125 percent to 28 percent. The 1978 law replaced the minimum tax on excluded long-term gains with an alternative minimum tax that is paid when it is greater than the tax computed in the regular way. The alternative minimum tax, designed to insure that all high-income taxpayers pay at least some tax, imposed marginal rates of up to 25 percent on capital gains. The Economic Recovery Tax Act of 1981 (ERTA) reduced the tax rates on long-term capital gains still further because it lowered the overall schedule of marginal tax rates. The maximum marginal tax rate on long-term gains is now 20 percent.

II. ECONOMIC EFFECTS OF CAPITAL GAINS TAXATION

This section outlines some of the ways in which the allocation of society's resources and the behavior of investors is affected by capital gains taxes. While there are many effects of capital gains taxation, this section will focus on the effects on saving and risk-taking. This section will also examine the lock-in effect, the impact of inflation, the bunching of gains, and the double taxation of gains on corporate stock.

Effects on Saving

Taxes on all types of income from capital have the potential to distort household decisions on saving. Both the amount of saving and the allocation of saving may be affected by capital gains taxes.

High tax rates on capital income may affect saving by reducing the after-tax rate of return to savers. From the standpoint of the individual household, the taxation of capital income increases the relative attractiveness of current consumption as compared to saving for the purpose of future consumption. Individual household decisions on saving and consumption may therefore become distorted. From society's standpoint, the return to savers would be less than the gross return on capital investment, and saving and investment would be reduced below desirable levels. Saving decisions are also affected by several factors other than rate of return, including the motives for saving (life cycle, precautionary, bequests), uncertainty about future income, inflation in consumer prices and the relative importance of substitution and income effects. Theory alone cannot tell us for certain whether taxes on capital income will increase or decrease private saving; the capital gains issue, therefore, becomes an empirical issue. While their findings are still highly controversial, several recent studies have found a significant response of savings to after-tax rates of return.[2] Even if these findings are correct, the effects of current capital gains taxes on saving are probably not great because preferential rates and the deferral of the tax until the gain is realized mean that expected after tax rates of return are not greatly reduced.[3]

There is a second avenue through which saving may be affected by capital gains tax rates. Tax sensitive corporations may respond to preferential taxation of capital gains by decreasing dividends and increasing retained earnings, which are ultimately reflected in higher stock prices.[4] This increases business saving, but households may see through the corporate veil and reduce their personal saving. This substitution between business saving and personal saving is not likely to be complete, however, and total private saving may increase by as much as 25 percent of the amount that is switched from dividends to retained earnings.[5]

In addition to affecting the amount of saving, taxes on capital income produce substantial distortions in the allocation of saving. Such distortion occurs because the tax treatment of capital income varies widely according to its source. While the real income from some types of saving is taxed at extremely high rates, other capital income is taxed at zero or very low effective tax rates due to deferral or exclusion from taxation of part or all of that type of capital income. Such differences in tax treatment produce substantial distortions in portfolio and intersectoral allocations.[6] For example, preferential tax rates on capital gains induce savers to choose investments that provide capital gains rather than ordinary income. For taxpayers in high tax brackets, stocks would be favored over bonds, and growth stocks would be favored over dividend paying stocks. Industries such as real estate and timber, which produce much of their income in the form of capital gains, would also be favored.[7]

In summary, it appears that capital gains taxes may reduce total private saving but that the effect is not large, due to preferential tax rates on gains, the benefits of deferral, and the substitution between corporate and personal saving. There are important welfare losses, however, due to the distortionary impact of capital gains taxes on intertemporal consumption decisions and the choice of savings instruments.

Effects on Risk Taking

It is commonly believed that high capital gains tax rates discourage venture capital and other high risk investments. A long tradition of economics literature has shown, however, that investment in risky assets can actually be increased by a proportional tax on capital gains, when losses are fully deductible.[8] The theoretical argument reasons that the effect of the capital gains tax is to make the government a partner in each investor's portfolio. The Treasury shares in realized profits and in losses as well. By sharing the risks, government reduces the variance of the expected after tax returns on the investment. Since the tax reduces the risk borne by the taxpayer, risk averse investors respond by increasing the proportion of high risk investments.

There are reasons why actual capital gains taxes may adversely affect risk-taking. The theoretical results apply to a proportional income tax with full offset of losses against other income. They are therefore not directly applicable to the current income tax system. A progressive tax system tilts the calculation of expected returns against the investor, since the tax rates on successful investments will be higher than those at which losses can be deducted. The limitation of the deduction of losses to $3,000 per year further reduces the attractiveness of high risk investments. With a high risk investment, the taxpayer may face the prospect of either a substantial gain or a large loss. The severe restrictions on the deduction of losses may cause investors to view the capital gains tax as a very one-sided arrangement and therefore to reduce their high risk investments. The tax may appear particularly one-sided in periods of high inflation, when part or all of the nominal gain may reflect the changing price level and not a real gain.

The response of the venture capital industry to changing capital gains tax rates seems to support the proposition that high capital gains tax rates tend to reduce high risk investment. New capital invested in venture capital firms and public underwritings in small companies declined substantially from 1969 through 1977, as capital gains tax rates were increased, and then increased dramatically in 1978-80, when capital gains taxes were reduced.[9]

Lock-in Effects and Total Tax Revenues

Under the U.S. income tax, capital gains are taxed only when realized. Taxpayers considering selling or switching investments must therefore include the capital gains tax when calculating their net returns from such sales. In such cases, when an otherwise desirable sale is not profitable after payment of the capital gains tax, the investor is said to be "locked-in" to current holdings. Advocates of reduced tax rates on capital gains have frequently argued that lowering capital gains taxes would unlock substantial amounts of gains and that the resulting increase in realizations would produce an increase in tax revenues. In addition, lock-in effects interfere with the efficiency of individuals' portfolio allocations and with the allocation of resources among competing uses.

Some of these lock-in effects are short-run or transitory in nature. Transitory lock-in effects are caused by two features of the taxation of capital gains: (1) sharp discontinuities in the marginal tax rates that apply to capital gains and losses and (2) the ability of taxpayers to determine the timing of the realization of gains and losses. Discontinuities in marginal tax rates are associated with the holding period requirement to qualify for taxation at the lower rates on long-term gains, the use of loss carryovers, and the limitation on the amount of losses that may be deducted from ordinary income. From 1970 through 1978 additional discontinuities could result from the limitation of the alternative tax to $50,000 of long-term capital gains, the minimum tax on preference income, and the spoiling of the benefits of the maximum tax on earned income.

Discontinuities in the tax rates on long-term gains as they existed in the 1970s for a taxpayer in the highest income bracket are illustrated in Figure 7-1. The tax rate on the first $50,000 of long-term gains was 25 percent. The rate jumped to 35 percent when the limit on the alternative tax was reached and then to 36.5 percent when the minimum tax was imposed. A taxpayer with a $10,000 short-term loss (or loss carryover) had a zero tax rate on the first $9,000 of long-term capital gains.[10] The next $1,000 was taxed at a 70 percent rate, since $1,000 of the short-term loss would otherwise be deductible against other income. The marginal rate then dropped to 25 percent, and additional long-term gains were taxed as in the case of no short-term losses. Under current law, the discontinuities due to the alternative tax, minimum tax, and maximum tax have been eliminated, but those related to losses still exist, although reduced in magnitude.

These short-run lock-in effects are well-known to investors, and they have been documented in several studies.[11] For example, the amount of short-term gains on sales of corporate stock declines as the six-month holding period approaches, but then jumps dramatically as soon as the gains qualify for tax treatment at the lower rates on long-term gains. While there appears to be no holding period effect for asset sales with losses, up to 30 percent of losses of high income taxpayers are realized in December, as taxpayers adjust their portfolios for tax purposes. Many taxpayers appear to be knowledgeable enough about their incomes to be able to use these end-of-the-year sales to even out their taxable income between the two years and thereby reduce their long-run tax liability. There is some evi-

128 Reform of the Federal Income Tax

Figure 7-1. Marginal Tax Rates on Long-term Capital Gains, Taxpayer in the 70 Percent Bracket, 1976–78.[a]

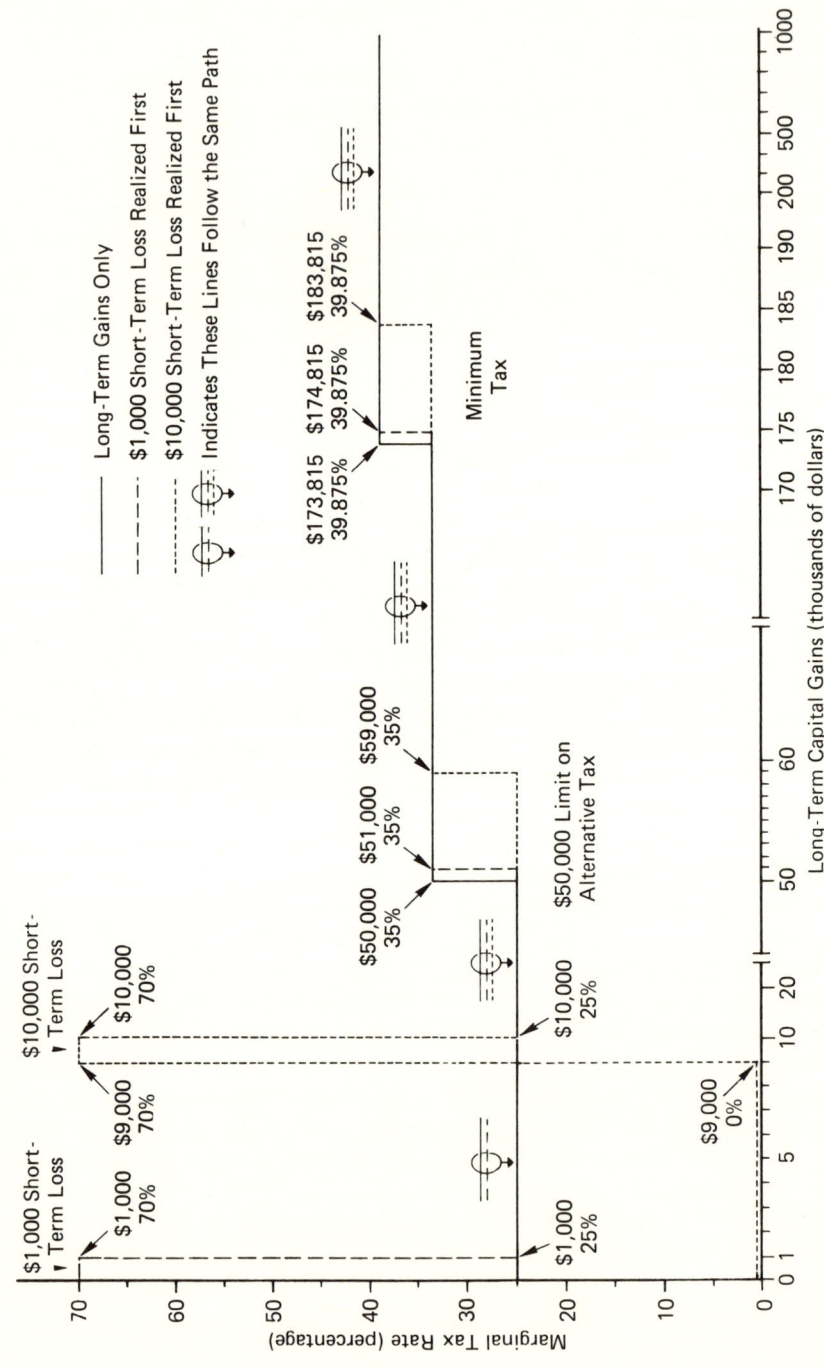

[a] The taxpayer is assumed to be married, filing jointly with taxable income from investments (not including capital gains) sufficient to be in the 70 percent marginal tax bracket for all examples. No allowance is made for the effect of the maximum tax or the value of loss carryovers to future years. The diagram shows 1976 when a maximum of $1,000 of capital losses could be deducted from ordinary income. The maximum deduction was increased to $2,000 in 1977 and $3,000 in 1978.

dence that taxpayers responded to the $50,000 maximum on the 25 percent alternative tax on capital gains that was in effect from 1970 through 1978 by taking gains over several years, so as not to exceed the $50,000 maximum. A recent study (Kaplan 1981) has shown that the holding period requirement for long-term capital gains may actually reduce government revenues by inducing taxpayers to take their losses as short-term and their gains as long-term.

Although the existence of short-run or timing effects is widely accepted, the question of long-run lock-in effects has generated much more controversy.[12] Over many years, those on one side of the debate argued strongly that reduced rates would generate substantial increases in realizations and even in total revenues, while partisans on the other side contended just as strongly that any such long-run effects were highly unlikely.[13] Until the last few years, however, little empirical evidence existed on the issue. Several studies by Martin Feldstein (with Slemrod and Yitzhaki) were among the first to attempt to measure long-run lock-in effects.[14] Feldstein's studies found strong lock-in effects on the sale of corporate stock. Simulations using the estimating equations developed in these studies predicted that reducing capital gains tax rates from 1973 levels would increase total tax revenues from capital gains, while taxing capital gains as ordinary income would decrease tax revenues. A study by Joseph Minarik is perhaps best known for pointing out an important error in one of the Feldstein studies that led to a substantial overestimate of the effects of capital gains taxes. However, Minarik did confirm the existence of substantial lock-in effects.[15]

Substantial evidence has now been accumulated demonstrating that both transitory and long-run lock-in effects exist and that, at the tax rates in effect during the 1970s the lock-in effects were quite large. An important question arises: What are the real economic implications of the lock-in effect? One important result of lock-in is to induce individual investors to continue holding portfolios of assets that they might find less desirable than some other portfolio. Some investors may be induced to assume more risk than they want because they are reluctant to sell appreciated investments to diversify their portfolios. At retirement, investors may wish to switch their investments from stocks with low dividends and high expected capital gains to stocks that provide a high dividend income but a lower expectation of capital gains. Thus, the lock-in effect may have a significant impact on the well-being of particular investors.

The lock-in effect may also reduce the efficiency of allocation of investment. For example, the lock-in effect reduces the ability of an entrepreneur to withdraw from an enterprise and use the funds to start a new venture. The owner/manager of a firm that is becoming less competitive may wish to sell out but feel constrained from doing so by capital gains taxes. These effects may not be important for large firms with thousands of stockholders, but they could be highly significant for smaller firms without good access to capital markets and where ownership and operation go together.[16]

Inflation

Inflation distorts the taxation of capital gains and of other forms of capital income. Inflation is particularly harsh in its impact on capital income because it distorts not only the real values of the tax brackets and exemptions but also the measurement of capital income itself. The capital gains tax applies to the entire gain from the sale of an asset even though much of that gain may only reflect increases in the general level of prices. The effect of taxing nominal capital gains is to substantially increase the effective tax rate on real capital gains. Table 7-1 shows summary data on nominal and real capital gains for assets sold between 1971 and 1975. It is interesting to note first that the $25 billion of nominal capital gains on stock sold in this period actually represents a loss of $420 million after adjusting for inflation. This problem is most severe for taxpayers with lower and middle incomes. The real capital gains of taxpayers with adjusted gross incomes over $500,000 are more than 80 percent of their nominal gains. In contrast, taxpayers with incomes under $50,000 have nominal gains but substantial losses in real terms.

It might be expected that these inflation induced real losses would be greatest for long-held assets, but the real losses are actually concentrated in stocks held less than five years. The longer held stocks have net positive real capital gains. An important reason for this result is the high rate of inflation in recent years as compared to earlier years. A commonly suggested remedy for the effects of inflation is to lower tax rates the longer an asset has been held. The results demonstrate that this solution would be inappropriate for correcting for inflation in recent years.[17]

Table 7-1 shows nominal gains for residential housing but real losses at all income levels, although the sample is too small for much reliability. For rental properties, nominal gains of $13 billion were reduced to real gains of $5 billion. For a miscellaneous group of other assets for which holding periods could be calculated, real gains were about 62 percent of nominal gains. The taxation of nominal gains thus means that inflation substantially increases the taxation of capital gains and in some cases leads to effective tax rates of over

100 percent of real gains. It should be noted, however, that realizing negative real gains does not mean that an investor realizes no benefit from holding an asset. Most assets having negative real gains also generated a flow of dividend or rental or other income that should be included in the total return on the investment.

The Bunching of Gains

One of the traditional arguments for preferential treatment of capital gains relates to the problem of the bunching of gains. When assets that have been held a number of years are sold, the resulting gain may be relatively large compared to the taxpayer's normal income. Under a system of progressive tax rates, the bunching of gains can lead to a significantly higher rate of taxation than on an equal amount of income spread over the holding period of an asset. Minarik (1981) found that averaging capital gains over a seven-year period would reduce tax liabilities about 5 percent for the population as a whole.[18] The impact would, of course, be larger for many individual taxpayers.

The bunching problem is more serious to the extent that realized capital gains are sporadic or once-in-a-lifetime events and less serious if gains are a regular source of income. Table 7-2 presents some tabulations of the number of taxpayers that reported realized gains in one or more years between 1971 and 1975. Almost one-fourth of all taxpayers reported capital gains (or losses) in at least one year. Of those taxpayers with gains, 42 percent reported gains in only one year and another 22 percent had gains in only two years. This suggests that for the majority of taxpayers, realizations may well be occasional events.

Among taxpayers with income other than gains under $20,000, nearly half had gains in only one year. The proportion of returns with gains in more than one year increases at higher income levels, with 68 percent of taxpayers earning over $200,000 non-capital gains income reporting gains in all five years. For taxpayers with gains in only one year, the gain increased taxable income by an average of 17 percent. The average increase in taxable income was largest for taxpayers with less than $20,000 of non-capital gains income. This phenomenon suggests that bunching is not a serious problem for the average taxpayer, although it may be a problem in particular cases. Whether one concludes that bunching is a serious problem depends on whether one believes it more significant that gains are occasional events for much of the taxpaying population or that most high income taxpayers realize gains almost every year.

Table 7-1. Nominal and Real Long-Term Capital Gains, 1971-75.

Income Class AGI (in thousands)	Number of Returns with Gains	Nominal Gains	Real Gains	Real Gains by Holding Period			
				1-5	5-10	10-20	Over 20
		(millions of dollars)					
Corporate Stock Sales							
Negative AGI	87,887	$ 186	$ -192	$ -209	$ -43	$ 26	$ 34
$ 0- 20	5,803,695	5,444	-3,792	-2,799	-2,920	-887	2,813
$ 20- 50	3,867,614	3,086	-4,546	-4,576	-362	266	126
$ 50-100	803,178	4,504	1,012	-1,961	2,184	379	411
$100-200	214,048	2,580	369	-1,434	420	672	711
$200-500	47,011	3,309	2,083	-298	1,265	680	437
$500 and Over	10,109	5,533	4,642	-22	2,289	1,305	1,070
Total	10,833,542	$24,622	$ -420	$-11,287	$ 2,832	$2,440	$5,603
Real Estate							
Negative AGI	53,146	$ 434	$ 112	$ -29	$ 126	$ 9	$ 6
$ 0- 20	1,032,134	3,544	1,120	397	-71	204	589
$ 20- 50	587,988	6,875	2,994	1,478	-61	85	1,493
$ 50-100	85,539	1,148	528	78	200	85	165
$100-200	29,771	740	297	208	61	71	-44
$200-500	7,483	359	163	59	25	95	-16
$500 and Over	1,181	121	82	10	24	27	19
Total	1,797,242	$13,230	$ 5,295	$ 2,201	$ 305	$ 577	$2,213
Residences							
Negative AGI	8,849	$ 2	$ -66	$ -7	$ -3	$ -14	$ -43
$ 0- 20	601,767	1,435	-1,623	-406	-481	-441	-295
$ 20- 50	259,745	1,239	-1,048	-96	-405	-255	-293
$ 50-100	17,162	285	-19	7	16	-102	60
$100-200	7,458	131	-18	20	6	-28	-18
$200-500	1,540	21	-10	2	7	-17	-2
$500 and Over	651	3	-.5	1	-.5	-.1	-1
Total	896,772	$ 3,115	$-2,785	$ -478	$ -859	$ -857	$ -591

Other Transactions

Negative AGI							
$ 0- 20	96,695	$ 606	$ 395	$ 101	$ 104	$ 25	$ 165
$ 20- 50	1,184,786	3,673	1,972	634	734	418	186
$ 50-100	535,878	5,045	3,402	1,002	659	229	1,513
$100-200	129,315	1,291	643	282	70	270	20
$200-500	35,387	864	479	228	126	118	7
$500 and Over	8,622	397	82	44	-45	75	8
	1,333	174	86	38	32	13	3
Total	1,992,616	$12,049	$ 7,058	$ 2,329	$1,679	$1,147	$1,901

Table 7-2. The Bunching of Capital Gains, 1971-75.

Income Class[a]	Number of Returns		Percentage of Returns with Gains by Number of Years with Gains					Gains as Percentage of Taxable Income[b] Returns with Gains 1 Year Only
	Total Returns	Gains in One or More Years	1 Year	2 Years	3 Years	4 Years	5 Years	
Less than zero	88,638	49,161	79.0%	2.9%	7.2%	2.2%	8.7%	n.m.
$ 0- 19,999	48,038,016	8,844,749	46.9	23.1	13.0	7.1	9.9	23.9%
$ 20,000- 49,999	5,891,009	3,136,988	32.8	19.6	16.1	13.9	17.7	8.3
$ 50,000- 99,999	402,598	351,734	12.8	11.1	14.3	17.7	44.2	3.8
$100,000-199,999	58,869	56,195	9.5	8.1	13.0	15.8	53.5	3.5
$200,000 and over	10,536	10,153	3.7	4.7	8.6	15.0	67.7	8.8
Total	54,455,504	12,448,980	42.3%	21.7%	13.8%	9.1%	13.1%	16.8%
Total net gains in AGI (billions of dollars)	$16.32	$16.32	$2.78	$3.19	$2.45	$3.91	$4.05	

[a]Income is defined as average adjusted gross income (AGI) net of capital gains over the five year period.
[b]This column shows net capital gains as a percentage of taxable income on income other than capital gains for returns with gains in only one year.
Source: 1971-1975 Capital Gains Panel.

Double Taxation of Gains on Corporate Stock

One argument supporting preferential taxation of capital gains concerns an element of double taxation on gains on the sale of corporate stock. It is said that corporate dividends are taxed twice: once at the corporate level, and a second time as they are received by the individual. A similar argument can be made for capital gains, since one dollar of retained earnings should be translated into one dollar (or slightly less than one dollar) of increased market value for the firm's shares. The double taxation argument is not as significant for capital gains, since they are taxed later and at lower rates; the argument does not apply to other types of assets.

III. EFFECTS OF THE 1978 AND 1981 REDUCTIONS IN CAPITAL GAINS TAX RATES

The initial effects of the 1978 and 1981 reductions of capital gains tax rates are now fairly well known. The volume of trading on stock exchanges has increased dramatically. One study has estimated that, as a result of the 1978 law, the volume of trading increased by 50 percent on the New York Stock Exchange and by more than 100 percent on the American Stock Exchange.[19] The total value of corporate stock held by individuals and financial institutions increased by $220 billion or 24 percent from the beginning of 1978 to the end of 1979 and then rose an additional 33 percent during 1980.[20] The amount of new private capital committed to venture capital firms has been estimated to have increased from an average of $45 million per year in 1976 and 1977 to an average of nearly $600 million per year from 1978 through 1980.[21]

In 1979 total realized capital gains increased by 45 percent, which more than offset the reduction in tax rates. Taxes paid on capital gains increased from $9.3 billion to $11.2 billion, approximately 21 percent. In the second year under the new tax rules, total capital gains increased by an additional 2 percent, and taxes from capital gains are estimated to have increased by about 7 percent.

The effects of the 1978 reductions in capital gains tax rates on tax revenues seem to confirm the Laffer Curve idea that lower marginal tax rates can lead to increases in tax receipts. Of course, these year-to-year comparisons exclude the effects of trend increases in realizations and the effects of other economic variables. They also fail to distinguish the extent to which the increased realizations come directly, from changes in the propensity to realize gains, or indirectly, through the effects of tax rates on securities and asset prices. These questions can be examined within the framework of a time series model.

The time series model, which is described in more detail in the Appendix to this paper, incorporates several key aspects of the effects of capital gains taxes. First, capital gains taxes affect the propensity to realize gains out of a given stock of accrued but unrealized gains. The lock-in effect of high capital gains tax rates induces investors to turn over their portfolios at a slower rate and to hold appreciating assets for the benefit of heirs, since any accrued gains on assets held at death are not taxed. Second, capital gains taxes may affect the stock of unrealized gains. The stock of unrealized gains at any point in time is the sum of all past appreciation in the values of capital assets, less previously realized gains and gains that escape taxation due to the step-up in basis at death. Capital gains affect the stock of unrealized gains to the extent that they affect the prices of corporate shares and other assets. Third, capital gains taxes affect the allocation of new investment among various types of assets. Low capital gains tax rates induce investors to allocate more of their portfolios to stocks and less to other investments. High capital gains taxes cause investors to allocate a larger part of their wealth to owner occupied housing, since gains on housing can be deferred and in most cases avoided altogether.

The equations of the model can be used to analyze the effects of the 1978 and 1981 tax cuts for capital gains. A summary of the results of simulations of what would have happened in the absence of the tax cuts is shown in Table 7-3. The simulations imply that without the 1978 tax cut, realized capital gains would have increased by about 11 percent in 1979 and then would have declined slightly in 1980. The effect of the first two years of the tax cut was therefore to increase realizations by an average of 33 percent over what would have otherwise taken place. My revenue estimates suggest that taxes collected on capital gains would have increased in 1979 and 1980 to $10.3 billion and $10.4 billion without the tax cut. The results imply that tax revenues were increased in 1979 by about $0.9 billion and in 1980 by about $1.6 billion over the revenues that would have been obtained under the old law. It is interesting to note that nearly 88 percent of the increase in realized gains was the result of an increase in the propensity to realize gains, while the rest of the increase resulted from the higher values of corporate stock and other assets.

The model can also be used to estimate the effects of the Economic Recovery Tax Act of 1981, which reduced the maximum tax rate on long-term gains to 20 percent. Assuming that the tax cut was

Table 7-3. Simulation of the Effects of the 1978 and 1981 Tax Cuts on Capital Gains.

	Results of Tax Cuts			Simulation Results: No Tax Cuts			Simulation Results: 1978 Cut Only		
Year	Stock of Gains	Realized Capital Gains	Taxes Paid on Capital Gains	Stock of Gains	Realized Capital Gains	Taxes Paid on Capital Gains	Stock of Gains	Realized Capital Gains	Taxes Paid on Capital Gains
				(billions of dollars)					
1978	$2309	$50.5	$ 9.3	$2309	$50.5	$ 9.3	$2309	$50.5	$ 9.3
1979	2769	73.4	11.2	2679	56.2	10.3	2769	73.4	11.2
1980	3368	74.6	12.0	3291	54.8	10.4	3368	74.6	12.0
1981	3523	82.8	11.7	3368	53.9	10.3	3399	75.5	12.1

in effect for half of 1981, realized gains are projected to increase to about $83 billion in 1981. This is an increase of 11 percent over 1980 and 10 percent over what would have occurred without this tax cut. Revenues from capital gains taxes are estimated to decline slightly from 1980 levels and from what would have been collected under tax rates in effect in 1980. If the simulation result proves to be accurate, it would provide an interesting perspective on the position and shape of the Laffer Curve. In order to break even, realizations would have to increase to about $86 billion, well within the possible range of error of these estimates.

IV. CONCLUSIONS: THE APPROPRIATE TAXATION OF CAPITAL GAINS

The arguments in the earlier sections pointed up some of the adverse effects of high marginal tax rates on capital gains. These effects included reduced saving and risk-taking, lock-in, and reduced tax revenues. If these adverse effects are to be avoided, some kind of preferential treatment of capital gains is required, as long as the United States maintains a system of high marginal tax rates on income.

On the other hand, there are a number of persuasive arguments for taxing capital gains at the same rates that apply to other income. A brief list of these arguments follows:

1. Horizontal equity requires that capital gains be taxed at the same rates as other income because a dollar of capital gains will buy just as much as a dollar of ordinary income.

2. Vertical equity is violated by having lower rates on capital gains, which accrue mostly to high-income families.

3. Even if capital gains were taxed at the same rates as ordinary income, they would have a lower effective tax rate because of the benefits of the deferral of the tax on accrued gains. Deferral represents an interest-free loan of the tax that would be paid on the accruing gains under accrual taxation.

4. The special treatment of capital gains substantially complicates the income tax Code.

5. The arguments for special treatment of capital gains are based on productive investments, but the benefits of the preferential rates go to the profits on gold, antiques and other non-productive investments. Capital gains tax treatment is accorded to transactions that do not represent true capital gains.

6. There are numerous unproductive tax games invented to keep lawyers and accountants busy. Such games include tax straddles and borrowing to finance investments (interest is deducted currently but the capital gains tax is paid later and at lower rates).

How Should Capital Gains Be Taxed?

There are four main options for the taxation of capital gains. Within the framework of the current income tax system with high and progressive marginal tax rates, the two basic options are full taxation and taxation at preferential rates. Additional options relate to the taxation of capital gains within the framework of a flat rate income tax or a consumption tax.

The first option is to move toward full taxation of capital gains within the framework of the current income tax system. This option would have merit in improving horizontal and vertical equity and tax simplification. It would still provide an *ex ante* preference for capital gains due to the benefits of deferral. To reduce some of the inequities of full taxation, there should be (1) indexing of the basis of assets to correct for inflation and (2) either liberalized income averaging or prorating of capital gains over the holding period to reduce the bunching problem.[22] However, as discussed earlier in this paper, high marginal tax rates lead to increased distortions and adverse effects on saving, risk-taking, venture capital, and lock-in. The experience of the 1970s shows that tax rates of 30 percent or more have significant adverse effects and that full taxation of gains at current rates would probably decrease tax revenues from capital gains. Any method (such as an alternative tax) that tries to achieve full taxation but eliminate the highest marginal rates would primarily benefit high income taxpayers.

The second option is to continue to give preferential treatment to capital gains through the exclusion of some fraction of long-term gains. This option does not directly or correctly treat the problems of bunching, inflationary gains or lock-in for any particular transaction or even on the average. The option does, however, reduce the magnitude of these problems. It also eliminates the adverse effects of high marginal rates and produces more tax revenue than full taxation would likely yield. Even with some part of long-term gains excluded, indexation of capital gains for inflation may be desirable as a matter of equity.

Within the framework of an income tax, another option is an income tax with flat rates or mildly progressive rates of no more than about 25 percent. Such a tax would seem to offer the opportunity for full taxation of capital gains (desired by many income tax purists) without most of the bad side effects produced by high marginal rates.

Under a consumption tax or expenditure tax, capital gains would not be taxed except as they affect consumption. Two basic approaches have been suggested for the treatment of capital gains within the framework of a consumption tax: the use of special qualified accounts, and the so-called prepayment method. Under the qualified accounts method, taxpayers would take a deduction on their consumption tax return when they invest in a qualified account. When funds, including any capital gains, were withdrawn from the accounts, presumably for consumption, the amount withdrawn would be taxed under the consumption tax.[23] The qualified accounts would be similar to the current IRA type accounts, except that more flexibility would probably be permitted. A lock-in effect for asset sales that result in withdrawals from qualified accounts would exist, but no lock-in effect would result from switching investments within an account. Under the second method, capital gains would not be taxed, but no deduction would be permitted for the initial investment. With proportional tax rates, a constant discount rate and a market price for investments that always correctly reflects the present value of their income, the present value of the taxes are the same under the two approaches. However, under the prepayment method, a taxpayer whose investment accrues at an above normal rate would be able to consume more gains without any additional tax. The prepayment approach is likely to evoke two primary responses: that it would provide desirable incentive effects and that it would create an inequity primarily benefitting the rich and the lucky. It may be hard to persuade many people that allowing capital gains to go untaxed is actually equivalent to establishing a system of qualified accounts.

In the final analysis, the "correct" approach to taxation of capital gains depends on two fundamental questions: (1) What is the basic type of tax system that is most desirable? Income or consumption? High, progressive rates or low marginal rates? (2) Which of the conflicting goals of taxation should be given the most weight? Horizontal and vertical equity, neutrality, simplicity, or effects on stabilization and economic growth?

APPENDIX

The equations of the model used to analyze the effects of changes in capital gains tax rates are shown in Table 7-4. The model is estimated for 1951-1980 using annual data. Because of interactions between the equations, the equations of the model are estimated simultaneously using full information maximum likelihood estimation.

The first equation of the model estimates total realized capital gains as a function of the stock of accrued but unrealized gains (UG), the predicted tax rate on long-term capital gains (TX), the rate of increase of income other than capital gains (OY), and the percentage of the population over age sixty-five ($P65$). The last three variables are entered multiplicatively times the stock of unrealized gains, so that their effect is to modify the propensity to realize gains out of the stock of gains. High capital gains tax rates reduce the propensity to realize gains. The income variable is included because there may be some types of reported gains (such as timber gains) that are not adequately accounted for in the stock of gains variable but that may be related to income. The income measure used is adjusted gross income net of capital gains. Increases in the percentage of the population over age sixty-five reduce the propensity to realize gains. This may be due to the lock-in effect created by the step-up in basis on assets held at death or because older investors tend to be less active traders.

Any measure of the actual tax rates on capital gains would be endogenous to the amount of gains realized and therefore would produce biased estimates in regression analysis. Following the practice of previous studies, the tax variable is a predicted tax rate on long-term capital gains. The predicted tax rate is determined using the average amount of gains over the sample period for the five highest income classes. The tax rate calculations include the effects of the minimum tax, the alternative tax, the changing exclusion ratio, and income tax surcharges.

Equations 2, 3, and 4 determine the market values of three major categories of assets that generate capital gains: corporate stock, other gains producing assets, and owner occupied housing. The other assets category includes real estate, farm and other land, and business property. The market value of each asset depends on a trend increase in the value over the previous year, capital gains tax rates, a share of new investment in all gains producing assets, and additional variables that are expected to affect the market values of these assets. For example, the value of corporate stock is also a function of increases

Table 7-4. Equations of the Capital Gains Model.

1. Realized Capital Gains

$$RG_t = -7.452 + (.157 - .0452 \frac{TX_t}{100 - TX_t} + .0912 \frac{OY_t - OY_t}{OY_t} - .0114\, P65)\, UG_t$$
$$(8.3)(17.8)(8.2)\phantom{\frac{TX_t}{100-TX_t}}(9.1)\phantom{\frac{OY_t-OY_t}{OY_t}}(16.0)$$

$$R^2 = .984$$

2. Market Value of Stock

$$ST_t = 1.641\, ST_{t-1} - .0257 \frac{TX_t}{(1+r)^4}\, ST_{t-1} + 38.629\, CDIV_t + 5.901\, CRE_t + (6.571 - 22.307 \frac{TX_t}{100 - TX_t})\, NI_t$$
$$(7.0)\phantom{ST_{t-1}}(2.6)\phantom{\frac{TX_t}{(1+r)^4}}(4.1)(3.0)(6.7)(10.6)$$

$$R^2 = .907$$

3. Market Value of Other Gains Producing Wealth

$$OW_t = (.995 - .00145 \frac{TX_t}{(1+r)^8} + .0794\, (\frac{FP_t}{GNPD_t} - 1) + .0116 \frac{GNPD_t - GNPD_{t-1}}{GNPD_{t-1}})\, OW_{t-1}$$
$$(73.8)(4.7)\phantom{\frac{TX_t}{(1+r)^8}}(5.3)\phantom{\frac{FP_t}{GNPD_t}}(9.8)$$

$$+ (-2.734 + 11.418 \frac{TX_t}{100 - TX_t})\, NI_t$$
$$(3.8)(7.5)$$

$$R^2 = .999$$

4. Market Value of Owner-Occupied Housing

$$OO_t = (.975 + .740 \frac{CPI_t - CPI_{t-1}}{CPI_{t-1}} + .627 \frac{RYD_t - RYD_{t-1}}{RYD_{t-1}})\, OO_{t-1} + (3.837 + 10.889 \frac{TX_t}{100 - TX_t})\, NI_t$$
$$(62.9)(8.6)\phantom{\frac{CPI_t-CPI_{t-1}}{CPI_{t-1}}}(5.0)\phantom{\frac{RYD_t-RYD_{t-1}}{RYD_{t-1}}OO_{t-1}}(5.3)(9.0)$$

$$R^2 = .999$$

5. Equation for Calculating the Stock of Unrealized Gains

$$UG_t = (ST_t - ST_{t-1}) + (ST_{t-1} - ST_{t-2}) + (OW_t - OW_{t-1}) + (OW_{t-1} - OW_{t-2}) + .5\, (OO_t - OO_{t-1})$$
$$+ .5\, (OO_{t-1} - OO_{t-2}) - NI_t - NI_{t-1} - RG_{t-1} - RG_{t-2} + UG_{t-2}$$

Definition of Variables

- RG — Total realized capital gains
- UG — Stock of unrealized capital gains
- TX — Marginal tax rate on long-term capital gains
- OY — Other income, adjusted gross income other than capital gains
- P65 — Percentage of the population over age sixty-five
- ST — Total market value of corporate equities
- CDIV — Change in dividends paid by corporations
- CRE — Corporate retained earnings with inventory valuation adjustment
- NI — Net new investment in gains producing assets
- OW — Total market value of other gains producing assets
- FP — Index of food prices in the Producer Price Index, raw materials stage
- GNPD — Gross National Product Implicit Price Deflator
- OO — Total market value of owner occupied housing
- CPI — Consumer Price Index
- RYD — Real disposable personal income

Sources: Tax data are from the Internal Revenue Service *Statistics of Income*, 1950–1980, asset data are from the Federal Reserve Board Flow of Funds Annual Balance Sheet Data, 1950–1981, and economic data are from the 1982 *Economic Report of the President*.

in dividends and retained earnings. The value of other gains producing assets is positively related to the general inflation rate and the relative price of farm products. The rate of increase in the value of owner occupied housing depends on the rate of increase of real disposable income and consumer prices.

The tax rate variables included in the stock and other asset equations are the prospective tax rates on real capital gains, assuming that existing trends will continue. Since the capital gains tax is deferred until the gain is realized, the tax rate is discounted to its present value using the interest rate on BAA bonds. On the other hand, purely inflationary gains are taxed, and this increases the effective tax rate on real capital gains. When these two effects are netted out, the tax rate is discounted by the real interest rate. Holding periods of four and eight years are assumed for stocks and for other assets. These are reasonable investment horizons comparable to average holding periods on these assets. The allocation of new investment among gains producing assets is affected by the tax rate on capital gains. The coefficients imply that high capital gains tax rates cause investment to flow out of corporate stock and into housing and other assets. It is interesting to note that the net investment figures for 1979 show an especially large outflow of funds from the stock market. Many individuals apparently took advantage of the reduced tax rates to realize capital gains and use their funds elsewhere.

The final equation is an identity that calculates the stock of unrealized gains. This variable is based on a series developed by Nelson McClung and uses flow of funds data on asset holdings by individuals. The calculation adds the increases in market values of assets less the amount of new investment and less the gains realized in previous years. Only one-half of the gains on owner occupied housing are included, since much of the capital gain on housing is never taxed.

Although the model is highly simplified, it does seem to work well. Coefficients on all included variables have the expected signs and are statistically significant. The R^2 for the equations range from 0.907 for corporate stock to 0.999 for the other wealth and housing equations. The results of the simulations should be treated cautiously, however, because the model is highly simplified. Similarly, the revenue estimates are only approximations using effective tax rates for aggregate data on six broad income classes.

NOTES TO CHAPTER 7

1. A marginal tax rate of 49.125 percent was extremely rare, however, because it required a combination of the effects of the minimum tax and the spoiling of the benefits of the maximum tax. A rate of 39.875 percent was more

common among high income taxpayers because it resulted from only the minimum tax.

2. Although the traditional view has been that savings are not significantly affected by the rate of return, recent estimates by Boskin (1978) and others suggest a rather large response of savings to the after-tax rate of return.

3. Feldstein (1978) demonstrated that the welfare loss from the distortionary effects of taxes on capital income may be substantial even when the amount of saving is totally insensitive to the interest rate.

4. Brittain (1966) and Feldstein (1970) provide evidence that corporations do respond to differential tax rates on dividends and retained earnings.

5. See von Furstenberg (1981:356) and Howrey and Hymans (1978:681). Another finding that supports this view is that the marginal propensity to consume out of dividends is not significantly different from that on other income but that the response of consumption to retained earnings is smaller (Feldstein 1973).

6. For evidence on the effects of taxes on portfolio allocation see Feldstein (1976) and Galper and Zimmerman (1977).

7. Steuerle (1982) shows that the average effective tax rate on capital income is low, largely because much of the income from capital is either taxed at preferential rates or not taxed at all. This is at least partly due to the fact that investment tends to flow toward areas where the income is lightly taxed.

8. See Domar and Musgrave (1944), Stiglitz (1969), and Atkinson and Stiglitz (1980).

9. *Savings and Investment Incentives: Hearings* (1981:179) (statement of Michael Bell).

10. This analysis does not include the discounted present value of using the loss carryovers in future years to offset ordinary income or capital gains. Also ignored is the effect of long-term gains in "spoiling" the benefits of the maximum tax.

11. Fredland, Gray, and Sunley (1968), Kaplan (1981), and Auten (1982).

12. The step-up in basis on assets bequeathed to heirs at death is often thought to be the most important cause of long-run lock-in effects. It is sometimes suggested that taxing accrued gains at death would therefore eliminate much of the lock-in effect. The effect of the step-up in basis and the effect of constructive realization of accrued gains at death can easily be exaggerated, however. In order to fully offset the lock-in effect, a tax on accrued gains at death would have to be at rates higher than those on realized gains. Furthermore, the life expectancy of individuals is long enough up through the age of seventy-five or so that the lock-in effect created by the step-up in basis is likely to be relatively small.

13. For contrasting views see New York Stock Exchange (n.d.) and Heller (1956).

14. Feldstein and Yitzhaki (1978) and Feldstein, Slemrod and Yitzhaki (1980).

15. Other recent studies that have found lock-in effects include Brannon (1974), Woo (1981), Minarik (1981), Auten (1982), and Auten and Clotfelter (1982).

16. There are several ways in which some lock-in effect may be desirable. First, to the extent that realized gains are consumed to a greater extent than

accrued gains, lock-in increases personal saving. Second, lock-in effects may discourage excessive churning of portfolios that does not add to real national output. The recent volatility of the stock market due to increases in trading by nontaxable institutional investors suggests that unproductive churning does occur and that some lock-in effect or other transaction cost may be desirable. The third possible benefit results from the fact that from the standpoint of an idealized Haig-Simons income tax, the deferral of taxes on accrued gains represents an interest-free loan from the government to the investor. This notion of an interest free loan is often used as an argument for accrual taxation of capital gains. Government may profit from this "investment," however, if the investment accrues at a faster rate than the government's discount rate.

17. Although contradictory to most people's intuition, it will generally be true that the real portion of the total gain increases as the holding period increases. This can be seen by a simple numerical example. Consider an asset that increases in value at 10 percent per year with 5 percent inflation. The calculations for $1 held for one and two years are shown below:

Year	Market Value	Nominal Gain	Indexed Basis	Real Gain	Real Gain as Percentage of Nominal Gain
0	1.0		1.0		
1	1.1	.10	1.05	.05	50.0
2	1.21	.21	1.1025	.1075	51.1

For a mathematical proof and further discussion, see Brinner (1976). With inflation accelerating sufficiently rapidly, the real portion may decrease with longer holding periods.

18. Minarik also found that some taxpayers would have their tax liabilities increased by averaging capital gains (but not other income) over a seven-year period. These taxpayers apparently use capital gains to offset fluctuations in deductions and other income sources, and thus do their own income averaging.

19. See Slemrod (1982).

20. Of course some of these gains are inflationary gains. After adjusting for inflation, the real value of corporate stock rose about 7 percent in 1978-79 and 22 percent in 1980. The real value of corporate stock was still 25 percent below the peak value at the end of 1968.

21. *Savings and Investment Incentives: Hearings (1981:179)* and data provided by the *Venture Capital Journal*. This increase includes increased investments both by individuals and by institutions, some of which were not directly affected by the capital gains tax cuts.

22. Prorating could work as follows for a taxpayer with a $10,000 gain on an asset held for ten years: Divide the gain by the holding period, and calculate the extra tax from including the $1,000 in taxable income. Multiply the extra tax on the $1,000 by ten and pay this amount of tax on the whole capital gain. Prorating has the effect of reducing the effect of the progressive rate structure in imposing high marginal tax rates on long-held assets. For additional discussion of prorating see Wetzler (1977).

23. Note the similarity of this approach with the suggestion for rollover of capital gains when the proceeds are reinvested.

BIBLIOGRAPHY

Atkinson, Anthony, and Joseph Stiglitz, *Lectures in Public Economics*, New York: McGraw-Hill, 1980.

Auten, Gerald, *Estimation of the Effects of Capital Gains Taxes on Realizations of Capital Gains*, Washington, D.C.: Report to the Office of Tax Analysis, March 1980.

Auten, Gerald, and Charles Clotfelter, "Permanent versus Transitory Tax Rate Effects and the Realization on Capital Gains," *Quarterly Journal of Economics* XCVI (November 1982): 613-632.

_____ , "Recent Empirical Work on Capital Gains," *Proceedings of the 73rd Annual Conference on Taxation*, Columbus, Ohio: National Tax Association, 1980.

Bailey, Martin, "Capital Gains and Income Taxation," In A. Harberger and M. Bailey, eds., *The Taxation of Income from Capital*, pp. 11-49. Washington, D.C.: Brookings Institution, 1969.

Boskin, Michael, "Taxation, Saving, and the Rate of Interest," *Journal of Political Economy* 86, no. 2, Part 2 (April 1978): S3-S27.

Brannon, Gerard, *The Lock-In Problem for Capital Gains: An Analysis of the 1970-71 Experience*, Washington, D.C.: Fund for Public Policy Research, 1974.

Brinner, Roger, "Inflation and the Definition of Taxable Personal Income," In Henry Aaron, ed., *Inflation and the Income Tax*, pp. 121-149. Washington, D.C.: Brookings Institution, 1976.

Brittain, John, *Corporate Dividend Policy*. Washington, D.C.: Brookings Institution, 1966.

David, Martin, *Alternative Approaches to Capital Gains Taxation*, Washington, D.C.: Brookings Institution, 1968.

Domar, Evsey, and R. A. Musgrave, "Proportional Income Taxation and Risk-Taking," *Quarterly Journal of Economics* 58 (May 1944): 387-422.

Feldstein, Martin, "Corporate Taxation and Dividend Behavior," *Review of Economic Studies* 37 (January 1970): 57-72.

_____ , "Personal Taxation and Portfolio Composition: An Econometric Analysis," *Econometrica* 44 (July 1976): 631-650.

_____ , "Tax Incentives, Savings and Capital Accumulation in the U.S." *Journal of Public Economics* 2 (April 1973): 159-171.

_____ , "The Welfare Cost of Capital Income Taxation," *Journal of Political Economy* 86, no. 2, Part 2 (April 1978): S29-S51.

Feldstein, Martin, and George Fane, "Taxes, Corporate Dividend Policy, and Personal Saving: The British Postwar Experience," *Review of Economics and Statistics* LV (November 1973): 399-411.

Feldstein, Martin, and Joel Slemrod, "Inflation and the Excess Taxation of Capital Gains on Corporate Stock," *National Tax Journal* XXXI (June 1978): 107-118.

Feldstein, Martin; Joel Slemrod; and Shlomo Yitzhaki, "The Effects of the Capital Gains Tax on the Selling of Corporate Stock and the Realization of Capital Gains," *Quarterly Journal of Economics* XCIV (June 1980): 777-791.

Feldstein, Martin, and Shlomo Yitzhaki, "The Effects of the Capital Gains Tax on the Selling and Switching of Common Stock," *Journal of Public Economics* 9 (February 1978): 17-36.

Fredland, Eric; John Gray; and Emil Sunley, "The Six Month Holding Period for Capital Gains: An Empirical Analysis of Its Effects on the Timing of Gains," *National Tax Journal* XXI (December 1968): 467-478.

Galper, Harvey, and Dennis Zimmerman, "Preferential Taxation and Portfolio Choice: Some Empirical Evidence," *National Tax Journal* XXX (December 1977): 387-397.

Green, Jerry, "The Taxation of Capital Gains," In Michael Boskin, ed., *Federal Tax Reform: Myths and Realities*, pp. 75-90. San Francisco: Institute for Contemporary Studies, 1978.

Heller, Walter, "Investors' Decisions, Equity and Capital Gains Taxes," In Federal Tax Policy for Economic Growth and Stability, Joint Committee on the Economic Report, 84th Congress. Washington, D.C.: U.S. Government Printing Office, 1956.

Holt, Charles, and John Shelton, "The Lock-in Effect of the Capital Gains Tax," *National Tax Journal* XV (December 1962): 337-352.

Howrey, Philip, and Saul Hymans, "The Measurement and Determinants of Loanable Funds Saving," *Brookings Papers on Economic Activity*, no. 3, 1978.

Kaplan, Steven, "The Holding Period Distinction of the Capital Gains Tax," Working Paper No. 762. Cambridge, Massachusetts: National Bureau of Economic Research, 1981.

Minarik, Joseph, "Capital Gains," In Henry Aaron and Joseph Pechman, eds., *How Taxes Affect Economic Behavior*, pp. 241-277. Washington, D.C.: Brookings, 1981.

New York Stock Exchange, "The Effects of Reducing the Capital Gains Tax Rate on Locked-In Capital and Federal Revenues," Summary of a 1965 Study of Investor Attitudes by Louis Harris and Associates. New York, n.d. Mimeo.

Slemrod, Joel, "Stock Transactions Volume and the 1978 Capital Gains Tax Reduction," *Public Finance Quarterly* 10 (January 1982): 3-16.

Steuerle, Eugene, "Is Income From Capital Subject to Individual Income Taxation?" *Public Finance Quarterly* 10 (July 1982): 283-303.

Stiglitz, Joseph, "The Effects of Income, Wealth and Capital Taxation on Risk-Taking," *Quarterly Journal of Economics* LXXXIII (May 1969): 263-283.

U.S. Congress. Senate. Committee on Finance. *Savings and Investment Incentives*. Hearings before the Subcommittee on Savings, Pensions and Investment Policy. 97th Cong., 2d Sess. (May 4, 1981).

von Furstenberg, George, "Saving," In Henry Aaron and Joseph Pechman, eds., *How Taxes Affect Economic Behavior*, pp. 327-390. Washington, D.C.: Brookings, 1981.

Wetzler, James, "Capital Gains and Losses," In Joseph Pechman, ed., *Comprehensive Income Taxation*, pp. 115-153. Washington, D.C.: Brookings, 1977.

Woo, Mai Nguyen, *A Time Series Analysis of the Lock-In Effect of Capital Gains Taxation in the United States*. Ph.D. diss., Georgetown University, 1981.

Discussants:

THE OPTION OF A TAX DEFERRED ROLLOVER ON CAPITAL GAINS

Alan Cranston

As one who teamed up with Senator Clifford Hansen in 1978 to play a key part in reducing the capital gains tax to 28 percent, I am pleased to hear from Gerald Auten of the great success our effort had in helping to stimulate greater formation of venture capital. The results of the 1978 capital gains tax reduction would be an even greater record of accomplishment had the economy been in better shape. We have not really had a fair test. When the economy revives, evidence that shows the great significance of what we wrought in 1978 will, without question, be forthcoming.

At the time we enacted the Revenue Act of 1978 there was a virtual drought of venture capital in California. Only $6 million was raised in 1977, an incredibly low figure. The reduction in capital gains taxes either caused or coincided with a great surge in venture capital investment the following year. In any case, partners in venture capital firms affirm that the tax change did make it possible for persons interested in venture capital investments to argue persuasively to their principals that they could afford to risk greater sums in such investments. That is precisely the result that Cliff Hansen and I and those with whom we worked were seeking, so we did accomplish what we set out to do.

However, the disappointing experience of the Reagan tax cuts should humble all of us who predict great things to come simply as a result of some changes in the tax laws. Perhaps, of course, dire predictions of the consequences should also be discounted. Necessity is still the great engine of the economy. An assembly line worker is not going to quit his or her job just because of tax rates. As to how hard people will work, it is more likely that individual attitude and pride in one's work and ownership are far more powerful motivators than tax rates. Tax rates, however, do affect choices of investment and whether one spends, saves, or invests capital at risk. There is an ongoing historic debate over whether tax policy should be neutral on such decisions or actively affect them, or seek to do so. I take the view that tax policy should be activist, should reflect the values of society, and should encourage investment in expenditures that are generally deemed beneficial to the economy.

In considering the Economic Recovery Tax Act of 1981 (ERTA), I preferred direct cuts in the capital gains rate for individuals and, importantly, for corporations, as well. I did not think that a pro-investment policy was well served by reducing the differential investment and passive receipt of income. I introduced then, and I will introduce again in this Congress, legislation establishing tax-deferred treatment of rollovers on long-term capital gains. Gerald Auten, in his paper, has described the concept under the term "special qualified accounts."

Under such a plan, as Dr. Auten describes it, a taxpayer is given the option of being taxed on capital gains within the framework of a consumption tax. This concept, which was introduced to me by my good friend and very persuasive fellow Californian, Bill Ballhaus of SmithKline Beckman Corporation, has always made sense to me. It contains the characteristics that should be found in sound proposals for investment incentives. It rewards wise, useful investment insofar as tax treatment is concerned. It does not unfairly shelter other ordinary income. Artificial accounting losses are not rewarded. It permits investment income to be taxed when consumed rather than when realized.

This plan constitutes a fair balance between the needs of the general economy for long-term access to capital and the necessity of equitably sharing the burden of paying for government. There has not been enough support for the rollover approach thus far. Its time will come, however, if we generate support for the proposal. I urge you to help do so.

LOWER CAPITAL GAINS TAX RATES AND THE STOCK MARKET

Steven R. Resnick

My remarks deal with the interaction between employment, sales growth, and capital formation. The objective is to describe certain intuitive relationships between these concepts using some statistical observations and a conventional valuation formula.

Table 7-5 shows a clear cut correlation between employment growth, capital spending growth, and sales growth for the 444 industries making up the U.S. manufacturing sector. The rankings are grouped according to decile of employment growth in manufacturing over the period 1972 to 1980. While correlations do not prove causation, we can intuitively accept a chain of causation linking growth in capital spending to sales growth, and growth in employment to both capital spending and, especially, sales. Note that half of the manufacturing industries suffered declining employment in the observation period. Causes of this phenomenon varied from negative shifts in demand (for example, wood television and radio cabinets and asbestos products) to increasingly tough foreign competition (lace goods, for example).

It is not always true that increasing capital investment in an industry in decline can reverse the course of decline in sales. Analysis by Merrill Lynch suggests, however, that an intuitive observation can be made: Encouragement of fast growth industries would help create jobs. Tools to achieve that objective could include the acceleration of the growth rate of capital spending through "incentives" for capital formation. The top forty-five industries, out of 444 ranked by employment growth, provided just over 75 percent of the total new jobs in manufacturing over the 1972 to 1980 period. Stated another way, the top forty-five industries, out of 444 ranked by shipments growth, provided just over 40 percent of the total new jobs in manufacturing

Table 7-5. Employment, Capital Spending, and Sales are Linked.

Employment Growth Decile[a]	Employment Growth[a]	Capital Spending Growth[a]	Sales Growth[a]
1	7.1	24.9	17.5
2	3.7	15.9	14.1
3	2.4	16.0	13.0
4	1.6	15.3	12.7
5	0.7	14.3	11.2
6	-0.1	13.9	10.4
7	-0.8	13.3	8.7
8	-1.7	12.2	9.2
9	-2.7	9.0	6.0
10	-6.0	-0.1	3.7

Note: Sales are measured as current dollar shipments.
[a]Compounded growth rate, 1972-80.
Sources: Bureau of the Census, *Annual Survey of Manufacturers, 1972-80* (Washington, D.C.: U.S. Government Printing Office, 1972-80); Department of Commerce, *1972 Standard Industry Classification Manual* (Washington, D.C.: U.S. Government Printing Office, 1972).

in the observation period. Clearly, the creation of a positive environment for the development of fast-growing industries would have a beneficial effect on employment.

During the 1972 to 1980 period, employment growth was negative for only one industry among the twenty highest growth industries (defined in terms of current dollar shipments). During the same period, employment growth was negative in all twenty of the lowest growth industries (defined in terms of current dollar shipments). Growth in capital spending was also negative in three-fourths of these low-growth industries. Double digit growth in capital spending occurred in only one of these low-growth industries; in this case, the industry attempted to save itself through the substitution of capital for labor. During the same 1972 to 1980 period, the forty-five highest growth industries displayed high rates of increase in capital spending and big rates of growth in employment.

Analysis by Merrill Lynch suggests that the lowering or elimination of capital gains taxes would increase the market value of both high and low growth stocks by increasing the after-tax return to investors. As shown in Exhibit 7-1, the value of high-growth stocks will rise more than the value of low-growth stocks when the tax rate on capital gains is reduced. Lowering or eliminating capital gains taxes would benefit employment by increasing the market value of high-growth stocks. Such an effect would tend to facilitate capital formation through both equity and debt. Hence, higher market values for stock could encourage higher levels of capital spending and tend to increase employment, particularly in high-growth industries.

The market value of public companies listed on the New York Stock Exchange (NYSE) was $1.3 trillion as of November 1982. Approximately half of the market is owned by individual taxpayers; half is owned by institutions paying zero or very low tax rates. Estimates by Merrill Lynch show that the effect of the elimination of the capital gains tax on the value of NYSE stocks alone would be about $85 billion if theory were fulfilled in practice. The impact on the value of all public and privately held companies would exceed $100 billion. Such an effect would also theoretically raise the debt capacity of corporations by about $50 billion, since the debt-equity ratio of corporate balance sheets is about 50 percent. It is interesting to note that over time in excess of $150 billion in new capital—or over one year's worth of current capital spending in the manufacturing sector (about $120 billion in 1982)—could theoretically be created by reducing the capital gains tax rate to zero.

This $150 billion in new capital creation is meant to represent a "what if" extreme point potential rather than a forecast. Propor-

Exhibit 7-1. Theoretical Effect of Reduction in Capital Gains Tax Rate.

	High-Growth Stock	Low-Growth Stock
Pretax Return		
Appreciation	15.0	6.0
Yield	3.0	8.0
Investor tax rate—Capital gains	15%	15%
Ordinary	40%	40%
After-Tax Return		
Appreciation	12.8	5.1
Yield	1.8	4.8
Investor total return	14.6	9.9
Elimination of Capital Gains Tax		
After-Tax Return		
Appreciation	15.0	6.0
Yield	1.8	4.8
Investor total return	16.8	10.8
Percent increase in investor total return	15.1%	9.1%
	(16.8 ÷ 14.6)	(10.8 ÷ 9.9)

Note: The exhibit portrays how a change in the capital gains tax rate would theoretically affect the valuation of a stock for taxable investors. Examples are provided for both high-growth and low-growth stocks, which are represented by long-term growth rates of 15 percent and 6 percent respectively, and current yields of 3 percent and 8 percent respectively. At a 15 percent capital gains tax rate, the stock would generate after tax appreciation of 12.8 percent and 5.1 percent respectively, assuming that pretax appreciation matched long-term growth rates. Assuming a 40 percent ordinary tax rate on dividend income, total return would then be 14.6 percent for the high-growth stock, versus 9.9 percent for the low-growth stock.

A reduction in the tax rate on capital gains to zero would allow the investor to recapture the portion of appreciation which had formerly been taxed away. The after-tax return on the dividend yield would not change. Total return would be 16.8 percent for the high-growth stock and 10.8 percent for the low-growth stock. Although both types of stocks would generate a higher after-tax return, the higher growth stock would benefit to a greater degree—a 15.1 percent increment in total return, versus a 9.1 percent increment for the low-growth stock.

Source: Statistical distribution analysis of growth rates and yields for Standard & Poor's 500 companies where growth rates are projected by Merrill Lynch & Co. Inc. Tax rates are representative for higher income investors.

tionally greater increments in equity value should accrue to those industries that have the fastest growth rates. These sectors of the economy generally have the highest rates of employment and tax revenue growth. Of course, this analysis is imprecise and not meant to be a formal recommendation; nevertheless, the sensitivity of potential market responses to potential changes in capital gains decisions is remarkable.

PROPOSALS TO INDEX CAPITAL GAINS

James W. Wetzler

The appropriate tax treatment of capital gains and losses involves trading off considerations of tax equity, complexity, and economic efficiency. The issues are very difficult ones, and we have to resign ourselves to the fact that, in an income tax, no system for taxing capital gains will be entirely free from problems.

In stark contrast with the experiences of 1969 and 1976, capital gains taxation was not a major topic of discussion during the Congressional search for "revenue enhancement" in 1982. This may have been so because several of the predictions made by the advocates of lower capital gains taxes in 1978 have come true. The venture capital industry has revived, although not to the levels of the mid-1960s, and there has been an impressive increase in realizations of long-term capital gains.

Data on realizations of capital gains and losses appear in Table 7-6, the right-hand column of which measures the direct contribution of capital gains and losses to the individual income tax base. This rose by 22 percent between 1978 and 1979, despite the reduction from 50 to 40 percent in the proportion of long-term capital gains included in taxable income. (The 1978 tax cut became fully effective on January 1, 1979.) This increase in realizations was sustained in 1980, and the preliminary data indicate that 1981 was a good year for realizations as well.

The data in Table 7-6 provide only the economic equivalent of circumstantial evidence that taxpayers responded to the 1978

Table 7-6. Capital Gains and Losses on Returns with Tax Liability (*billions of dollars*).

Year	Net Capital Gain in Adjusted Gross Income	Net Capital Loss Deducted in Computing Adjusted Gross Income	Excess of Net Capital Gain over Net Capital Loss
1975	$14.0	$1.6	$12.5
1976	18.4	1.5	16.9
1977	23.4	2.6	20.8
1978	24.4	2.7	21.7
1979	29.1	2.6	26.5
1980	30.5	2.7	27.7

Source: Internal Revenue Service, *Statistics of Income: Individual Income Tax Returns* (Washington, D.C.: Government Printing Office, various issues).

tax cut by sharply increasing their realizations of capital gains. Dr. Auten's statistical work is an attempt to cull more information from the time series data by estimating the magnitude of the tax-rate effect after allowing for other factors that might affect the amount of capital gains realizations, such as growth in the size of the economy. Dr. Auten estimates four equations: three to predict the amount of accrued but unrealized gains and a fourth to predict realizations given the stock of accrued but unrealized gains. He concludes that the capital gains tax rate affects realizations in two ways: by increasing the propensity to realize a given amount of accrued gain and by inducing investors to shift their portfolios out of common stock and into housing, where they expect to receive larger capital gains.

This last conclusion is surprising. Most people on Wall Street have favored cutting capital gains taxes in the belief that lower taxes would induce investors to buy more stock, not less. During the 1970s, however, real estate outperformed stocks. We cannot rule out the possibility that Dr. Auten's result does reflect investor behavior and that the 1978 tax cut had the unintended effect of reducing the market value of stock owned by individuals.

While the data in Table 7-6 and Dr. Auten's equations are important evidence, further analysis is needed before we can conclude that the 1978 capital gains tax cut paid for itself through an increase in realizations. Some of the long-term capital gains observed in the data are offset elsewhere in the tax system by deductions against ordinary income. For example, some of the reported long-term capital gains may represent gain legs of tax straddles in Treasury bills, offset elsewhere by ordinary losses. Also, some of the reported gains resulted from corporate acquisitions in which the acquiring corporation will receive depreciation or depletion deductions against ordinary income that more than offset the capital gain reported by the selling shareholders. These gains were especially important in 1981, the year of the Marathon and Conoco acquisitions.

The 1978 increase in the gap between the tax rates on ordinary income and long-term capital gains probably bears some responsibility for the increased private sector activity in both tax straddles and mergers and acquisitions that drew public attention to these areas. Congress has adopted legislation that appears to deal with the worst abuses, as part of the process of "fine-tuning" the 1978 changes in the capital gains tax. There will probably be additional areas in which taxpayers will step up attempts to convert ordinary income into long-term capital gains; these cases will have to be examined. For example, a recent tax-shelter syndication, involving one-half billion dollars worth of used billboards, appears to depend for its attractiveness on the use of cost recovery deductions against ordinary income and the expectation of subsequent long-term capital gains.

Worldwide, the hottest topic in capital gains tax policy appears to be whether to measure the taxable capital gain after indexing the cost (or other basis) of the asset for inflation. The House of Representatives passed such an indexation proposal for corporate stock, real estate, and tangible personal property (the Archer amendment) in 1978, and the Senate passed a similar proposal limited to stock and real estate (the Armstrong amendment) in 1982. The United Kingdom recently enacted indexation for all assets. In Canada, the new budget contains an ingenious plan whereby Canadian owners of listed Canadian stocks could elect to put them into an Indexed Security Investment Plan (ISIP). Stocks in an ISIP would be "marked to market" (i.e., taxed on an accrual basis) each year with an indexing adjustment and full offset of net losses against ordinary income. A percentage of indexed, accrued gain would be taxed each year.[1] The Canadian proposal, of course, bears some resemblance to the mark-to-market system that the United States adopted in 1981 for regulated futures contracts.

Analytically, any indexation proposal requires some difficult trade-offs. A comprehensive indexation for all types of investment income would improve the equity of the income tax, but it would be a significant complication. The treatment of interest would be especially troublesome because the indexation adjustment for borrowers would generally require an increase in their taxable income. (The United Kingdom Indexing Act does not include an indexation adjustment for borrowers.) Limiting indexation to certain assets, which is the strategy of the Archer and Armstrong amendments and the Canadian proposal, would greatly reduce but not eliminate the complexity problem. It would, however, create a new problem of tax incentives to purchase the favored assets. One's assessment of indexation must ultimately depend on how much inflation one expects. At low rates of inflation, indexation is not worth the complexity; at sufficiently high rates of inflation, an income tax would be grossly unfair and inefficient without indexation.

Let me conclude by commenting on the treatment of capital gains under the so-called flat tax proposals. Assume, for the moment, that we wish to adopt the basic principles of the "Fair Tax Act of 1983" proposed by Senator Bill Bradley and Representative Richard Gephardt—that is, a broad-based income tax that attempts to approximate the present level and distribution by income class of the income tax burden. The authors of the bill studied three alternative ways to treat capital gains under such an approach: (1) including all capital gains in taxable income and setting the top tax rate at 30 percent, (2) providing some exclusion for long-term capital gains and raising the top tax rate to compensate for whatever revenue loss is assumed to result, and (3) adopting indexation and a higher top tax rate. They chose option (1) because they wanted to lower the top tax rate as much as possible, were concerned about the complexity of indexation, and believed that the sharply lower tax rates on interest and dividends would more than compensate for the higher capital gains tax rate. Perhaps, however, we should begin to study a broader range of options, such as variants of the indexed mark-to-market approach about to be enacted in Canada.

NOTES

1. See the Honorable Allan J. MacEachen, *Inflation and the Taxation of Personal Investment Income* (Ottawa: Department of Finance, Canada, June 1982); *Report of the Ministerial Advisory Committee on Inflation and the Taxation of Personal Investment Income* (Ottawa, September 30, 1982); *Budget Speech* (Ottawa, Department of Finance, Canada, April 1983); and *The Indexed Security Investment Plan* (Ottawa, Department of Finance, Canada, April 1983).

WAS THE 1978 CAPITAL GAINS TAX CUT SUCCESSFUL?

Ed Zschau

We are asking the right question: Was the 1978 tax cut on capital gains successful? Now we have to establish the appropriate criteria for assessment. Gerald Auten mentioned that we should examine simplicity and equity of various kinds. We also have to evaluate tax policy in terms of what it does for job creation. What does it do for economic expansion? What does it do for productivity? What does it do for competition in international trade? The 1978 Act was extremely successful in addressing those issues.

In making that case, I would like to address three questions and look a little beyond. First, what was the promise of 1978? What were we expecting? Second, what were its specific results? And finally, where do we go from here? Is there a future direction that we should be following?

I came to Washington to testify in favor of the tax cut on capital gains in 1978. The leadership in the Congress was provided by the late Representative Bill Steiger, Senator Cranston, Senator Hansen, and the American Council for Capital Formation, as well as the American Electronics Association and the National Venture Capital Association. Essentially, the bases of our arguments pointed out that the problems the electronics industry and other high technology industries faced were severe and that they were caused by a lack of risk capital. People were simply not willing to put their money into these risky enterprises. Therefore, three bad things were happening: Companies were not getting started; they were not expanding; and most importantly, a lot of us, including my own company, were selling our technology to the Japanese in order to get money to meet the payroll. We feared that America would lose her leadership position in technology unless actions were taken to stimulate investment in high technology companies that could do much for job creation.

We conducted a survey to which two hundred and twenty-five companies responded. It showed that young companies, not the more mature companies, created jobs at the fastest rate in terms of absolute number of jobs per firm. These young companies were the job-creating engines in our economy. In order to create jobs, these young companies required constant injections of risk capital. They needed people to buy their stock and to invest in them. Risk capital was drying up, and the high tax rate, which could go as high as 49 percent in the mid-1970s, was a substantial disincentive to investment in these companies. This survey also showed that companies were raising less capital per firm than at any time in the last twenty years.

The most startling statistic we found was that every $100 invested in a young company generated $30 per year in tax revenue to the federal government. We said, "Amazing! This is like the goose that lays the golden egg! If you can get people to invest, you will create jobs, and you may even create more tax revenue." That was the basis on which the tax cut was sold. We sat back after 1978 and waited, but the investors did not wait. They poured into the marketplace. Within eighteen months after the capital gains tax cut was signed into law by President Carter, $900 million in new venture capital poured into venture capital funds. That figure was more than double the amount that had been raised by such funds over the prior eight years.

To cite some specific statistics: Between 1970 and 1978, when the maximum rate on capital gains was about 49 percent, about $58 million of new venture capital was being generated each year to be invested in young companies. In each of the five years since then, we have generated, on the average, $960 million, sixteen times the amount of venture capital per year going into firms that can then invest in young companies. Stanley Pratt, of *Venture Capital Journal* (January 1983, "Special Report: Capital Transfusions 1982," p. 6), estimates that last year $1.7 billion of new venture capital was made available for investment in young companies. Over $1.7 billion was invested in young companies, much of that money going into start-ups.

The new issue market took off. Tax revenues did not fall, as predicted. In fact, it appeared that, because of some of the effects that James Wetzler has talked about, tax revenues increased, at least temporarily, rather than declining, as the Treasury had predicted. The Revenue Act of 1978 and the results from it appear to be the bright spots in what otherwise has been our economic malaise. The money being poured into high-growth industries suggests a potential for job creation for the future.

This last year, a General Accounting Office (GAO) study surveyed seventy-two companies funded in the 1970s with about $200 million of venture capital that created 130,000 jobs. Today, those seventy companies generate about $6 billion in revenue and about $1 billion in exports. Because of the lower capital gains tax rate, money going into young companies is creating a potential for enormous economic expansion, for risk-taking, and for new technological development, which is what is needed to make us competitive with foreign countries.

Where do we go from here? I feel that we should continue to lower the tax on capital gains, perhaps by targeting—that is, by focusing on equities and new investments so that we are not lowering the tax on gains that come from investing in collectibles or nonproductive assets. We have done such targeting in California. We eliminated the capital gains tax on investments in small, private companies that are held over three years; this provided increased targeted incentives for investment in those companies that have the greatest record for job creation.

Talk about reducing the tax on capital gains and increasing the distinction between ordinary income and capital gains still further raises the issue of fairness. Is it fair for some people, particularly those that have accumulated wealth, to pay lower taxes on their gains? My feeling is that there is nothing fair at all about being unemployed, and if lowering the tax on capital gains can create new jobs, as it has in the past, that is the fairest thing we can do. There is nothing fair about losing our market share and our jobs to foreign competitors. We need to create incentives for risk-taking, job creation, and expansion. We ought to go further than we have, perhaps in a targeted way, to reduce still further the tax on capital gains.

Chapter 8

The State of the Corporate Income Tax: Who Pays It? Should It Be Repealed?

Arnold C. Harberger

The corporation income tax is one of the most fascinating species produced by the processes of economic legislation around the world. Most governmental authorities, legislators, and political leaders around the world have only good words to say about the promotion of capital formation, the fostering of savings, and so forth. This is in stark contrast to their actions, however. As is well known, the personal income tax is in effect a double tax on savings, taxing the income from which savings are generated and at the same time taxing the proceeds of such savings. In the United States we add to this double tax on savings a third tax, that on real property, and a fourth, that on the income of corporations. My first point is that this treatment is objectionable, particularly in light of the lip service that is constantly being paid to saving and investment.

My second point is that the corporation income tax lacks an economic rationale. Income from labor and income from capital are, indeed, distinct and political motivation leads, from time to time, to the differential taxation of these two types of income. (When, under the Nixon Administration, the maximum federal income tax rate in the United States was first reduced to 50 percent, the reduction applied only to so-called *earned* income. Income from capital still faced a maximum rate of 70 percent until very recently.) It is relatively easy at least to understand, if not endorse, this distinction in the mode of taxation between income from capital on the one hand and income from labor on the other. It is not at all easy to see how income from *corporate equity capital* came to be specially and separately taxed at an exceedingly high rate that for decades has hovered around 50 percent—especially considering that it rests at the top of a pile of at least a fourfold taxation of income from capital.

Why is the income produced by corporate equity capital a prime object for separate and special taxation? There is no sound *economic* underpinning for the corporation income tax. The tax originated because corporations are legal persons—but so, too, are three-year-olds, eighty-five-year-olds, manic depressives, blonds, and idiots. Why select out this particular class of legal person as the object of special (and harsh) taxation? There is no respectable *economic* answer to this question. Some say that the state has a claim to a part of the income of corporations because it granted them the right to limited liability; but this is not an economic argument. An economic argument would have to justify the tax either as a payment to the government for the resources involved (in granting limited liability) or as an offset for the costs that corporations (presumably because of their limited liability) imposed on the citizenry at large. Neither of those grounds can plausibly justify a corporation income tax of the magnitude that has prevailed in the United States since the 1930s. Hence, the tax must be viewed as arbitrary and capricious at best.

To a degree, the effects of the tax have been offset by various loopholes and offsets. Accelerated depreciation, the Investment Tax Credit, and debt finance are the three most prominent ancillary measures that have eroded some of the force of the corporation income tax. If carried to its extreme of immediate expensing of investment outlays, accelerated depreciation would in effect repeal the tax. (With immediate expensing, the government for practical purposes shares t percent of the costs of any investment [t is the relevant tax rate], then subsequently takes t percent of its proceeds. It is, therefore, effectively a t percent partner in the business.) In its present form, accelerated depreciation affects the corporate income tax unequally for different types of assets. Thus, although the full expensing of investment outlays would be nondiscriminating and nondistorting, accelerated depreciation both discriminates and distorts.

The second main vehicle for offsetting the effects of the corporation income tax is the Investment Tax Credit. This plays the role of a bonus that the government pays to investing firms *each time* they invest in eligible assets. From an economic point of view, it is a piece of legislation with no sound technical underpinning. Its only saving grace is the relatively low rate of the tax credit, which, of course, helps to limit the damage it does. To better see the underlying flaw in the tax credit system, imagine a similar system applied to the purchase of government bonds. Suppose that buyers of bonds would get a 10 percent tax credit each time they bought a government obligation. Obviously, under such circumstances, buyers would flock to buy bonds of the shortest eligible term so as to be able to roll over their investment and take advantage of the tax credit as many times as possible within a given period. So it is with the current tax credit—it gives a premium, within the periods stipulated in the law, to investment in assets of shorter life. No one has yet produced an economic (or other) argument as to why this is a desirable social or economic objective.

Finally, debt financing is an escape route from the corporation income tax because interest on debt is deductible in the calculation of profits and therefore not subject to the tax. It can be viewed in two different ways. One way is to consider the fact that less risky activities (such as public utilities) have easier access than more risky activities to the bond market and enjoy higher credit limits (in relation to their total capital) from banks and other financial institutions. Firms engaged in relatively safe activities might be able to get 75 or 80 percent of their capital through debt financing, while those in relatively risky operations might obtain only 20 to 25 percent of their capital from this source. The former set of firms would thus have to pay corporation income tax on the income from, say, 20 percent of its capital, while the latter would have to pay it on the income from, say, 80 percent of its capital. A corporation income tax of 50 percent on the earnings from *equity* capital thus might work out to be something like a 10 percent tax on the earnings from *all* capital in the first case and something like a 40 percent tax on the earnings from all capital in the second. This differential taxation of income from all capital introduces serious distortions in the allocation of capital among uses.

The second way of looking at the use of debt financing as an escape route emphasizes the fact that individual firms can vary, up to a point, their relative use of equity and debt as sources of capital. This device artificially distorts the capital structure toward the greater use of debt and carries with it additional (though much more subtle and difficult to measure) costs in terms of economic efficiency and resource allocation.

Faced with the combination of so many mechanisms for offsetting the effects of the corporation income tax, I have modified the emphasis I place on those aspects of the analysis. My early work on the subject emphasized the differential treatment of the corporate versus the noncorporate sector (with the corporation income tax discriminating significantly against investments in the corporate sector).

Today I stress at least equally the welter of distortions within the corporate sector itself—distortions caused by (1) the interaction of differential asset lives with both accelerated depreciation and with the Investment Tax Credit; (2) differential access to debt finance by different firms and different activities; and (3) differential possibilities of altering the financial structure of the firm in response to the existence of the tax. To these I might add, though I have not analyzed them here, the distortions created by the asymmetrical treatment of gains and losses as well as by other detailed, specific provisions of our tax system.

INCIDENCE IN A SUBSTANTIALLY CLOSED ECONOMY

Most of the traditional work in the field of public finance (including macroeconomic countercyclical fiscal policy) has been done in the context of a substantially closed economy. Some treatments were carried out with no attention paid to imports, exports, or international capital movements. Other treatments explicitly dealt with imports and exports, but effectively assumed international capital movements to be zero. Still other treatments modified the above by taking international capital movements into account but treating them as exogenous.

I consider all of the above cases to be covered by what I call a substantially closed economy. In particular, the scheme of general equilibrium incidence analysis that I helped to initiate in the late 1950s and early 1960s can be handled under any of the three alternative sets of assumptions described above.

Let me briefly describe that scheme. Take a country with a given labor force—that is, a labor force that may change for demographic reasons, even including international migration, but *not* as a direct or indirect consequence of the imposition of a corporation income tax. This, for practical purposes, means a labor force that is not responsive to changes in the real wage—an assumption that fits the facts dramatically well for the male labor force (and I believe that this is increasingly true for the female labor force, as well). Consider that this country possesses, in the same sense, a given capital stock. This means that the capital stock can move over time—through saving and through international capital movements—but that it, too, does not respond to the imposition of a corporation income tax. This, for practical purposes, means that neither national savings nor international capital movements are significantly responsive to changes in the domestic rate of return to capital. This assumption fits the facts quite well for national savings—but it is questionable as far as international capital movements are concerned.

Within the context of a given labor force and a given capital stock in the above sense, divide this economy into two sectors, corporate and noncorporate, and impose a special tax on the earnings of capital in the former sector. If markets work reasonably well in this economy, there will be a reshuffling of resources, with the important end result that equilibrium is restored in both the labor and capital markets, as well as in the markets for final products.

Without going into any technical details of the analysis, let me just state the "normal" end result. Normally (i.e., under plausible assumptions about the relevant parameters), taxing capital in one sector will lead to a rise in its gross-of-tax return but to a fall in its net-of-tax return. This will work out to a market equilibrium situation through a shift of some part of the capital stock from the taxed (corporate) to the nontaxed (noncorporate) sector, where the rate of return will fall so that it corresponds to the net-of-tax return in the corporate sector.

The burden borne by capital is simply the fall in the net-of-tax rate of return multiplied by the *entire* capital stock. The full burden of the tax is simply the effective tax rate per unit of capital multiplied by the *corporate* sector's capital stock. These can easily be equal to each other and thus produce the result that capital bears the full burden of the tax. When this happens consumers end up paying more for corporate sector products, but this is offset by their paying less for the products of the noncorporate sector.

When the reduction in the net-of-tax rate of return to capital times the *entire* capital stock is smaller than the effective tax rate times the *corporate* sector capital stock, this has its counterpart in consumers losing more through the rise in the price of corporate products than they gain through the fall in noncorporate goods. A wide range of outcomes for the incidence of the corporation income tax is theoretically possible, but under the assumptions made (of what I have called a substantially closed economy) the notion that capital bears something like the full burden of the tax (perhaps a bit more or a bit less) seems to be close to fitting the facts.

INCIDENCE WITH AN OPEN CAPITAL MARKET

I believe there have been times in our relatively recent history when the assumptions of a substantially closed economy seem to fit the facts pretty well. Cases in point are when international capital movements are dominated by capital controls designed to stem capital flight (as is common in certain less developed countries [LDCs] or, as in the case of the Marshall Plan years, by a virtual one-way movement into economies with substantial capital controls, absence of currency convertibility, and so forth.

Things change, however, across time and among places. As we moved out of the Marshall Plan years and the European economies recovered, their capital controls were gradually dismantled, the Common Market was established, multinationals began to grow in influence throughout the world, and the Eurocurrency market was not only born but quickly became a major element in the world financial scene. These changes create a new set of rules governing the international movement of capital. At the levels of the movement of short-term capital among major international financial institutions (and as between major countries, such as the United States, the United Kingdom, Switzerland, Germany, and so forth), the integration can be said to be complete, in the sense that short-term interest rates (adjusted by covered interest arbitrage in the currency futures market) are equalized. At other levels, the degree of integration is probably not complete, but it is obviously much greater than it was in, say, the 1930s or the immediate postwar years.

These facts of modern life require a reexamination of the incidence question in the context of an open capital market. This I have done on the assumption that the labor force is given (in the sense indicated earlier) but that as far as capital is concerned it is the net rate of return that is given.

This very assumption dramatically alters the conclusion reached for the case of a substantially closed economy. For if the net rate of return is given in the international market place, the burden of a tax on the income from capital in one country will not (in the middle or long run) end up being borne by capital (which can flee) but by other factors of production (land, labor, and to a degree, perhaps, old fixed capital, which cannot flee). General incentives to save, which depend on net rates of return, will not be impaired, but wages will be driven down. In the end, for tradable corporate products the other factors mentioned must absorb the full burden of the tax. If, as I believe, land is not an important input into *corporate* tradable products in the United States, then labor must bear more than the full burden of our corporation income tax.

The logic is as follows. If the corporate tradables sector is to continue to exist, wages must fall in order to absorb the corporation income tax because the prices of these tradables are not going to rise as a result of the tax. In the middle to long run, the labor market has to find its own equilibrium. This will happen when the wage levels (for equivalent labor) in other sectors have fallen by a similar amount. This, in turn, means that product prices will also stay put in the corporate nontradables sector (here implicitly assumed to have similar capital intensity).

As far as the noncorporate sector is concerned, this simple approach runs into trouble if the tradable noncorporate products are in infinitely elastic supply. Fortunately for the relevance of the example, the principal tradable noncorporate products in the United States come from agriculture, which faces a rising supply curve because of the land factor. Thus, in this open capital market case the supply of products from the tradable noncorporate sector will increase, owing to lower labor costs.

With respect to nontradable goods, the likelihood is that nontradable, noncorporate products will fall in price (relative to tradables), owing to lower real wages. On the other hand, the price effect on nontradable corporate products is uncertain, since this sector would face, simultaneously, a fall in wages and a rise in the cost of capital (owing to the tax). As alluded to above, the net effect depends on the relative capital intensities of the two corporate sectors.

SOME JUDGMENTS ON INCIDENCE

The United States was never in a situation characterized *fully* by the assumptions of the substantially closed economy and we are not now and are not likely ever to be in a world that *fully* meets the assumptions used in my analysis of incidence in an open capital market. We have been and are still somewhere in between, but we have moved a good distance from the more closed to the more open case.

It seems clear to me that the major trading nations of the world, *taken together*, come close to the substantially closed economy model. Therefore, if all of these nations together were to raise or lower their respective corporation income taxes, the burden of a rise (or the benefit of a reduction) would fall mainly on the owners of capital all over the world.

We must expect significantly different effects if only the United States raises or lowers its tax, however, and those effects will be substantially of the type indicated by our analysis of incidence with an open capital market. Since in the open capital market case the tax could easily be more than fully borne by labor (with wages falling not just in the corporate sector to reflect the tax but across the whole economy), the burden of an increase in the corporation income tax could be fully or nearly fully borne by labor. For example,

168 Reform of the Federal Income Tax

to test your intuitions on this subject, think of a substantial rise in the corporation income tax of, say, the state of Illinois. How much of it would likely be borne by owners of land and real estate and by labor in Illinois? In the middle or long run, nearly all, and this would be especially certain if there were severe impediments to labor's moving out of Illinois to other states, as is the case with international movements of labor.

SOME SUGGESTIONS FOR REFORM

On more than one occasion I have been a discussant in debates between partisans of consumption taxation on the one hand and income taxation on the other. At other times I have commented on the virtues of eliminating the corporation income tax entirely or fully integrating it with the personal income tax, which amounts to much the same thing. My economist's instincts lie with the consumption tax, and I favor in some ideal world the elimination of the corporation income tax or its full integration with the personal tax. (This must be obvious from the slant of my comments on the choice of the income from corporate equity capital as a tax base.)

At the same time as I hold these positions, I live in this world. I have worked with governmental agencies and private organizations in many countries and have acquired great respect for realism and practicality. I am therefore not likely (consciously at least) to go overboard for an "ideal" solution that is impractical or otherwise beyond reach in the context of the present or the near future.

I do think that the principal move should be toward full expensing of investment outlays, together with the total elimination of the Investment Tax Credit. Actually, the moves made under the Economic Recovery Tax Act of 1981 (ERTA) (in setting up three classes of depreciable assets) and under the Tax Equity and Fiscal Responsibility Act of 1982 (TEFRA) (in effectively canceling a part of the Investment Tax Credit by permitting subsequent depreciation of only 95 percent of the asset price) were moves in this direction. Consider the subsequent steps listed in Table 8-1. The steps could (indeed should) be several years apart (e.g., new assets should not enter at zero class lives before older assets are pretty much fully depreciated). There could be intermediate steps in between to reduce possible transition difficulties, but the idea is perfectly straightforward and workable.

All this could be done without changing the rate of the corporation income tax and without giving systematic capital gains or imposing systematic capital losses on owners of existing assets. This program would eliminate all problems in connection with incentives for

Table 8-1. Method of Phasing in Expensing and Eliminating the Investment Tax Credit.

	Depreciation Class Levels (years life)			Investment Tax Credit (percentage)	Subsequent Depreciation (percentage)
Current	15	5	3	10	95
Next Step	10	4	2	5	95
Following Step	5	2	1	0	100
Ultimate Step	0	0	0	0	0

differential types of assets and, at least in principle, the existing discrimination in favor of debt financing.[1]

Once these steps are taken, the move toward integration with the personal income tax is easy and can also be done gradually. Corporate accounting would be relatively simple in a world without depreciation allowances. It would be no problem at all to have shareholders include in their income, say 10 percent of the corresponding corporate earnings and then have 10 percent of the tax on those earnings treated in the same way as withholdings from salaries and wages are now. This percentage could be moved up over time (keeping in mind, among other things, the revenue needs of government), ending with total or partial integration as the case may be.

I do not believe that the corporation tax should be abolished (even though full expensing of investment is in many respects equivalent to it) because of complications with regard to the earnings of transnational companies. My instinctive judgment is that it is best for any one country to keep its legally operative corporate rate in the same general neighborhood as those of the rest. In this way, it can accomplish up to full integration as far as its national taxpayers are concerned without giving away gratuitous tax revenue to foreign treasuries.

If most major countries adhered roughly to this general principle, the most natural path to the actual elimination of the tax would be through concerted action by them. Please note, however, that full integration of the corporate and personal tax can be done unilaterally and accomplishes for any one country essentially the same result as a zero corporate rate.

NOTES TO CHAPTER 8

1. To accomplish this requires the symmetrical treatment of investment outlays vis-à-vis loan receipts on the one hand, and of gross returns to investment vis-à-vis gross payments (interest plus amortization) on loans on the other. On an investment financed fully by equity, the government would share in t percent of the investment outlays and in t percent of the subsequent flows of gross return. If the investment were financed 60 percent by debt, the government would share in only $0.4t$ percent of the costs and in t times each year's gross return to capital minus interest and amortization (t is the relevant tax rate).

Discussants:

IS REPEAL OF THE CORPORATE INCOME TAX POSSIBLE?

Robert F. Dee

Arnold Harberger has argued forcefully that the corporation income tax is a poor tax from the point of view of economic theory and, indeed, from the point of view of economic practice. The chief objection is that it holds back growth in the more dynamic sectors of the economy and tends to put a brake on capital formation. On the other hand, this tax is easy to administer and is politically popular. It is easy to administer because corporations necessarily maintain standard accounting records. It is politically popular because most citizens look upon corporations as relatively wealthy institutions and expect them to pay their share of the country's tax load.

Dr. Harberger has explained, however, in his earlier published comments on corporate taxation, that the tax is, in fact, discriminatory because corporate net income is the tax base. As a result, the tax tends to be most onerous for activities with low ratios of debt to equity because interest on debt is deductible. Consequently, this system of taxation favors operations that are financed by debt capital over those that are not, thereby distorting the economy in a way that probably is not beneficial in the long term.

It is interesting to compare tax rates by industry group as a percentage of pretax income. The Securities Exchange Commission (SEC) tax data show that the average tax rate for all U.S. industry is 20 percent. Some industries, such as commercial banks, have negative tax rates. The variability in rates appears to support the view that the income tax rates have uneven effects, from those negative rates that I just cited for banking to others that are paying up to 40 percent.

My company can see the theoretical merit of repealing the corporate income tax, but we have questions, of course, about how that goal is to be achieved. We are aware of the present heavy dependence in developed countries on revenues from the corporate sector.

The SEC tax chart to which I referred shows the foreign rate on foreign income as a percentage of pretax income to be 52 percent. We also recognize the practical difficulties inherent in replacing these revenues from some alternative source or sources.

In considering the repeal of the corporate income tax, the practical questions may well outweigh any consideration of theory. Chief among these practical problems is the political difficulty of explaining a change in corporate taxation in today's economic climate. It seems likely that any radical change will be strongly opposed, certainly by the media and unquestionably by populist politicians, of whom one or two come readily to mind. For this reason, it seems practical to commit our energies and resources to modifying the system we now have rather than pressing for repeal. Unless the President champions this repeal—along with other changes in tax policy, such as the introduction of a flat rate tax system or a value added tax or some other system that is seen as an efficient generator of revenues—it would not be politically realistic to press for radical change.

Changes in the existing corporate tax system should be checked by principles of equity and neutrality. Although no tax system can be devised that will not favor certain industry groups at the expense of others, evenhanded administration of the corporate income tax is certainly a goal that we all should pursue. My own experience over the years with our own industry group and with others convinces me that meaningful tax rate reduction is probably the only universally acceptable goal. Once it is attained, business requires the assurance that tax rates and the system of taxation will not be changed from Congress to Congress. For example, one of the main elements of current taxation, the foreign tax credit, is frequently subject to debate. Because of this credit, American business continually faces double taxation, which reduces the ability of U.S. companies to compete in foreign markets and discourages American exports.

A steady, predictable, equitable environment of taxation is vital. Only in such an environment can corporations plan for the future with any reasonable degree of certainty.

THE ENERGY INDUSTRY AND FEDERAL TAX POLICY

Tor Meloe

Economists generally agree that broadly based consumption taxes have the smallest negative effect on savings and investment and, therefore, on economic growth.[1] Corporate income taxes, which fall particularly heavily on capital intensive industries, and other business taxes have the greatest negative impact on investment. Business taxes include employer social security contributions and the windfall profits tax on petroleum producers.

The following data illustrate the fallacy of depending on corporations for an increased share of the tax burden.

- Corporate pretax income is only 7.2 percent of total national income. This represents nearly a postwar low. After-tax income is equivalent to only 4.8 percent of the national income.

- Corporate profits are about one-third below their first quarter 1980 peak, despite hundreds of billions of dollars of new investment. In constant dollar terms, profits are lower than in 1965 after inventory and capital consumption adjustment (see Figure 8-1).

- Rate of return on stockholders' equity for all American manufacturing corporations was only about 9.2 percent in the third quarter of 1982. A recent study by Data Resources, Inc., estimates that, based on increased costs of capital, an adequate return on shareholders' equity must be at least 18.6 percent over the next five years for an average risk-taking company, and more than that for higher risk companies.[2]

- Ratios of corporate liquidity and capital structure have been weakening, thus impairing the ability of companies to expand investment and creating many bankruptcies.

It is ironic that in the United States the corporation is viewed as an important source of tax revenue, whereas some other industrial nations provide heavy subsidies to make their industries competitive on world markets. This contrast in industrial policy is a major reason why many U.S. companies are losing out to foreign competitors.

The petroleum industry is an example of the impact of this U.S. industrial policy. In recent years, petroleum companies have stepped up their investment for exploration and production and modernized their downstream operations. U.S. oil industry capital and exploration expenditures totaled almost $47 billion in 1980, the last year for which complete data are available. This figure is about four times the 1973 level.[3] With profits falling off, many oil companies are cutting back on their investment budgets and will be forced to reduce them even further if taxes on the industry are increased. This is unfortunate in view of the massive investment oil companies will have to make in years ahead to replace domestic petroleum reserves and to modernize downstream facilities.

Figure 8-1. Adjusted After-Tax Profits of U.S. Corporations (*1972 dollars*).

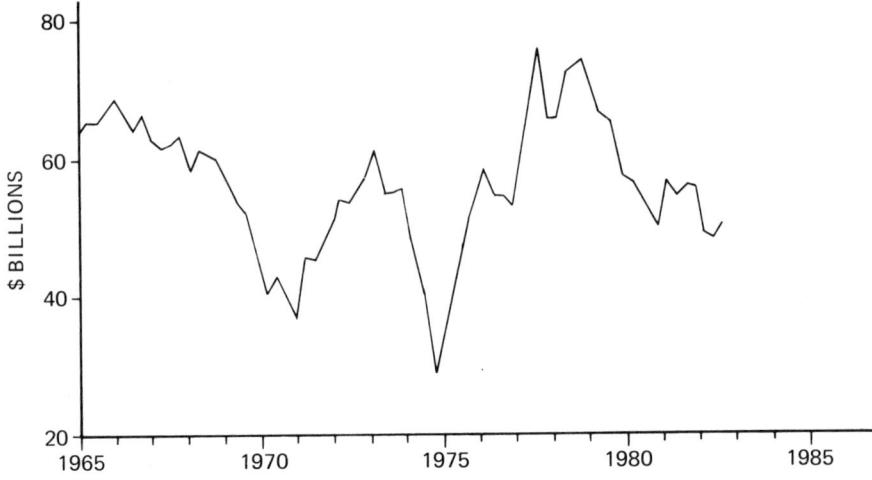

Note: U.S. corporate profits with inventory valuation adjustment and capital consumption adjustments.

Figure 8-2. U.S. Petroleum Industry Capital and Exploration Expenditures (*billions of dollars*).

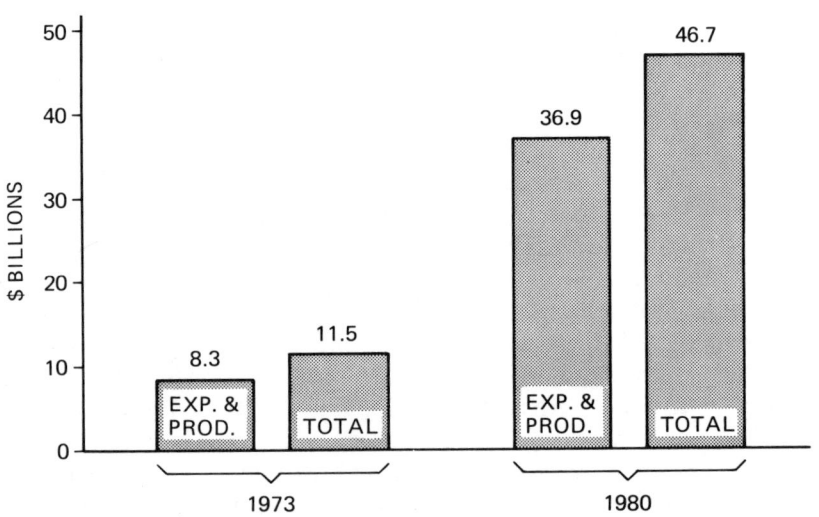

Source: Chase Manhattan Bank, *Capital Investments of the World Petroleum Industry*, 1980.

The Chase Manhattan Bank has estimated that the U.S. petroleum industry will need to invest $1.3 trillion in the 1980s,[3] compared with actual investment of $170 billion in the 1970s. Clearly, higher taxes on the oil industry would inhibit industry efforts to replace domestic petroleum reserves and to reduce dependence on imported oil.

OIL INDUSTRY TAX BURDEN

Despite the depressed condition of the oil industry, increased taxes are a real possibility for the petroleum industry. It probably pays the highest taxes of any major American industry. In 1981, twenty-three leading U.S. oil companies paid current U.S. federal, state, and local income taxes equivalent to 33 percent of their U.S. net income before provision for income tax (assuming no windfall profits tax). By comparison, one hundred leading non-oil industrial companies paid only 26 percent of their net income. When the windfall profits tax is included, the tax burden on the oil companies becomes 51 percent of U.S. net income before provision for taxes. Also, oil producers pay billions of dollars in severance taxes on oil production and property taxes on oil and gas reserves.

Despite this already huge burden, the petroleum industry was again taxed heavily under the Tax Equity and Fiscal Responsibility Act (TEFRA). Ironically, one reason for some of the current sentiment for increases in petroleum taxes is the misconception held by some that the petroleum industry escaped relatively unharmed under TEFRA.

Actually, the petroleum industry will pay a large share of the taxes raised under TEFRA. According to a recent study by the accounting firm of Price Waterhouse concerning the direct revenue effects of TEFRA, the cumulative impact of TEFRA on the petroleum industry over the five-year period (1983-87) will range from $11.5 billion to $22.7 billion, depending upon assumptions made on industry growth.[4] Also, depending upon the economic scenario, the petroleum industry will pay on average 11.1 percent to 22 percent of all revenues raised through the business tax provisions under TEFRA.

In addition, a five-cents-per-gallon excise tax was recently enacted on motor fuels, bringing the total federal excise tax to nine-cents-per-gallon as of April 1, 1983. While this is a tax at the pump, there is no assurance that oil companies will not have to absorb some of the tax under today's weak market conditions. This tax will direct billions of dollars out of the spending stream and return them later through expenditures for road repairs, increased subsidies for mass transport, and other transfer payments. The excise tax will reduce demand for gasoline and refinery operating rates. The tax will not create a single new job and in the short-term, will increase unemployment because of the lag in spending the tax revenue. In addition to the federal government, many states facing serious financial pressures are also looking to the oil industry for greater tax revenues. In 1982, a total of thirty-three states enacted tax legislation that applied only to the petroleum industry.

This massive taxation of the oil industry is not based on good economics. Rather, it reflects the fact that legislators find it politically popular to tax oil companies and let them absorb the tax or pass it on in price to individuals.

The economic impact of proposed taxes on oil—and of taxes in general—must be evaluated in terms of tax criteria that are consistent and that promote widely accepted objectives of economic policy. In view of the highest U.S. unemployment rate in over forty years and the stagnation of the past three years, the primary objective of tax policy today should be to reverse this trend and restore strong long-term growth to the U.S. economy.

If new taxes must be imposed in order to reduce the federal deficit, a tax on consumption does the least harm to economic growth. A consumption tax should be broad-based and borne equally by all consumers. However, before new taxes are imposed, efforts to reduce government expenditures should be stepped up.

NOTES

1. For general discussions of the incidence and effect of taxes, see Richard A. Musgrave, *Theory of Public Finance* (New York: Krieger, 1959); Joseph A. Pechman, *Federal Tax Policy* (Washington, D.C.: Brookings Institution, 1977); and Earl R. Ralph and George F. Break, *Public Finance* (New York: The Ronald Press, 1961).

2. Donald McLagen; Allen Sinai; and Michael Hergert, "What is an Adequate Return on Equity for the 1980s?" In Data Resources, Inc., *U.S. Long-Term Review* (Spring 1982), p. 1.52.

3. Chase Manhattan Bank, *Capital Investment of the World Petroleum Industry* (New York, 1980), p. 4.

4. Price Waterhouse, *The Direct Revenue Effects of the Tax Equity and Fiscal Responsibility Act of 1982 on the Petroleum Industry—Final Report* (Washington, D.C., 1982), Exhibit A.

ANOTHER VIEW OF THE CORPORATE INCOME TAX

Joseph A. Pechman

As Arnold Harberger's paper reveals, he believes that the U.S. tax system bears excessively heavily on capital. He attributes part of the excess burden to the corporate tax and would like the tax to disappear.

Professor Harberger's description of the prevailing view of the incidence of the corporate tax—a view that he helped originate—is accurate, and his extension of the analysis to a corporation income tax in a world economy is also correct. Briefly stated, both in a closed economy and in an open economy in which all nations impose the same tax, the corporate tax is probably borne by capital; but a nation that gets out of line will burden workers and other citizens rather than just the owners of capital.

I disagree, however, that there is no sound underpinning for the corporation income tax. The major practical justification is that the corporation income tax is needed to safeguard the individual income tax. Without it, individuals could amass huge amounts of wealth in corporations that would never be subject to tax or would be taxed at preferential rates. It is true that economists have designed elegant systems to substitute for the corporate tax (for example, full taxation of unrealized capital gains annually or periodically) or to integrate the corporate with the individual income tax (for example, partnership treatment for corporate shareholders). All of these systems have been found impractical, however, and most nations either have a classical corporate tax (that is, one that is not integrated with the individual income tax) or some form of dividend relief. It may be that Professor Harberger would not regard this defense of the corporate tax as an *economic* argument, but it is still a valid basis for keeping the tax.

Another reason for having a corporate tax is the economic interdependence that Professor Harberger stresses so much. In a world with vast capital flows across international borders, all nations would at least want to tax profits that are exported to absentee owners abroad, simply to get a share of the economic return generated within their own borders. Even though he bludgeons the corporate tax in most of his paper, Professor Harberger agrees that abolition of the corporate tax is impractical "because of complications with regard to transnational companies."

Although I agree with Professor Harberger's analysis of the incidence of the corporate tax, I fail to see how he arrives at the conclusion that the U.S. corporate tax is a tax on U.S. labor, landowners, and owners of old fixed capital. To be sure, he doesn't quite say that, but he does ask us to test our intuition by thinking of a substantial rise in the corporate income tax in the state of Illinois. The same intuition, he implies, should tell us that the U.S. corporate tax is borne by U.S. citizens.

The trouble with this argument is that we have been *reducing*, not increasing, the effective rate of the corporate tax in this country for many years. And Professor Harberger believes that the reductions enacted in 1981, even though they were modified somewhat in 1982, were in the right direction. Some careful studies made before the enactment in 1981 of the Accelerated Cost Recovery System (ACRS) at the International Monetary Fund concluded that the pre-1981 capital recovery provisions of the United States were already more liberal than those of most industrial countries.[1] The enactment of ACRS reduced the U.S. corporate tax even more relative to those that are levied elsewhere. On this basis, I suppose Professor Harberger would have to say now that recent tax action in the U.S. has probably increased real wages rather than reduced it, as his paper infers.

However, I don't want to quibble about such fine points, because in the end Professor Harberger becomes quite reasonable. Professor Harberger recognizes that, in our zeal to give still more incentives to investment, we have badly botched the corporate tax. For corporate investment as a whole, ACRS plus the investment credit plus other preferences are more than the equivalent of expensing of capital investment for tax purposes. Instead of taxing in a neutral way, however, we introduced large subsidies in some industries and left other industries paying significant taxes. The economic cost of the distortions to the corporate tax introduced by this system probably exceed the costs attributed by Professor Harberger and others.

Harberger's solution is to cut through all the complexity by substituting full expensing for ACRS and the investment credit. This has the advantage of treating equally assets with different economic lives. It has the added characteristic that, in effect, the corporate tax on new fixed investment is entirely eliminated.

I would prefer to retain some vestige of the corporate tax for reasons mentioned earlier. To improve its structure, I would allow an immediate deduction for the present value of the future economic depreciation that firms could claim if there were no inflation.[2] If a neutral stimulus for investment is desired, the stimulus could be provided through an initial allowance, which would be deducted from the cost of the asset before the depreciation allowance is calculated.[3] This has the virtue that, as under expensing, no adjustment for inflation would ever be needed because the depreciation deduction would be taken in the same year in which the asset was purchased.

A major point about recent changes in the corporate tax, which is unfortunately relegated to a footnote in Professor Harberger's paper, is that something must be done to the subsidy to debt financed investment if we go as far as expensing. The early part of his paper mentions that the interest deduction gives a great advantage to debt finance, but the latter part treats it as a peripheral matter. As Arnold Harberger points out, full expensing should be coupled with complete denial of the deduction for interest.[4] If economic depreciation is used, the first-year allowance could be calculated to offset the effect of the denial of the interest deduction.[5]

If nothing is done about the interest deduction and ACRS and the investment credit remains unaltered, the existence of the interest deduction becomes a vast subsidy for firms able to borrow money for new investment. Let us assume that, for a particular firm, ACRS plus the investment credit is exactly equivalent to expensing. Assuming full loss offsets, the rate of return on the investment is not affected by the corporate tax. Since in equilibrium the rate of interest will equal the rate of return on capital, the corporate tax is offset twice: once by expensing and the second time by the interest deduction. Not a bad deal: Given a 46 percent corporate tax rate, if you can borrow $100 million for an investment that will yield 15 percent, the government will give you a tax break of $6.9 million on top of the $15 million the lender will earn net of corporate tax on his investment![6]

In conclusion, I believe that the corporate tax should continue to play a role in the U.S. tax system; that recent legislation has gutted the tax and introduced huge distortions in the system; that ACRS should be replaced by a deduction for the present value of economic depreciation plus a uniform initial allowance; and that something needs to be done immediately about the interest deduction to eliminate the unwarranted subsidy to borrowing.

NOTES

1. See George F. Kopits, *IMF Survey* (October 27, 1980, and April 20, 1981).

2. This idea, which was originally conceived by Nicholas Kaldor, was recently rediscovered by Alan J. Auerbach and Dale W. Jorgenson. See their "Inflation-Proof Depreciation of Assets," *Harvard Business Review* 58, no. 5 (September-October 1980): 113-18.

3. For an explanation of why an initial allowance that is deducted from the cost basis of the asset is neutral, see Arnold C. Harberger, "The Neutrality in Investment Incentives," in Henry J. Aaron and Michael J. Boskin, eds., *The Economics of Taxation* (Washington, D.C.: Brookings Institution, 1980), pp. 299-316.

4. For an explanation of why the interest deduction should be denied under full expensing, see Robert E. Hall, "Tax Treatment of Depreciation, Capital Gains, and Interest in an Inflationary Economy," in Charles R. Hulten, ed., *Depreciation, Inflation and the Taxation of Income from Capital* (Washington, D.C.: Urban Institute, 1981), pp. 149-66.

5. Ibid., p. 165.

6. The interest deduction at a 15 percent rate is $15 million. The tax value of this deduction is 0.46 × 15 or $6.9 million.

POLITICAL REALITY AND THE CORPORATE INCOME TAX

Steven D. Symms

We should work toward elimination of the corporate tax. I caution, however, that the chances of exterminating that dinosaur in the Ninety-eighth Congress are close to zero. Because of the political infeasibility of achieving the best option, I recommend efforts toward creation of a corporation tax that is as neutral as possible. Since the only purpose of taxation is to raise enough revenue for the necessary functions of government, we should aim toward a neutral tax Code. That is, taxes should distort as few economic decisions as possible.

The Economic Recovery Tax Act of 1981 (ERTA), which included an innovative new system of capital cost recovery, was a major step in the right direction, but we should now move toward expensing for capital equipment, which is tax neutral. I agree with Arnold Harberger when he says we should continue to reduce the length of depreciation schedules in order to move toward expensing. In my opinion, expensing would make the Investment Tax Credit (ITC) undesirable because the ITC causes distortions in investment patterns. For many industries, however, the Investment Tax Credit represents up to 50 percent of cash flow. In these hard times, when there is a significant amount of debt in the economy and long-term capital is very expensive, I doubt that this issue can be resolved easily.

In addition, incentives to use debt financing should be eliminated from the tax system. Present law, on both the corporate and individual side, rewards debt and penalizes saving. The inherent bias against saving and investment must be reduced and then eliminated from the tax Code.

Having reviewed some of the objectives for corporate tax reform, I want to discuss some of the political realities that will influence these reforms and some of the dangers that I see lurking ahead. First, we are faced with tremendous deficits that will not allow near-term reductions in corporate taxation. On the other hand, I am confident that Congress will not enact major new corporate tax increases in the next few years.

Second, there may be changes made in the corporate tax area that will not be in the best long-run interests of the country. Specifically, I am concerned that if a number of large firms in the nation's basic industries go bankrupt, efforts will be mounted to establish a Reconstruction Finance Corporation (RFC). The RFC would provide loan guarantees or credits to industries for specific types of investments. In short, we would be taking a major step toward nationalization of our basic industries. We would not, however, be addressing the basic problem in our economy, which is high levels of entitlements spending. I do not believe the long-term capital markets will be revitalized until Congress solves the entitlements problem.

In conclusion, I think any progress in the corporate tax area will be determined by progress in controlling the federal budget. The terrifying deficits we face over the next few years give us the opportunity to do something right for a change. They give us the opportunity to address entitlements spending and, thus, bring the budget under control. Once the budget is under control, then we can begin to undertake some of the important corporate tax reforms that are so badly needed.

PART III

SOLUTIONS TO THE PROBLEM WITH THE TAX SYSTEM
Restructuring The Federal Tax System

 Chapter 9

Value Added Tax: Has the Time Come?

Charles E. McLure, Jr.

I. INTRODUCTION

In 1963 the Fiscal and Financial Committee on Tax Harmonization in the Common Market (Neumark Commission) recommended that the members of the European Common Market (six, at that time) replace their highly defective gross receipts or turnover taxes with Value Added Taxes (VAT).[1] Interest in this form of tax, largely unknown on this side of the Atlantic before then, spread to the United States, fueled, in part, it seems, by the mystique of this new fiscal device, and in 1966 the influential Research and Policy Committee of the Committee for Economic Development proposed that the corporate income tax be replaced by a VAT.[2] Advocates of the VAT argued that such a switch in revenue sources would stimulate saving and investment and would improve the U.S. balance of payments, an objective that had only recently assumed importance. Opponents of the VAT disliked the distributional implications of replacing the corporate income tax with a sales tax, which they presumed would be regressive, and they doubted the claims made for the VAT on the basis of stimulus to saving and investment and its supposed international effects.[3] The entire debate was hampered by theoretical and empirical uncertainty about the incidence of the corporate income tax. By comparison, there was little dispute that a VAT would be borne by consumers of taxed products.

Another flurry of interest in the VAT occurred in the early 1970s when President Richard Nixon suggested that revenues from a federal value added tax might be used to replace part of those from the existing local property taxes that comprised the primary means of financing public primary and secondary education.[4] A presidential task force studied the VAT and in its 1970 report concluded that the VAT should not be adopted as a partial or total substitute for any existing tax. It recommended that if the federal government were to need substantial additional revenue, it should turn to the VAT or other indirect tax rather than increase income taxes.[5] The distributional issues were much the same as before, in that a tax on capital would have been replaced with a tax on consumption. As before, there was some debate about tax incidence—this time about the incidence of the property tax.[6] This episode also resulted in no action, perhaps in part because White House interest in the VAT became one of the casualties of Watergate.

The next notable appearance of the VAT in the American press occurred in 1979, when Chairman Al Ullman of the House Ways and Means Committee suggested the tax as a partial replacement for the corporate and personal income taxes. Though hearings were held,[7] the Ullman bill never reached the floor of the House, and Ullman's subsequent defeat suggested to some that the VAT was not particularly popular with the American electorate. The VAT has also recently been mentioned as a means of raising general revenue to finance social security.[8]

During the two decades since the Neumark Report, the value added tax has become one of the revenue workhorses of the world. Virtually every important country in Europe imposes the tax, and it has spread throughout the Third World.[9] Though the United States is joined by Canada and Australia in resisting this tidal wave of adoption of the VAT, it is reasonable to ask whether the time has finally come for the United States to adopt the tax.

This paper examines that question. Since virtually all of the conceivable arguments for and against the VAT (and a few that are hard to conceive) have been amply documented in previous rounds of the debate, they are not presented in great detail.[10] The outcome of the exercise—whether or not the United States should adopt a VAT—depends crucially on views on such issues as the proper size of government and equity in taxation, matters about which there can reasonably be disagreement.

Much of the early debate about the relative merits of a VAT was clouded by confusion about the nature of the tax. In particular, it was thought by some that imposition of the tax would automatically improve the balance of payments because the tax is imposed on imports and rebated on exports. More careful observers realized, however, that exactly the same argument could be made about the retail sales taxes levied by the American states; they are also applied to imported goods and, for the most part, they do not apply to exports.[11] Yet hardly anyone would say that the state sales taxes significantly affect the balance of payments.

This illustrates a basic lesson of this paper. Though the VAT and the retail sales tax differ importantly in the way they are administered, *the VAT is merely a sales tax.*[12] Except for administrative issues, and economic effects related thereto, there is virtually no question about the effects of the value added tax that cannot be adequately answered by asking exactly the same question about a federal retail sales tax.[13] This basic truth is important, because it allows Americans who are familiar with retail sales taxes, but not with the VAT, to appraise the economic effects of the latter without being led astray by its administrative novelty or by mindless and unfounded assertions that the VAT is not a sales tax. Moreover, it helps us to realize that the most important issues in the VAT debate involve not that tax but the taxes it might replace or the spending it might finance.[14]

This paper discusses briefly the context in which the VAT is currently being considered, principles of taxation against which taxes are commonly judged, and public rankings of various sources of tax revenue. Then it discusses the likely tax base, rates, and revenue yield of an American VAT, the advantages of uniform rates, the distribution of the tax burden by income classes, effects on economic neutrality and growth, international effects, the issue of preemption of a state tax base, and transition problems. Key administrative aspects of the tax are covered briefly in the appendix.

II. PUTTING THE DISCUSSION IN CONTEXT

In appraising the case for a VAT, it is important to consider the context in which it is being discussed. When most of the European countries first adopted the VAT, they were replacing preexisting national taxes levied on gross turnover at all (or many) stages of economic activity. Since these taxes were notorious for their stimulus to vertical integration and the difficulty of making accurate border tax adjustments, the VAT was clearly a step in the right direction.[15] The necessary changes in methods of compliance and administration would be relatively straightforward, there would probably be little effect on the overall incidence of taxes or price levels, and any overall effect on the allocation of resources, including those on saving and investment, would be positive. Effects on the balance of payments could not be predicted accurately, but they were generally expected to be minimal.

The present situation in the United States is, of course, quite different. There is no defective national sales tax to replace. Rather, any substitution at the federal level would be for some combination of the corporate income tax, the individual income tax, or the payroll tax. (Replacing revenue from the local property tax does not seem to be under active consideration.) Or the VAT might be an alternative to a cash flow consumption tax. Any such substitution would involve a major change in tax structure that would have important ramifications for tax equity, neutrality, saving and investment, and administration and compliance; it would not be merely a clear improvement over an existing sales tax, as in most of Europe. But there is another major difference in the European and American debates, especially in the current round of interest in the United States.

The U.S. is currently facing a number of years of large federal deficits, even if the budget balance is calculated at high employment, rather than taken at its actual level. In this context, imposition of a VAT can be seen as the alternative to some combination of higher inflation, tighter monetary policy and higher interest rates, further budget cuts, repeal of even more of the 1981 tax cuts, and other tax increases. Deciding whether to impose an American VAT, rather than choosing one of these other alternatives, is a much more complicated task than the one that faced the Europeans, and it is even more difficult than the more limited question of alternative tax structures in which the issue of an American VAT has most commonly been posed. Needless to say, this paper is not the place to attempt a comprehensive comparison of the various economic effects of a VAT with those of inflation, higher interest rates, budget cuts, and various other taxes. Rather, since *any* tax increase will reduce the deficit, reduce inflationary pressure, allow monetary policy to be looser and interest rates to be lower, and reduce pressure for further budget cuts, I concentrate on the basic structural issue of choosing between alternative ways to raise more public revenue. In limiting the discussion in this way, however, I do assume away many of the most important macroeconomic fiscal issues facing the nation.

III. PRINCIPLES OF TAXATION AND THE VAT

Taxes are generally judged by their performance under two alternative standards: the benefit principle and the principle of ability to pay. The first of these is satisfied when beneficiaries of public services pay the costs of providing them. Ability-to-pay is a shorthand way of saying that taxes should be progressive, in the sense that tax payments rise proportionately more rapidly than income; how much more rapidly depends on public views of vertical equity—a matter on which economists have little to say.[16] A third important goal of tax policy is that, to the extent that tax payments diverge from benefits received, they should distort the use of economic resources as little as possible—that is, taxes should be neutral.[17] Finally, it is important that taxes be collected without excessive costs of compliance and administration. The growth in both the underground economy and the complexity of the income taxes underscores the importance of this last principle.

Because it is generally impossible to assess the benefits of public spending accurately, except for those of services that closely resemble privately provided services, it is impossible to implement the benefit principle precisely. Yet it may not be too far wide of the mark to believe that, on average, citizens receive benefits from public services that bear a roughly proportionate relationship to private consumption.[18] If so, then the value added tax probably would not fare too badly under the benefit principle. By comparison, the VAT is generally given low marks on ability-to-pay grounds, since it is likely to be regressive, unless levied at highly differentiated rates.

If VAT could be levied at the same rate on all consumption, it probably would not greatly distort consumption choices, and it would probably be roughly neutral with regard to the choice of saving versus consumption.[19] For practical reasons discussed later (see section IV) the tax cannot be levied on all consumption, and political pressures and considerations of vertical equity may further prevent it from being imposed on all consumption that could realistically be taxed. Thus, any real-world VAT will almost certainly rank lower on neutrality grounds than will an idealized flat rate VAT—probably the more so, the more various items are taxed at different rates. Finally, experience in Europe and elsewhere clearly indicates that the VAT can be administered without exhorbitant expense but that it is not the self-enforcing levy that some of its greatest fans would have us believe.

Many of the propositions stated in the previous two paragraphs are explained in greater detail below. At this point, it is worth commenting further on how the appraisal of the VAT on grounds of benefits, vertical equity, and neutrality depends on the context in which the tax is considered.

Suppose, first, that the VAT is being considered as a means of financing a general increase in the size of the public sector. In such a case, the VAT may rank fairly high on benefit grounds, but those who prefer greater redistribution of income through taxation would argue that the tax does poorly on ability-to-pay grounds. On the other hand, the VAT would generally fare poorly as a benefit tax if used to finance an increase in services to a limited group, but some might like (or dislike) the redistributional effects of any given tax expenditure package.

Suppose, now, that the VAT is being considered as a replacement for some existing tax. In such a case, it is difficult to judge the tax substitution on benefit grounds because one does not know what part of the budget is being financed. Different observers, however, can readily judge the substitution from the viewpoint of ability-to-pay, depending on the tax being replaced and their views of vertical equity.[20] Similarly, they can judge the trade-off between the relative equity effects and the neutrality of various taxes.[21] Finally, note that even the appraisal of the tax as a means of financing a *given* increase in public spending can generally usefully be conducted in these differential terms, since there are alternative ways of financing the increase.[22]

In attempting to assess the desirability of imposing a VAT, either as a direct substitute for present taxes or as a means of avoiding increases in other taxes, it is useful to go beyond the views of economists, to those of the public. This can be done with the help of surveys of public attitudes toward taxes conducted over the past decade by the Advisory Commission on Intergovernmental Relations.[23] While interpretation of such surveys is inherently risky, it does appear that the public might favor greater reliance on the VAT, relative to the federal income taxes.

The May 1982 survey by the ACIR found that the "federal income tax" was considered by 40 percent of those expressing an opinion to be "the worst tax—that is, the least fair," and another 12 percent felt that way about state income taxes. By comparison, only 15 percent of those with a view accorded that dubious distinction to the state sales taxes, the kind of tax most similar to the VAT.[24] While the state sales tax has grown in relative popularity since 1973, the federal income tax has suffered a slight decline in popularity over that period.[25] Even if the group surveyed is broken down into socioeconomic groups, the federal income tax is reported by all groups to be far less popular than the state sales tax. In 1982 those with "high school incomplete" and those with household income below $15,000 per year voted for the federal income tax over the state sales tax as the worst tax by a margin of 1.75 to 1.[26]

Though now somewhat dated, results of earlier survey questions dealing directly with the VAT are consistent with these results. In a

1972 survey of whether and how to reduce local property taxes, 32 percent of respondents favored imposing a federal value added tax, while only 14 percent favored raising individual income taxes.[27] Similarly, in the same year, 34 percent of respondents chose a VAT on things other than food and similar necessities as the best way to raise federal taxes substantially, while 10 percent chose an increase in individual income tax rates.[28] Finally, in both 1972 and 1976 the state sales tax was favored over the state income tax by a margin of almost two to one as the best way to raise substantial additional revenue at the state level.[29]

IV. TAX BASE, RATES, AND REVENUE

Consumption expenditures in 1981, the last year for which we have data, were $1,843 billion. (See Table 9-1.) This is a useful place to begin in attempting to quantify the potential base of a value added tax.[30] As argued in section V below, there are important economic and administrative reasons to levy the tax at a single rate on as much of this consumption spending as possible. But there are also strong administrative and political reasons that all consumption cannot be taxed. First, the figure for total consumption includes such items as food produced and consumed on farms, which would be almost impossible to tax.[31] Food, especially that consumed at home, is sometimes also excluded from the tax in the interest of equity—that is, to reduce the progressivity of the tax. Table 9-1 considers two alternatives: full taxation of food not consumed on farms and exemption of food consumed at home as well as on farms.[32]

The imputed income from owner-occupied housing would also be very difficult to tax, for both administrative and political reasons, and no European country attempts to tax it. Failure to tax this item of consumption means that owner-occupied housing would be favored relative to rental housing unless (1) residential rents were also excluded from tax or (2) the capital value of new owner-occupied housing were taxed. The European countries do not tax residential rents, but in some countries the capital value of housing is burdened, to some extent, by taxes paid on construction materials.[33] The original Ullman bill would have taxed housing at one-half the rate applied to other items; housing was totally exempt in the revised bill. Table 9-1 assumes no taxation of housing services or construction.[34]

Inclusion of health care (medicine, doctors, hospital care, and so forth) in the tax base would be unpopular politically, and it would probably increase the regressivity of the tax.[35] Similarly, it is unlikely

Table 9-1. Estimated Base of Consumption-Type Value Added Tax with Limited and Liberal Exemption at 1981 Levels of Consumption (*billions of dollars*).

	Personal Consumption Expenditures	Estimated Tax Base	
		Limited Exemptions	Liberal Exemptions
Food and tobacco	$ 398.4	$ 391.7[a]	$121.1[b]
Clothing, accessories, and jewelry	136.4	136.3[c]	136.3[c]
Personal care	24.6	24.6	24.6
Housing	295.3	—	—
Household operation	256.5	249.4[d]	152.9[e]
Medical care expenses	194.6	194.6	—
Personal business	99.8	41.0[f]	20.7[g]
Transportation	260.8	260.8	256.3[h]
Recreation	117.2	117.2	111.2[i]
Private education and research	29.3	29.3	—
Religious and welfare activities	25.4	—	—
Foreign travel and other, net	5.2	13.7[j]	13.7[j]
Total personal consumption	1,843.2	1,457.6	836.8
Percentage of personal consumption	100.0	79.1	45.4

[a] Excludes food furnished to government and commercial employees and food produced and consumed on farms.
[b] Includes only purchased meals, beverages, and tobacco products.
[c] Excludes standard clothing issued to military personnel.
[d] Excludes domestic services.
[e] Excludes domestic services and household utilities (except telephone).
[f] Excludes services furnished without payment by financial intermediaries except life insurance companies and expenses of handling life insurance.
[g] Excludes items in note *f* and legal services and funeral and burial expenses.
[h] Excludes bridge, tunnel, ferry, and road tolls; transit systems; and commutation railway expenses.
[i] Excludes admissions to legitimate theaters, opera, and entertainments of nonprofit institutions; clubs and fraternal organizations, except insurance; and pari-mutual net receipts.
[j] Excludes foreign travel and expenditures abroad by U.S. residents, but includes expenditures in United States by foreigners and personal remittances in kind to foreigners.
Source: U.S. Department of Commerce, *Survey of Current Business* (Washington, D.C.: Government Printing Office, July 1982), pp. 40–41.

that educational expenses would be subject to tax. Table 9-1 thus considers two alternatives, inclusion and exclusion of health and education, from the tax base. Alternative assumptions are also made for such items as household utilities, public transportation, and legal fees. Religious and welfare activities are assumed to be tax-free in both estimates.

Many of the services of financial institutions are not sold on the basis of explicit fees or prices; rather, their cost is covered by differentials between earnings on investments and interest paid on deposits.[36] As a result, it is difficult to include the full value of these services in the base of a VAT.[37] Figures on consumption also include foreign travel and expenditures made abroad by Americans that would not be covered by the VAT, but exclude spending in the United States by foreign travelers that would be. Both columns of Table 9-1 reflect these considerations.

The figures in Table 9-1 indicate that once administrative realities are recognized, no more than about 75 to 80 percent of total consumption is likely to be taxed.[38] At a rate of 5 percent, a VAT on this base of roughly $1,400 billion would have yielded some $70 billion in 1981 or roughly 23 percent of the yield of the personal income tax in that year. A more realistic estimate of the base, once political realities—as reflected in likely tax expenditures under the VAT—are also taken into account, is on the order of $850 to $900 billion, or some 45 to 50 percent of all consumption. A tax of 5 percent on this base would have produced about $42 to $45 billion in 1981.

V. THE CASE FOR UNIFORM RATES

Economic theory tells us that welfare will be maximized if taxes do not interfere with choices over the disposal of resources. This has commonly been interpreted to mean that a tax levied at uniform rates is more nearly neutral than one levied at rates that differ between commodities. Unfortunately, it is virtually impossible to tax one important use of resources, leisure,[39] and various other commodities are difficult to tax, for administrative or political reasons, as noted above. In this second-best world, preference for a single rate on those items that can be taxed can be based only on unsupported faith that a uniform rate nonetheless fosters neutrality,[40] plus a healthy appreciation for the administrative disadvantages of differential rates.

Differentials in rates inevitably complicate compliance with a VAT and, therefore, administration of the tax. Most obviously, sales must be segregated into the various categories subjected to different rates. This can strain the record-keeping ability of small shopkeepers. Moreover, it becomes necessary to make hairline distinctions between products. For example, if soft drinks are taxed at the full rate, but juices are taxed preferentially as food, or even exempted, where along the spectrum do we draw the line?[41] How is the dividing line communicated to shopkeepers and their employees for hundreds, or even thousands of items, and how is it enforced?

Moreover, problems can occur if the same firm sells some items that are exempt and others that are taxed. If such a firm is allowed credit for tax paid on all its purchases, including those used as inputs to exempt sales, it will be at an advantage relative to a firm that sells only exempt items and that, being "out of the system," can take no credit for purchases on inputs. Some countries attempt to avoid this problem by requiring allocation of the costs of inputs between exempt and taxable items, allowing credit only for taxes paid on inputs to taxable sales. Where inputs and outputs are readily identifiable, this solution is workable. Many expenses, however, cannot be neatly categorized in this way, and problems of compliance and administration arise.[42] (For example, how does one treat the tax on the refrigerator used to cool both taxable soft drinks and exempt juice?)

It appears that the combination of low or zero rates on some items and extraordinarily high rates on other items can turn a sales tax that would otherwise be roughly proportional to consumption and regressive, when compared to income, into a tax that is progressive when compared to consumption and proportional or even mildly progressive when compared to income.[43] Yet most of the participants at a recent conference on the VAT held at the Brookings Institution who were favorably disposed to this reduction in progressivity did not think that it justified the complications in compliance and administration it entails.[44] Rather, they felt that, "on balance, the rate differentiation was a mistake, that in highly developed industrial countries with well-articulated systems of transfers and income taxes, it is better to keep the VAT clean ... and simple, and to take care of income redistribution questions with instruments other than the value added tax."[45]

VI. EQUITY, EFFICIENCY, AND ECONOMIC GROWTH

Given what has been said above, there is little need to dwell at length on the effects imposition of a value added tax would have on equity, efficiency, or savings, investment, and growth.

A. Equity

If it could and would be levied at a uniform rate on all consumption, a value added tax would be regressive; that is, the tax would take a smaller fraction of income as income rises.[46] Exemptions that are necessary for administrative reasons (primarily housing) would probably not greatly affect that conclusion. But exemption of food and medical care would reduce regressivity substantially, and differential rates applied to luxuries could, if European experience is any guide, turn the tax progressive. Differential rates, however, have such adverse effects on administrative feasibility and neutrality that they are a poor way of preventing regressivity. Any VAT that has acceptable administrative features would probably be regressive, in and of itself. This regressivity could, however, be reduced or eliminated by combining the VAT with a system of (or increases in) transfers to low-income households.[47]

Substituting a VAT for part of the payroll tax would probably have little net effect on the distribution of tax burdens between income classes.[48] It would, however, shift some of the tax burden from workers to nonworkers, that is, from the nonaged to the aged, from labor to capital, and from workers to recipients of transfer income. These horizontal shifts may, of course, be every bit as important from a policy point of view as would be vertical shifts.

The personal income tax is, on average, progressive. Thus, substituting revenues from a VAT for part of the personal income tax would clearly be regressive. For that matter, so would be relying on it rather than a graduated-rate personal consumption tax. This regressivity could, however, be reduced or even eliminated at the bottom of the income scale if a refundable credit were allowed low-income families. Finally, if the corporate income tax is borne by capital, reducing it further and replacing lost revenues with a VAT would substantially lessen the progressivity of the tax system. If the corporate tax is borne by workers or consumers, substituting a VAT for part of it would have little net impact on the incidence of taxes, by income class.

B. Neutrality

Taken by themselves, the payroll taxes are relatively neutral; the primary distorting effects are probably on the labor-leisure choice.[49] Much the same would be true of a VAT levied at uniform rates. A VAT levied at differential rates would probably be substantially more distortionary than the payroll taxes.[50]

The personal income tax, while relatively neutral, is probably less neutral than a uniform VAT. The same is probably true of a personal consumption tax, once one allows for tax expenditures. Comparison of the neutrality of the personal income or consumption tax with a differential rate VAT on a priori grounds is difficult.

The corporate income tax is notorious for the many distortions it produces: corporate versus noncorporate products; capital versus labor-intensive production; debt versus equity finance; saving versus consumption. Given this, replacing part of the corporate tax with a uniform VAT would almost certainly increase neutrality, and substituting even a VAT characterized by modest differentiation would probably do so.

C. Growth

The VAT, being a tax on consumption, is relatively neutral toward the saving-consumption choice. So, for that matter, are the payroll taxes and a personal consumption tax.[51] By comparison, the personal income tax and corporate income tax penalize saving. Substituting a VAT for part of either of the income taxes would therefore have a salutary effect on saving that would make possible greater investment and a higher rate of economic growth.[52] How much saving would increase as a result of substituting a VAT for part of the income taxes is difficult to predict because it depends crucially on the elasticity of saving with response to the interest rate, a figure about which there is no unanimity among economists.[53] If savings elasticities are near the high end of the range generally agreed to be reasonable, a tax substitution of this type could significantly increase saving.

VII. EFFECTS ON PRICES[54]

Imposition of a VAT is often opposed because of the fear of politicians that the tax will be inflationary. Unfortunately, this term is often misunderstood, and even if it is not, any impact on prices is likely to depend on the context in which the tax is imposed.

First, it can be expected that imposition of a VAT, unmatched by a reduction in other taxes and accompanied by accommodative monetary policy, will increase prices by roughly the average rate of tax.[55] But this will be only a one-time shift in the *level* of prices, not an increase in the *rate* of inflation, unless workers attempt to recoup part of the resultant loss in real income through wage negotiations. If wages are indexed to consumer prices, or otherwise increase to reflect the VAT, there may be subsequent rounds of higher rates of inflation before the inflation rate settles back to what it would otherwise have been.

According to this reasoning, substitution of a VAT for another general sales tax should have little effect on the average level or rate of increase of prices. Any effect would come about through such influences as asymmetrical movements in relative prices resulting from the change in tax policy—that is, if prices did not fall on average to reflect lower taxes by as much as other prices rose to reflect higher taxes.[56]

Finally, if the VAT were substituted for one of the direct taxes, the result would depend on whether the reduction in the direct tax would otherwise cause prices to fall (i.e., whether the tax is shifted to consumers and is "unshifted" when removed). If the tax is unshifted, the result would resemble that for replacing an equal-yield indirect tax, meaning little effect on prices; if not, the VAT should be reflected in higher prices. The VAT would be more likely than a personal consumption tax to raise prices.

Given the variety of circumstances in which the VAT has been imposed it is difficult to summarize experience in this area satisfactorily. Yet a study done at the International Monetary Fund indicates that in twenty-one of thirty-one countries introduction of the VAT resulted in no major impact on prices. In five more countries there was a one-time shift in the consumer price index (CPI) but no important effect on its rate of increase. In only one country (Norway) was there an acceleration of the rate of increase in the CPI that could not be associated with expansionary wage and credit policies.[57] In short, this experience appears to bear out the theoretical expectations. Evidence reported at the Brookings conference is broadly consistent with these findings, but it does seem to suggest a wage-price spiral.[58]

VIII. INTERNATIONAL ISSUES

The claim that U.S. employment of the value added tax would improve the nation's balance of payments can be appraised at several levels.[59] The crudest version of this argument is that imposition of the VAT would, in and of itself, improve our competitive position because the tax is rebated on exports and imposed on imports. (These are often called border tax adjustments.) As noted in the introduction, this argument is so ridiculous that it deserves little comment. The analogy is presumably to export subsidies and import duties, fiscal measures that would improve our competitive position if exchange rates were fixed, but unlike import duties, the VAT is levied on consumption from domestic production, as well as on imports. Similarly, unlike export subsidies, the rebate that occurs at export is to allow U.S. production to enter world markets free of the tax on domestic production, not to subsidize it. In other words, the VAT is no more likely to stimulate exports and reduce imports than is a retail sales tax.

A more sophisticated argument is that the VAT would have positive international effects if it were substituted for an existing tax. This argument could be valid in a world of fixed exchange rates if, for example, the corporate income tax were shifted forward to consumers in the form of higher prices and were thus just a complicated form of sales tax. In such a case the two taxes might have generally similar effects domestically, but only the VAT would provide border tax adjustments. This argument suffers on at least two grounds. First, economists disagree on the incidence of the corporation income tax, but most probably do not think that it is shifted forward through higher prices.[60] If the tax is borne by shareholders, or by workers, as Arnold Harberger has suggested at this conference, replacing it with a VAT would have little effect on the international competitiveness of American industry or on the balance of trade.[61] There is a more fundamental objection to this entire line of reasoning, however. Exchange rates have not been fixed since the breakdown of the Bretton Woods agreement in 1971. In a world of flexible exchange rates it makes little sense to speak of tax effects on the balance of payments, since any such effects would presumably be reflected in exchange rates, at least in the intermediate to long run.[62]

Perhaps the most persuasive theoretical argument for an effect on international competitiveness is one that is seldom made. Substitution of a VAT for the corporate income tax would improve the after-tax return from domestic investment.[63] This could encourage American firms to invest at home rather than abroad and might also encourage capital inflow from foreign investors. While theoretically attractive, this argument has lost some of its practical relevance.[64] The Economic Recovery Tax Act of 1981 (ERTA), as modified by the Tax Equity and Fiscal Responsibility Act of 1982 (TEFRA), has greatly reduced corporate income tax on income derived from new investment in depreciable assets.[65] Much of the corporate income tax is being paid primarily on income from other sources, including that from investments in depreciable assets made before 1981. This being the case, replacing the corporate tax with a VAT would have less effect on the expected profitability of future American investment than it would have had before ERTA.[66]

In summary, then, there appears to be little reason to expect much improvement in the international economic position of the United States from adoption of the VAT. At their worst, arguments that there would be substantial improvement are simply fallacious. At best, they are based on incidence assumptions that are unlikely to be valid, relevant only in a world of fixed exchange rates, or less applicable in the world of ERTA and TEFRA.

IX. VAT AND THE GROWTH OF GOVERNMENT

Both liberals and conservatives face interesting dilemmas in deciding whether or not they should favor an American VAT. A key feature of the VAT that has not been captured adequately by the discussion to this point is the fact that its imposition would put a large new source of revenue at the disposal of the federal government. Because the base of a VAT would be large, even with fairly liberal exemptions, enormous amounts of additional revenue could be raised with relatively small increases in rates. If foreign experience is any guide, introduction of a VAT would facilitate growth in the relative size of the federal government, whether the VAT was initially introduced to raise additional revenue or only as a substitute for existing taxes.[67]

Thus, conservatives must weigh the advantages a VAT might have in reducing projected deficits, marginal tax rates, and various distortions, including penalties to saving, against the prospect that it would facilitate the growth of government. Liberals must balance the regressivity of the VAT against the fact that it could be used to finance programs they support.

X. STATE PREEMPTION

Much has been said about the fact that the federal government would be "poaching" on the fiscal preserve of state (and some local) governments if it were to levy a value added tax, because forty-six states and the District of Columbia already occupy the sales tax field. There is much truth to the general principle that the federal government, which has the greatest facility to tax *any* base, should be cautious about preempting revenue sources that are particularly suited to use by the states.[68] There is, however, a potential advantage from federal entry into the sales tax field that is commonly overlooked.

Although most states tax retail sales, they do not tax a base that is defined consistently, and many do not provide adequate allowance for tax-free purchases by business. In addition, states have difficulty in collecting their taxes on mail-order sales from outside the state. Adoption of a federal sales tax would create the possibility of bringing more rationality to this field, through a commonly defined base and through universal coverage of consumption expenditures by residents of a given state, whether made from in-state suppliers or out-of-state firms.[69]

The federal government of West Germany shares revenues from its VAT with the German *Laender* (states). The same could be done here. In Germany the federal/state split of revenues is a continuing source of friction. Similar controversy could be avoided in this country by allowing the states to piggyback a state tax on the federal sales tax rather than simply to share revenues from the state tax. This approach allows the states to levy higher or lower rates of tax on the commonly-defined base, rather than forcing them into the straight-jacket of fixed rates or revenue sharing based on uniform shares. Note, however, that piggybacking a federal value added tax is not particularly easy.[70] By comparison, experience with local supplements to state taxes has demonstrated that piggybacking a federal retail sales tax would be quite feasible.

This discussion of the state preemption issue concludes that (1) the disadvantages of federal preemption must be weighed against the advantages of piggybacking a federal levy could bring and (2) piggybacking is easier if the federal sales tax is a retail sales tax, rather than a VAT.

XI. TRANSITIONAL PROBLEMS

When the European countries switched from turnover taxes to the VAT, there was a severe problem of equity and neutrality toward investment made before the switch. If no transitional measures had been taken, taxpayers would have received no credit for turnover taxes incurred before the switch, but they would have received credit for VAT paid after the switch. Besides being unfair, this difference in tax treatment would have encouraged firms to delay investment expenditures until after the switch. The problem could have been handled by allowing some credit against VAT for turnover taxes paid on investment goods, but only at the cost of substantial revenue loss. Instead, some countries levied a special tax on investment for a period following imposition of the VAT.[71]

Since the United States would not be replacing another sales tax, there appear to be few transitional problems of this type. As long as the chain of credits was not broken, all sales at retail occurring after the switch would bear exactly the statutory rate of tax, regardless of when value added occurred.[72] There would, therefore, be no incentive to alter the timing of economic activity other than retail sales— that is, there would be no intertemporal substitution effects on imports, exports, or investment.[73] There would, however, be an incentive for consumers to advance purchases of consumer durables in order to avoid the tax. The same problem would occur, of course, with imposition of a retail sales tax.

That there would be no transitional problems of the kind encountered in Europe does not mean that the tax could be imposed quickly, without substantial preparation. An entirely new administrative apparatus would be required, and taxpayers would need to be trained to collect the tax. Moreover, countless minute decisions would need to be taken before the tax could be imposed, in order to avoid confusion, revenue loss, and even litigation.

XII. CONCLUDING REMARKS

In appraising the desirability of an American VAT, several features of the tax should be kept in mind. It would be regressive, unless levied at distortionary and administratively complicated differential rates or accompanied by some sort of refundable tax credit or transfer scheme. The payroll taxes are also regressive, but the income taxes are progressive. A VAT would be more nearly neutral than the present income taxes, if levied at a uniform rate (and perhaps even if levied at differential rates), but probably not more neutral than the payroll taxes. It would be more favorable to saving, investment, and economic growth than the income taxes but probably similar to the payroll taxes in this respect. The VAT would probably be reflected in higher prices but not necessarily in a higher rate of inflation. In and of itself, the VAT would have little effect on international competitiveness and the balance of payments, and substituting it for any of the other taxes would probably also have little effect. Finally, and perhaps most important of all, the VAT would provide the federal government with a new source of revenue that could easily grow to equal the personal income tax in yield. In virtually no country have initial VAT rates not risen over time.

Whether the United States should have a national sales tax depends in large part on one's view of equity, efficiency, growth, and the role of government. Nor do all the arguments conveniently run in the same direction. For example, many who would favor the implications for neutrality and economic growth and who would not object to the regressivity of the tax might be uneasy about opening up this large pot of untapped federal revenue. Conversely, many who would prefer to rely more heavily on less regressive taxes might, nonetheles, favor a VAT if the alternative were fewer public services. Finally, I would conclude by noting that given American familiarity with retail sales taxes, there is little reason that *if* a national sales tax is to be levied at modest rates, it should be a VAT, rather than a retail sales tax.

APPENDIX
MECHANICS OF THE VAT

Table 9-2 illustrates the mechanics of the VAT, its basic similarity to a retail sales tax, and its superiority over the gross turnover taxes used in Europe before the switch to VAT. Suppose there are three stages in the production-distribution process: manufacturing, wholesaling, and retailing. For now, assume that there is a simple unidirectional passage of goods through this process on the way to consumers who buy only from retailers.

The first three lines of the table show that value added at a given stage is the difference between sales and purchased inputs (capital and intermediate goods).[74] However, the tax is not actually implemented by applying the tax rate to value added calculated in this way, as line 4 might suggest. Rather, the credit or invoice method illustrated in lines 5 through 7 is commonly employed. Gross liability (line 5) is calcualted by applying the tax rate to sales. The firm is then allowed a credit for sales paid on purchases (line 6) as documented by invoices, producing the net liability shown in line 7. In

Table 9-2. Three-Stage Example of 10 Percent Value Added Tax.

	Stage of Production			
	Manufacturing	Wholesale	Retail	Total
	Calculation of Value Added			
1. Sales	$300	$700	$1,000	$2,000
2. Purchased inputs	—	300	700	1,000
3. Value added (line 1 minus line 2)	300	400	300	1,000
4. Tax on value added (10% of line 3)	30	40	30	100
	Calculation of Tax Liability			
5. Gross tax liability on sales (10% of line 1)	30	70	100	200
6. Credit for taxes on purchases	—	30	70	100
7. Net tax liability (line 5 minus line 6)	30	40	30	100
	Illustration of Alternative Sales Taxes			
8. Retail sales tax (10% of retail sales)	0	0	100	100
9. Gross receipts tax (5% of line 1)	15	35	50	100

the simple case in the example, the liability calculated in this way is exactly the same as in line 4. This credit method is widely believed to improve compliance and facilitate administration, because of the possibility of cross-checking credits claimed for taxes paid against actual payments, but this feature is easily overrated.[75]

Line 8 indicates that the same revenue could have been collected through a retail sales tax levied at the same rate. Thus, the consumption-based VAT is best seen as merely an alternative means of collecting this more familiar tax.

Line 9 shows that in the present example the same revenue could also have been raised by imposing a tax of 5 percent on gross receipts (turnover), but one should not conclude that it is a matter of indifference whether the turnover tax is used or the VAT or retail sales tax is levied. To see this, suppose that the manufacturer in the example integrated forward (or the retailer integrated backwards). In that case only $50 of taxes would be collected. Moreover, it is easily seen that the aggregate tax burden depends on the pattern in which value added occurs, as well as on the degree of vertical integration. By comparison, total revenues under both the VAT and the retail sales tax are totally insensitive to these differences. This helps to explain the European switch from turnover taxes to VAT.

An additional defect of the turnover tax is the difficulty of making border tax adjustments. Note that no matter at what stage imports occur (unless consumers import directly and avoid paying tax), total tax is $100 under either the VAT or the retail sales tax. Similarly, if either the manufacturer or the wholesaler exports, goods enter world markets free of tax, under either of these approaches. (See also the discussion of zero rating below.) By comparison, exact border tax adjustments (compensating import taxes and export rebates) cannot be made under the gross receipts tax because the tax that has been paid by the time a given stage is reached depends on the extent of vertical integration and the pattern of value added.

An important administrative feature of the VAT is the difference between exemption and zero rating. Though these two terms may sound synonymous, they have quite different effects. A firm selling zero-rated items is a registered taxpayer ("in the system") and can therefore receive credits for taxes paid on purchases. Thus, its sales really occur free of tax. By comparison, a firm selling only exempt items is not registered. As a result, it obtains no credit for taxes paid on inputs. This means that though exemption involves less administrative effort and compliance costs than zero rating, it is also less favorable. This is easily seen in two examples. In the top panel of Table 9-3 exempt sales are made at retail; such sales contain a tax

Table 9-3. Illustration of Exemption and Zero-Rating of Retailer under Credit-Method Value Added Tax.

	Stage of Production			
	Manufacturing	*Wholesale*	*Retail*	*Total*
Exemption of Retailer				
1. Gross tax liability	30	70	0	100
2. Credit	0	30	0	30
3. Net tax liability	30	40	0	70
Zero Rating of Retailer				
4. Gross tax liability	30	70	0	100
5. Credit	0	30	70	100
6. Net tax liability	30	40	-70	0

Source: Based on Table 9-2.

Table 9-4. Illustration of Exemption and Zero-Rating of Wholesaler under Credit-Method Value Added Tax.

	Stage of Production			
	Manufacturing	*Wholesale*	*Retail*	*Total*
Exemption of Wholesaler				
1. Gross tax liability	30	0	100	130
2. Credit	—	0	0	0
3. Net tax liability	30	0	100	130
Zero Rating of Wholesaler				
4. Gross tax liability	30	0	100	130
5. Credit	0	30	0	30
6. Net tax liability	30	-30	100	100

Note: Based on Table 9-2.

component from previous stages that were taxed. This can be contrasted with zero rating of the final stage. As shown in the bottom panel of Table 9-3, the sales to consumers are totally free of tax. Export sales are virtually always zero rated.

Even worse is the situation when exemption occurs before the last stage, as in the top panel of Table 9-4. Because no credit can be taken for taxes paid before the exempt stage, the total tax load is actually increased by exemption. By comparison, zero rating of the middle stage has no effect on ultimate liability, as shown in the bottom panel of Table 9-4. Not surprisingly, many observers believe that zero rating is far preferable to exemption.[76]

NOTES TO CHAPTER 9

1. Report of the Fiscal and Financial Committee (1963).
2. Committee for Economic Development (1966).
3. For a summary and appraisal of the arguments for and against a value added tax, see McLure (1972) or (1973a). The early American debate on the VAT is surveyed in McLure (1973b).
4. This was just after the *Serrano v. Priest* decision had cast a pall of uncertainty over the legal feasibility of continuing to rely so heavily on the local property tax to finance public education.
5. Report of the President's Task Force on Business Taxation (1970: 60). Two of the fifteen-member task force, Dan Throop Smith and Norman Ture, dissented, arguing that the VAT should be introduced at once.
6. Mieszkowski (1972) had only recently published his important article arguing that, on average, the property tax is borne by owners of capital and is not shifted to consumers.
7. See *Tax Restructuring Act of 1979: Hearings* (1979). For a summary and examination of the Ullman proposal, see McLure (1980a).
8. McLure (1981) examines the possibility of employing the VAT to finance social security.
9. Experience with the VAT in selected European countries is discussed in Carlson (1980) and in Aaron (1981). For an early appraisal of experience with the VAT in developing countries see Lent et al. (1973). More recent information on foreign systems of VAT is contained in Price Waterhouse (1979).
10. Standard treatments of the administration and economic effects of the VAT include Shoup (1969a: ch. 9); Smith et al., (1973); McLure (1972), (1973a), (1980a), and (1981); and Prest (1980). Given the nature of the present discussion, many assertions are made in the text without substantial elaboration. Explanations are found in the footnotes or in references cited there.
11. For a more detailed statement of this view, see section VIII below and McLure (1973a). Export prices may incorporate minor amounts of retail sales tax, as noted, for example, in Shoup (1973).
12. Strictly speaking this assertion is accurate only if the tax is imposed on the *consumption* basis, under the *destination* principle. This is the approach used in Europe and the only one likely to receive serious consideration in the United States.
13. Because of differences in the ways the two taxes are administered, they can occasionally have somewhat different economic effects. In particular, it is easier to free capital goods and exports of tax. See also Shoup (1969b). Moreover, it is often argued that a VAT can be administered effectively at higher rates that can a retail tax.
14. See also note 22 below.
15. Border tax adjustments are the compensating import taxes and export rebates required to place indirect taxation on a destination basis. See also section VIII. The difficulty of accurate border tax adjustments is explained a bit more fully in the appendix. For further detail, see McLure (1972).

16. For a textbook discussion of these principles, see Musgrave and Musgrave (1980: ch. 11). One strand of the theory of optimal taxation may suggest that the optimal degree of progressivity can be determined scientifically; but behind any such seemingly exact determination lies a description of the social utility of income at various levels of income—something no economist knows.

17. Taxes related precisely to benefits received would not distort choices, just as prices determined in fully competitive markets do not. Three other goals are sometimes included in lists of objectives of taxation: macroeconomic stability (high employment and price stability), a high rate of economic growth, and external stability (international competitiveness and the balance of payments). The second and third of these are discussed below; the first was set aside in section III above.

18. I make this assertion with some trepidation, given that one of my discussants is co-author of an important theoretical article (Aaron and McGuire 1970) arguing that a public good that is equally available to all is of greater value, the higher one's private consumption.

19. This is not the place for an extended discussion of the conditions under which a uniform consumption tax is neutral or how rates must be differentiated for welfare maximization if those conditions are not met. See, for example, King (1980) on taxation and the saving-consumption choice and, more generally, Atkinson and Stiglitz (1980: lectures 12 and 14).

20. This is not quite true, since there is no unanimity about the incidence of some taxes, as noted in the introduction.

21. Again, this is not entirely accurate, since economists disagree on the magnitude of distortions caused by various taxes.

22. But taking the spending increase as given may be granting too much, for as Henry Aaron (1982: 5) has written, "The most important question about a value added tax concerns what its revenues are used for."

23. The latest of these, ACIR (1982) summarizes important results of previous surveys.

24. The other 33 percent voted for (or against) the local property tax. These figures have been adjusted to reflect that 9 percent of respondents offered no opinion. See ACIR (1982: 4). Some of these differences may reflect differences in revenue yields: $250 billion for the federal personal income tax in fiscal 1980 and $80 billion for state and local sales taxes. Unfortunately, this source does not indicate whether attitudes were being expressed on only the individual income tax, or on the corporate tax as well.

25. Though the first ACIR study was conducted in 1972, the figures for that year are not used in these comparisons because they differ markedly from those for the years immediately following.

26. ACIR (1982: 13). The lowest margin by which the income tax was voted worst was 1.6 to 1, by those not married. The highest margin was 4.4 to 1, by those with annual household income above $35,000.

27. ACIR (1982: 45). 44 percent favored no federal action, and 10 percent expressed no opinion.

28. ACIR (1982: 48). 40 percent favored reducing special treatment of capital gains and various itemized deductions, and 16 percent did not express an opinion.

29. ACIR (1982: 36).

30. It is common to note that, in principle, a VAT could be based on national income or even gross national product rather than on consumption. It does not seem worthwhile to examine the income-based VAT for the following reasons: (1) It involves greater costs of compliance and administration because it requires accounting for depreciation of capital assets, whereas under a consumption-based tax all purchases of firms, including those of capital goods, are expensed; (2) it is less favorable to capital formation than a consumption-based VAT; and (3) virtually every other country with a VAT uses the consumption base. The GNP-based tax is even worse. Since it does not allow even depreciation allowances for capital goods, important questions of definition (repair versus investment) occur, and saving and investment are affected even more adversely than under the income-based tax. For a detailed explanation of the difference in the income and consumption bases, see McLure (1972).

31. The problem in agriculture can go even beyond this. For administrative and political reasons some countries exempt agriculture but also exempt selected agricultural inputs. This might not be necessary on administrative grounds in the United States.

32. An important element (17.4 percent) of expenditures on "food and tobacco" is actually devoted to alcoholic beverages and tobacco products. Since these items are presently subject to excise taxes, it is difficult to know how to treat them in the present context.

33. Aaron (1981: 10).

34. If housing construction were zero rated, this would be the correct estimate. If it were exempt, the tax base would be understated. See the appendix for the important distinction between these terms.

35. While the taxation of health care purchased directly by individuals would almost certainly be regressive, so much of expenditures of this type are covered by insurance that the incidence of the tax is more difficult to appraise. Finally, much health care for low-income families is provided or financed publicly.

36. As financial institutions become more aggressive in competing with money market institutions for the funds of investors, a tendency toward charging for services may increase.

37. On the other hand, such institutions may pay tax on purchased inputs that they cannot recoup via tax credits. See also the appendix. The same may be true of tax-exempt nonprofit institutions.

38. These estimates are intended to provide only rough guesses of the potential tax base under liberal and narrow definitions of the tax base. Because of the difficulty of knowing how controversies over the treatment of various items would be resolved, they are not predictions of what the base would actually be. Nor has any effort been made to take account of VAT paid at intermediate stages on exempt consumption, including that by governments and by tax-exempt organizations.

39. Note that a tax on leisure is equivalent to a subsidy on labor. Thus (in a world with no saving), a tax on leisure would result in an expenditure on the subsidy to labor exactly equal to the yield of a tax levied at the same rate on consumption from labor income!

40. Aaron (1981: 6) has written, "Even in theory, . . . a case can be made for the differentiation of tax rates. . . . In practice, the required differentiation would be hard to carry out, and the view persists that the potential neutrality (in other words, uniformity) of the value added tax is one of its chief advantages."

41. Aaron (1981: 7) refers to other examples of hair-splitting noted in the papers presented at the recent Brookings conference on the VAT.

42. Writing about German experience, Pohmer (1981: 99) says, "The most troublesome problems involve the need to distinguish between deductible and non-deductible input taxes when some outputs are taxable and some are exempt."

43. Aaron (1981: 8).

44. Aaron (1981: 9). For an even stronger statement to this effect based on experience in the Netherlands, see Cnossen (1982).

45. Aaron (1982: 4-5).

46. Among early efforts to estimate the distributional impact of a VAT and its substitution for other taxes are McLure (1973a), Schultze et al. (1972), and Pechman (1977). None of these estimates or the statements about incidence in the text take account of the view expressed in Browning (1978) and Browning and Johnson (1979) that the VAT is progressive since it would be reflected in increased transfer payments, which are received primarily by low-income families. Economic policy under the Reagan Administration casts doubt on the basic assumption of the Browning analysis that transfers are automatically indexed for tax increases.

47. See Schultze et al. (1972). Provision of transfers to offset the regressivity of VAT would, of course, be made more difficult if income maintenance were shifted from the federal government to the state and localities, as under the Reagan Administration's "new federalism."

48. See, for example, Pechman (1977: 207).

49. The often heard argument that payroll taxes discriminate against labor-intensive activities is theoretically invalid for taxes with universal coverage, unless labor supply responds significantly to price; if it does not, the tax is simply borne by labor. Once benefits (of retirement, disability insurance, etc.) are taken into account, there may be little net effect on the labor-leisure choice. For purpose of the present discussion benefits are held constant.

50. The problem is not merely that differential rates levied on retail sales to final consumers would distort consumer choices; it goes deeper than that. Suppose that a given commodity (food, for example) can be consumed directly, in which case it is exempt, or can be used as an input to production for taxed consumption (restaurant meals). Suppose that food represents 50 percent of the value of restaurant meals and the tax rate applied to such meals is 10 percent. The effective rate of tax on value added in restaurant activity is 20 percent! Thus the potential distortion is far greater than nominal tax rates suggest. See also Hemming and Kay (1981).

51. The social security system has often been argued to reduce national saving, most notably by Martin Feldstein. But those arguments pertain to the benefit side of social security. Considered by themselves, the payroll taxes used to finance social security are basically neutral in this regard.

52. Since this paper is not the place to enter into a consideration of the efficacy of macroeconomic policy, this discussion is based on the assumption that increased saving would result in increased investment.

53. For a survey of the empirical evidence in this field, most notably the debate between Michael Boskin (1978) and Phillip Howrey and Saul Hymans (1978), see McLure (1980c).

54. See also Tait (1980).

55. Thus, if a 15 percent tax is imposed on two-thirds of consumption, consumer prices should rise, on average, by roughly 10 percent. Whether this is reflected exactly in the consumer price index (CPI) depends on the construction of the index and is beyond the scope of the present discussion.

56. This might occur, for example, if wages were sticky downward and monetary policy were accommodative. It is more difficult to know what to make of arguments that prices rise because of "uncertainty" or businessmen taking the opportunity to grab greater profits through higher prices.

57. Tait (1980).

58. Aaron (1981: 12-13). The conclusion that imposition of VAT (usually in the context of an equal-yield substitution) did not raise prices is consistent with subsequent tax increases leading to higher prices and even to a wage-price spiral.

59. Much of this discussion repeats McLure (1972 and 1973a).

60. Whereas the incidence of the corporation income tax was hotly debated ten to twenty years ago, the topic seems largely to have disappeared from the professional literature in economics. Given the difficulty of determining empirically the incidence of the tax, economists seem to have retreated to using theoretical analysis to argue that the tax is not likely to be shifted forward through administered prices. On the other hand, following Harberger (1962), they are likely to argue that the tax is borne by all capital, rather than only by shareholders. Harberger (this volume) notes that in a world in which both goods and capital are highly mobile between countries, the tax is likely to be borne by workers and landowners. Harberger (1973) had previously made this argument for small, open developing countries. For a similar argument, in a somewhat different context, see McLure (1979).

61. The Harberger analysis does, however, suggest that substituting a VAT for the corporate income tax would induce movements in the relative prices of corporate and noncorporate output. In a world of fixed exchange rates the switch to a VAT could therefore produce a positive competitive effect, since so many of traded goods are produced in the corporate sector. But, as noted in the text, exchange rates are no longer fixed.

62. See also McLure (1968).

63. In addition, for some firms it would reduce the extent to which credit could be taken against U.S. taxes for taxes paid abroad, thereby also decreasing the attraction of foreign investment.

64. The same argument (except for the part in the previous note) could be made for replacing part of the local property tax.

65. For estimates of effective tax rates on income from new investments, see U.S. Treasury Department (1982).

66. By the same token, there is little reason to expect the remaining tax to have much effect on relative prices, as in the Harberger (1962) analysis.

67. Cnossen (1981:59) writes, "One motive for the introduction of the value added tax in the United States is a desire to use some or all of the proceeds to reduce other taxes. If Dutch experience is any guide, such shifts, however, desirable they may be in theory, would not occur." Aaron (1981:16) offers this similar appraisal, "While the value added tax might be used to reduce other taxes and as part of a program of fiscal retrenchment, . . . the United States would be blazing a trail of fiscal forbearance not traversed by any of the countries covered in this book."

68. This assignment principle has not deterred the states from taxing corporate income, something most economists who have considered the issue would probably agree they should not do. For an elaboration of this argument, see McLure (1982).

69. Of course, there is always the risk that a federally imposed base would make less sense than many of the present state bases.

70. This is explained further in McLure (1980b). For a contrary view, see Cnossen (1982).

71. Germany and the Netherlands followed this route; on the other hand, Italy allowed temporary deduction of investment from the base of the turnover tax. See Cnossen (1981), Pedone (1981), and Pohmer (1981).

72. Note that this is a feature of the credit method of administering the tax (explained in the appendix). Under either the subtraction or addition methods of implementing the tax, value added after imposition of the tax would be taxed, whereas that occurring earlier would not be. See McLure (1972) for an explanation of the differences in the results of using these three approaches.

73. Aaron (1981:9) notes, however, that if the VAT replaced part of the corporate income tax there might be some incentive to make investments before the switch, when they would result in more tax saving.

74. In this example we make no distinction between purchases of intermediate goods and capital goods, as is entirely appropriate for a consumption-based VAT. See McLure (1972) for illustrations of the treatment of capital goods under an income-based VAT, as well as the mechanics of implementing a VAT through the addition and subtraction methods.

75. For a similar assessment, see Aaron (1981: 9). For more detail, see Cnossen (1981).

76. For example, Cnossen (1981:58) writes, "The neutrality of the tax would be improved . . . if exemptions were replaced by zero rating."

BIBLIOGRAPHY

Aaron, Henry, ed. *The Value Added Tax: Lessons from Europe*. Washington, D.C.: The Brookings Institution, 1981.

Aaron, Henry. "The Value Added Tax: Some Lessons and Issues." *The Brookings Review* 1 (Fall 1982): 4-5.

Aaron, Henry J., and McGuire, Martin C. "Public Goods and Income Distribution." *Econometrica* 38 (April 1970): 907-20.

Advisory Commission on Intergovernmental Relations (ACIR). *Changing Public Attitudes on Governments and Taxes*. Washington, D.C.: ACIR, 1982.

Arthur Andersen & Co. *VAT in Other Countries*. Chicago: 1980.

Atkinson, Anthony B., and Stiglitz, Joseph E. *Lectures on Public Economics*. New York: McGraw-Hill, 1980.

Boskin, Michael J. "Taxation, Saving, and the Rate of Interest." *Journal of Political Economy* 86, no. 2 (April 1978, part 2): S3-S27.

Browning, Edgar K. "The Burden of Taxation." *Journal of Political Economy* 86 (August 1978): 649-71.

Browning, Edgar K., and Johnson, William R. *The Distribution of the Tax Burden*. Washington, D.C.: American Enterprise Institute, 1979.

Carlson, George N. *Value-Added Tax: European Experience and Lessons for the United States*. Washington: U.S. Government Printing Office, 1980.

Cnossen, Sijbren. "The Netherlands." In Henry J. Aaron, ed., *The Value Added Tax: Lessons from Europe*, pp. 43-59. Washington: The Brookings Institution, 1981.

_____. "What Rate Structure for a Value-Added Tax?" *National Tax Journal* 35, no. 2 (June 1982): 205-14.

_____. "Harmonization of Indirect Taxes in the EEC." In Charles E. McLure, Jr., ed., *Tax Assignment in Federal Countries*. Canberra, Australia: Centre for Research on Federal Financial Relations, forthcoming.

Committee for Economic Development. *A Better Balance in Federal Taxes on Business*. New York: CED, 1966.

Due, John F. "The Case for the Use of the Retail Form of Sales Tax in Preference to the Value-Added Tax." In Richard A. Musgrave, ed., *Broad-Based Taxes: New Options and Sources*, pp. 205-14. Baltimore: Johns Hopkins Press for the Committee for Economic Development, 1973.

Harberger, Arnold C. "The Incidence of the Corporation Income Tax." *Journal of Political Economy* 70 (June 1962): 215-40.

_____. "The Panamanian Income Tax System—A Heterodox View." University of Chicago, 1970. Mimeo.

_____. "The State of the Corporation Income Tax." (This volume.)

Hemming, Richard, and John A. Kay. "The United Kingdom." In Henry J. Aaron, ed., *The Value Added Tax: Lessons from Europe*, pp. 75-89. Washington, D.C.: The Brookings Institution, 1981.

Hoefs, Richard A. "The European Experience with Value-Added Tax." Statement on the Tax Restructuring Act of 1979 before the Committee on Ways and Means of the U.S. House of Representatives, 96th Cong., 1st Sess., November 15, 1979. (Washington: U.S. Government Printing Office, 1980), pp. 140-45.

Howrey, E. Phillip, and Hymans, Saul H. "The Measurement and Determination of Loanable-Funds Saving." *Brookings Papers on Economic Activity* 3 (1978): 655-85.

King, Mervyn. "Savings and Taxation." In G.A. Hughes and G.M. Heal, eds., *Public Policy and the Tax System*, pp. 1-35. London: George Allen and Unwin, 1980.

Lent, George E.; Milka Casanegra; and Michele Guerard. "The Value-Added Tax in Developing Countries." *International Monetary Fund Staff Papers* (July 1973): 318-78.

McGuire, Martin C., and Henry Aaron. "Efficiency and Equity in the Optimal Supply of a Public Good." *Review of Economics and Statistics* 51 (1969): 31-39.

McLure, Charles E., Jr. "Taxes and the Balance of Payments: Another Alternative Analysis." *National Tax Journal* 21, no. 1 (March 1968): 57-69.

_____. "The Tax on Value Added: Pros and Cons." In Charles E. McLure, Jr. and Norman B. Ture, *Value Added Tax: Two Views*, pp. 1-68. Washington: American Enterprise Institute, 1972.

_____. "Economic Effects of Taxing Value Added." In Richard A. Musgrave, ed., *Broad Based Taxes: New Options and Sources*, pp. 155-204. Baltimore: Johns Hopkins Press for the Committee for Economic Development, 1973.

_____. "A Federal Tax on Value Added: U.S. View." In Proceedings of the 66th Annual Conference of the National Tax Association, pp. 96-103. Toronto: National Tax Association-Tax Institute of America, 1973.

_____. "The Relevance of the New View of the Incidence of the Property Tax in Developing Countries." In Roy Bahl, ed., *The Taxation of Urban Property in Less Developed Countries*, pp. 51-76. Madison: University of Wisconsin Press, 1979.

_____. "The Tax Restructuring Act of 1979: Time for an American VAT?" *Public Policy* 28, no. 3 (Summer 1980a): 301-22.

_____. "State-Federal Relations in the Taxation of the Value Added." *The Journal of Corporation Law* 6, no. 1 (Fall 1980b): 127-39.

_____. "Taxes, Saving, and Welfare: Theory and Evidence." *National Tax Journal* 33, no. 3 (September 1980c): 311-20.

_____. "VAT versus the Payroll Tax." In Felicity Skidmore, ed., *Financing Social Security*, pp. 129-64. Cambridge, Mass.: MIT Press, 1981.

_____. "Assignment of Corporate Income Taxes." *Canadian Tax Journal* 30, no. 6 (November-December 1982): 840-59. Also forthcoming in Charles E. McLure, Jr., ed., *Tax Assignment in Federal Countries*. Canberra, Australia: Centre for Research on Federal Financial Relations.

Mieszkowski, Peter. "The Property Tax: An Excise Tax or a Profits Tax?" *Journal of Public Economics* 1 (April 1972): 73-96.

Musgrave, Richard A., and Peggy B. Musgrave. *Public Finance in Theory and Practice*. New York: McGraw-Hill, 3d ed. 1980.

Pechman, Joseph A. *Federal Tax Policy*. Washington: Brookings Institution, 3d ed. 1977.

Pedone, Antonio. "Italy." In Henry J. Aaron, ed., *The Value Added Tax: Lessons from Europe*, pp. 31-42. Washington: The Brookings Institution, 1981.

Pohmer, Dieter. "Germany." In Henry J. Aaron, ed., *The Value Added Tax: Lessons from Europe*, pp. 91-101. Washington: The Brookings Institution, 1981.

Prest, A.R. *Value Added Taxation: The Experience of the United Kingdom.* Washington, D.C.: American Enterprise Institute, 1980.

Price Waterhouse. *Value Added Tax.* New York, November 1979.

Report of the Fiscal and Financial Committee. *The EEC Reports on Fiscal Harmonization.* Amsterdam: International Bureau of Fiscal Documentation, 1963.

Report of the President's Task Force on Business Taxation. *Business Taxation.* Washington, D.C.: Government Printing Office, September 1970.

Schultze, Charles L.; Edward R. Fried; Alice Rivlin; and Nancy H. Teeters. *Setting National Priorities: The 1973 Budget* Washington, D.C.: The Brookings Institution, 1972.

Shoup, Carl S. *Public Finance.* Chicago: Aldine Publishing Co., 1969a.

_____. "Experience with Value Added Tax in Denmark, and Prospects in Sweden." *Finanzarchiv* 28 (March 1969b): 236-52.

_____. "Factors Bearing on an Assumed Choice Between Federal Retail Sales Tax and a Federal Value-Added Tax." In Richard A. Musgrave, ed., pp. 215-26. *Broad Based Taxes: New Options and Sources.* Baltimore: Johns Hopkins Press for the Committee for Economic Development, 1973.

Smith, Dan Throop; James B. Webber; and Carol M. Cerf. *What You Should Know about the Value Added Tax.* Homewood, Ill.: Dow Jones-Irwin, Inc., 1973.

Tait, Alan A. "Is the Introduction of a Value Added Tax Inflationary?" Washington, D.C.: International Monetary Fund, processed, 1980.

U.S. Congress, House of Representatives Committee on Ways and Means, 96th Congress, 1st Session, *Hearings on the Tax Restructuring Act of 1979* (Washington: U.S. Government Printing Office, 1980).

U.S. Treasury Department, Office of Tax Analysis. "Treasury Interprets Its Effective Tax Rate Tables." *Tax Notes* (December 6, 1982): 779-83.

Discussants:

THE VALUE ADDED TAX: A TRIUMPH OF FORM OVER SUBSTANCE

Henry Aaron

Few writers know as much as Charles McLure does about the Value Added Tax (VAT)—how it works, its virtues and flaws, the history of its adoption abroad, and its tacit dismissal here. If anyone can make a case for the serious consideration of the value added tax, it is someone, like McLure, who understands fully all sides of the question. He presents a remarkably balanced and sophisticated picture of where the debate on the value added tax ought to take place.

In my comments, I shall try to persuade you that the value added tax has engendered more enthusiasm from its supporters than its real economic advantages justify and more denunciation from its critics than its economic shortcomings warrant. In short, I shall argue that from an economic standpoint the intensity of feeling about the economics of the value added tax is a triumph of form over substance. To establish this point, I shall underscore some of the observations that McLure has made, and again quibble a bit with a few relatively minor points, and, finally, argue that the politics of the value added tax is far more interesting and important than the economics.

Among the more important, and frequently unrecognized, points about the value added tax that McLure makes is his assertion that the value added tax cannot be expected to do much for the balance of trade. McLure correctly dismisses the contrary claim, frequently heard in political circles, as without any substance. Under floating exchange rates, no sustained improvement in the balance of trade can be expected. What McLure does not stress sufficiently is that replacement of any tax by the value added tax will help the trade position of some industries and hurt that of others. While U.S. industry as a whole would find its foreign trade position neither better nor worse, industries that would pay more in value added taxes than they pay under our current tax structure would find themselves at a competitive disadvantage relative to the present situation. This fact may explain why some business leaders support the value added tax, but others oppose it.

Second, McLure points out that the possible uniformity of effective rates, once regarded as a strength of the value added tax, may not be a virtue after all. Because any practical tax distorts some important choices that individuals or businesses must make, the analysis of optimal second-best taxes has shown that uniform sales taxes are not in general optimal. Charles McLure understands that there is no reason to think that observed variations in rates, either in actual European practice or as proposed in such draft legislation as former Congressman Al Ullman's, are motivated by concerns for economic efficiency. Rather, their purpose seems to be to make the distributional effects of the value added tax more palatable than those of a uniform tax. While uniform rates are inconsistent with either economic efficiency or distributional goals, Dr. McLure correctly summarizes European experience as showing that variable rates are not worth the administrative pain and suffering they cause. So we are left with the spirit-dampening news that a uniform tax is likely to be inferior in its allocative and distributive effects to a tax with differentiated rates but that the administrative consequences of differentiation are troublesome.

This introduces the third point. In practice, the VAT seems to have had little effect on the distribution of tax burdens or of incomes—or on much of anything else—in those countries that have adopted it. This is the central lesson that European experience seems to teach us. The key word in the preceding sentences is "seems." In Europe, the VAT replaced taxes that had similar distribution, a point stressed frequently at the recent Brookings Institution conference that Dr. McLure generously cites. Actual value added taxes seem to be roughly proportional over most of the income distribution. We cannot be sure, however, that the alternative measures that would have been taken if the value added tax had not been adopted would have had similar effects on the income distribution—and this is the real test of how any tax affects the distribution of income. Would the countries that have relied increasingly on the value added tax have raised other taxes (and, if so, *which* other taxes) or cut government expenditures (and, if so, *which* programs) if they had not imposed the value added tax? Thus, the claims that the value added tax undercuts progressivity or adds to regressivity are virtually impossible to prove or disprove.

In the department of minor quibbles, I have only two. First, Dr. McLure may be a bit low on his estimates of the revenue a value added tax could yield. His Table 9-1 vividly portrays how easy it is for well-intentioned exclusions from the value added tax base to reduce its yield and, incidentally, to destroy the ballyhooed uniformity of rates. But, as Dr. McLure well knows, final sales can be excluded from tax either by exemption or zero rating. If the former method is used, the loss of revenue is much smaller than Table 9-1 suggests. Table 9-1 is correct only if all spared final sales are zero rated, so that they receive a rebate of all prior stage taxes. To the extent that they are simply exempted, the revenue yield would be higher than McLure suggests. European experience also attests that the use of exemptions rather than zero rating would cause some of the VAT to fall on investment or government purchases, rather than entirely on consumption.

Second, while I share many of the misgivings about the corporation income tax that McLure states and that most of the economics profession would endorse, it is important to distinguish flaws inherent in the corporation income tax and those added by legislative ineptitude. Many of the distortions in the corporation income tax arise because, as work by Robert Hall, Don Fullerton, and the Council of Economic Advisers has amply demonstrated, the corporation income tax is a vehicle for subsidy to selected forms of investment at the same time that it heavily taxes others. A corporation income tax on debt-financed investment with fair economic depreciation or with expensing, if deduction of interest is disallowed, is nondistorting. In fact, when pure economic profits are earned, a tax on such profits is an essential element of a minimally distorting tax system. The capricious variation in effective rates caused by ridiculous depreciation rules is to be deplored, but it calls for reform of the corporation income tax and does not imply its repeal. If there is a case for repealing the corporation income tax, it should rest on some fact other than the appalling mess that Congress has made of it.

It is ironic that many who are most skeptical of Congressional capacity to deal rationally with the corporation income tax nonetheless envision the immaculate passage of an unsullied value added tax through the politically lecherous hands of 535 "dirty old men and women." The once strapping corporation income tax stands emaciated and atrophied after amendments to depreciation rules on equipment and many other preferences have made it a subsidy at prevailing rates of inflation, rather than a tax.

The political prospects of the value added tax will not rest on its supposed economic strengths or weaknesses. Rather, they will center on the political questions of what is to be done with the revenue and what other political or economic objectives the value added tax will serve. Recall that the value added tax was adopted in Europe as part of a package deal built around economic integration among countries that in varying degrees relied on that most pilloried impost, the turnover tax, or on other equally unappealing revenue sources. Moreover, it was introduced for the most part in nonfederal governments at a time when the size of the public sector was increasing and when inflation was an economic cold, not pneumonia.

The United States now suffers from inflation, indetectable economic growth, and a widespread suspicion of the public sector. It is composed of states undergoing fiscal travail and groggy from attempts by the Reagan Administration to cut grants of all kinds. Against this background, it would take extraordinary events, far beyond the persuasiveness of arguments concerning efficiency or tax structure that economists customarily make, to cause Congress to introduce a big new tax.

My point is really quite simple: The value added tax is a proven success as a revenue raiser, but there are major political obstacles to its adoption in the United States. The only thing that can overcome those obstacles is a general consensus about the need to raise revenues by a large amount—to finance some major new expenditure program, to close an intolerable deficit (and in this connection, a value added tax has to be obviously better than all expenditure cuts and all other tax increases), or to replace a tax that most segments of the nation have come to regard as intolerable.

None of these conditions is satisfied or in prospect of being satisfied. Proposals for large new expenditures, other than for national defense, seem to be a drug on the market; and no one has argued persuasively that the value added tax is the uniquely right way to pay for refurbishing battle ships or for MX silos. The deficit is a serious problem that needs to be faced, but for every person proposing to use the VAT to close it, there are legions to advocate cuts in domestic spending, cuts in military spending, closing tax loopholes, or other measures. Short of an expensive and popular war that creates both the economic need and political acceptance for a new tax, a precondition most of us would prefer to escape, it is hard to picture how a value added tax could be adopted. In short, the value added tax seems destined to remain among that honored list of ideas good enough never to be wholly forgotten, but not good enough ever to be adopted. The answer to the question in McLure's title, "Has the time come?" is "Certainly not now, and perhaps not ever."

A RETAILER'S PERSPECTIVE ON THE VALUE ADDED TAX

Donald V. Seibert

Introduction

I would like to discuss advantages and disadvantages of the Value Added Tax (VAT) from an overall perspective, as well as from that of a retailer. Retailers are particularly sensitive to a VAT, or any similar tax, that would position us as a tax collector.

While the federal deficit continues to grow, and financing of the social security system remains uncertain, the public attitude toward taxation seems to have remained unchanged. A 1982 study by the Advisory Commission on Intergovernmental Relations, "1982 Changing Public Attitudes on Governments and Taxes," indicates that from May of 1979 to May of 1982 about 36 percent of those polled felt that the worst tax (that is, the least fair) was the federal income tax. In contrast, only 14 percent considered the sales tax the least fair; while 11 percent considered the state income tax least fair. These data reflect the taxpayer's perception that our progressive income tax is unfair.

Since the people who count most, the taxpayers, are not happy with the federal income tax, it is appropriate to explore alternatives such as a value added tax. While I am neutral with respect to a VAT, I am decidedly partisan on one aspect. I do not see the VAT, a similar consumption tax, or other taxes solely as either partial or complete replacements for existing taxes, such as the personal and corporate income taxes. (I am assuming that if introduced today, a VAT would resemble Al Ullman's Tax Restructuring Act of 1980, a consumption VAT similar to that in place throughout the European Common Market.)

Background on the Value Added Tax

From time to time during the last sixty years, and as early as 1921, there have been proposals that the United States adopt a VAT tax system. In 1940 a bill calling for a federal VAT was introduced in the Congress. From 1953 to 1967 Michigan imposed a variation of the VAT and in 1975 adopted a single business tax, which functions somewhat like a VAT. This Michigan single business tax is levied at the corporate level and has been a relatively stable source of revenue. In 1970 a presidential task force on business taxation examined the concept of a VAT in connection with its study of major tax policy issues. The task force concluded that a VAT system should not be substituted in whole or in part for existing federal taxes but that should the need for substantial federal revenues arise, the government should turn to a VAT or some other form of indirect taxation.

As Charles McLure's paper indicates, in certain respects a VAT is similar to a retail sales tax. The rate of tax is fixed and certain products and users are exempt. However, the similarity stops there. Where a retail sales tax applies only to the final sale, a VAT applies to each sale in the commercial process: from the supplier of raw materials to the manufacturer, to the wholesaler, then to the retailer, and ultimately to the consumer. While in theory VAT relates to the increase in value added at each level, in practice it is measured by the increase in the sales price at each level. Ultimately, the full weight of the tax falls on our favorite person, the American consumer.

The Effects of a VAT on Tax Equity

A principal concern is that the main burden of a VAT would fall on those who could least afford to pay it. Since the tax would be based on consumption, lower income groups would be forced to spend an inordinate portion of their income on taxes in buying basic necessities. In answer to this, VAT proponents point out that the regressivity of VAT could be offset by credits or exemptions slanted toward low-income taxpayers. While this latter effort would tend to dilute VAT revenues, it would probably be a political necessity and would add to the administrative costs.

There are other approaches to softening the impact of a VAT on lower income groups. A multirate VAT could be devised, similar to those that other countries have designed. In such systems, instead of a single comprehensive rate, a standard rate applies to the purchase of most goods and services, a steeper rate applies to carefully defined luxury items, and a reduced rate applies to such necessities as health care services, hospital care, food products and home rentals.

It should be recognized that any approach to providing relief from the burden of taxation will itself create problems. Building multiple rates into a VAT, for example, would cause administrative complexities and raise the cost of administering the program.

The Effect of a VAT on Economic Efficiency and Growth

Among the advantages offered by a VAT would be its effect on the neutrality of the tax system. A VAT would have less of an impact on business decisions than does our current federal income tax because it favors neither capital nor labor intensive industries. Our present tax structure, while improved since the enactment of the Economic Recovery Tax Act of 1981 (ERTA), is not conducive to capital formation. The progressive tax system on individual income has encouraged investments based largely on tax motivation and has accentuated the temptation to cheat. At the corporate level, high tax rates on income increase product costs and tend to exert an undue influence on business judgment. The institution of a VAT could enable Congress to reduce the top rates for both individual and corporate taxpayers to more reasonable levels, thereby restoring investor confidence in business and enabling business management to base decisions primarily on business motives. A broadly based tax, such as the VAT, could compensate for the loss in government revenues, yet it would apply ultimately only to those who opt to buy taxable goods and services—our customers. Since customers incur the VAT only when they spend, an incentive to save would be created. Under a progressive income tax, the consumer has few alternatives but to pay his tax or to invest in sometimes uneconomical tax shelter schemes. While the VAT may collect the same amount of total revenue and reduce direct taxes, the consumer does not have to spend his money on items that will be taxable. He has more of an incentive to invest and to save.

A VAT may also encourage businesses to cut costs in order to operate more efficiently. Since the VAT is a fixed percentage of the price to the consumer, there is an incentive to reduce the total costs of producing the good or service. If a business could lower its costs, it could reduce prices and maintain the same profit margin. A reduced sales price would also reduce the VAT and improve the competitive position of the business. It has been argued that the same results could be achieved under an income tax system, but when income taxes take 46 percent of any savings, incentives to attempt to control costs are reduced. If a VAT were coupled with a reduction in income tax rates or an elimination of the corporate income tax, incentives to cut costs would be significant.

The effect of a VAT on U.S. export volume would depend ultimately upon the exporter and on how the VAT were factored into the overall U.S. tax structure. Since a VAT does not increase product costs, the forgiveness of the tax on exports does not give the exporter a direct benefit, although it might make his price more competitive in world markets. However, if the country of import imposes a VAT, that offsets the advantage of the home-country tax remission, assuming the tax rates are equal. Where the exporter may receive an advantage would be in the reduction of other taxes that affect the product sales price. If the government levies a smaller income tax on profits and wages, the exporter could reduce his selling price and maintain the same profit. It is the potential reduction in sales price that can help the exporter.

Opponents of the VAT often raise the argument that a VAT, taken by itself, is inflationary. They claim that since the VAT is an indirect tax that is added to the price of goods and services, it ultimately increases consumer prices. However, if accompanied by reductions in direct taxes, a VAT might not lead to higher wage demands that would, in turn, fuel the inflationary spiral. Experiences from abroad are inconclusive. It should be remembered, however, that in Europe the VAT replaced various turnover type taxes, which were taxes applied to gross sales at each stage in the production-distribution process, without allowance for taxes paid on productive inputs.

Still another argument often raised against a VAT is that new or marginal businesses might not receive the same benefits from a reduction in income tax rates or other direct taxes that would accompany the VAT in pricing their products. The effect may be to weaken the competitive position of new or marginal businesses, since older and more profitable businesses might be able to reduce prices. The present income tax system, which taxes profits, provides a better competitive opportunity for newer or marginal concerns.

Administrative Aspects of a VAT

Since the tax would be based on consumption of goods and services, it might be less susceptible to the fluctuations inherent in a system that relied on taxing profits. The flow of revenue might be more uniform, enabling government to more accurately forecast its budgets and plan its cash expenditures. The precise impact of a VAT is, of course, unknown and serious disagreement exists among economists, as well as politicians and businessmen.

If all invoices to taxable producers would state the VAT separately, the wizardry of modern computers could simplify the task of data accumulation, while monthly reporting would limit the period covered and the time required for data accumulation. By its nature, though, a VAT would require the filing of millions of returns periodically. This could place a severe strain on government systems and employees and on the private sector. Most especially, small and medium-size businesses would incur added costs.

Because it would be a broadly based tax on consumption, a VAT has the potential of raising large amounts of revenue with a low rate of tax. Based on Table 9-1 of Dr. McLure's paper, estimates of the tax yield from a broadly based VAT range from $8 to $15 billion for each 1 percent rate. It is logical to assume that the amount would continue to increase each year, as a result of real economic growth and inflation. Coupling a VAT with a spending limitation such as the Balanced Budget Amendment would avoid the potential danger of wasteful spending of VAT-generated revenues.

A last cautionary statement about administering a VAT: There is a natural reluctance on the part of state and local officials to have the federal government impose a tax on something that they consider their private preserve. With state sales tax collections approaching $80 billion, it is natural that they would be wary. Any increase in the base price (such as a VAT could cause) could have an adverse effect on sales and, thus, on state and municipal revenues.

Conclusion

It is clear that the considerations involved in evaluating a value added tax are varied and complex. There are no obvious answers to some of the complex issues that must be considered, and careful study is needed by business, labor, government, and various private and public interest groups. Corporations and industry groups should undertake in-depth analyses of the potential impact of VAT on their operations. The results of these studies should be useful to government decisionmakers in Congress and in the Administration.

Eventually, discussion and study of the value added tax as but one element of a restructured tax system might provide a basis for an overall change in U.S. tax policy. The objective is, of course, to meet more efficiently the challenges facing our economy today and in the future.

WHY CONGRESS WILL NOT ACCEPT THE VALUE ADDED TAX

James M. Shannon

There is talk in the country and in the Congress about the need to adopt some form of consumption tax. The recent discussion began with the introduction in the Ninety-sixth Congress by Al Ullman, then chairman of the House Ways and Means Committee, of a comprehensive reform bill that included a Value Added Tax (VAT). This paper addresses some of the political problems that must be confronted when considering a value added tax and compares the current situation in Congress to the time when the VAT was considered in the Ninety-sixth Congress.

In the past, the value added tax has been proposed in tandem with some kind of major reduction in income taxes or corporate taxes or some kind of phasing out of the payroll tax. Chairman Ullman's bill would have reduced income and corporate taxes by about $115 billion. In light of the budget deficits that we are facing today and, given the need for new revenues, responsible people are coming forward to recommend adoption of a value added tax. The last time Congress considered the VAT, we learned how politically sensitive the subject can be, even when the VAT is being considered as a replacement tax. Now that the VAT is being considered as an additional tax, I think the political problems are much more complex.

In the Ninety-sixth Congress, when the value added tax was last considered, tax reduction was a forceful cry in the country. Proposition Thirteen was popular in California. Many people feared that Congress would use VAT as an additional tax rather than as a substitute for other forms of taxation. Inflation was very high in 1979 and 1980. Charles McLure is right that the value added tax does nothing to the rate of inflation; the VAT simply raises the level of prices in one shot and for one time only. It was difficult, however, in times of double-digit inflation to propose a VAT because of the immediate increase in prices. Fortunately, the problem of inflation is not nearly so serious today as it was in 1979 and 1980.

Administration of the tax is an important question to consider. It would be more difficult, as Professor McLure pointed out, to go to a value added tax in the United States than it was in Europe. We have no comparable federal tax. We would not be going from some kind of sales tax to a value added tax. We would be adding a completely new tax and doing so would create many new problems.

Increasing the complexity of the tax structure at a time when more and more Americans are equating complexity of the tax laws with unfairness would be difficult. After all, the goal of simplicity is the big impetus behind the flat tax proposals. People say that the laws are complex and difficult to administer and that the public does not understand them—and that, therefore, the tax laws are not fair. While it can be argued that we could administer a value added tax, administration would be a big problem. Although a simple, straightforward VAT could be administered, any actual VAT that emerged from the political process would likely be expensive to collect.

The important question of preemption of state sources of revenues also arises. This Administration's economic policies have resulted in real cuts in federal aid to the states. When Congress recently proposed a five cent increase in the gas tax, we heard from some of the state governments that we would be preempting their revenue sources at a time when those revenues were particularly needed. Any attempts to enact a value added tax at this particular moment would run into tremendous opposition from the state legislatures and governors.

One of the most serious problems with any consumption tax is the problem with regressivity. The Brookings Institution considered this whole issue in 1980 and concluded that because of the political decisionmaking process and the incremental nature of the VAT, we should consider a VAT in tandem either with some kind of effort (1) to make the rest of the tax system more progressive or (2) to help those at the lower end of the scale through some kind of direct expenditure program.

Perhaps the biggest concern—and one that has not been adequately addressed either by the Congress or by those who have looked at this issue outside the political system—is the question of how to insulate the VAT from the political and legislative pressures that weigh on the present federal tax system. Clearly, this audience could deliberate and agree today on reasonable exemptions and candidates for a lower rate of taxation under a value added tax. We should not, however, underestimate the ingenuity of the Members of Congress and the people they represent in arguing for further exemptions, loopholes, and differentiations. What might begin as a relatively clean, simple, easy to understand, neutral tax system would emerge from the political process looking very different from what had been expected. Until the question of how the VAT can be insulated from political and legislative pressures is resolved, it is going to be difficult to instill confidence in the VAT.

We thus face many issues when looking at a VAT. We must consider the issues of administrability, preemption of state sources of revenue, regressivity, and political pressures. Finally, we must face the issue of the basic skepticism of many Americans concerning a full switch from one tax to another. People fear that enactment of the VAT would simply mean more taxes and additional sorts of taxes for the average taxpayer. Americans are also concerned that the VAT is a hidden tax, and that once enacted it would be easy for the Congress to raise the tax. Indeed, it would be politically easier to raise the VAT than to raise income taxes.

Now, having noted all the reasons why it would be difficult to adopt a VAT in this Congress, I must tell you why it probably will be discussed, if not seriously considered. The reason is simple. It is the same reason that the Congress was able to pass a 1982 tax increase within ninety days of an election. We have a desperate search for new revenues occurring on Capitol Hill. Unfortunately, there are no easy ways of finding these revenues. In this context, a VAT is one among many potential approaches that will be examined.

THE POTENTIAL OF THE VALUE ADDED TAX

Al Ullman

It is significant, I think, that the Value Added Tax (VAT) is one of the principal features on the agenda of this conference on New Directions in Federal Tax Policy for the 1980s. Consumption taxes are now being discussed at most tax policy conferences, reflecting a new interest since I first introduced my VAT bill in 1979.

To analyze a VAT correctly, we must first determine what kind of a VAT we are discussing. My own thinking has changed since I introduced my far-reaching tax restructuring bill in 1979. In my judgment today, the value added tax should be a noncumulative transaction tax applied on all business transactions, irrespective of the form of business organization. The tax should essentially be a fee for doing business in the free market. It should be levied on all transactions in the stream of services and production and should be applied as a flat tax on added value, with only the cost of products and services subject to the tax. Capital expenditures should be deductible. Other business taxes, particularly the corporate tax, should be phased out as the VAT is added.

There are two points in Charles McLure's paper with which I disagree. First, I do not agree that the VAT is a sales tax. The political and economic impact of the VAT would be greatly different. As a matter of fact, I would not support a national sales tax, since sales taxes have been preempted by the states, and the federal government should not venture into that area.

Second, I disagree with Drs. McLure and Aaron in their evaluation of the value added tax as a stimulus to exports. That is certainly not the most important reason for imposing the tax, but if a tax on added value were substituted for a corporate tax, under international agreements both a border tax on imports and a subsidy on exports could be imposed in the amount of the VAT. One argument against the trade benefits accruing from a VAT is that the increased value of the dollar under floating currencies would offset the stimulus to exports. This effect, in my judgment, would be short-term in nature, with the nation's total economic credentials determining the dollar's valuation in the long term.

There are many reasons for moving to a broadly based tax on added value, including the VAT's effectiveness in encouraging work, saving, investment, and trade. However, a major reason behind the current consideration of a consumption tax, including the value added tax, is the federal government's desperate need for revenue. We are trapped in a budgetary nightmare. The inadequacies of the income tax system are obvious; moreover, most of its problems can only be corrected by measures that involve revenue loss, that is, abolishing the so-called "marriage penalty." This nation cannot survive without a strong and viable revenue system adequate to pay for necessary government expenditures.

I think there is no question that the deficits demand new and increased federal revenues. The idea of increasing federal revenues was a moot point in 1982, and the issue was even more debatable when I introduced by VAT bill in 1979. Today, however, the problem is self-evident. We are now looking at deficits rising above $200 billion in each of the next several years, even optimistically assuming 4 percent real growth in the out years. There is now strong sentiment in Congress and elsewhere in favor of increasing revenues.

What are the options that would raise new revenues? First, it has been suggested on Capitol Hill that tax loopholes should be closed. I believe the Congress should always be on the lookout for abuses in the tax Code and should correct them. It is totally counterproductive, however, to look at loophole closing as a revenue-raising mechanism. I hope Congress refrains from that exercise this year.

Second, enactment of a surtax would raise revenue. Congress passed a temporary surtax in 1967, but in my judgment a surtax is wrong for these times. It would only exaggerate the inequities in the income tax system. An on and off surcharge would compound the cyclical tendencies of a tax system already overloaded in that direction.

Third, additional excise taxes could be considered. During the Korean War, this country used a number of excise taxes; by now, we have eliminated most of those, with minor exceptions. I think excise taxes are an unwise method of raising revenue, as they place a disproportionate tax burden on special segments of the economy.

Fourth, the widely discussed flat rate tax could be considered as a way to raise new revenue. In my judgment, however, it is on the consumption side that a flat tax should be applied. There is no way our income tax system can be structured within a flat tax framework without a major loss of both equity and revenue.

I must conclude, then, that if we want to narrow the projected deficits, there are no realistic options other than a value added tax such as that which I propose.

The concept of a value added tax creates substantial political problems. When I first introduced my tax restructuring bill, which would have instituted a VAT, few Members of Congress supported my position at that time. I doubt if many would do so now. I do think, however, that we are now nearing the point where the issue of providing a workable revenue system for our government and our economy can no longer be avoided.

Further, along with its other virtues, a VAT would make it politically possible to eliminate the corporate tax. The corporate tax cannot be eliminated unless it is replaced by some other kind of tax. This is a political reality. If all forms of business, including corporations, paid a simple tax on added value, this would be a strong argument for eliminating the corporate income tax. Eliminating the corporate income tax is high on my list of priorities in attempting to get back to some kind of sane tax system in this country.

Finally, it is essential that we recognize the major dimensions of America's fiscal crisis. It is time we find structural solutions to the revenue problem because we *must* find them. Patchwork and stopgap answers will no longer suffice. Restructuring the revenue system will not solve all of America's problems, but, in my humble judgment, unless we solve the revenue problem, we will be unable to solve the others.

 Chapter 10

The Choice Between Income and Consumption Taxes

David F. Bradford

INTRODUCTION

This paper is intended to form the basis for discussion among tax practitioners of the potential advantages of adopting a consumption basis, rather than an income basis, for the principal individual tax system. It begins by describing the problem of individual tax base design in general terms. It then defines income and consumption bases and discusses ways in which consumption appears a superior guide for tax policy. The final section summarizes the actual data required to implement a practical consumption base. An appendix elaborates on the definitions of income and consumption in a tax accounting framework.

THE PROBLEM OF TAX DESIGN

Under what may be called an individual tax system the tax authorities periodically (say, once per year) send a bill to each individual. The bill requests payment of an amount of money determined by applying a tax schedule to a number called the individual tax base. The schedule applied may depend upon characteristics of the individual subject to tax (for example, age, family status, health). Conceivably, the procedures for determining an individual's tax base may also depend upon these or other characteristics. However, the larger the tax base of an individual with given characteristics, the larger his tax liability.

Although both the tax schedule applicable and the rules for calculating an individual's tax base may depend upon characteristics such as family status, I shall for the most part ignore such distinctions in the following. This means neglecting such interesting questions as how to aggregate the tax burdens of family members. It will, however, enable us to focus on the issues of primary concern if we look at the choice of individual tax base as though there were but one type of individual taxpayer.

The impact of a fiscal system on individuals is only partly determined by the individual tax system. Other tax instruments and expenditure programs may be equally or more important. The Value Added Tax and the corporation income tax are two significant taxes affecting relative individual tax burdens, although these are not individual taxes. In assessing the merits of one or another individual tax base it may be pertinent to consider interactions with such other tax institutions.

We are accustomed to think of an income tax as *the* individual tax. However, there are others fitting my definition to some degree. An estate or inheritance tax is an example. A payroll tax is another. Although the individual typically does not get the bill, the payroll tax in the United States does recognize individual circumstances. (Earnings are taxed only up to a specified maximum level in a given year.) More importantly, the whole structure of social security taxes and benefits can be viewed as an individual tax system. An interesting question, which I shall not pursue here, is how social security design is affected by the characteristics of the primary individual tax.

THREE CRITERIA

What are the criteria by which we should judge individual tax systems? Probably first and foremost is the objective of fairness across taxpayers. Applied over and over through time, the rule defining the tax base (together with a specification of tax schedules through time) will produce a series of tax assessments for each individual. We would like it to be the case that people who deserve to bear less of a burden of tax experience "better" (mainly lower) sequences of tax liabilities. Note that this description stresses not simply the effect of applying the rule in a single period; it also takes into account its operation on individuals over time.

A second criterion is economic efficiency. Presumably, an ideal rule would assign tax burdens according to what we might call exogenous features of an individual's circumstances—innate intelligence, for example. Practical rules must rely on endogenous features—outcomes resulting from individual choices under the exogenously given features. For example, a practical tax would typically be positively related to labor earnings, a quantity depending on innate earning power (arguably exogenous) and intensity of effort (presumably endogenous). Such rules inevitably distort the individual's choices, and some potential value is lost as a result. Other things being equal, these losses should be minimized.

A third important consideration is administrability. One could imagine a concept of relative deservingness-to-pay tax based on elaborate psychological tests or close scrutiny of an individual's diet or some such thing, wholly impractical to implement. What we call "income" for tax purposes is basically an aggregate of market transactions. These transactions may be more or less easy for the tax authorities to monitor. They may impose more or less difficult recordkeeping and calculation burdens on taxpayers. They may require more or fewer arbitrary decisions or judgment calls.

INCOME AND CONSUMPTION TAX BASES DESCRIBED

This general description of the problem of tax design is the basis for a considerable and growing literature in economics. It is not surprising that, depending upon the details of the formulation, formal models may imply a wide variety of different tax systems. Instead of attempting to derive a tax base from first principles, it will be more useful for us to review the properties of the two major contending ideals for practical systems: the consumption and income bases. The following description borrows heavily from my paper, "The Case for a Personal Consumption Tax" (1980a). I have also provided as an appendix a somewhat more elaborate discussion, emphasizing the accounting aspects.

Income is usually defined by tax theorists in terms of the *uses* to which the individual puts his resources during the year. This definition looks like the familiar accounting identity

$$Y = C + \Delta W \qquad (10.1)$$

where Y, C and ΔW stand for income, consumption, and change in net worth over the accounting period ("savings"), respectively. To employ income as a tax base requires putting operational flesh on the concepts of consumption and savings. For example, it must be determined whether outlays for medical treatment constitute consumption. Similarly, it must be decided what sort of wealth will be included in net worth; for instance, human capital is usually not included. It should be emphasized that the terms "consumption" and "wealth" are not operationally defined a priori; they are defined in the process of determining tax policy.

Practical calculation of either a consumption or an income tax base normally starts with the individual's receipts rather than his outlays. This can readily be seen by starting with the assumption that the wealth entering the definition of the tax base is an asset like a savings account. We think of a savings account as having a readily identifiable current yield. The yield is simply the interest rate, r, times the account balance. Let W_t stand for the wealth at the beginning of period t, and E_t for the "nonwealth receipts" (wages, transfers, and so forth), understood as occurring at the end of period t. The yield on wealth, rW_t, and consumption, C_t, are also regarded as occurring at that time. For these concepts to form a satisfactory accounting system, it is necessary that

$$W_t + 1 = W_t + E_t + rW_t - C_t \qquad (10.2)$$

or

$$C_t + \Delta W_t = E_t + rW_t \qquad (10.3)$$

The left side of (10.3) is income as we have defined it. The right side, the sum of nonwealth receipts and returns on wealth, is the usual calculation base. It is what the layman thinks of as income.

The same approach is normally taken to calculate a consumption tax base. Savings are subtracted from the sum of nonwealth receipts and returns on wealth:

$$C_t = E_t + rW_t - \Delta W_t \qquad (10.4)$$

<u>The difference between an income base and a consumption base lies entirely in the treatment of savings.</u> A common view is that a <u>consumption tax would treat various nonsavings transactions differently than would an income tax.</u> For example, it is sometimes suggested that gifts and bequests received would necessarily be treated differently in income and consumption accounting. This is not so. Assuming their anticipated value is not counted in wealth, these receipts are simply included in E_t in the appropriate period. Referring to accounting relationships (10.3) and (10.4), one sees that such an increment in nonwealth receipts leads to the same change in both income and consumption.

For another example, consider the treatment of gifts and bequests given. It may be argued that amounts given away are not consumed. If this approach were taken, the corresponding amount would need to be deducted from nonwealth receipts in the period in question. But the procedure follows whether it is income or consumption we are trying to measure. Whether or not one regards gifts and bequests as consumption has nothing inherently to do with the choice between income and consumption bases. In thinking about this choice, all that should concern us is the treatment of savings.

Both income and consumption are reasonable choices as tax bases. Both seem likely to lead to relative tax burdens among individuals that are broadly consistent with the degree of well-off-ness as it might be independently specified. Consumption is typically a large fraction of income, and the ordering of taxpayers by income and consumption is likely to be highly correlated. I have argued at various times that consumption is the preferable base, however, and in the following sections I shall try to recapitulate those arguments briefly.

EQUITY AND THE CHOICE BETWEEN INCOME AND CONSUMPTION BASES

Let us suppose we could as easily implement either of these two taxes. Why favor the consumption base as far as fairness or equity is concerned?

A part of the answer has to do with formal optimal tax theory. Consider, for example, a world in which all individuals have the same preferences about consumption of goods at different times but have different abilities. The ability differences are reflected in wage rates. Suppose that taxes can be levied on income or consumption or both. Now pick tax schedules to raise a required amount of revenue and to maximize some weighted sum of the utility levels obtained by individuals.

The solution to such a problem depends upon various parameters of the preferences and the distribution of abilities. It is not unreasonable to describe the parameter values implying the consumption base as a kind of midpoint of the plausible set. Other values imply more taxation of savings (in the direction of an income tax or beyond) or less (that is, subsidy to savings). (Readers interested in a more extensive discussion may find my 1980b paper helpful.)

To me, the more compelling part of the answer follows from reflection on the principle underlined earlier that *the difference between an income base and a consumption base lies entirely in the treatment of savings.* Imagine a situation without either tax and with two individuals we regard as similarly endowed. Then think about raising revenue either by imposing an income tax or a consumption tax. In general, the results will not be the same for our two individuals. One will be seen to be burdened more heavily by the income tax, the other by the consumption tax. The one burdened the more heavily by the income tax will be the one who saves more. (This may be because of a preference for postponing consumption or because the individual's nonwealth receipts occur late in life.) One of the two tax bases must relatively burden the greater saver. Forced to choose, I tilt toward the saver.

One reason for this tilt is an externality. Accumulation by individuals is socially desirable: I am better off when my neighbor has a reserve against future needs. But even without this externality, it seems to me there is something appealing about the neutrality toward savings characteristic of a consumption base.

Suppose, for example, we are comparing the results in a system in which the lifetime pattern of nonwealth receipts is fixed for each individual. People may differ in initial wealth, in the time path of nonwealth receipts, and in the use made of these endowments. How should they be compared? Since people having the same aggregate of initial wealth and present value of nonwealth receipts have the same consumption possibilities, it seems compelling that they should bear the same tax burden, measured in present-value terms. Put another way, because of the lifetime budget constraint, the principle of horizontal equity calls for equal reductions in the discounted value of consumption by people for whom this total would be equal in the absence of tax. The discounted value of nonwealth receipts added to initial wealth might be labeled "lifetime wealth," the operative constraint on lifetime consumption. The principle of horizontal equity amounts to the idea that people should be taxed according to lifetime wealth. (We can interpret the tax burden as the present value of lifetime tax payments.) Vertical equity, in turn, calls for positively relating tax burdens to lifetime wealth (and, one might add, the principle of progressivity requires that the tax burden as a fraction of lifetime wealth be larger as lifetime wealth is larger).

IMPLEMENTING EQUITY PRINCIPLES BY A CONSUMPTION TAX

These principles of horizontal and vertical equity are readily implemented by a consumption tax along lines to be described below. Under this scheme each person will confront a constant expected rate of tax on his annual tax base, with the level of the rate a positive function of his lifetime wealth. Further, by the use of a progressive schedule of taxes on the annual base, the burden, measured by the present value of taxes discounted at the rate of interest (the pre- and posttax interest rates are the same) will be progressively related to lifetime wealth.

By contrast, an annual income tax generates tax burdens that are somewhat haphazardly related to individual circumstances, as measured by lifetime wealth. A flat rate income tax, unlike a flat rate consumption tax, systematically biases the distribution of tax burdens. Given two persons with the same lifetime pattern of nonwealth receipts, the income tax imposes the lighter burden on the one who consumes early in life, the heavier burden on the one who postpones consumption. Given two persons with the same lifetime wealth, the income tax imposes the lighter burden on the one whose nonwealth receipts occur late in life. If the income tax is levied according to a progressive schedule, the relationship between lifetime wealth and lifetime tax burden will be even less systematic. Not only does the timing of receipts and consumption enter the result in the way described, but also other characteristics of their time profile now influence relative tax burdens.

All this discussion is based on a simplified example. Other aspects of individual circumstances might be considered relevant. For example, it might be desirable to make a distinction between nonwealth receipts due to labor and those due to inheritance or gift. Attention to family status is presumably in order. Imperfect capital markets and uncertainty complicate the picture. Yet none of these complications seem to point to a preference for income over consumption taxation.

EFFICIENCY AND THE CHOICE BETWEEN INCOME AND CONSUMPTION BASES

One efficiency issue is commonly regarded as critical to the income versus consumption tax choice. Does society save too little because of the income tax? A great deal of effort has been devoted to attempting to measure the responsiveness of aggregate private savings to the rate of return on saving. The conventional wisdom still seems to be that there is not very much responsiveness. A commonly drawn implication is that we might as well tax income.

This is not a proper implication at all. At best the conventional wisdom concerning aggregate saving would hold that consumption and income taxes are equivalent as far as the level of saving is concerned. But I would go further and suggest that once government accumulation (or decumulation) is allowed, the link is broken between any aggregate saving objective and the choice between income and consumption bases. (This assumes government accumulation does not generate an equal and opposite reaction in private saving.)

A concern with aggregate saving is not readily justified by the usual analysis of efficient resource allocation. Economists normally focus on losses due to the distortion of individual choices arising from the tax-caused divergence between social and private trade-offs. An example is the spread between the yield on savings and the return to the saver under an income tax. Even in this context the responsiveness of saving to the rate of return is not the key parameter. It is not difficult to construct examples in which a consumption tax leads to a minimum of distortion even where savings are totally insensitive to the yield.

More important than any of this is the inference I draw from the following three propositions:

- Unlike the ideal model, the real world treats very differently savings transactions that are economically very similar. Real world income taxes generate large intersectoral and portfolio distortions.
- Problems of implementation assure that *any* real world income tax will induce significant distortions of this type.
- A consumption type tax that is substantially free of these distortions would be easy to implement.

My guess (difficult to substantiate) is that efficiency losses associated with divergences from consistency in a practical income tax system are unavoidable and large. Such losses may exceed those that might be at stake in the choice between ideal income and consumption taxes. Because this view is tied up with problems of implementation, let us turn to that subject now.

THE CHOICE BETWEEN INCOME AND CONSUMPTION BASES: IMPLEMENTATION ISSUES

For a time, conventional wisdom among many economists was that a consumption base might well be preferable to an income base in principle but would be too difficult to put into practice. The currency of this view is somewhat surprising since one of the early and influential advocates of a consumption tax, Nicholas Kaldor (1955), stressed precisely the opposite. In my view, a consumption type tax would be easy to implement and an equally consistent income type tax very difficult to implement. (Other recent studies concur. See for example, Lodin [1978], the Meade Report [Institute for Fiscal Studies, 1978], Kay and King [1978].)

The reason for this is that a great many of the most severe problems of measurement in the income tax fall away in a consumption tax, while the latter adds virtually no new ones. The difficulties in the income tax arise when we attempt to use data on transactions to attach numbers to the symbols in expression (10.3). Here are three examples:

- It is clear that an employee who receives wages has experienced a nonwealth receipt. But so also has an employee who obtains a promise of future pension benefits from his employer. The first is easy to measure, and the second difficult.

- If an individual holds a savings account untouched during the year, it is clear and easily measured how much has been his return from this part of his wealth (although correcting for inflation is *not* simple). But no comparably simple data arise to allow us to measure the return in direct consumption services he enjoys from ownership of a house, an automobile, a work of art, jewelry, and so forth.

- Similarly, it is difficult to measure the return in direct accrual of wealth he experiences as a consequence of holding ownership in a farm, a small business, even shares of stock in a corporation.

These three examples illustrate three categories of measurement difficulties: (1) the problem of measuring the value of receipt today of claims that will generate cash flows only in the possibly distant, possibly uncertain, future; (2) the problem of measuring the value of consumption services rendered by assets, corresponding to which no actual cash transaction ever occurs; and (3) the problem of measuring accruing value of assets corresponding to which the cash transaction will occur in the possibly distant, possibly uncertain, future.

These are not trivial economic phenomena. Mention of additions to retirement rights under category 1 and owner occupied housing under 2 should suffice to demonstrate their significance. Category 3 accounts for the need in the tax law for rules relating to depreciation of business structures and equipment and for rules relating to capital gains. In the United States, these are very complex and contentious aspects of the law. Category 3 also encompasses the taxation of accruing retirement value even in fully funded retirement plans (untaxed in the United States) and the accruing value of life insurance policy claims (taxed in a very complicated way in the United States.) Finally, category 3 may be the intellectual basis for the taxation of corporate profits, as a proxy for the otherwise untaxed accrual of wealth at the shareholder level. (I shall return briefly to this point below.)

Measurement difficulties in categories 1 and 3 vanish if consumption is the desired tax base. Because what is involved is both postponed cash receipt and postponed consumption, the failure to measure correctly nonwealth receipts (E_t) and returns on wealth (rW_t) in (10.3) or (10.4) corresponds precisely to an equal and opposite mismeasurement of savings ($\triangle W_t$). Under a consumption tax one could simply dispense with the rules relating to depreciation, capital gains, special treatment of retirement savings and life insurance, corporation income measurement and taxation, and innumerable complex procedures for dealing with business transactions. Acquisition of an asset would result in a deduction on the right side of (10.4). Accruing asset value changes or receipt of claims on future payments can simply be ignored until they actually generate cash flow. The result is an extremely simple system of tax accounts for these problem categories.

Measurement difficulties in category 2, direct consumption services generated by wealth, are also easily dealt with under a consumption base system by taking advantage of a technique based on the equivalence in present value of the following: recognizing a deduction from the tax base for acquisition of an asset but including in the tax base all return flows of value (the standard approach to implementing a consumption base); and ignoring for tax purposes *both* the acquisition of an asset *and* the return flow of value. Intuitively, the second approach has the effect of paying in advance (by foregoing the deduction) the taxes that would become due subsequently under the first approach. For this reason, it may be called the tax prepayment method of accounting. For assets with ordinary cash yields, the choice between the two methods is a matter of indifference (provided the applicable tax rate is the same). The tax prepayment method is tailor-made, however, for investments generating hard-to-measure noncash yields.

INFLATION AND THE CHOICE BETWEEN INCOME AND CONSUMPTION BASES

One of the most serious current problems of income measurement is how to deal with inflation. My guess is that inflation has been the main factor leading to the abandonment in the United States of any serious attempt to tax on the basis of a consistent income concept.

The difficulty of measuring income in a time of inflation arises because of the need to use market transactions made, actually or implicitly, at different times. In calculating the gain from sale of an asset, for example, it is necessary to subtract the purchase price from the current sales proceeds. If substantial inflation has occurred in the interim, adjustments are necessary to express both transactions in common units. Failure to adjust such items as capital gain and depreciation calculations may enormously distort the tax base.

Inflation also produces an "inflation premium" in interest rates. Unfortunately, it is not easy to determine what that premium is, since it depends upon hard-to-observe anticipations of future price level changes. But failure to adjust interest payments and receipts can produce astounding distortions of incentives when the inflation rate is large. To illustrate, take the case in which the interest rate in the absence of inflation is 2 percent, and suppose that with an inflation rate of 10 percent an interest rate of 12 percent prevails. Consider now the price today for which a dollar of real purchasing power thirty years hence can be bought (or sold). Table 10-1 shows how this price in column (1) varies with the tax rate on interest in the absence of inflation. The same figures apply with inflation if interest payments and receipts are adjusted for tax purposes by subtracting out the 10 percent inflation premium. Column (2) shows the price without inflation adjustment. Prices in excess of 1 in column (2) for tax rates of 20 percent or more reflect the fact that, in the absence of inflation adjustment, the after-tax rate of interest is negative

Table 10-1. Illustration of the Effect of Inflation on the Price (via Borrowing or Lending) of a Dollar of Purchasing Power Thirty Years Hence.[a]

Individual Tax Rate (percentage)	(1) No Inflation or Inflation Plus Adjustment of Interest for Tax Purposes	(2) 10 Percent Annual Inflation and No Adjustment
0	$0.55	$0.55
10%	0.59	0.79
20	0.62	1.13
30	0.66	1.62
40	0.70	2.34
50	0.74	3.40

[a]Entries show the present amount one would have to pay to purchase a claim on one dollar (in present purchasing power) thirty years from now. In the illustration the interest rate with no inflation is assumed to be 2 percent; with inflation at 10 percent the interest rate is assumed to be 12 percent.

under the illustrative conditions. The example illustrates rather dramatically the strain imposed by inflation on an income tax system that has no corrections for the inflation factor in interest payments.

Neither type of inflation correction would be needed under a consumption type tax. This is because the calculation of the tax base involves only current year transactions. The tax base and tax liabilities are always measured in consistent units. To illustrate, consider a person who purchases a share of stock for $100 that grows in real value to $110 by the next period, when it is sold and the proceeds are consumed. (The same reasoning would apply to the interest rate illustration in the previous table.) If the taxpayer's tax rate is 50 percent, under the standard treatment he or she sacrifices $50 of consumption in the first period in return for $55 extra consumption in the second period. If the tax prepayment approach is chosen, the taxpayer sacrifices $100 of consumption in the first period in return for $110 extra consumption in the second period. The same 10 percent return is obtained in both cases. If the price level doubles between the two periods, and the price of the stock with it, the second period outcomes will be $110 and $220, respectively, under the two treatments, exactly the same in real terms as when there is no inflation.

AVERAGING

Before turning to the question of how the choice of individual tax base bears on the taxation of corporations, I would like to mention the neglected matter of tax averaging. The advantages of the sort of uniformity of treatment accorded a wide range of investment or savings transactions by either a consistent income or consumption base depend upon constancy over time of the applicable rate of tax. In a graduated rate income tax system, the marginal rate is likely to vary over the individual's lifetime. (Averaging provisions may be provided, as in U.S. law, but they typically do little to mitigate this pattern.)

Ideally, one would like to have a single flat rate applicable, or more precisely *anticipated* to be applicable, to an individual's transactions, with a higher rate of tax applicable to better endowed individuals. Interestingly, just this result follows from the availability in a consumption type system of the two methods of treating savings—the standard one involving current deduction followed by taxation of return flow, and the tax prepayment method involving neither deduction of the amount saved nor taxation of the return. It is in the interest of the taxpayer to choose the balance of the two approaches in just such a way as to maintain a constant marginal tax rate over time. Furthermore, a progressively graduated schedule of rates means that the constant rate attainable by a taxpayer will be higher, the greater his endowment.

THE INDIVIDUAL TAX BASE AND THE TAXATION OF CORPORATIONS

Corporations are taxed under a variety of different methods in different countries. Among the varying features are the definition of taxable income, the treatment of dividends at both the corporate and shareholder level, the deductibility of interest payments, the applicability of investment incentives, and the methods of accounting for foreign earnings. It would take me far afield to attempt to discuss these aspects in any detail in this paper.

On the other hand, certain general propositions about the systems of corporate taxation most readily compatible with progressive individual income or consumption taxation seem reasonable:

First, in the context of a genuine accrual income tax at the individual level, any corporate level taxation of income—defined in the same way as individual income but with "distributions" replacing "consumption"—will distort the allocation of investment between corporate and noncorporate forms, the structure of corporation finance, and the legal form of business organization. It seems rather difficult to justify such a tax if the underlying choice of individual income is accepted as the correct measure of deservingness-to-pay-tax. Under an accrual income tax, wealth changes associated with share ownership would be most naturally measured by changes in market value of shares. The sum of dividends and share value change would enter the calculation of rW in (10.3). There would be no need for corporate level income accounting for tax purposes.

Second, corporate level accounting is needed if markets for shares are insufficiently active to permit regular revaluation. The natural procedure in that case is to allocate income calculated at the corporate level to individual shareholders. The practical problems of implementing methods to allocate corporate income to shareholders are formidable in the context of actual tax systems. (I think the difficulties are largely attributable to the fact that actual systems do not attempt to tax individuals on the basis of our definition [10.1] of income.)

Third, under a system of individual income taxation that makes no attempt to follow the accrual of wealth due to holding assets, a tax on income imposed at the corporate level may make sense. It is a kind of proxy for the individual level tax. A flat rate tax, however, will be a bad approximation to the allocation of income to the shareholder if there is substantial variation in individual marginal rates. Furthermore, the approximation will tend to be the worse the higher the rate of return on corporate capital.

Fourth, the double taxation of dividends as practiced in the United States seems to me hard to justify. (But then, U.S. corporations' practice of *paying* dividends is equally hard to explain.)

Finally, with a thoroughgoing consumption base at the individual level there would be no logic to a tax on income at the corporate level. However, an extra flat rate tax on corporate cash flow to and from public equity holders would be wholly compatible with an individual consumption base. Such a tax might be useful as a method of capturing corporate wealth in the context of a transition from the present rules to a consumption base.

HOW CAN AN INDIVIDUAL CONSUMPTION TAX BE IMPLEMENTED?

As has been emphasized repeatedly here, the difference between a consumption and an income base resides in the treatment of savings. In other respects they are, or can be, the same. As we have also already emphasized, two basic methods of accounting, the standard and the tax prepayment approaches, produce the effect of exempting savings from tax. Implementation of an individual consumption base, then, requires developing methods for keeping track of savings given the standard treatment (deduction), so that the returns will be taxed, and isolating savings undertaken on a tax prepaid basis, so that the associated returns will be exempt from tax.

The following simple rules will accomplish this:

- All assets purchased for direct personal use (house, automobile, and so forth), must be treated on a tax prepaid basis (no deduction). This treatment is currently followed in the income tax. It avoids the problem of measuring the returns taking the form of direct services.
- All assets purchased for use in closely held business enterprises must be given standard treatment (immediately expensed). In other words, unincorporated business enterprises must be accounted for on a cash flow basis. This procedure precludes the necessity of separating out the earnings of capital and labor.
- Financial assets may be purchased or sold via qualified accounts. A qualified account is supervised by a fiduciary institution, such as a bank. Net deposits to a qualified account during the account-

ing period are reported to the tax authorities and deducted from the depositor's tax base. Net withdrawals in an accounting period are similarly reported and are added to the depositor's tax base. It is permitted to borrow via a qualified account, in which case the proceeds of the loan are added to the tax base; repayments are deducted. Nothing transpiring inside the qualified account has direct tax consequences, only deposits and withdrawals.

- Transactions with respect to financial assets other than via qualified account, including payment and receipt of interest, receipt of dividends, purchases and sales, have no consequences for the tax base.

Table 10-2, which in a sense represents the summing up and conclusion of this paper, shows the data that might be used to implement a consumption type base, called a Cash Flow Tax (CFT). For comparison, I have also included in the table an indication of the data needed to implement a reasonably consistent individual income base called a Comprehensive Income Tax (CIT). As expected, many of the data items are common to the two taxes. Items preceded by a bullet are included in one and excluded in the other. Rather than provide a point-by-point commentary, I urge the reader to work through the illustrative tax return information. It will be readily apparent that those bulleted items presenting significant problems (requiring inflation adjustment, for example) are required for the income base and not for the consumption base. In some cases, for example, in the treatment of pensions or gifts and bequests, alternative rules might be employed, but the consistent alternatives would not simplify the CIT. The items included in the consumption base and not in the income base are typically readily measured cash flows.

(Table 10-2 commences on page 244)

Table 10-2. Information on Tax Returns for Illustrative Comprehensive Income and Cash Flow Taxes.

(Items preceded by a bullet are treated differently under the comprehensive income tax [CIT] and the cash flow tax [CFT].)

	Household Receipts and Deductions	An Element of C.I.T.	An Element of C.F.T.
Receipts:			
R-1	Wages, salaries, tips, royalties, and so forth, subject to tax[a]	Yes	Yes
R-2	Receipts of pensions, annuities, disability compensation, workman's compensation, and sick pay[b]	Yes	Yes
• R-3	Gifts, inheritances, trust distributions and life insurance death benefits received[c]	No	Yes
• R-4	Interest received on financial assets, *adjusted for inflation*	Yes	No[d]
R-5	Dividends received on corporate earnings	No[e]	No[d,f]
• R-6	Allocated share of *inflation corrected* corporate earnings	Yes	No
• R-7	Policyholder claim on earnings from life insurance, annuity, and pension plan reserves, *adjusted for inflation*	Yes	No
• R-8	Increase in value of the claim on a trust, beyond allocated share of amounts given or bequeathed to the trust, *adjusted for inflation*	Yes	No
• R-9	Proceeds from the sale, exchange or distribution of capital assets	Yes	No[d,f]
• R-10	Imputed service value attributable to owner-occupied housing and other household durables	Yes	No
R-11	Gross receipts from unincorporated business enterprises	Yes	Yes
• R-12	Withdrawals from qualified accounts (including withdrawals of borrowed funds)[g]	No	Yes
R-13	Total receipts (sum of included items R-1 - R-12)		
Deductions:			
D-1	Special items as a matter of policy (e.g., charitable contributions, medical expenses)	Yes	Yes
D-2	Contributions to qualified retirement plans	Yes	Yes
• D-3	Gifts and bequests made to an identified taxpayer or trust with eligible beneficiary (cf. receipts item R-3)	No	Yes
• D-4	Interest paid on indebtedness (including interest on home mortgages) *adjusted for inflation*	Yes	No[h]

Table 10-2. continued

	Household Receipts and Deductions	An Element of	
		C.I.T.	C.F.T.
Deductions: (continued)			
• D-5	Net life insurance premiums	No	Yes
D-6	Employee business expense (includes qualified travel expenses, union and professional association dues, tools, materials and qualified educational expenses)	Yes	Yes
• D-7	Basis of assets sold, exchanged or distributed (cf. receipts item R-9), *adjusted for inflation*	Yes[i]	No
D-8	Current expenses associated with unincorporated business enterprises	Yes	Yes
• D-9	Capital outlay associated with unincorporated business enterprises	No	Yes
• D-10	Depreciation allowances for current and past capital outlays associated with unincorporated business enterprises, *adjusted for inflation*	Yes	No
• D-11	Deposits to qualified accounts (including repayment of borrowed funds)	No	Yes
D-12	Total deductions (sum of included items D-1 - D-11)		
Tax Base:			
B-1	Total receipts less total deductions (R-13 minus D-12)		

[a] The definition of "wages subject to tax" could incorporate differential rules according to individual characteristics (for example, marital status might be used to mitigate the marriage tax problem). This item would *exclude* social security taxes attributable to retirement benefits and contributions to retirement plans. It would *include* employer-paid health and life insurance premiums and similar employee benefit outlays.

[b] This item would probably include social security benefits of all types. Pensions and annuities for which there has been no exclusion under R-1 or deduction under D-2 or D-11 would be excluded under R-2.

[c] The exclusion of gifts and inheritances received under the illustrative Comprehensive Income Tax may be rationalized by the difficulty in measuring accruing wealth from anticipated inheritance. Correspondingly, the giver, bequeather, or life insurer receives no deduction from the Comprehensive Income Tax Base (deduction item D-3 and D-5). The same system could be applied to the Cash Flow Tax. Alternatively, with appropriate modification of the treatment of life insurance and trusts, the Comprehensive Income Tax could follow the illustrative Cash Flow Tax usage, and vice versa.

[d] Under the illustrative Cash Flow Tax, a significant distinction is made between assets owned on a tax prepaid basis, the return on which is excluded from the base, and assets owned via qualified accounts, the return on which is ultimately included on the base when withdrawn. See footnote g.

(*Table 10-2. continued overleaf*)

Notes to Table 10-2. continued

[e]The exclusion of dividends under the Comprehensive Income Tax is a corollary of the allocation of all corporate income to shareholders. Dividends result in a reduction in the basis of the shares for purposes of calculating gain from sale or exchange (capital gain).

[f]Under the Cash Flow Tax, qualified account treatment would be obligatory for closely held corporations. See footnote g.

[g]"Qualified accounts," which are similar to IRAs and H.R. 10 accounts in current U.S. income tax law, play a critical role in the Cash Flow Tax. All inflows are deducted from the tax base, and all outflows are included. Nothing transpiring inside the account has direct tax consequences.

[h]Borrowing via qualified account (cf. fn. g) is included in the tax base and *all* consequent return payments into the account, whether of principal or interest, are deducted. However, neither interest on nor repayment of borrowing outside of a qualified account has tax consequences under the Cash Flow Tax.

[i]The deduction of adjusted basis would have to be limited, as at present, in relation to sales proceeds in R-9. Unused deduction of net losses could be carried forward.

APPENDIX[1]

Income and Consumption: Operational Definitions

An operational tax base of the income tax type is not a quantity like water in a closed hydraulic system, wherein the total remains constant regardless of how it is directed by valves and pumps. Rather, it is an aggregation of transactions, usually voluntary, although sometimes implicit. The transactions that take place will depend in part upon how they are treated by the tax system. The choice of a tax base is a choice about how to tax certain transactions.

An operational tax base is necessarily defined by a set of accounting rules that specifies the use of actual and implicit transactions in reaching the total to which a tax schedule is applied to determine the taxpayer's liability. The concept of income generally used in discussion of tax reform has been called an accretion concept. It is supposed to measure the command over resources acquired by the taxpayer during the accounting period, that command having been either exercised in the form of consumption or held as potential for future consumption in the form of an addition to the taxpayer's wealth. Hence, the apparently paradoxical practice of defining income by an outlay or uses concept—consumption plus change in net worth.

Everyday usage, on the other hand, tends to associate income with the sources side of the accounts. Thus, one speaks of income "from labor," such as wages, or income "from capital," or "from proprietorships," such as interest and profits. Because sources and uses must be equal in a double entry accounting system, the result should be the same whichever side is taken for purposes of measurement, provided that *all* uses are regarded as appropriate for inclusion in the tax base.

Definitions of Income and Consumption

To illustrate, it may be helpful to outline a rudimentary classification of transactions to define income and consumption. The accounts considered first are those of a wage earner whose only sources of funds are his wages and his accumulated balance in a savings account.

In the simplest case, the possible applications he can make of these funds may be divided into the purchase of goods and services for his immediate use and additions to or subtractions from his accumulation of savings. Thus, an account of his situation for the year might be the following:

Sources	*Uses*
Wages	Rent
Interest	Clothing
Balance in savings account at beginning of period	Food
	Recreation
	Balance in savings account at end of period

The two sides of this account are, of course, required to balance. Of the uses, the first four are generally lumped under the concept of consumption. The last constitutes the net worth of the household. Thus, the accounts may be schematically written as:

Sources	*Uses*
Wages	Consumption
Interest	
Net worth at beginning of period	Net worth at end of period

The concept of income concerns the *additions* to sources and their application during the accounting period. These can be found simply by subtracting the accumulated savings (net worth) at the beginning of the period from both sides, to give:

Addition to Sources	Uses of Addition to Sources
Wages	Consumption
Interest	Savings (equals increase in net worth over the period)[a]

[a]Note savings may be negative.

Income may be *defined* as the sum of consumption and increase in net worth. Note carefully that this involves a uses definition as a measure of differences in individual circumstances. This approach to the concept of income has substantial advantages as a device for organizing thinking on particular policy issues. With this uses definition of income, the situation of the illustrative individual may be represented by:

Addition to Sources	Uses of Addition to Sources
Wages	Income
Interest	

The last version of the accounts makes clear the way in which information about sources is used to determine the individual's income. To calculate his income for the year, this individual obviously would not add up his outlays for rent, clothing, food, recreation, and increase in savings account balance. Rather, he would simply add together his wages and interest and take advantage of the accounting identity between this sum and income.

This classification of uses into consumption and increase in net worth is not sufficient, however, to accommodate distinctions commonly made by tax policy. It will be helpful, therefore, to refine the accounts to the following:

Addition to Sources	Uses of Addition to Sources
Wages	Consumption
Interest	Cost of earnings
	Certain other outlays
	Increase in net worth

An individual's outlay for special work clothes needed for his profession requires the category "cost of earnings." These are netted out in defining income. Note that the decision about which outlays to include in this category is a social or political one. Thus, under U.S. income tax law, outlays for specialized work clothes are deductible, but commuting expenses are not. There is no independent standard to which one can appeal to determine whether such outlays are consumption (and, hence, a part of income) or work expenses (and, hence, out of income).

Similarly, a judgment may be made that some outlays, while not costs of earning a living, are also not properly classified as consumption. The category of "other outlays" is introduced for want of a better label for such transactions. For example, in everyday usage, charitable contributions would not be an application of funds appropriately labeled "personal consumption," much less "increase in net worth." Thus, using the definition of income as the sum of consumption and the increase in net worth, we now have:

Addition to Sources	Uses of Addition to Sources
Earnings (Wages + Interest)	Income (Consumption + Increase in net worth)
	Cost of earnings
	Certain other outlays

Again, to calculate income it is generally convenient to work from the left (sources) side of the accounting relationship described above. In this case,

Income = Earnings
minus
Cost of earnings
minus
Certain other outlays.

Similarly, consumption may be calculated by starting with source data:

Consumption = Earnings
minus
Cost of earnings
minus
Certain other outlays
minus
Increase in net worth.

One further addition to the accounting scheme is needed at this point: the item "gifts and bequests given." This is a use of funds that some would regard as consumption, but I reserve the term consumption, without modifier, for the narrower notion of goods and services of direct benefit to the individual in question. The accounts now have the following structure:

Addition to Sources	Uses of Addition to Sources
Wages	Consumption
Interest	Gifts and bequests given
Gifts and bequests received	Cost of earnings
	Certain other outlays
	Increase in net worth

It must be decided whether gifts and bequests given are to be regarded as income, that is, as a component of the total by which taxpayers are to be compared for assigning burdens. The term "ability-to-pay" is used to describe the income concept that considers income to be the sum of consumption plus gifts and bequests given plus increase in net worth, because it is within the taxpayer's ability to choose among these uses and, hence, all three measure taxpaying potential equally. The label "ability-to-pay" is intended to be suggestive only. There is no agreed upon measure of the idea of a taxpayer's ability to pay. Because of this, I employ quotation marks when I use the term "ability-to-pay" in its role as a label for an income or consumption concept.

"Ability-to-pay" income or consumption would also generally be calculated by starting on the sources side:

"Ability-to-pay" income = Earnings
plus
Gifts and bequests received
minus
Cost of earnings
minus
Certain other outlays.

"Ability-to-pay" consumption = Earnings
plus
Gifts and bequests received
minus
Cost of earnings
minus
Certain other outlays
minus
Increase in net worth.

The difference between consumption and income is the savings or increase in net worth over the period. Thus, equivalently:

"Ability-to-pay" consumption = "Ability-to-pay" income
minus
Increase in net worth.

Finally, there is the pair of income and consumption concepts that exclude gifts and bequests given from the category of uses by which tax burdens are to be apportioned. These are given the label "standard-of-living" because they are confined to outlays for the taxpayer's direct benefit. As with the term "ability-to-pay," this label is intended to be suggestive only. The "ability-to-pay" and "standard-of-living" concepts are related as follows:

"Standard-of-living" income = "Ability-to-pay" income
minus
Gifts and bequests given,

"Standard-of-living" consumption = "Standard-of-living" income
minus
Increase in net worth.

This discussion leads to a four-way classification of tax bases:

		Gifts Given	
		Included	*Excluded*
Increase in net worth	Included	"Ability-to-pay" income	"Standard-of-living" income
	Excluded	"Ability-to-pay" consumption	"Standard-of-living" consumption

NOTES TO CHAPTER 10

1. This Appendix is adapted from U.S. Treasury Department, *Blueprints for Basic Tax Reform* (Washington, D.C.: Government Printing Office, January 1977). An earlier version of the essay appeared in *Tax Notes* 16 (August 23, 1982): 715-723.

BIBLIOGRAPHY

Bradford, David F. "The Case for a Personal Consumption Tax." In Joseph A. Pechman, ed., *What Should Be Taxed: Income or Expenditure?* Washington, D.C.: The Brookings Institution, 1980a.

_____. "The Economics of Tax Policy Towards Savings." In George M. Von Furstenberg, ed., *The Government and Capital Formation*. Cambridge, Mass.: Ballinger Publishing Company, 1980b.

Institute for Fiscal Studies. *The Structure and Reform of Direct Taxation: Report of a Committee Chaired by Professor J.E. Meade*. London: George Allen and Unwin, 1978.

Kaldor, Nicholas. *An Expenditure Tax*. London: Allen and Unwin, 1955; Westport, Conn.: Greenwood Press, 1977.

Kay, John A., and King, Mervyn A. *The British Tax System*. Oxford: Oxford University Press, 1978.

Lodin, Sven-Olof. *Progressive Expenditure Tax—An Alternative? A Report of the 1972 Government Commission on Taxation*. Stockholm: LiberForlag, 1978 (originally published as *Progressiv utgiftssakatt—ett alternativ?* Stockholm: Statens Offentliga Utredningar 1976:62).

U.S. Treasury. *Blueprints for Basic Tax Reform*. Washington, D.C.: Government Printing Office, January 1977.

Discussants:

POLICIES, PROBLEMS, AND POLITICS OF THE CONSUMPTION BASED TAX

David L. Boren

I would not presume to analyze David Bradford's paper from an academic point of view. There are others on the panel far more qualified than I to offer that perspective. Instead, I will focus my discussion on the broader policy questions presented and the practical problems associated with the political acceptance of the proposal for a consumption based tax.

First, it should be emphasized that Dr. Bradford makes several good points about our present income based tax system. There is no doubt that it has penalized the saver in our country. The after-tax return on savings and dividends has been low, indeed, over the past two decades. In some cases, because of inflation, it has been negative. At the same time, while saving has been discouraged by the tax Code, borrowing and the expansion of debt have been encouraged. The combined effects of inflation and generous tax deductions for borrowing costs have encouraged the creation of more and more debt. I would certainly not quarrel with Dr. Bradford's assertion that we would all be better off if our neighbors had saved more and borrowed less. We would have a more secure society and one in which those beyond their working years would be better able to take care of themselves and less dependent on the viability of government programs like social security.

In addition, if borrowing had been more restrained, we would be facing a less dangerous situation in critical sectors of our society. In agriculture, for example, we now face a critical situation, largely because the huge deficit incurred by that sector over the past twenty years can no longer be serviced. This threatens not only the farm community but the entire economy. In the past twenty years, farm debt has increased from approximately $12 billion to over $200 billion, while real annual farm income has declined by 3 percent nationwide. The combination of huge debt, shrinking equity against which to borrow, and virtually no income with which to service debt is a disastrous combination encouraged by the government's tax and agriculture policies of the last decade. Examples in many other sectors of the economy could be cited, as well.

Another great benefit of increased saving would, of course, be the creation of capital for productive investment. It is becoming clear that the viability of our economy depends upon our ability to compete in international markets. With our high wage scale, we must use the latest technology to produce our products efficiently. It is well known that in the past ten years we have saved and reinvested only 3 or 4 percent of our national income in research and new plant and equipment. In West Germany, the rate of investment in research and new plant and equipment has been three or four times as high; in Japan, the rate has been as much as five or six times as high. A broad political consensus has been formed behind the goal of increasing our rate of investment. This consensus was reflected in the nearly unanimous support in the Senate Finance Committee and House Ways and Means Committee for improved and accelerated depreciation and cost recovery procedures.

While it is clear that Dr. Bradford is correct in wanting to further encourage saving and investment, it is less clear that a massive change in our approach to taxation is the best way to accomplish the objective in the shortest time. Several questions would be raised about a system that makes such a major change. The first immediate political question concerns how such a change would affect the relative tax burdens among lower, middle, and upper income citizens. With the huge deficits we now face, it is clear that the new tax system would have to continue, at last in the present, to raise about the same amount of revenue as the present system. If the taxes collected from corporations are virtually removed—and if large amounts placed into savings of one form or another are no longer taxed and much of the return is tax free—how would the lost revenue be reclaimed? Assuming that upper income persons have a much greater ability to choose to save after making necessary purchases, the burden would appear to shift dramatically. In difficult times of high unemployment, with more and more people living at the margin, there would be extreme political pressure against any major shift of additional tax burdens to the middle and lower income taxpayers.

The need to answer the first objection in regard to a major shift in the tax burden leads to the second possible objection. It is not clear that such a consumption based system would end up being any less complex than the present system. Surely, simplicity should be a primary goal, since a lack of faith in the tax Code and reduced voluntary compliance are becoming increasing problems. If political reality dictates that there can be no major shift of tax burdens, the consumption based tax would be framed by the political system to prevent such a shift. This could add much complexity to the system. Questions would immediately arise about exemptions from a consumption tax for the so-called necessities. Are charitable contributions or medical expenses necessities? In this day and time, is telephone service a necessity? What about the ability to use an automobile? What about home ownership, to which a vast majority of voters and office holders attach great value? There is the further question of whether certain kinds of consumption are more desirable than others, in order to encourage the expansion of some sectors of the economy. The questions and complications are endless, and they certainly bring into doubt any assertion that a consumption based tax system would automatically be less complicated.

A third question, which follows from the second, comes to mind. Would it be as easy in a consumption based system as in an income based system to encourage the kind of spending, particularly by the business sector, that would help us maintain our technological edge? With corporate tax burdens virtually nonexistent, would the consumption based system be as effective in encouraging corporate investment in research and plant modernization? There may be sound economic efficiency reasons for considering total elimination of the corporate tax, so that we no longer treat as the taxable entity the corporation as well as the individual stockholder. However, a question arises as to whether under that system there would be as much direct and effective incentive for capital investment as under the current corporate income tax system, which includes Investment Tax Credits.

A fourth question is closely related to the question of providing the proper incentives for certain preferred investments. Not only do we want to encourage certain types of investment, but we also want to encourage the generation of income from some sources more than from others. Could a consumption based system do that as effectively as our present system? For example, is it clearly in our national interest to encourage additional export income in order to improve the balance of trade and to expand our world markets? The current system uses foreign tax credits, DISCs, and other devices to encourage companies to generate income through export sales. More incentives are currently being considered. It is unclear how we could reach this goal effectively under a consumption based system.

Fifth, the consumption based system, as proposed by Dr. Bradford, would strongly bias the tax system against debt creation by reducing the ability to charge off borrowing costs. While some adjustment needs to be made to encourage more saving and less borrowing, a proper and reasonable balance must be maintained. All borrowing is not bad. Clearly, long-term debt can, and often does, serve an extremely important function. The damage done by the disruption of long-term fixed rate financing, caused by government deficits and unstable interest rates, is convincing proof of that statement. The ability to obtain access to long-term financing is especially important to the small enterprise and to new entrepreneurs in our economic system.

Finally, one reaches perhaps the most important objection of all. A massive change in our tax system would create uncertainty. The last thing our economy needs right now is the injection of a further element of uncertainty. Investment decisions are already made difficult for the businessman, who is buffeted by fluctuating interest rates, divided economic forecasts, retroactive government regulatory decisions, and constant changes in the tax Code. Given the slowness of the political system to resolve the details of new proposals, adding further uncertainty at this moment would be of questionable benefit and should be approached with great caution. While I agree that something must be done to encourage savings, there is a simpler way to change the tax Code without developing a new theoretical base for the tax system.

A strong and growing consensus has been built around the need for the encouragement of saving and the need to promote capital formation. Instead of confusing this issue by injecting a debate about a major shift in the tax structure, an evolutionary change in the present system may well be preferable. Additional tax incentives for saving and for investment could be added to the present system, while carefully crafted consumption tax increases could be used to recoup the revenues lost in the process. The consumption taxes could be framed to minimize their regressive features; luxury taxes or taxes on nonnecessity items come to mind. At the same time, the movement for the simplification of our present tax Code could be continued. It is also now very clear that for Congress to have an opportunity to consider tax policy in any kind of coherent context, we must have a broad, bipartisan agreement on deficit reduction; otherwise, we will be faced with a repetition of the Band-Aid approach, which calls for a laundry list of "revenue enhancements." Such a simple approach focuses on coming up with a dollar figure instead of on sound economic principles. Recent imposition of the withholding tax on interest income is a glaring example of the evil of that approach. A blended approach aimed at moving us toward Dr. Bradford's goal of increasing saving without injecting a sweeping change in fragile and uncertain economic times is well worth considering.

AN EQUITY CASE FOR CONSUMPTION TAXATION

Lawrence H. Summers [1]

Oliver Wendell Holmes once wrote that "taxes are what we pay for civilization." Demand curves slope downward, however, and as our tax system is seen as more and more burdensome, we may choose to purchase fewer of the benefits of civilized society and to spend less to protect that society from foreign adversaries. An idea of this sort must be behind the rising antipathy of the American people toward taxes—manifested in tax revolts in many states, increasing tax evasion and avoidance, and the election of Ronald Reagan.

Our tax system has come under attack from many sources. Two strands of criticism have permeated popular discussions. One strand focuses on what are seen as tax loopholes or provisions in the tax Code that primarily benefit the rich without conferring significant social benefits. The second strand, in ascendancy at the moment, emphasizes the grave consequences of our current tax system for economic efficiency and growth. To date, these strands of criticism have been largely dissonant. Measures seen by some as increasing fairness—such as full or accrual taxation of capital gains—are widely recognized to undermine economic efficiency in an unacceptable fashion. Measures necessary to restore adequate incentives—such as the reduction in the top bracket rate from 70 to 50 percent, are seen by many as inequitable and unfair. Our current tax law satisfies no one. Some regard its inequities as a disgrace to the human race; others say that it stunts the economic growth on which future prosperity depends.

I share David Bradford's conviction that the consumption tax offers an appealing solution to many of the dilemmas of tax policy. Keynes concluded his *General Theory* with the famous observation that even "Practical men, who believe themselves to be quite exempt from any intellectual influences, are usually the slaves of some defunct economist. . . . It is ideas, not vested interests, which are dangerous for good or evil." The pace of life has accelerated since Keynes wrote, and we may hope to see the *Blueprints* that David Bradford laid out at the Treasury put into practice, long before he or it is defunct. We may also hope that the powerful ideas contained therein will overwhelm the many vested interests that will inevitably oppose any tax reform.

I do not need to repeat the contribution that consumption taxation could make to economic growth. It would eliminate the many disincentives to savings and investment that remain in the tax Code and contribute greatly to reducing the efficiency cost of taxation. I want to amplify a theme Dr. Bradford touched on and suggest that, in several ways, a shift to consumption taxation would increase fairness and equity in our tax system.

First, there is the question of choosing a fair base for taxation. Thomas Hobbes argued that there was greater justice in taxing people on what they took from the social pot (their consumption) rather than on what they contributed (as measured by their income). In many cases, this value judgment seems compelling. Should not some tax be paid by a wealthy man who draws down his wealth to maintain a high rate of consumption? It is not unreasonable for a profligate borrower, who lives beyond his income, to pay taxes on his pleasures.

Critics of the consumption tax point to the apparent counter-example of the miserly millionaire who enjoys great wealth but pays little tax. This argument has never seemed very compelling to me. If an individual foregoes consumption and allows his wealth to be used to contribute to productivity and growth, why should he be taxed? This question is hard to answer convincingly, since any proceeds earned and the interest on them will ultimately be taxed, if they are spent.

I want to dwell on this argument for a moment because I think it is very important. A consumption tax is, in a very real sense, less coercive than an income tax. Under an income tax, persons who earn and save must pay tax. In the words of the old joke, "The reward of energy, enterprise and thrift is taxes." Under a consumption tax, enterprise and thrift are unpenalized, and even energy and effort can escape taxation as long as their fruits are saved.

Fairness has many dimensions. A particularly important dimension is what economists call vertical equity—the notion that the rich should pay more than the poor. It is often thought that because many of the rich save more than the poor, a shift toward consumption taxation is necessarily regressive. This need not and probably would not be so. Obviously, a rate structure could be legislated to achieve any given degree of progressivity in either an income or a consumption tax regime. Beyond this observation, however, there are several features of the consumption tax that would make its ultimate effect more progressive than is the current income tax system. Four aspects of the consumption tax support this conclusion.

First, a consumption tax is favorable to capital accumulation and growth. The incentive for Americans to save would be enhanced by increases in the rate of return that would be received. Similarly, with the removal of burdensome taxes, foreign capital would flow into the United States. The consequences of increased capital accumulation for the pretax income distribution are progressive. Increased capital accumulation means higher productivity and higher wages for workers. The law of diminishing returns implies that increases in capital drive down the returns earned by the owners of capital.

How great are these effects? Before coming to Washington, I completed a study of the response of saving to rates of return. I concluded that the response of saving to the rates of return was substantial. If this conclusion is correct, it is reasonable to estimate that, in the long run, a shift to consumption taxation might raise wages by more than 15 percent and reduce pretax capital returns by more than 40 percent. Thus, reductions in the taxation of capital would largely be shifted to the long-run benefit of workers.

Second, consumption taxation would offer a viable framework for attacking tax shelters. We frequently think that the important characteristic of consumption taxation is that it exempts capital income from tax, but consumption taxation also disallows the deductions for borrowing and business losses upon which most tax shelters depend. Let me offer some statistics. In 1979 total interest deductions under the individual income tax came to $71 billion, while total interest income came to $73 billion. In the same year, total net profits from business activities were equal to $8.7 billion, and total net losses came to $11.5 billion dollars. Because a consumption tax would avoid taxing capital income, it would obviate the need for the loss allowances from which so much mischief springs.

The significance of this effect is difficult to gauge. Those who are most successful in sheltering income show up in our tax statistics as poor, with very low AGIs, but some indirect evidence suggests that capital is increasingly escaping current taxes. The spread between municipal and taxable bond yields has narrowed greatly in the last two years. Undoubtedly, this has many causes, but the current and prospective availability of methods to avoid capital income taxation must have reduced the attraction of their tax exemption for investors. No similar reduction in tax subsidies to borrowing seems to have taken place.

Third, a properly implemented consumption tax would offer an opportunity to tax accumulated wealth, which to date has escaped taxation under the individual income tax. It would be terribly unfair to tax an individual once when income is earned, twice when it is invested, and then thrice when it is consumed. On the other hand, when income is successfully sheltered in the first place and accumulates tax-free interest, there is justice in taxing it when it is spent. A proper consumption tax would focus on providing maximum incentives directed at encouraging new acts of saving, but there is little efficiency cause for exempting consumption financed from past savings. As a consequence, consumption taxes would offer an improved way of attacking current concentrations of wealth.

In addition, consumption taxes would probably lead to some asset revaluations. These should probably be minimized by a gradual phase-in. In some cases, however, they would offset windfall gains attributable to our income tax system and its interaction with inflation.

Further, under a consumption tax, saving decisions would no longer be distorted. This would surely mitigate one of our major barriers to increased progressivity under the income tax. Progressivity could no longer be opposed on the grounds that high marginal rates excessively interfere with saving decisions. Under a consumption tax, the higher marginal propensity of the rich to save would not constitute a justification for opposing progressivity. In economists' language, the optimal tax is likely to be more progressive if efficiency costs can be minimized. A related point is that the perceived cost of public sector spending, which tends to be egalitarian in its incidence, would be reduced by moving toward a more efficient tax system.

These four considerations—increased productivity and higher wages, reduced tax shelter abuses, increased ability to tax existing wealth, and the reduced efficiency cost of progressivity—lead me to believe that consumption taxation is a reform that deserves support from equity-oriented tax reformers as well as from those concerned with economic growth. David Bradford, in his current paper and his other writings over the past few years, has helped show us the way. I hope and believe that tax reforms will build from his *Blueprints* in future years.

NOTES

1. These remarks represent my personal opinions and do not necessarily represent the opinions of any other organization or individual.

THE CONSUMPTION BASED TAX: PROSPECTS FOR REFORM

Perry D. Quick

It is common these days for proponents of a consumption tax to say that recent innovations in tax policy—IRAs and Keoghs, for example—have moved us halfway toward a consumption tax. Other observers would respond skeptically, saying that there is considerable work to be done and many problems to be addressed before a consumption tax system would be workable, either in an economic or political sense.

This conference presents a real opportunity to accelerate adoption of broad-based tax reform, whether that reform ultimately results in a consumption based tax or some other system. Addressing a string of massive structural deficits requires more than just a change in the economics of tax policy. It also may require tax legislation politics to focus our political energies on real improvements in the tax system, improvements that add up to significant reform.

We want a system that encourages work, saving, and investment. The best way to make our tax system more efficient and less distortional is to reduce tax rates on these activities. Academic economists argue over the theoretical efficiency gains of a comprehensive income tax system versus a consumption tax system. I would like to endorse Senator Boren's evolutionary approach to reform. I suspect that continuing to attack the problems of our current system and to move in the direction of broadening the base and lowering tax rates, without deciding what system we ultimately want, would give us the bulk of the efficiency benefits we might gain from adopting more drastic measures now. For example, most alternatives for base broadening that are "on the table" today are consistent with moving toward either a consumption tax or a comprehensive income tax. We could decide later which system would give us a second round of efficiency gains.

We also want a system that is fair. Recently, we have seen many attempts to design flat income taxes, "almost flat" income taxes, and other systems, and to assess the distributional effects of these alternatives. Depending on the system, and depending on one's point of view, these systems have been shown to be more or less fair than each other or than what we have now. Before coming to the Roosevelt Center, I worked with Senator Gary Hart to put together several structures for an expenditure tax system that attempted to keep the distribution of the tax burden roughly similar to the existing tax system. (The distributional effects of the two possible systems are shown in Table 10-3.) Clearly, expenditure tax systems can be constructed that improve efficiency and, at the same time, keep the distributional impacts roughly the same as the current one.

We want a system that can be implemented and administered. Professor Bradford has done as much as anyone to show that an expenditure tax system could be put in place and that most of the administrative difficulties could be handled satisfactorily. I think it is time that the practitioners take a closer look at this system to see whether it is workable and where the pitfalls in the system remain.

It seems that many people already have a fairly clear impression of what they want as tax reform. Now consider for a moment what is needed to get the bipartisan support to move the system toward real reform. We still have work to do in demonstrating to the public that the benefits of reform are worth the costs.

First, academics and practitioners must both demonstrate more concretely to the public the generalized benefits of tax reform. What can we say about the improvement in the average growth rate of the economy, about unemployment, or about the average individual's personal income, if these reforms were to be enacted?

Second, academics and practitioners must demonstrate that the new system will not generate undesirable side effects. Many people, for example, are concerned that a consumption tax will allow new dynasties of "miserly millionaires" and unfair accumulations of wealth and power to develop over time. This issue can be handled intellectually, but are policymakers prepared to explain the issue?

Third, it must be demonstrated that the changes associated with reform will not be too disruptive. As noted earlier, we can construct systems where the distributional effects are not very different from the current system. We also must develop more fully the workable transition mechanisms that would smoothly convert the existing system to the new one.

There are several things we can do today that would set the stage for future reforms, regardless of whether those reforms move us toward a consumption based tax or some other system. The key to this process may be lower tax rates matched with base broadening. The lower the tax rates, and the less special preferences are worth, the easier it will be to do away with such preferences over time. And base broadening would allow us to decrease tax rates while raising adequate revenue.

To this end, I'd like to offer an alternative approach to the surtax "trigger" or "standby" proposal currently under consideration in

Table 10-3. Tax Revenue Estimates.

			Consumption Tax	
Consumption Class (thousands of dollars)	Number of Filers (millions)	"Present Law" Tax (billions of dollars)	Low Exemption, 24 Percentage Rate (billions of dollars)	High Exemption, 30 Percentage Rate (billions of dollars)
$ 0-5	40.7	$ 1.2	—	—
5-10	24.3	9.5	$ 2.1	—
10-15	17.9	17.8	23.1	$ 12.7
15-20	11.8	22.9	28.9	25.5
20-30	8.7	32.6	35.4	36.5
30-50	3.7	22.8	26.5	30.0
50-100	1.3	16.5	19.0	22.6
100+	0.3	13.3	9.3	11.3
Total	108.7	$136.6	$144.3	$138.6

Note: 1976 consumption levels; 1982 levels would be 50 percent higher. Tax revenues under "Present Law" do not reflect ERTA or TEFRA. Low exemption is equivalent to applying a zero bracket amount of $10,000 in 1982 dollars; High exemption is equivalent to $15,000. Based on U.S. Treasury, *Blueprints for Basic Tax Reform* (Washington, D.C.: Government Printing Office, January 1977).

Washington. To relieve the uncertain fiscal pressures that we may face in 1985 and beyond, it has been proposed that Congress pass a law that would trigger a surtax—in other words, an increase in tax rates—if the deficit in 1985 is greater than 2 percent of GNP. This surtax approach would help to cut the deficits in future years, but it fails to address the underlying structural problems with our tax system. I suggest that we keep a trigger type of approach because it may be helpful in these uncertain times. I also suggest that we change the target. We should put in place some structural improvements, such as a base broadening attack on some special preferences, to go into effect in 1985 and beyond. We could thereby raise our future revenue potential. Then, if the deficit were *below* 2 percent of GNP in those years, we could trigger additional cuts in tax rates or an expansion of IRAs. In this way, we can aim at both short-term fiscal prudence and longer-term tax reform.

Chapter 11

The Comprehensive Income Tax: Advantages and Disadvantages

Richard Goode

The individual income tax has been the leading source of federal revenue, by a wide margin, ever since the end of World War II. It also generates substantial amounts of revenue for state and local governments. Probably the tax never lived up to the sanguine prediction of the House Ways and Means Committee in 1913 that "all good citizens" will "cheerfully support and sustain" it,[1] but in recent years dissatisfaction appears to have become so acute that one may ask whether the income tax can or should retain its leading role. My answer is, yes, the individual income tax is better than the alternatives. By reforms long discussed by specialists, the tax can be greatly improved. It is excessively naive, however, to expect that the changes can be easily or quickly made or that their adoption would quiet all complaints.

The percentage of total tax revenue that the United States obtains from the personal income tax is slightly above the median for industrial countries. In relation to gross domestic product, the yield of the tax in the United States is virtually equal to the median for those countries. (All levels of government are included; see Table 11-1.) These facts may come as a surprise to those who have inferred from recent political debates that the income tax is unusually heavy in the United States.

Table 11-1. Personal Income Tax Revenue in Relation to Total Tax Revenue and Gross Domestic Product, Selected OECD Countries, 1978-80.

Country	Percentage of Total Tax Revenue[a]	Percentage of Gross Domestic Product[a]
Australia	43.9%	13.1%
Austria	23.3	9.6
Belgium	35.2	15.9
Canada	33.3	10.6
Denmark	51.0	22.8
Finland	43.9	15.6
France	12.8	5.3
Germany	29.6	11.1
Ireland	30.2	10.3
Italy	22.9	7.2
Japan	23.3	5.8
Luxembourg	27.1	12.6
Netherlands	26.4	12.0
New Zealand	59.7	18.6
Norway	35.9	16.7
Sweden	41.8	21.1
Switzerland	35.7	11.1
United Kingdom	31.4	10.8
United States	35.9	11.0
Median	33.3	11.1

[a] Unweighted arithmetic means of annual percentages; includes all levels of government.

Source: Organisation for Economic Co-Operation and Development, *Revenue Statistics of OECD Member Countries, 1965-1981* (Paris, 1982), p. 72.

ADVANTAGES OF THE INCOME TAX

The great capacity of the income tax as a revenue raiser ensures that it will continue to receive much attention from governments. But the role of the tax cannot be explained merely by its fiscal productivity. Revenue could be obtained more simply from some form of sales tax, value added tax, or gross receipts tax. The income tax owes its place in modern revenue systems to its recognized advantages—advantages that induced the Ways and Means Committee to call it the "fairest and cheapest of all taxes" when the first income tax in the United States was enacted after adoption of the Sixteenth Amendment in 1913.

An advantage of the income tax over other major taxes now in use is that it takes account of the personal circumstances of taxpayers and incorporates progressive rates. Thus, it applies the principle of ability to pay. Furthermore, the income tax has the economic advantages associated with its wide coverage. A comprehensive income tax can avoid nonfunctional discriminations between activities and industries, which are an inherent feature of more narrowly based taxes. To be sure, an income tax discriminates against income-producing personal exertion and investment as compared with leisure and hoarding; but a comprehensive income tax avoids discrimination between sources of income and forms of consumption.

CRITICISMS AND COMPLAINTS

The same characteristics of the income tax that lend its appeal as a means of tapping ability to pay, however, lead to many of our current discontents. Provisions that favor certain activities or sources and uses of income are easily introduced, which necessitates high nominal rates if adequate revenue is to be raised. The height and progressivity of tax rates become contentious political issues.

There may be lessons here for both the supporters of a comprehensive income tax and the advocates of a flat rate tax. Omissions from taxable income and rate graduation are deeply enough embedded in the history of the income tax to indicate that they must respond to enduring beliefs and preferences.

The principal complaints against the U.S. income tax are familiar. They can be briefly enumerated and require little explanation. They are that the tax is too complex, that rates are too high, that incentives to work and assume responsibility are damaged, that saving and investment are curtailed and economic growth thus retarded, that avoidance and evasion are extensive and unfair. A complaint more recent than these perennial ones is that the income tax interacts unfairly and harmfully with inflation. This newest criticism may have had the greatest impact on opinions of influential members of the middle class, and it is technically the most difficult with which to deal.

The public dislikes the income tax. Far from endorsing the judgment of the 1913 Ways and Means Committee, 36 percent of respondents to an opinion poll conducted in 1982 said that the federal income tax was the worst tax. The rate reductions and other provisions of the Economic Recovery Tax Act of 1981 did not mollify people. In 1981, and also in 1980, 36 percent of respondents again said that the federal income tax was the worst tax. This may appear to be a stable and tenaciously held opinion. But in 1972, only 19 percent of those interviewed held it, and the income tax was ranked the fairest tax of all. (The local property tax was rated the worst tax in 1972.) By 1982, the poll-takers apparently no longer thought it worthwhile to ask which tax is fairest.[2]

The polls do not tell us what people dislike about the income tax. Some may be displeased because the present tax fails to live up to the high standards that can be attained by a well-administered, comprehensive income tax. Others might be even more displeased if administration were tightened and exclusions and deductions from taxable income narrowed. We can only speculate.

As already intimated, it seems likely that one explanation of the more critical attitude toward the income tax is its interaction with inflation. The most obvious result of this interaction with inflation is bracket creep, which has pushed many people into higher rate brackets. Less obvious, but much more difficult to rectify, is the distortion of the measurement of interest income and expense, capital gains and losses, and business profits. Resentment of inflation itself and, lately, discontent with the country's general economic performance may have rubbed off on the income tax.

A unique feature of comments on the income tax is the extent to which criticisms come from both those who favor progressive taxation and those who dislike it. Indeed, supporters of income taxation have been most assiduous in documenting the shortcomings of the present tax. I have participated in that documentation myself. To be sure, I never went so far as President Jimmy Carter, who, with an infelicitous combination of hyperbole and rhyme, called the income tax "a disgrace to the human race." Many comments are hypercritical and unrealistic. They play into the hands of irreconcilables who date the decline of the republic from the adoption of the Sixteenth Amendment.

A COMPREHENSIVE BASE

Most specialists believe that the income tax base should be comprehensive in order to attain the greatest advantages of the tax. In pure form, a comprehensive income tax base would include all accretions to economic power or wealth—that is, the sum of consumption and the increase or decrease in a person's net worth. This would comprise not only earnings and investment returns, including accrued capital gains and losses, but also gifts, bequests, and transfer payments received. Not all income so defined would be subjected to tax; much of it would be relieved by personal exemptions. Deductions, however, would be limited to costs of acquiring income.

It is generally conceded that this pure form of comprehensive income tax is not a practical possibility. Short of it, there are several versions of a broad-based tax that might deserve the name comprehensive income tax. One version begins with the accretion base but omits gifts and bequests received, unrealized capital gains, and imputed rent of owner-occupied dwellings. Put another way, to adjusted gross income, as now defined, is added the omitted part of capital gains; employers' contributions to pension funds, health insurance, and life insurance on behalf of employees; interest on life insurance savings; half of social security benefits; unemployment compensation; veterans' benefits; contributions to IRAs and Keogh plans; interest on state or local bonds; and a few other items. Personal deductions are limited to those miscellaneous items that can plausibly be classified as costs of obtaining income. Several tax credits are eliminated. The measurement of business profits also should be adjusted, but that topic relates preeminently to the corporation tax and is not discussed in this paper.

A second version of a comprehensive income tax starts with the base just described but allows some personal deductions. These include state and local income taxes, unusual medical expenses, and large casualty losses. Interest payments are regarded as a cost of obtaining property income and are deductible up to the amount of taxable property income reported. In recognition of costs incurred when both husband and wife work outside the home and to alleviate the so-called marriage penalty, married couples are allowed to deduct part of the earnings of the spouse with lower earnings, say, 25 percent, up to a limit. This may as closely approximate a pure comprehensive income tax as is worth discussing. Many would say that it is outside the limits of practicality.

A third version of a comprehensive tax differs from the second version by allowing personal deductions for home mortgage interest, subject to a limit, and charitable contributions that are large relative to income. Interest on state or local bonds outstanding at the time the law was changed continues to be excluded. Still other versions can easily be imagined, but they depart farther and farther from the concept of a comprehensive income tax.

RATES IN A COMPREHENSIVE TAX

With a comprehensive income base it is possible, of course, to cut nominal tax rates without sacrificing revenue. The cuts can be made in many different ways, and therein lies an obstacle to reform. Differences of opinion about the appropriate degree of progressivity may block action. The best approach probably is to separate the issues of comprehensiveness and progressivity by adopting rates that maintain the existing degree of progressivity. This requires deeper cuts of nominal rates in high brackets than in low and middle brackets because high-income persons benefit more, on average, than others do from the present exclusions, personal deductions, and credits.

Estimates by Pechman and Scholz, based on projected 1984 income levels, show what could be done.[3] Individuals and families below the estimated poverty lines in calendar year 1984 could be freed of income tax by personal exemptions of $1,750 per capita plus $1,750 for heads of households and a zero bracket amount of $4,000. Adoption of those provisions, together with a base similar to the second version of the comprehensive income base described above, would allow the present revenue yield and approximately the present effective progressivity of the individual income tax to be maintained under a rate schedule ranging from about 9 to 28 percent. With other broad, but less comprehensive, income bases, schedules with beginning rates between 9 and 12 percent and top rates between 28 and 30 percent might be required.

ADVANTAGES OF A COMPREHENSIVE TAX

A comprehensive income tax with lower nominal rates has substantial advantages over the present system. It is more equitable, in my view. It greatly reduces complexity. Under it, time and energy now devoted to tax compliance—and even more to tax avoidance—become available for productive activities; some of the differences in taxation related to income sources and uses are eliminated, while others are reduced. In my estimation, it would help improve economic efficiency.

Under a comprehensive income tax, large changes would occur in relative taxation of the yields of different forms of saving and investment. Items less favorably treated would include saving through life insurance, employer financed pension funds, IRAs and Keogh plans, as well as investments preferred by the institutions administering these saving programs. Also less favorably treated would be investment in state or local securities and all assets that are expected to throw off a large part of their total return in appreciation (and not dividends or other recurrent payments). Investment in owner-occupied residences would be less favorably treated because of the elimination or curtailment of personal deductions for property taxes and mortgage interest. Many other forms of saving and investment would be more favorably treated.

Saving and investment flows to previously favored outlets could be expected to diminish in relation to flows to other outlets. Hence, the prices of assets associated with the former flows would tend to decline relative to prices of assets associated with the latter flows.

Some forms of saving and investment would be more favorably treated than others. To the degree that one believes that individual decisions and the financial markets generally tend to result in the most efficient allocation of investment, the consequences of a closer approach to neutral tax treatment should be welcomed. A significant offsetting social cost can be attributed to more uniform taxation only to the extent that one believes that the special tax provisions serve high priority objectives and are more effective than other means of advancing them. I share the widespread skepticism on these points.

It is tempting to anticipate increased incentives to work, save, and invest because of the lower marginal rates of the comprehensive income tax. But I doubt whether that effect would be very significant. If the degree of progressivity is not changed, it seems that true marginal rates would remain unaltered for representative taxpayers, with decreases in rates on income from some sources being balanced by increases in rates on income from other sources. To be sure, the lower marginal rates would be automatically available under the comprehensive tax, rather than being dependent on the separate actions of taxpayers to take advantage of tax saving provisions. Hence, the lower rates would be more clearly discernible and, possibly, more attractive.

CAPITAL GAINS AND LOSSES

Something more should be said about the implications of changes in the tax treatment of capital gains and losses. The termination of the exclusion from taxable income of 60 percent of long-term capital gains would raise effective rates of tax on this form of income, despite lower nominal rates. Often it is asserted that low taxes on capital gains are desirable because they encourage investment in new and growing firms and risky enterprises. It is true that a large part of the return on investment in new and growing firms tends to take the form of appreciation because profits are reinvested rather than distributed. But whether favorable taxation of realized appreciation is needed to encourage new and growing firms or is conducive to economic vigor when applicable to all kinds of firms, new and old, is debatable. Preferential taxation of capital gains may have done more to foster highly leveraged real estate ventures than to encourage innovative enterprises. Better opportunities for especially risky investments to offset capital losses should mitigate the effect of heavier taxation of gains.

In many cases, the distinction between investment returns in the form of dividends, interest, rent and realized capital gains is economically artificial. For example, it is hard to believe that any significant policy objective is served by taxing at different rates the capital gain realized at the maturity of a bond bought at a discount and its coupon yield.

An old argument about capital gains taxation is that a tax limited to realized gains will discourage realizations and will tend to lock investors into their holdings and damage the efficiency of the capital market. This contention is qualitatively valid, though often overemphasized. At present, an important lock-in factor is the escape from taxation of appreciation of assets transferred at death; the termination of that opportunity would considerably alleviate the problem.

A more serious objection to full taxation of capital gains is that the gains are overstated because of inflation. It would not be difficult to correct nominal gains for inflation by applying a general price index. Perhaps simultaneous adoption of the two provisions would be a reasonable trade-off. An inflation correction for capital gains but not for business profits and interest income and payments, however, could not be rigorously justified on equity and economic grounds, in view of the absence of a clear functional distinction between capital gains and other investment returns. A fully satisfactory adjustment for all kinds of income probably is not practicable because of technical difficulties.[4] However, unless inflation is kept at much lower than recent levels, the subject should be addressed with a more open mind than it has been in the past.

SAVING AND INVESTMENT

Taken as a whole, the changes involved in transition to a comprehensive income tax would tend to increase taxation of property income relative to labor income. The question arises whether this would discourage saving and wealth accumulation, with adverse effects on productive investment and growth. The question cannot be confidently answered. On theoretical grounds, we cannot predict how a reduction in the rate of return on saving would affect its volume. On the one hand, the lower rate of reward would tend to make saving less attractive relative to immediate consumption, but, on the other hand, a person who is saving for retirement or for specific future expenditures would need to save more to satisfy his needs. Statistical studies have not resolved the issue.

Furthermore, it appears highly likely that any differences in saving propensities resulting from the fairly small increase in effective income tax rates that is under consideration would be overshadowed by macroeconomic factors affecting national saving and investment. Among the most important of these factors is the budget deficit. Over the ten calendar years 1973-82, the federal deficit (national income and product accounts definition) equalled 47 percent of total personal saving in the United States. It fell below 10 percent of personal saving in only one year.[5] The deficit may be looked at either as a negative entry in national saving or as an absorber of private saving. If our goal is to increase savings available for private investment, we need to check our tendency to run federal deficits year in and year out. It is important to bear in mind, however, that a smaller federal deficit will result in greater investment in the United States only if monetary policy, tax provisions, and other conditions ensure a high level of activity and make investment here attractive relative to foreign investment.

A FLAT RATE TAX

An alternative to a comprehensive income tax with lower graduated rates is a flat rate tax. This idea has attracted some attention lately. A flat rate tax is simpler and avoids the harm to incentives done by progressivity, but it necessarily involves a huge redistribution of taxation from high-income to low- and middle-income groups.[6] I do not believe that the country is willing to discard a feature of the income tax that is essential to reach ability to pay, that has been present in the U.S. tax for the past seventy years, and that appears in almost every other income tax.

A particular version of the flat rate tax proposed by Robert E. Hall and Alvin Rabushka imposes a flat rate tax on income earned by personal effort.[7] Under it, business profits (including interest on borrowed capital) are virtually exempt. This is true because all outlays for fixed investment and inventories would be immediately deductible from business gross receipts, regardless of the length of useful life of depreciable assets or the amount of inventory accumulation. Under a 19 percent flat rate tax, as suggested by Hall and Rabushka, investment goods or inventory selling for $100 would have a net cost of $81, and the after-tax return would equal 81 cents of every dollar of before-tax return. For established firms that are able to take full advantage of the immediate deductions, the rate of return would be equal to that under full tax exemption. Furthermore, no tax would be paid on reinvested profits.

For the business sector in a closed economy, the base of the tax proposed by Hall and Rabushka closely resembles that of the European model value added tax. That tax is universally recognized to be a consumption tax. Under those conditions, the Hall-Rabushka plan simplifies the income tax out of existence and substitutes a consumption tax. Whether in practice the outcome would be virtually equivalent to a value added tax (with personal exemptions) depends on how international trade and international flows of capital and investment income are treated.

AN EXPENDITURE TAX

Another alternative to a comprehensive income tax that has been discussed in recent years, especially in academic circles, is an expenditure tax. This is a direct tax on consumption expenditures, incorporating personal exemptions and graduated rates. The idea has received an occasional comment by a few writers over a long period of time but was generally considered impracticable. Lately, some writers have taken a different view, asserting that the expenditure tax would be simpler to administer than the income tax. I do not agree and note that the expenditure tax has been tried only in India and Sri Lanka, where it was a failure. I consider the income tax superior to an expenditure tax, but in this paper, there is no space to elaborate on my reasons. Rather, I shall make some assertions that could be more convincingly supported in an extended discussion.[8]

In my opinion, the income tax is fairer than an expenditure tax because income is a better measure of ability to pay than is consumption. The difference between income and consumption, of course, is saving (or dissaving). Saving results from personal decisions that do not diminish one's ability to support the commonwealth. The expenditure tax would allow unchecked accumulation of wealth during a person's lifetime and would allow the perpetuation of a family fortune, unless stringent taxes were applied to gifts and bequests. By permitting untaxed compounding of property income, the expenditure tax favors recipients of that kind of income over those earning income by personal effort. That clashes with a long tradition holding that earned income should be taxed more lightly. Abrupt transition to an expenditure tax would be unfair to persons who, having accumulated retirement savings from taxable income, find themselves taxed on the basis of consumption as they used up their savings.

Complications arise concerning the taxes of persons who move into the country or out of it.

Progressive income and expenditure taxes have similar effects on incentives to work. The concentration of taxation on earned income, however, entails higher tax rates on it, if revenue is to be maintained. The effect on the amount of work done is indeterminate on theoretical grounds. Available statistical studies suggest that single persons and first earners of married couples would not be much affected, but that second earners of married couples would work less.

The rate of return on savings would be increased. Although the size of the change would be greater than the reduction discussed previously in connection with the comprehensive income tax, the uncertainty of the economic consequences is similar. My inclination is to believe that personal saving would be stimulated, but probably by only a small amount. As pointed out above, even sizable changes in personal saving propensities may be outweighed by macroeconomic factors, particularly the size of the budget deficit.

CONCLUSION

I conclude that movement toward a more comprehensive income tax, with lower nominal rates, is a far more attractive route to tax reform than pursuit of either a flat rate tax on income or an expenditure tax. What are the prospects? I have to concede that experience offers small grounds for optimism. The erosion of the income tax base has been going on a long time and has accelerated in the recent past. Almost the first measure that occurs to any group that wishes to foster a worthy purpose or a selfish end is a tax credit, personal deduction, or exclusion from taxable income. Congress has responded to many such appeals and, in trying to do too much with the income tax, has weakened its structure, complicated compliance, and brought it into disrepute. In the aggregate, the special provisions advance no coherent set of policies.

Transition to a comprehensive income tax would bring widely shared gains in lessened complexity and greater economic efficiency. Of course, not everyone would be a net gainer. Those who—because of clever tax planning or other reasons—enjoy large amounts of exclusions, personal deductions, and tax credits would lose. Often those who would lose advantages as a result of generally beneficial legislation, being more aware of their prospective losses than the broad public is of its gains, are able to block action.

Some of the provisions of a comprehensive income tax would affect many people and would be highly sensitive; for example, the taxation of part of social security benefits and of veteran's benefits and unemployment compensation would arouse controversy. Others might appear strange; for example, the taxation of interest on life insurance savings of policyholders would stimulate discussion. Many Members of Congress and others would object that the curtailment of deductions for charitable contributions would retard socially desirable activities. Limitation of interest deductions would arouse the opposition of homeowners, the real estate industry, and the producers of automobiles and other consumer durables. Abolition of IRAs and Keogh plans, together with termination of the tax sheltered status of employer financed pension plans, would be seen as a threat to the business of many financial institutions and would upset many personal plans.

I cannot pretend to expertise on political strategy. I see my role as a tax specialist being to expound and support measures that I am convinced would be advantageous, even though their prospects for immediate adoption appear dim. Those of us who have special interest in taxation and knowledge of it can contribute to sharper analyses and better public understanding of a subject on which there is much confusion.

I leave it to others to decide whether more progress can be made through a broad campaign that, by proposing many simultaneous changes, will offer significant immediate gains and possibly divide the opposition, or along the arduous path of attacking vulnerable provisions a few at a time. Perhaps a pressing need for revenue will unite the minds of members of the Executive branch and Congress. The passage of the Tax Equity and Fiscal Responsibility Act of 1982, which limited deductions for medical expenses and casualty losses and increased the minimum tax on preference items, is an encouraging sign. But even a small flock of fiscal swallows does not make a comprehensive tax summer.

Whatever strategy is followed, patient and persistent efforts will be needed to make progress. Support will be needed from technicians, opinion leaders, and members of both the legislative and executive branches of government.

NOTES TO CHAPTER 11

1. Quoted from my book, *The Individual Income Tax* (Washington, D.C.: The Brookings Institution, rev. ed. 1976), p. 2.
2. Advisory Commission on Intergovernmental Relations, *1982, Changing Public Attitudes on Governments and Taxes* (Washington, D.C.: 1982).

3. Joseph A. Pechman and John Karl Scholz, "Comprehensive Income Taxation and Rate Reduction" (Statement prepared for the Senate Finance Committee, September 30, 1982), *Tax Notes* 17 (October 11, 1982): 83-93. See also Joseph J. Minarik, "The Future of the Individual Income Tax," *National Tax Journal* 35 (September 1982): 231-41.

4. See Henry J. Aaron, ed., *Inflation and the Income Tax* (Washington, D.C.: The Brookings Institution, 1976); Vito Tanzi, *Inflation and the Personal Income Tax, An International Perspective* (Cambridge: Cambridge University Press, 1980).

5. Both the deficit and personal saving are deflated by the implicit price deflator for GNP. Statistics from *Economic Report of the President, February 1983*, pp. 166, 190, 250, and *Economic Indicators*, October 1982.

6. For statistics, see Pechman and Scholz (1982) and Minarik (1982) (note 3 above).

7. Robert E. Hall and Alvin Rabushka, "A Proposal to Simplify Our Tax System," *Wall Street Journal* December 10, 1981.

8. See my paper, "The Superiority of the Income Tax," in Joseph A. Pechman, ed., *What Should Be Taxed: Income or Expenditure?* (Washington, D.C.: The Brookings Institution, 1980), pp. 49-73.

Discussants:

THE ACHILLES' HEEL OF THE COMPREHENSIVE INCOME TAX

William D. Andrews

Richard Goode's paper is an eloquent description of a noble ideal. The comprehensive income tax has also proved to be a durable ideal; its classic formulation was in Henry Simons' *Personal Income Taxation*, which was published in 1938, and the basic idea has changed very little since then.

But our failure to live up to the comprehensive income tax ideal has also proved to be remarkably durable. All the major departures from a true accretion base decried by Henry Simons are still with us forty-five years later. Capital gain rates have varied but currently stand at only 40 percent of ordinary income rates. Tax-free step-up of basis at death was repealed in 1976 but quickly restored in 1978. Simons' proposal to tax unrealized appreciation when property is given away, during life or at death, has made no progress. And the municipal bond interest exemption has proved resistant to change even in the form of a provision that would allow a municipality, with respect to each bond issue, to elect a direct interest subsidy in lieu of tax exemption. Meanwhile, the magnitude of the exemption has grown immensely, and ways have been devised to utilize it in connection with industrial and residential construction, as well as municipal facilities in any strict, functional sense.

Dr. Goode's paper affirms, indeed, that discrepancies between our actual practice and the preaching of a comprehensive income tax have proliferated, not abated. We need to know why. Perhaps the comprehensive income tax ideal belongs in a category with the Ten Commandments, which have similarly failed, over an even longer period of time, to eradicate sin.

But perhaps something more than political fallibility (or venality) stands in the way of achievement of a comprehensive accretion income tax. Suppose, for a moment, that the body politic were quite willing to make all the changes involved in adopting such a tax. Still, is that a goal capable of practical achievement? I think not.

Dr. Goode's paper, indeed, confirms this conclusion in an interesting way. The moment the paper turns to implementation, it talks of a variety of departures from a true accretion base, apparently in the nature of concessions to practicality. The paper mentions several versions of a practical tax, but, at a minimum, it suggests three omissions from total accretion: (1) gifts and bequests received, (2) imputed rent of owner-occupied dwellings, and (3) unrealized capital gains. Let us consider the extent to which the noble goals of a comprehensive income tax may be undermined by any of these three concessions.

(1) *Gifts and Bequests.* If one considers accretion quite literally from the standpoint of an individual taxpayer, then the definition of accretion would seem to require inclusion of gifts and bequests received. Yet if gifts and bequests were taxed, and no deduction allowed the donor, the result would be that a single cycle of earning and spending or earning and saving would be taxed twice, instead of once, whenever the earner and the beneficiary were different individuals. It is hard to believe, even in principle, that there is twice as much consumption to be included in taxable income if part of one's salary is spent sending a parent on an extended trip, for example, rather than taking the trip oneself. In the case of a gift of property, the donee is indeed enriched, but no more than the donor is impoverished, and the pleasure the donor presumably derives from the transaction is not the kind of using up of resources that generally characterizes the consumption component of taxable income.

What is intrinsic in the comprehensive income tax ideal is that every element of consumption and accumulation of resources be subject to tax. The exclusion of gifts and bequests does not undermine that objective at all.

(2) *Imputed Rent from Owner-Occupied Dwellings.* This is a much tougher problem. It is perfectly clear, in principle, that occupation of a dwelling is consumption of scarce economic resources and that an owner-occupied home provides consumption services for the occupant as a return on the owner's investment, all combined in one transaction. If other forms of investment return are taxed, and personal rent is not deductible, then there is no principled reason for omitting imputed rent from the taxable income of the owner-occupier. Advocates of a comprehensive income tax have sometimes urged that our tax should be amended to include imputed rent.[1]

But that would involve a formidable practical problem of measurement. Noncash transactions are always a source of trouble. The introduction of a substantial noncash component into the taxable income of every homeowner would represent a radical transformation in the practical aspects of the tax.

Perhaps, moreover, housing services are a more or less uniform fraction of disposable income and not a ready substitute for other wants and needs. In theory, it might be enough if housing services represent a uniform and fixed share within income classes, since differences between classes could be made up by adjustments in the rate schedule. If that were the case, then omission of the return-on-capital portion of housing services from everyone's income might be a relatively benign departure from the ideal. At least there is some limit on what portion of total income a taxpayer will devote to housing services, even if those services are exempt from tax.

One might well conclude, therefore, that while omission of imputed rent from a comprehensive income tax base is quite wrong in principle, it is probably rather tolerable in practice; it certainly does not undermine the whole enterprise. If we are to exempt imputed rent of homeowners, however, then perhaps we should allow renters a compensatory deduction for some portion of their rent, which Dr. Goode's paper does not recommend, and continue the deduction for mortgage interest, which he would repeal. His proposed version of a comprehensive income tax would have the effect of preserving the owner-occupied housing exclusion from income, but only to the extent one is wealthy enough to own a home free of mortgage.

(3) *Unrealized Capital Gains.* Omission of unrealized appreciation from current income is a common feature of practical plans launched under the banner of comprehensive income taxation. It sounds innocent enough; after all, it is not a matter of exemption but only of deferring gain until realization (assuming something is done to change the present rule permitting step-up of basis at death). Moreover, the valuation problems involved in any comprehensive current taxation of unrealized appreciation would raise enormous practical problems, virtually insuperable in some circumstances and much greater than those arising from imputed rent. A tax on unrealized appreciation would also raise severe problems of liquidity, particularly for those whose assets are invested in active businesses rather than passive portfolios.

But unrealized appreciation has proved, in fact, to be the Achilles' heel of the whole comprehensive income tax ideal. Deferral of gain is not as serious as outright exemption, but it is the next best thing, as sophisticated taxpayers and their counsel are now well aware. Deferral for a generation, in a 6 percent world, is tantamount to three-fourths exemption. In a 12 percent world, it is tantamount to fifteen-sixteenths exemption. Furthermore, the omission of unrealized appreciation and its correlatives can be magnified by leverage to produce exemptions from income way beyond mere accumulation.

At least one of the sources of the malaise to which Dr. Goode's paper refers is the sense that even quite respectable people do not pay their share. Such a sense is reinforced when it appears that even the Attorney General has thought it appropriate to make investments for which a deduction was to be claimed of four times the amount invested. Some of the tax shelters for which such deductions are claimed will undoubtedly not stand up, but it is clear that some investments, like highly leveraged real estate with a full recourse mortgate, may readily produce exactly that kind of result. A leveraged tax shelter depends, of course, on depreciation deductions, not just omission of unrealized appreciation, but it rests directly on the same underlying tolerance for disparity between real and conventional values and our willingness to levy taxes as if the disparity did not exist.

Even without intensive exploitation, the omission of unrealized appreciation is a severe defect. Prudent, wealthy people are urged to live on income without dipping into principal and to invest for capital appreciation as well as for current income. Their consumption needs will therefore be met from income, while their accumulation takes the form of appreciation on which taxes may be indefinitely deferred. Under a practical comprehensive income tax, it is only those without capital, who have to save from income, that are taxed on their accumulation as well as their consumption.

Borrowing aggravates the matter. If one puts wealth into property that appreciates, and then borrows against the appreciation, the result may be that even current consumption, as well as accumulation, goes untaxed. We have limits, of course, on what one can borrow against corporate securities, but that is just one of the reasons tax-aggressive, wealthy investors favor real estate.

Intensive exploitation of the failure to tax on current value involves deductions for capital costs as well as exclusion of unrealized appreciation, but the difficulty underlying these deductions is essentially the same—the practical necessity of computing taxes by reference to conventional rather than true values. Dr. Goode's paper apparently refers to these deductions when it refers to problems of computing business income, but then declines to discuss them since they are more involved in computing corporate than individual income.

In theory, as Dr. Goode's paper repeats, a comprehensive income base consists of consumption and accumulation. Accumulation in any real sense perfectly clearly includes unrealized appreciation—

that is, "the change in the value of the store of property rights between the beginning and the end of the period in question," in Henry Simons' words.[2] Clearly, then, omission of unrealized appreciation in a comprehensive income tax is wrong in principle.

More importantly, unrealized appreciation has none of the intrinsic redeeming limitations that make omission of imputed rent a tolerable defect. Unrealized appreciation is not a uniform fraction of income or accumulation; many taxpayers have none of it, while others have more than enough to live on. Even worse, unrealized appreciation can readily be substituted for other forms of income through complex and sometimes unnatural investment arrangements now widely distributed under the once pejorative label of "tax shelters."

A comprehensive income tax ideal with an immediate concession that taxation is not to be based on actual value is like a blueprint for constructing a building in which part of the foundation is required to be located in quicksand. If the terrain cannot be changed, the blueprint had better be amended.

If we cannot tax accretion comprehensively, for practical reasons, then what? The general answer reflected in comprehensive income tax proposals has been to tax as much as is practical, since that will take us as near the ideal goal as we can get. But this is not a happy answer. Insofar as the virtue of the whole idea was one of uniformity of treatment, then taxing some taxpayers on the whole amount of their accretion, while omitting substantial portions for others, may well be worse than taxing all on something else. Mathematicians and economists have put a similar idea more rigorously in the theory of second best.

Accretion, according to Goode and Simons, consists of two components: consumption and accumulation. While comprehensive income tax proponents would tax the sum of both, without differentiation, a little reflection will confirm that they are analytically and practically distinct. The difficult real problems in constructing a sound income tax sort out readily, indeed, into problems of defining consumption, on the one hand, and accumulation on the other. The taxability of fringe benefits like free travel, for example, and the deductibility of travel and entertainment expenses are consumption issues. The taxability of imputed rent from owner-occupied dwellings is also a consumption issue. Taxability of unrealized appreciation and deductibility of capital costs, on the other hand, are accumulation issues. The problem of what to do about the disparities that result from omitting unrealized capital gains, therefore, is a problem of coming up with a better way to treat accumulation.

It is feasible, as it turns out, to deal uniformly and comprehensively with accumulation by excluding it from the tax base instead of including it. One must simply account for business and investment transactions uniformly on a cash flow basis. This is not just a feasible alternative; it offers enormous opportunities for simplification by eliminating problems of capital cost measurement and of distinguishing between realized and unrealized gain. These problems plague present law and would persist under any version of a comprehensive income tax in which property values are to be conventionally determined.

The possibility of equity or uniformity (the idea of uniform treatment as measured against a single, unitary base) makes the comprehensive income tax base a noble ideal. But uniformity in relation to the accumulation component of accretion cannot be achieved unless assets are constantly restated at current fair value. Since any such constant revaluation of investment and business property is impractical, then the best policy is to exclude accumulation comprehensively.

Uniformly eliminating accumulation from the comprehensive accretion base is like redrawing unworkable blueprints to eliminate the portion of a proposed building whose foundation would fall in quicksand. Even if one preferred the original blueprint in the abstract, the building itself would be vastly improved by the revision. It is also possible that the revision would be better yet; perhaps it would produce a building even handsomer than the one originally imagined.

The result of excluding accumulation comprehensively from an accretion base would be to put the personal income tax entirely on a consumption base. This is, of course, not a new idea. Hobbes and Mill are among the philosophers who have concluded that aggregate consumption expenditure would be superior to total accretion as a personal tax base, if only it could be satisfactorily measured. Only relatively recently has it become clear, however, that a comprehensive consumption base is quite feasible, and that it is the only way of avoiding the quite intractable problems of measuring accumulation comprehensively.

There is not space here for extended discussion of a personal consumption tax, but two points in Dr. Goode's paper call for comment. First, there has been much important work done in the last decade by lawyers as well as economists from which I think most careful readers have concluded that a personal consumption tax would be at least as feasible and uncomplicated as a comprehensive income tax.[3] I remain convinced that it would be incomparably simpler.[4]

Skeptics have demonstrated that implementation of a personal consumption tax could be impeded by sabotage if left to clumsy or unfriendly workmen. The consumption tax could be made unnecessarily complicated and more readily subject to subversion even by well-motivated departures from simple cash-flow accounting. A more important fact, which has in no way been refuted, is that a consumption tax would simply eliminate the intractable complications and opportunities for subversion by taxpayers involved in trying to measure accumulation, whether by reference to true values (which is impractical) or to conventional values (as under existing law and under any comprehensive income tax scheme that excludes unrealized gains).

There is a view of tax policy that focuses on *departures* from a comprehensive tax base without worrying much about difficulties in defining the base itself. These departures are sometimes called tax expenditures. If one views tax expenditures as resulting simply from a legislative decision to pursue some extraneous objective—such as subsidizing municipal borrowing or energy-saving personal expenditures—then there is no apparent reason why the same legislators could not pursue the same objectives by introducing specious exclusions, deductions, and credits into a consumption tax. The municipal bond exclusion, for example, could be continued in exactly its present form under a consumption tax if there were overriding, nontax reasons for continuing a subsidy in that form.

But the creation of tax expenditures has often been more complicated than simple adoption of a subsidy. Many of them have their origin partly in real or imagined difficulties in income measurement, such as separation of capital from current expenditures and selection of amortization periods and methods. Moreover, they take the form of solutions to these difficulties: accelerated deductions or deferred recognition of gains. A consumption-based income tax would eliminate many of these difficulties, thus removing part of the reason and part of the mode of implementation of the tax expenditures involved.

Second, on the general question of fairness, Dr. Goode's paper says: "By permitting untaxed compounding of property income, the expenditure tax favors recipients of that kind of income over those earning income by personal effort."

Putting the personal income tax on a consumption base would, indeed, have the effect of allowing accumulations to compound tax-free. Economists have often regarded this as an advantage because the rate of substitution between present and future consumption is undistorted by this form of tax. Further, the rates of return on particular investments are similarly undistorted, and deadweight losses from the tax might, accordingly, be reduced.

But, of course, the burden of the tax falls on people, not categories of income, and it is a mistake to discuss distributional consequences as if recipients of property income were one group while those earning income by personal effort were another. The vast majority of people who pay substantial taxes have both kinds of income, in varying proportions, over a lifetime.

A more revealing comparison would be between those people who inherit wealth and those who depend over a lifetime on their personal earnings plus the product of saving and investing some part of those earnings. The proposal in Dr. Goode's paper would clearly increase taxes substantially for the earner group (if rates were held constant) by rescinding the provisions for tax-free retirement saving in the present law. On the other hand, the combined effect of exempting gifts and bequests received plus unrealized appreciation would be to permit a substantial number of those in the first category, the inheritors, to continue escaping tax on the accumulation component of their income. Comprehensive exclusion of accumulation from the tax base is much more consistent with the dictates of uniformity underlying the comprehensive tax base ideal than is the erratic and discriminatory inclusion of accumulation accomplished by an accretion base with an exclusion for unrealized appreciation.

NOTES

1. Richard Goode, *The Individual Income Tax* (Washington, D.C.: The Brookings Institution, rev. ed. 1976), p. 12.
2. Henry C. Simons, *Personal Income Taxation* (Chicago: The University of Chicago Press, 1938), p. 50.
3. "Complexity and the Personal Consumption Tax," Report by the Committee on Simplification, Section of Taxation, American Bar Association, *Tax Lawyer* 35 (1982): 415.
4. William D. Andrews, "A Consumption-Type or Cash-Flow Personal Income Tax," *Harvard Law Review* 87 (1974): 1113.

THE POLITICAL PROBLEMS OF IMPLEMENTING A COMPREHENSIVE INCOME TAX

Barber B. Conable, Jr.

The comprehensive tax is a modest evolution from the idea of a flat rate tax. The same general principles apply, and, thus, the same criticisms can be found embedded in the idea, if one looks carefully. The current manifestation of a comprehensive income tax, developed by

Senator Bill Bradley and Congressman Richard Gephardt, has been changed a great deal, and will continue to be changed. It is, however, a significant and desirable public practice for us to discuss our tax system in radical terms—that is, seeking major change—because informed discussion tests an institution that is of great significance to the people of this country. The major issue between the government and the people remains taxation.

I do believe that we can focus too much on the form and not consider the reason behind taxation—namely, the level of government spending. The differences in the mode of taxation usually have only marginal impact on the overall effects of taxation. It is easy to get bright-eyed about the fine points of the collection system and to ignore the fact that the tax burden is ultimately *the* tax matter with which we should be most concerned.

Richard Goode's paper is an interesting disquisition on the comprehensive tax. I must say that, as a politician, I look for the political constituency for a proposal of this sort and find it difficult to locate. If there is no political constituency, the tax will not be enacted. This is a concept that many people do not understand. President Carter did not understand it. When he ran for President, he got a great hand on the lecture circuit in his call for a simplified tax system. What he did not understand was that he was talking to people who itemize their deductions, and that in excess of 70 percent of all taxpayers are on the short form already and have little to gain from simplification. That being the case, if simplification is a major goal, a substantial part of the potential constituency has been lost before the campaign can begin. Granted, many people who make out the short form think that it is too complicated. However, it is homeowners who tend to itemize, and they generally represent the upper income classes, who are not usually the greatest concern of the politicians who have to change the tax system, if it is to be changed.

I also think that many people forget that the system has evolved into a complex and increasingly narrow-based system, as Dr. Goode describes it, not because of a desire to confound or to confuse taxpayers, but because equity is the enemy of simplicity. I will acknowledge that many of the items in the tax Code would no longer be considered equitable in a changing economy, but there was a reason for them at the time they were instituted. It should surprise no one that government is a very conservative institution. Once some item is placed in something as sensitive as the tax Code, that item becomes very difficult to remove, even though it has become merely historical and no longer has its previous relevance. In fact, many of the complexities in the tax Code are still viewed as equitable. Anybody who has ever claimed a deduction will consider it as American as apple pie and will fight to the death to defend it before he will let his friendly local Congressman take it out of his hopes for the next April 15. These are two basic facts, then: First, the constituency is a narrow one for major simplification; and second, equity is the enemy of simplicity.

As to the tax base and what has happened as we have narrowed it with tax preferences, it can be dealt with in ways other than by radical surgery. The Tax Equity and Fiscal Responsibility Act of 1982 (TEFRA) reduced some of the deductions available. The original concept of the Reagan tax plan of 1981 was to leave the tax base alone, rather than narrowing it, and to reduce the rates across the board, not in any complicated way but for everyone. That thinking was radical enough. Many thought the Economic Recovery Tax Act of 1981 (ERTA) favored the rich because the rate reduction was the same for them as for others. In my view as a tax writer, it represents a dramatic change from the past, when we constantly created new preferences in order to shift the flow of capital or savings from one direction to another to give a slight edge in the attraction of capital to one particular type of activity as opposed to another. Instead of following that course in 1981, we left the base alone, originally anyway, rather than narrowing the base.

Future tax reform, as in the past, is probably going to have to be bought. We achieved structural changes in the past and certified reform to the people who were calling for tax reform measures primarily through reducing the rates. In other words, we were buying reform in that, when people looked at the bottom line, they would see that their taxes had gone down. If you eliminate a deduction, those who claimed it will see their taxes go up. Reform is an attractive word. Nobody will believe that reform has been real unless the bottom line is reduced taxes, because everyone thinks he pays more than his share of taxes and therefore believes that any reform worthy of the name should reduce his taxes.

As a result of the indexing provision included in ERTA, it is going to be increasingly difficult to have either broad-based rate reductions or the elimination of preferences. The indexing provision eliminates inflation as a factor in pushing an individual into higher tax brackets. In the past, the impact of inflation on the graduated income tax has permitted us to buy a great deal of reform because inflation provided an automatic increase in government revenues—part of which could be used to finance growth in federal spending, and the rest of which could be diverted into buying different types of tax reform that would be attractive to taxpayers. If indexing remains, we are certain to have tax increases, not reductions, because fiscal dividends resulting from real economic growth will probably be insufficient to provide for any degree of tax reduction.

Many people have not yet focused on the impact of indexing. Perhaps when they do, they will want the measure repealed. Certainly the budget people will want it repealed, but I think the taxpayers, once they understand what indexing means, will clasp it to their bosoms and defend it as a great American concept.

Indexing does mean that we will have honest taxation from now on. When I came to Washington eighteen years ago, the federal budget was $116 billion. In all that period of time, I voted for five separate tax reductions and for a simple one-year temporary increase. I was so effective as a tax cutter that now the federal budget is in excess of $620 billion. The difference, of course, is more bracket creep than real economic growth.

I think this is the context of the new indexation that will take effect in 1985. It will force us to consider what is achievable in the way of major tax changes. Major tax change will not be popular or acceptable unless, in the view of the people, it will have the ultimate effect of reducing their tax burden. I think that reform is going to be difficult to achieve and that therefore, from a purely political viewpoint, an effort moving toward a comprehensive tax is going to be extremely difficult. Certainly, it is a goal to be debated and to be desired. Simplicity is an attractive administrative characteristic. It is certainly far preferable for Americans to understand their tax system than to consider it an instrument of torture or of confusion. If we continue to complicate the Code, of course, the time will come when it will be considered unconstitutional, because of its complexity.

I conclude with this note of caution. Do not expect much leeway for reducing the total tax burden, based on additional revenues, and a sharp reduction in demand for government services. Do not expect a lot of maneuvering room for the tax writers to achieve dramatic change and to accrue unto themselves heroic status or public support, or even, ultimate political survival. It is always timely to talk about taxes; but whether it is timely to expect a millennium—a substantially new tax system—is the question I raise.

BROADENING THE TAX BASE THROUGH A COMPREHENSIVE INCOME TAX

Emil M. Sunley

Richard Goode has outlined the case for a comprehensive income tax. It would improve equity, eliminate differences in taxation related to income sources and uses, permit a reduction in marginal tax rates, and reduce the time and energy now devoted to tax planning and compliance. Dr. Goode rejects the consumption tax base because savings, which would be exempted under the consumption tax base, result from personal decisions that do not diminish one's ability to support the commonwealth.

The most recent interest in a comprehensive income tax has taken the form of proposals for a broad-based, low-rate income tax. These proposals, I believe, provide a road map for how the income tax should evolve. When Congress is able to reduce taxes, priority should be given to reducing marginal tax rates instead of providing new exclusions, deductions, and credits. When Congress must raise tax revenue, priority should be given to base broadening; that is, tax incentives that are no longer needed or are of a low priority should be removed.

Today, the need is to restore the revenue base. Federal revenues are expected to decline from 21.1 percent of gross national product (GNP) in fiscal year 1981 to 18.9 percent in fiscal year 1985. To balance the budget, then, without increasing revenues, expenditures must fall to 18.9 percent of GNP, but expenditures are currently running at over 24 percent of GNP. Given that outlays for defense, social security, and interest payments will soon equal over 70 percent of total expenditures, it is unlikely that the gap between expenditures and revenues, even at high employment, can be closed without increasing revenue. But any tax increases should not have their major impact in 1983, or even possibly the beginning of 1984. Given the softness of the economy, tax increases are not needed at this time.

To restore the revenue base, Congress will have to survey the entire federal revenue system, not just the individual income tax. But what are the major alternatives currently under discussion for broadening the individual income tax? Most of these alternatives, it is interesting to note, would also be included in a proposal for a broad-based consumption tax.

Itemized Deductions

As part of the Tax Equity and Fiscal Responsibility Act of 1982 (TEFRA), Congress cut back the deductions for medical expenses and casualty losses. Now Congress should consider pruning other itemized deductions.

Consistent with the goal of increasing the incentive to save, Congress could repeal the deduction for consumer interest, which is an incentive to consume. This would increase federal revenues by $8.6 billion a year. It must be recognized, however, that about half of all consumer interest is incurred on automobile loans. Given the depressed state of the automobile industry, this may not be the time to end the deductibility of interest on these loans. Also, if limitations are placed on consumer interest, many will avoid the limitation by taking a second mortgage on a home. An alternative to limiting the deductibility on consumer interest would be limiting the deductibility of all nonbusiness interest to the extent it exceeds property income. An exception might be made for interest on first mortgages.

This year, Congress considered repealing or limiting the deduction for sales and personal property taxes. Most taxpayers who itemize determine their sales tax deduction from a table. The allowable deduction bears little relationship to sales taxes actually paid. Repealing the sales tax deduction, however, would have very uneven effects. For example, it would favor Oregonians, who are subject to a state income tax but not a sales tax, while penalizing neighboring Washingtonians, who are subject to a sales tax but not a state income tax. If Congress wants to reduce the tax subsidy for state and local spending by increasing the out-of-pocket cost to taxpayers of state and local government, Congress could repeal or limit the deduction for all state and local taxes. This would not discriminate against states that rely more heavily on sales taxes. It would also reduce the incentive for investment or over investment in housing provided by the deduction for property taxes. Permitting only 75 percent of state and local taxes to be deductible would increase federal revenues by $9.4 billion in fiscal year 1985.

In 1981, Congress extended the charitable deduction to taxpayers who do not itemize their other personal deductions. For the years 1982 to 1984, the amount of contributions a nonitemizer is allowed to take into account is subject to a dollar cap. The cap is $100 for the years 1982 and 1983 and $300 for 1984. Congress could repeal the deduction for charitable contributions by nonitemizers. The zero bracket amount already allows for an assumed amount of charitable giving by nonitemizers. Compared to present law, repeal of the deduction would increase federal revenues by $2.7 billion in fiscal year 1986 and by almost $5 billion in fiscal year 1987.

Employee Benefits

The principal employee benefits that receive special tax treatment are retirement plans; health, disability and life insurance plans; and workers' compensation. Employer contributions to these plans now equal 13.5 percent of wages and salaries, up from 5.9 percent in 1970. (See Table 11-2.) The tax law encourages the substitution of tax-favored employee benefits for wages and salaries. The tax-favored status of certain employee benefits leads not only (1) to misallocation, but also (2) to a given amount of tax exemption increasing in value as the employee's tax bracket rises.

The appropriate tax treatment of employee benefits under a broad-based income tax involves a number of complex issues. There are no easy answers to the question of how employee benefits should be valued and assigned to individual employees for purposes of taxation.

To reduce the tax-favored status of employee benefits, Congress could consider imposing an excise tax on employer payments for group health insurance, group life insurance, and workers' compensation.[1] The rate of the tax might be equal to 11 percent, which is the first bracket rate for the individual income tax. An 11 percent excise tax on these employee benefits would increase federal revenues by about $9 billion a year.[2]

As an alternative to the excise tax on employer contributions, Congress could consider placing a limit on the tax exclusion for employer-paid health insurance premiums. Though many factors account for rapid increase in health care costs, one is certainly the fact that the federal income tax provides an incentive to purchase comprehensive health insurance. This leads both individuals and their doctors to treat health services as if they were free, resulting in an overuse of these services and little concern for their costs. A limitation on the exclusion for employer health plan payments would encourage both the employee and employer to economize on health care plans, favoring lower-cost plans with high deductibles and significant coinsurance provisions, which, in turn, would increase cost consciousness. Alternatively, the employee may choose to use an innovative health care delivery system, such as a health maintenance organization (HMO), which would result in lower health care costs.

A major problem with proposals to place a limit on the exclusion for employer health plan payments is how to allocate employer payments to individual employees. Should the allocation depend on age,

Table 11–2. Employer Contributions for Major Employee Benefits, 1970 and 1981.

	1970		1981	
	Amount of Employer Contributions (millions of dollars)	Percentage of Wages and Salaries	Amount of Employer Contributions (millions of dollars)	Percentage of Wages and Salaries
Pension and profit sharing	$12,972	2.4%	$60,244	5.9%
Group health insurance	11,801	2.2	55,497	5.4
Group life insurance	2,848	0.5	6,439	0.6
Workers' compensation	3,696	0.8	15,834	1.5
Total	$31,317	5.9%	$138,014	13.4%

Sources: U.S. Department of Commerce, *National Income and Productivity Accounts of the U.S. 1929–1974.* Washington, D.C.: Government Printing Office, 1974; U.S. Department of Commerce, *Survey of Current Business* 62, no. 7 (July 1982).

marital status, or number of covered dependents? For companies with insured plans, the allocation could depend on the company's contribution for each employee. Allocation of income to employees of companies with self-insured health plans would remain a problem. Limiting the exclusion to $1,800 per year per family would produce $5 billion in revenue from twenty-three million individuals. A $2,400 cap would produce $2 billion in revenue from eleven million individuals.[3] The cap should be indexed for inflation.

Instead of, or in addition to, placing a limit on the employee exclusion, Congress could seek to achieve certain health policy goals by providing an employee exclusion only for "qualified" plans. Presumably, a qualified plan would have a high deductible and a significant coinsurance rate, or it would have to provide health services through an HMO.

Fringe Benefits

In addition to the major statutory employee benefits, employees also receive tax-favored fringe benefits, such as subsidized cafeterias, free parking, company cars, employee discounts, business lunches, and the like. These fringe benefits may serve the business purpose of the employer, but they also involve an important component of personal consumption. Though taxing these benefits would present difficult problems of valuation and administrative feasibility, Congress nevertheless may want to reduce or limit some of these tax-favored fringe benefits. In deciding which benefits should be taxed, consideration should be given to the importance of the fringe benefit to the employee, the ease in valuing it, and the problems of recordkeeping. For most fringe benefits, average cost to the employer would be an adequate approximation of the value of the fringe benefit to the employee.

An alternative to taxing employees on certain fringe benefits would be to deny a business deduction for the cost of the fringe benefits. In the Senate-passed version of TEFRA the deduction for business meals would have been limited to 50 percent of expenses, unless the meal was connected with business-related travel away from home. In the United Kingdom, no business deduction is permitted for the cost of company-provided automobiles.

Unemployment Benefits

Prior to 1979, unemployment insurance benefits were not taxable. The Revenue Act of 1978 provided that a portion of unemployment benefits would be included in the recipient's gross income if the recipient's total income, including unemployment benefits, exceeded a base amount of $20,000 for single individuals and $25,000 for married couples. For every dollar of income exceeding the base amount, the taxpayer was required to include fifty cents of unemployment benefits in income. TEFRA increased the taxation of unemployment benefits by lowering the base amounts to $12,000 for single individuals and $18,000 for married couples.

The basic case for taxing unemployment benefits is to improve equity by imposing the same tax on families with equal incomes and to increase the incentive for finding a job. Current law may be quite perverse for those taxpayers subject to the phase-in for taxing unemployment benefits. For these taxpayers, an additional dollar of income will make an additional fifty cents of unemployment benefits taxable. In effect, the marginal tax rate on additional earned income is 50 percent higher, because of the phase-in rule for unemployment benefits. If all unemployment insurance benefits were included in taxable income, most low-income families would not be affected much; however, the perverse effect of the phase-in would be eliminated, equity would be improved, and federal receipts would increase by $1.0 billion a year.

Net Interest Exclusion

As part of the Economic Recovery Tax Act of 1981 (ERTA), Congress enacted a number of new tax incentives for savings, including a new exclusion of 15 percent of net interest earned. This exclusion, which begins in 1985, is superior to most savings incentives in that it is limited to *net* interest (interest earned less interest paid) and thus would not reward taxpayers who borrow merely to make tax-favored investments.[4] Nevertheless, it should be recognized that reduction in marginal tax rates is the strongest savings incentive. It increases the reward for saving while reducing the tax benefits of borrowing. Given the budget situation and the recent marginal tax rate reductions, Congress may want to repeal the net interest exclusion before it takes effect. This would annually recapture $3 billion of revenues beginning in fiscal year 1986.

Shifting Income to Children

Significant tax minimization can be achieved by shifting property income to minor children. Parents may make outright gifts or interest-free demand loans to their children or to trusts established for their children's benefit. When such gifts or loans are invested in high-yield securities, the resulting income is shifted to the children where it is taxed at lower rates. Congress may want to consider placing some limits on the ability of taxpayers to use their children for purposes of tax minimization. One possibility would be to include in the parents' taxable income the property income of minor children, including any trust income. A child would be taxed only on earned income. This proposal would increase federal revenue by $500 million.[5]

NOTES

1. The excise tax would not apply to employer contributions to pension plans, inasmuch as these contributions are later taxed when retirement benefits are paid. If the tax were extended to pension contributions, it would have to be viewed as a charge for the privilege of deferral. Also, the workers' compensation payments that replace lost wages could be included in the workers' taxable income. The employer payments to fund this portion of worker's compensation would, then, not be subject to the excise tax.

2. Alternatively, the rate of tax could be set equal to combined employer/employee social security tax rate and the resulting revenues transferred to the social security trust funds.

3. Amy K. Taylor and Gail R. Wilensky, "Tax Expenditures and the Demand for Private Health Insurance," Jack Meyer, ed., *Market Reforms in Health Care: Current Issues, New Directions and Strategic Decisions* (Washington, D.C.: American Enterprise Institute, 1983), p. 175.

4. Mortgage interest and trade and business interest would not be taken into account in determining net interest.

5. This is a very rough estimate, but it is consistent with the assumption that each family with adjusted gross income of over $100,000 or more on average save as much as $500 in taxes by shifting property income to minor children.

Information in this article was originally published in *Budget and Policy Choices 1983: Taxes, Defense, Entitlements* (Washington, D.C.: Center for National Policy, 1983), pp. 13-23.

※ Chapter 12

The Flat Rate Tax: A Proposal for Tax Simplification
Robert E. Hall and Alvin Rabushka

Despite recent progress in lowering rates, the American tax system remains a disgrace, in dire need of simplification and reform. It is inordinately lengthy, filling volumes of tax codes, and complicated by hundreds of credits, exemptions, and special provisions. Many taxpayers require expensive professional help to fill out their tax returns correctly. Each act of Congress further complicates the system. Political promises of real simplification and reform of the tax system remain unfulfilled.

The tax system consists chiefly of the personal income tax, the corporate income tax, and the payroll tax for social security. The personal income tax has steeply progressive rates, rising to a maximum marginal rate of 50 percent under the new tax law. The income base to which these progressive rates are applied has steadily eroded over the years through a wide variety of exclusions, deductions, and exemptions to the point where it now constitutes no more than half of total national income. The personal income tax discourages saving. Income is first taxed when earned and again when savings earn interest. Even worse, the returns to savings put into the corporate sector are taxed twice, once as corporate profits and again at the household level when dividends are paid. A growing chorus of criticism contends that the current system attenuates individual incentives to work, save, and invest. For many taxpayers, saving a dollar in taxes is worth twice as much as earning another dollar in income.

Prior to the twentieth century, federal revenues, comprising about 3 percent of gross national product (GNP), were largely collected from customs duties. With the adoption of the Sixteenth Amendment in 1913 and the payroll tax in the 1930s, federal revenues have grown to consume 22 percent of GNP. Escalating inflation in the 1970s pushed growing numbers of taxpayers into high tax brackets that twenty years ago were meant only for the very rich. Costly side effects have begun to surface.

Scholarly research, along with Internal Revenue Service reports, reveals widespread evidence of tax evasion on interest, dividend, and other forms of household or professional income. Tax shelters are now a commonplace feature of the financial landscape. Estimates of the underground economy range from several tens of billions to several hundred billion dollars. In the eighteenth century, customs duties exceeding 100 percent made England into a nation of smugglers. Today, marginal tax rates of 50 percent from the personal income tax, 46 percent from the corporate tax, and 14 percent from the payroll tax are converting Americans into tax avoiders and channeling their investments into tax shelters. The current system fosters contempt for the law, while simultaneously discouraging productive economic activity.

Why is it so difficult to reform the tax system? Most scholars, lawmakers, and practitioners routinely claim that it is politically infeasible to simplify and radically reform the tax system. They believe talk of simplification is unrealistic. Congress would, it is alleged, never abolish the exemptions and deductions for mortgage interest payments, charitable contributions, and excess medical care costs, or remove the many benefits and credits enjoyed by low-income households and a bevy of special interest groups. The American demand for justice means that the rich should pay higher taxes. As a result of these beliefs, changes in the tax Code are invariably incremental and represent slight modifications to the corporate or personal income tax.

We sense growing interest in the public and in Congress for drastic reform in the tax system. As a contribution to the debate and discussion on this important subject, we propose a simple income tax based on low marginal rates to replace the entire current system of separate tax rate schedules on corporate and individual income. The new tax would be a low, flat rate applied to all taxpayers, excluding the very poor, and to all types of income. It would be applied to a much larger tax base than the present system, thus generating similar amounts of revenue as the current high-rate system with its exemptions and deductions. The simple flat rate would end bracket creep, which is caused by inflation pushing people into higher and higher tax brackets. It would largely minimize the penalty current law imposes on two-earner households ("the marriage penalty"). It would be stable, predictable, and cease further proliferation of a variety of tax credits used to attain social goals. Most importantly, it would restore the incentives to work, save, and invest, thereby promoting growth and higher standards of living.

Our proposal does not include reform of the social security payroll tax and the retirement benefits it finances, though reform is long overdue. The social security tax cannot be discussed separately from benefits, and we would be taken too far from our basic subject of tax reform to go into the massive changes in social security needed to put the system on a sound footing.

BASIC PRINCIPLES OF THE SIMPLE INCOME TAX

The simple income tax rests on four basic principles:

1. All income should be taxed only once and as closely as possible to its source.
2. All types of income should be taxed at the same low rate.
3. The poorest households should pay no income tax.
4. Tax returns for both households and businesses should be simple enough to fit on a postcard or one page.

We propose the replacement of the existing corporate and personal income taxes with a business tax and a compensation tax. The business tax includes the earnings of corporations, unincorporated businesses, farms, professionals, and rental income. The business tax does not permit a deduction for interest payments, dividends, or other payments to the owners of the business. As a result, all income that individuals receive from business activity has already been taxed and should not be taxed again. The same holds for capital gains. The business tax is like a withholding tax; it means that the tax authorities do not have to track down all the interest, dividends, capital gains, and other business income received by the public. Compensation is the only element of household income not taxed under the business tax. We therefore propose a new compensation tax to replace the present personal income tax. The new compensation tax would have a set of personal allowances to insure that the poorest families pay no compensation tax.

Under our existing laws, tax rates can be as high as 50 percent for compensation and 80 percent for business income because income is taxed first under the corporate tax and again under the personal tax. To collect the same amount of revenue that the present system generates, assuming the same flows of income occur as today, the simple tax system would require a standard rate of only 19 percent.

THE BUSINESS TAX

The new business tax would rationalize the present hodgepodge of federal tax provisions for business income. It would reduce the high marginal rates currently paid on some types of income from capital. By eliminating interest deductions, it would also end the subsidies embodied in current tax shelters. A uniform rate of 19 percent would replace the current range of tax rates that stretch from actual subsidy of highly leveraged tax shelters with large interest deductions to rates as high as 80 percent imposed on income earned by corporate stockholders.

The new business tax applies equally to all forms of business income (corporate, partnership, professional, farm) and to rental and royalty income. The base for the tax is gross revenue less purchases of goods and services and compensation paid to employees. In addition, a capital recovery allowance is deducted for investment in plant and equipment. No deductions for depreciation, interest, or payments to owners are permitted. However, the self-employed may pay themselves salary in any amount they choose, provided they report it on the compensation tax form.

The business tax return would fit easily on a single page, even for a multibillion dollar corporation. Figure 12-1 shows what it would look like.

Gross revenue from sales does not include earnings the business may receive from its ownership of other businesses (provided these businesses file their own tax returns) or from its ownership of securities. These earnings have already been taxed in other businesses. Gross revenue does include sales of used plant and equipment. Businesses are not required to maintain inventory or depreciation accounts for tax purposes.

In place of the hodgepodge of investment incentives in the current tax system, we propose the use of straightforward first-year write-off of all business investment, both in new and used plant and equipment. First-year capital recovery is a great simplification over the complicated depreciation deductions and investment credits in present tax law. It also eliminates the present problem that depreciation

Figure 12-1. Hall-Rabushka Simplified Flat Rate Tax Form (*Business Tax*).

Form 2	Business Tax	1982
Business Name		Employer Identification Number
Street Address		County
City, State, and ZIP Code		Principal Product

1 Gross revenue from sales	1	
2 Allowable costs		
(a) Purchases of goods, services, and materials	2(a)	
(b) Wages, salaries, and pensions paid to employees	2(b)	
(c) Purchases of capital equipment, structures, and land	2(c)	
3 Total allowable costs *(sum of lines 2(a), 2(b), 2(c))*	3	
4 Taxable income *(line 1 less line 3)*	4	
5 Tax *(19% of line 4)*	5	
6 Carry-forward from 1981	6	
7 Interest on carry-forward *(14% of line 6)*	7	
8 Carry-forward into 1982 *(line 6 plus line 7)*	8	
9 Tax due *(line 5 less line 8, if positive)*	9	
10 Carry-forward to 1983 *(line 8 less line 5, if positive)*	10	

based on historical cost is not rapid enough to offset the effects of inflation. The first-year system avoids all distortions of inflation.

In 1981 the net revenue of U.S. business was $1,179 billion. Under the new business tax, capital recovery allowances would have been $349 billion, leaving net taxable business income at $830 billion. A tax rate of 19 percent would have yielded $158 billion, nearly triple the revenue from the actual corporate income tax in 1981 of $57 billion. The extra revenue, despite the much lower tax rate, comes from (1) the much wider tax base, including unincorporated business, and (2) taxing business income at its source.

Under the simple tax system, all business income would be taxed only once, at its source. Household receipts of interest, dividends, and capital gains would be after-tax income. Though wealthy households might receive large amounts of these types of income, it is important to understand that the taxes on this income have already been paid. The recipient household should not pay any more tax on business income. Taxing business income at its source has an important practical benefit. Under the present personal income tax, large amounts of interest and dividend income escape taxation through outright evasion and tax avoidance. Apparently, people find it easy to overlook these types of income when filling out personal income tax returns. Under our business tax, the only way dividends, interest, and other earnings of capital could escape taxation would be for the business to fail to file a tax return, which is easier to detect and punish.

Capital gains on rental property, plant, and equipment are taxed under the business tax. The purchase price is deducted at the time of purchase, and the sale price is taxed at the time of the sale. These provisions are most important for real estate, where they will eliminate the current abuses in which low capital gains tax rates create an incentive for artificial turnover of property. Every owner of rental real estate would be required to fill out the simple business tax return.

Capital gains in the overall value of a successful firm are also taxed under the new business tax and should not be taxed again at the household level. To see this point, consider the case of the common stock of a corporation. The value of the corporation's stock in the market is the capitalization of its future earnings. Because the owners of the stock receive the earnings after the corporation has paid the business tax, that tax depresses the stock's market value. When the market learns that future earnings are likely to be higher than previously thought, the stock rises in value and its owners receive capital gains. When the high earnings materialize in the future, they will be correspondingly taxed. To tax the immediate capital gains of the stock would be double taxation. Thus, with comprehensive taxation of business income at the source, capital gains should be excluded from taxation at the household level.

In order to impose the appropriate tax on banks and certain other types of business, it is necessary to separate the value of the service the bank provides to its customers from the interest the bank pays to the customer. Today, most banks net one against the other, so the customer gets free services in exchange for lending the bank funds at zero or below-market interest rates. Because the business tax is imposed on the value of the product sold by a business (the services provided by a bank, for example), but does not allow a deduction for interest paid out, it would not be permissible for a bank to report the net receipts from its customers as its sales. Instead, the bank must add in the difference between the interest it pays its depositors and the full market interest rate they could earn elsewhere. As a general matter, businesses would not be permitted to borrow from their customers and pretend that the value of sales was only the net charge after deducting interest; this violates the basic principle that interest payments are never deductible. Businesses, like banks, could continue to carry on their relations with their customers in any way they chose, but for tax purposes the full value of their services would be reported as their sales.

One other potential source of abuse of the business tax, the conversion of business assets to personal use, would need to be monitored. There is nothing new about this problem; under today's income tax, one can buy a car for business purposes at the end of the year, take the investment credit, and then convert the car to personal use at the beginning of the next year. Under the proposed business tax, conversion to personal use would be counted as a sale, and the market value of the asset would be included in the revenue of the firm. Auditors would check that the assets on the books of the firm were actually used by the firm and not for the personal use of the owners.

First-year writeoff of investment would create large tax losses in the startup years for almost all businesses and occasional large tax losses, even for established businesses, when they made significant investments. The business tax provides unlimited carry-forward of tax losses so that they reduce taxes in future, profitable years. Further, the balances carried forward earn interest at the market rate.

THE COMPENSATION TAX

Most income in the United States is compensation for work. We propose that compensation be taxed at the level of the individual or married couple. Compensation is defined as cash wages, salaries, and pensions received by workers from employers. Pension contributions and other fringe benefits paid by employers are not counted as part of compensation.

To limit the tax burden of poor families, we propose a set of personal allowances. Taxes would be 19 percent of compensation in excess of personal allowances. The proposed allowances for 1982 are:

Married Couple	$6200
Single	3800
Single head of household	5600
Each dependent	750

Except for the personal allowances, no deductions of any kind would be permitted, including interest deductions.

The tax return for the compensation tax would fit on a postcard. Figure 12-2 shows what it would look like.

In 1981, wages, salaries, and private pensions were about $1,503 billion. We estimate that personal allowances in 1981 would have been $481 billion, leaving taxable compensation of $1,022 billion.

Figure 12-2. Hall-Rabushka Simplified Flat Rate Tax Form (*Individual Compensation Tax*).

Form 1	Individual Compensation Tax		1982
Your first name and initial (if joint return, also give spouse's name and initial) Last name			Your social security number
Present home address (Number and street, including apartment number, or rural route)			Spouse's social security no.
City, town or post office, State and ZIP code	Your occupation ▶		
	Spouse's occupation ▶		
1 Compensation as reported by employer		1	
2 Other wage income, including pensions		2	
3 Total compensation *(line 1 plus line 2)*		3	
4 Personal allowance			
(a) ☐ $6200 for married filing jointly		4(a)	
(b) ☐ $3800 for single		4(b)	
(c) ☐ $5600 for single head of household		4(c)	
5 Number of dependents, not including spouse		5	
6 Personal allowances for dependents *(line 5 multiplied by $750)*		6	
7 Total personal allowances *(line 4 plus line 6)*		7	
8 Taxable compensation *(line 3 less line 7)*		8	
9 Tax *(19% of line 8)*		9	
10 Tax withheld by employer		10	
11 Tax due *(line 9 less line 10, if positive)*		11	
12 Refund due *(line 10 less line 9, if positive)*		12	

At a rate of 19 percent, tax revenues would have been $194 billion. By comparison, the personal income tax in 1981 yielded about $289 billion. The required revenue from the compensation tax is less than from the personal income tax it replaces, because the business tax covers part of the tax base of the current personal tax. The reasons that a low rate of 19 percent yields revenue reasonably close to that obtained from the current tax system are: (1) the business tax includes currently untaxed fringes in its base; (2) the current income tax fails to tax fully dividends, interest, and other forms of business income because of widespread evasion and avoidance; and (3) the current tax allows a number of deductions not included in our proposal, the most important of which is the deduction of state and local taxes.

INTERNATIONAL ASPECTS OF THE SIMPLE TAX

We favor the straightforward principle that the U.S. tax applies only to the domestic operations of all businesses, whether of domestic, foreign, or mixed ownership. Only the revenue from sales of products sold within the United States plus the value of products as they are exported is to be reported on the top line of the business tax form. Only the costs of labor, materials, and other inputs purchased in the United States or imported to the United States are allowable on the second line as deductions for the business tax. Physical presence in the United States is the simple rule that determines whether a purchase or sale is included in taxable revenue or allowable cost.

To see how the business tax would apply to foreign trade, consider first, an importer selling its wares within the United States. Its costs would include the actual amount it paid for its imports, valued as they entered the United States; this would generally be the actual amount paid for them in the country of their origin. Its revenue would be the actual receipts it obtained from sales in the United States. Second, consider an exporter selling to foreigners products produced in the United States. Its costs are all of the inputs and compensation paid in the United States, and its revenue is the amount received from sales to foreigners, provided that the firm did not add to the product after it departed the United States. Third, consider a firm that sent parts to Mexico for assembly and brought back the final product for sale in the United States. The value of the parts as they left the United States would count as part of the revenue of the firm, and the value of the assembled product as it entered the United States would be an expense. The firm would not be allowed to deduct the costs of its Mexican assembly plant.

Under the principle of taxing only domestic activities, the U.S. tax system would mesh neatly with the tax systems of our major trading partners. If every nation used the simple tax and followed the principle, all income throughout the world would be taxed once and only once. Because the principle is already in use in the many nations with value added taxes, it makes sense for the United States to adopt it as well. By the same principle, the compensation tax applies to the earnings of everyone working within the United States, whether or not they are Americans, but does not apply to the foreign earnings of Americans.

Choices about the international location of businesses and employment are influenced by differences in tax rates. The United States, wih the low marginal rate of 19 percent, would be much the most attractive location among major industrial nations, from the point of view of taxation. Although the simple tax does not tax the overseas earnings of American workers and businesses, there is no reason to fear a mass exodus of economic activity. On the contrary, the favorable tax climate in the United States would draw in new business from everywhere in the world.

BALANCING THE BUDGET
WITH A SIMPLE TAX

If federal spending can be held to the level proposed by the President in his budget for the 1983 fiscal year, or if any increases can be financed by user fees or earmarked taxes, then the 19 percent tax rate would balance the budget by 1985. Even if spending is at the high level projected in the baseline budget of the Congressional Budget Office (CBO), a tax rate of 19 percent would bring the federal deficit down to $75 billion by 1987. Under the President's spending proposals, the tax rates necessary to balance the budget starting in fiscal year 1983 would be 21 percent in that year, 20 percent in 1984, and 19 percent in 1985. Under the higher CBO baseline spending projections, the tax rates necessary to balance the budget would be 23 percent in 1983 and 1984, 22 percent in 1985, 21 percent in 1986, and 20 percent in 1987. Immediate adoption of the simple tax would bring moderate deficits during the current recession, but would commit the nation to a balanced budget within three years, provided spending is kept at reasonable levels.

The base for the simple tax is gross national product (GNP) less indirect business taxes and investment. In arriving at the conclusions just stated, we used projections of GNP from the President's budget and from the CBO. (See Table 12-1.) We approximated the base as 79 percent of GNP, based on detailed calculations for 1980.

The simple tax allows each taxpaying individual or family to deduct a personal allowance. These allowances are indexed according to the cost of living from the proposals for 1981. The total allowances for a husband, wife, and two children in 1983 would be $8,355. Our estimates of total allowances were derived from our estimate for 1981 by assuming 1 percent annual growth in the number of taxpayers and rates of increase of the cost of living from the President's budget and from the CBO baseline projections.

The simple tax replaces the personal and corporate taxes, but not the rest of the federal tax system (of which the social security payroll tax is by far the most important part). Our computations take a projection of total federal spending less a projection of revenue from the other taxes. If the simple tax yields exactly this amount of revenue, it would balance the budget.

The computations take account of the influence of past deficits on current spending through the interest on the national debt. We used the projections of the Treasury bill interest rate underlying the President's budget and the CBO projections in order to track the

Table 12-1. Income Flows and Tax Yields (*from U.S. National Income and Product Accounts for 1981*).

	Billions of Current Dollars
Gross domestic product[a]	$2,868
Federal indirect business tax[b]	57
Imputed items[c]	129
Wages, salaries, and pensions[d]	1,503
Investment[e]	349
Taxable business income[f]	830
Revenue from the business tax at 19 percent	158
Taxable compensation[g]	1,022
Revenue from compensation tax at 19 percent	194
Total tax revenue	352
Actual personal income tax[h]	289
Actual corporate income tax[i]	57
Total actual tax revenue	348

[a]*Economic Report of the President* (ERP) (Washington, D.C.: Government Printing Office, January 1982), Table B-8.
[b]*ERP* Table B-76.
[c]"National Income and Product Accounts, 1976-1979," *Survey of Current Business* (Special Supplement, July 1981): Table 8.8, p. 77.
[d]*ERP* Table B-21, plus our estimate of private pensions.
[e]Business investment is estimated as total investment in equipment, nonresidential structures, and farm investment, plus 20 percent of investment in residential structures (*ERP* Table B-15). The remaining 80 percent of residential structures are owner-occupied and not deductible under the business tax.
[f]Gross domestic product less federal indirect business taxes, wages, salaries, and pensions, imputed items, and investment.
[g]Wages, salaries, and pensions less personal allowances.
[h]Estimated as 75 percent of the revenue for fiscal year 1981 and 25 percent of the revenue for fiscal year 1982 (*ERP* Table B-19).
[i]Same as personal income tax.

effect of a reduced national debt on interest expense. We do not attempt to take account of the influence of tax reform on total economic activity and the corresponding augmentation of federal revenue, though we think these effects could be substantial.

Details of the future budgetary implications of the simple tax appear in Table 12-2. Table 12-2 presents our computations based on the economic assumptions and spending proposals in the President's February budget. The first four lines compute the level of taxable income on a calendar year basis. Line 5 gives taxable income on a fiscal year basis. Dividing the estimate of required revenue by taxable income yields the necessary tax rate under the simple tax.

Line 6 gives the Administration's estimates of the revenue from the personal and corporate income taxes, including the effects of the

Table 12-2. Computation of Flat Tax Yield over 1981-85 Period.

Line		1981	1982	1983	1984	1985
1	GNP	2922	3159	3522	3881	4257
2	Tax base	2314	2502	2789	3074	3372
3	Allowances	481	535	580	620	655
4	Taxable income (calendar year)	1833	1967	2210	2454	2717
5	Taxable income (fiscal year)	1790	1933	2149	2393	2651
6	Revenue from personal and corporate income taxes	347	345	370	407	450
7	Rate to raise same revenue	19.4	17.8	17.2	17.0	17.0
8	Rate to close deficit			21.2	20.0	19.0
9	Revenue at 19 percent tax rate			408	455	504
10	Deficit at 19 percent tax rate	58	99	51	29	8

Economic Recovery Tax Act of 1981 (ERTA) and the modifications proposed by the President in February 1982. Line 7 shows the rate under the simple tax necessary to yield the same revenue as the personal and corporate income taxes. Note that the rate declines from around 19 percent in 1981 to 17 percent in later years, as the major personal tax reductions of 1982 and 1983 go into effect.

Line 8 shows the simple tax rate necessary to eliminate the deficit starting in fiscal year 1983. Though this rate starts above 21 percent, it falls to 19 percent by 1985. Again, these computations take account of the favorable effect on interest costs of lower deficits in earlier years.

Line 10 shows the projected size of the federal deficit if the simple tax were adopted starting in fiscal year 1983 at a constant rate of 19 percent. The deficit is manageable in all years and essentially disappears in 1985.

Congressional Budget Office projections of real growth and inflation are less optimistic than those of the Administration through 1987, which means that a 19 percent flat tax will not completely eliminate the deficit by then. But even under CBO's pessimistic estimates, the projected deficit falls from $250 billion to less than $100 billion by 1987, a much more manageable figure.

THE FUTURE OF THE ECONOMY
UNDER THE SIMPLE INCOME TAX

At the outset, the simple income tax, with common flat rates of 19 percent on business income and compensation, would raise revenue equal to about 12 percent of GNP, the same as the current combination of corporate and personal income taxes. The personal allowances under our proposed tax system are raised from year to year in line with inflation, which would tend to hold its revenue constant as a fraction of GNP (the new law provides for this kind of indexation starting in 1985).

The switch from the current corporate and personal income taxes to the simple income tax would have some mild transitional effects on the U.S. economy. Briefly, the elimination of depreciation deductions for business would be costly to the owners of existing plant and equipment, but this largely would be offset by the reduction in the taxation of the earnings of capital assets. We do not think any special compensation is necessary for the loss.

Adoption of the simple tax would lower interest rates. Rates would fall immediately because investors would require a lower rate of interest when they were no longer paying tax on the interest. In the medium run, the investment boom set off by the more favorable tax treatment of capital formation might bring interest rates partway back to their earlier level. In the long run, interest rates would decline as capital accumulation proceeded. Prices of bonds would rise as soon as the tax was announced. None of these effects would be large, and none seems to call for any corrective action by the government. Compared to the gigantic capital losses inflicted on bondholders by inflation and rising taxes over the past decade, and the corresponding capital gains accruing to homeowners over the same period, neither of which has been offset by any government policy, the effects of the simple tax in the opposite direction are mild.

Though under the simple tax our system would stabilize revenue as a fraction of GNP, it would probably produce more revenue than the government needs to maintain existing programs. Low marginal tax rates would draw economic activities from the underground economy into the formal market, where they would be recorded as part of GNP. Businesses and individuals would spend less time worrying about the tax consequences of their actions and would concentrate instead on earning higher incomes. On these grounds, it is possible that the revenue needs of the federal government could be met with tax rates as low as 16 or 17 percent, rather than the 19 percent needed to reproduce current revenue at current levels of GNP.

Over the postwar period, cuts in marginal tax rates have coincided with episodes of vigorous economic growth and reduced inflation in the United States. Moreover, those nations with lower marginal tax rates have achieved the highest economic growth over the past decade. The growth stimulated by tax reform is favorable not only for the increased income it would bring to the American public but also because it would moderate and eventually eliminate the federal budget deficit.

The benefits of tax reform are not purely economic. The complexities of the federal tax system foster contempt for government and make petty criminals out of a large fraction of the population. A simplified tax with low marginal rates would help restore confidence in government and help uphold the basic honesty of the American people.

BIBLIOGRAPHY

Budget of the United States Government, Fiscal Year 1983. Washington, D.C.: Government Printing Office, February 1982.

Congressional Budget Office. *Baseline Budget Projections for Fiscal Years 1983-1987: A Report to the Senate and House Committees on the Budget—Part II.* Washington, D.C.: Government Printing Office, February 1982.

Discussants:

A FRAMEWORK FOR EVALUATING A FLAT RATE TAX

J. Gregory Ballentine

I will base my remarks on testimony given in September 1982 by John Chapoton, Assistant Secretary of the Treasury for Tax Policy, when he testified on the flat tax before the Senate Finance Committee. In his testimony, Mr. Chapoton stressed the need for an objective framework for analyzing tax policy. He noted the need for the Treasury Department to develop such a framework and the need for those examining tax policy to use such a framework.

In 1982 some of us at Treasury outlined two broad notions of what a pure tax system would involve: a uniform income tax and a uniform tax on consumed income. We did not imply, and we did not mean to imply, that we would necessarily develop a program moving toward one of those two systems immediately, or even that we would move toward a target of one of those two programs. We did, however, view those two paradigmatic tax structures as providing standards by which individual programs and major tax reforms, such as various flat tax proposals, could be evaluated.

Basically, both a uniform income tax and a uniform tax on consumed income would provide uniform treatment of income, no matter what the source. I stress the concept of uniform treatment of income because that was the theme of our testimony. The one type of uniformity not included in our framework was rate uniformity, or the use of a single tax rate. The concept of uniformity we discussed is characterized by the same treatment of income for individuals in equal economic circumstances, or the same treatment of their income or their consumption, no matter what the source. Our definition of uniformity did not imply that the same tax rate applied to income for different income groups.

Indeed, there are strong reasons why we would not want a single tax rate. As an example, Alvin Rabushka noted that the Hall-Rabushka plan would cause some redistribution of income. He mentioned a small loss below $40,000 and a small gain above $60,000 to $70,000. Frankly, we would not view the redistributional effects as being small. As I understand the numbers, for a family of four with a $20,000 income, including all wages with no tax shelters, no fringe benefits, and no particular tax breaks, the Hall-Rabushka plan would effectively repeal considerably more than the entire 25 percent 1981 tax cut. Higher income persons would break even or gain. For example, top grade government employees, earning on the order of $60,000, would just about break even. At incomes above $70,000, people would be getting significant tax cuts. That is not what we would label a small redistribution.

Single rate uniformity, with its marked redistribution of income, challenges the American public's notion of how rapid and how marked a change should be made in the relative economic circumstances of different income groups. The question takes on substantial political significance. It is one thing to talk about what changes one would like to make in an already existing flat rate system. It is an entirely different thing to talk about immediately and rapidly redistributing large amounts of income.

Because the Hall-Rabushka plan is designed to be revenue-neutral in the early years, for every person who experiences a tax cut, there would be another person or persons who experience equal dollar amounts of tax increases. In this case, the tax increases would be for those with incomes below $40,000. It is not a part of our framework for tax design to create a significant redistribution of income.

There are further uniformity problems with the Hall-Rabushka plan. The proposal would essentially ignore differences among individuals, except for their wage levels, levels of income, and exemption levels. For example, one of the costs of attaining this degree of uniformity is that cancer surgery or other major medical expenses would be treated as consumption because medical deductions would not be allowed. By ignoring medical deductions, the proposal treats major cancer surgery in the same fashion as the purchase of a villa.

There are other examples of the same phenomenon, although they are less dramatic. It is not necessarily true that the gains from uniformity outweigh the damages of ignoring the fact that, for example, some employees have legitimate employee expenses while others do not. At the same time, it is not appropriate for every employee to file as a business firm and thus receive business deductions. These are some of the cases where the concept of uniformity used in our framework do not carry over to the Hall-Rabushka plan. There are, however, many other places where it does. I can discuss these briefly.

First, all income should be taxed only once. Corporations do not pay taxes; only individuals pay taxes. The corporate income tax and the individual income tax should be viewed as taxes on individual income. Together they constitute a double tax on some income. Proposals that seek to reform the tax system but ignore the corporate income tax (The Fair Tax Act of 1983, proposed by Senator Bill Bradley and Representative Richard Gephardt, was one, in the initial stages) are not consistent with the broad definition of uniformity used in our framework. Further, proposals that attempt to reform both the personal income tax and the corporate income tax miss the point. The issue is not to reform the corporate income tax to make it work properly but to integrate the corporate and personal income tax. Again, I stress the importance not of immediate integration but of a framework to examine proposed changes.

Second, an important part of the uniform taxation framework is that real income, not inflationary income, should be subject to tax. A case in point is capital gains. To the extent that a capital gain is due simply to a rise in the nominal price level, it is not income. If one holds an asset valued at $100.00 for one year and the next year that asset is valued at $110.00, after the price level has risen by 10 percent, one has realized no real income. It would be a mismeasurement of income to define nominal gains as such. The measure of income itself must be corrected, i.e., indexed for inflation, and this is an important part of Treasury's framework. The indexation issue is no problem in the Hall-Rabushka plan. In a consumption based tax, capital gains are not subject to tax, and, therefore, the problem of inflation measurement does not exist. That is a significant advantage of consumption based taxes, whether of the flat rate or progressive nature.

Finally, there are other specific aspects of a consumption tax where the concept of uniformity does apply. A consumption tax or a consumed income tax, as discussed in the testimony, is a tax with a single general deduction for net saving.

In conclusion, I want to note that even the Treasury's analytical framework can be no panacea for handling the complexities of tax programs. A framework can be very idealistic, but there are still difficult issues that must be resolved. One such issue is the allocation of necessary business expenses. The classic example of the business lunch is a case of distinguishing a necessary business expense from renumeration to the employee that should be taxed. Another example is the treatment of tuition expenses. Are they business expenses or consumption? These issues must be faced. They do not go away.

Regardless of the enormous gains that we are able to perceive in the reforms and the frameworks that we devise, we cannot ignore the fact that it is a complex world. Therefore, any tax system able to deal with that world will inevitably also be quite complex.

THE FLAT RATE TAX AND THE FISCAL APPETITE

James M. Buchanan

I feel uncomfortable as a discussant of the Hall-Rabushka paper. I can accept almost everything they say about the current tax structure, and I agree with their argument concerning the advantages that might be offered by a dramatic shift to the flat rate tax *as they propose it*. Hall and Rabushka, like most of their peers in social science, find it challenging and rewarding to spin out idealized reforms. Most of the time, it does not concern us much if our fantasies never become political reality.

My objection to the Hall-Rabushka proposal stems from my fear that it will, in some form, secure widespread political support, and that as implemented the flat rate tax will not work out as Hall and Rabushka project. As Hayek reminds us, the task of the social scientist is to examine the unintended consequences of human action, and, in this instance, surely unintended consequences would emerge to haunt the advocates of the flat rate tax proposals, much as the withholding provision under the income tax is alleged to haunt Milton Friedman in his dreams.

We find it very difficult not to construct our ideal structures on the "as if" model of benevolent despotism. If, indeed, our politics are best described in the image of a benevolent despotism, we might find a sweepout of the encrusted overgrowth of the existing tax structure long overdue. As "advice" to such a despot, the introduction of the flat rate tax has almost everything to recommend it. Unfortunately, however, no such benevolent despot exists, and if we are proffering advice to government—warts and all, with politicians whom we recognize—to proceed "as if" is both naive and dangerous.

Each and everyone of us knows that a miraculous introduction, *tomorrow*, of the Hall-Rabushka proposal, down to its finest details, will insure that, over the long term, the share of national income diverted through the governmental sector will increase, and perhaps dramatically. One of the most important constraints on the further exploitation of taxpayers under our existing structure is surely the presence of loopholes. Remove these, and the constraint vanishes.

It does not take much public choice sophistication to recognize that elected politicians, in their natural inclinations to respond to constituency demands, will increase tax rates beyond efficiency limits. This result holds so long as we acknowledge that tax shares are more generally distributed than specific program benefit-transfer shares. Even within the complex fiscal structure that now exists, most economists would acknowledge that a high tax asymmetry or bias is present. The flat rate tax would guarantee that the high tax bias would be exacerbated. In the current order of fiscal affairs, organized pressures can emerge for specialized tax treatment, as well as for specialized program benefits. At least, in part, pressures for tax loopholes offset pressures for new and expanded spending programs. No such tax countervalence would remain under the flat rate tax, even if it should replace all other taxes, and dollar for dollar.

More importantly, of course, we also know that the flat rate tax would not replace, dollar for dollar, existing revenue sources. We know that, under any plausibly acceptable model of fiscal decision-making, the flat rate tax would become an additional instrument for massive revenue generation in the hands of government. It is folly to think otherwise.

As "advice to the truly benevolent despot," the equi-revenue assumption taken over from traditional normative tax theory is meaningful and perhaps useful. Equal revenues can be raised more efficiently and more equitably under the flat rate tax than under the structure that now exists. There is, of course, nothing at all new in this; normative tax theorists have been telling us this for decades. The political, external diseconomies of the flat rate tax must be incorporated into any serious analysis of its effects, however, and these make the equi-revenue assumption seem absurd. The appropriate comparison is not between a flat rate tax raising X dollars of total revenue and the current structure raising X dollars; the appropriate comparison is between X dollars of revenue raised under current structure and X and Y dollars raised under the flat rate tax *and* other sources.

Note that I have not introduced a Leviathan model of the fiscal process anywhere in my discussion to this point. In our book, *The Power to Tax* (Cambridge University Press, 1980), Geoffrey Brennan and I argued that, for questions concerning the constitutional authorization of the taxing power, it is appropriate to model government as a revenue maximizer, with a natural proclivity to exploit fully any revenue source granted to it. In this constitutional perspective, the availability of a *new* revenue source opens up prospects for massive increases in the share of national treasure to be commanded for the public sector. Make no mistake; politicians of all stripes would treat the introduction of a flat rate tax as a shift outward in their possibility frontier. (I should emphasize that everything I have said above in criticism of the flat rate tax applies—if anything, even more strongly—to proposals for other new impositions.)

As I indicated at the outset, I do not feel comfortable with this totally negative, even if very simple, critique. I feel under some obligation to suggest an alternative route to reform that is not so politically naive. Any such reform must be genuinely constitutional; it must constrain the fiscal appetite of modern government. To some extent, at least, this objective might be accomplished by passage of the balanced budget, tax limitation constitutional amendment approved by the Senate in 1982. If such a constitutional amendment were in place, I should, of course, adopt a totally different position on the flat rate tax. Within these limits, I might well be quickly convinced that the Hall-Rabushka plan offers genuine improvement. (And I am, indeed, surprised that Alvin Rabushka, in particular, who has been so solid in support of the amendment, does not make its passage a necessary precondition for advancing the flat rate tax proposition.) Without the prior existence of such constitutional limits on fiscal appetites, we must hope that such proposals as this fall on deaf ears, and that any new sources of revenues will be withheld from the fiscal reaches of government. Legislative passage of the flat rate tax, before any constitutional limits on spending or on total revenue intake, offers the path to fiscal ruin. For the economy to grow, the government must shrink. The flat rate tax insures just the opposite.

PROSPECTS FOR ENACTMENT OF A FLAT RATE TAX

James R. Jones

I think the Ninety-eighth Congress is going to have a considerable amount of discussion on basic tax reform. As I have been saying for the last four or five years, future tax reform will either take the form of a flat rate tax or a progressive flat rate gross income tax, or the form of a more consumption-oriented tax. A consumption-oriented tax would be similar either to the concepts Dr. Martin Feldstein discussed in an earlier paper, or to a value added approach, as was proposed a few years ago by Congressman Al Ullman, Senator Russell B. Long, and a few others.

In any event, I do think there is a desire on the part of the public for some basic tax reform. That tax reform should have two features: One, the reform should be simple, so that the average citizen can understand that he is getting a fair shake; two, the reform should make it clear to the public that everyone is paying his fair share of the tax load.

I have a certain bias in favor of a gross income tax or flat tax approach. In my first term on the Ways and Means Committee, I offered a proposal for a flat rate or gross income tax as an amendment to the tax bill of 1976. I think I garnered one other vote in favor of it. I cannot remember if my hand went up at the time the final vote was taken, but I do know that I received a great deal of mail from the Boy Scouts of America, the preachers, the churches, the private schools, and so forth. From this experience, I knew that it would not be easy to implement a flat rate tax approach.

Having said that my bias is toward a gross income tax approach, let me point out what I consider to be some of the major difficulties with the Hall–Rabushka plan. These problems indicate that it would not be easy to pass a flat rate tax in the Ways and Means and the Finance Committees in the Ninety-eighth Congress.

First of all, Congress will not be able to discuss tax reform measures until sometime in the late spring or summer because social security is going to dominate the Congressional agenda throughout the spring. Second, with talk of a more extensive summer recess this year, hope of an early adjournment, and recognition that 1984 is going to be a terribly partisan year, with a lot of Presidential politics involved, it is unlikely that we are actually going to put on the books a major tax reform bill.

Let me point out some of the concerns that I have about the Hall–Rabushka approach. First, I am concerned about the regressive nature of this tax. If we are going to have a gross income tax or a flat rate tax approach, it is much preferable to have two, three, or four progressive levels of taxation. To do otherwise would create redistribution of the tax burden that I think would be unfair. I think the question of fairness will come up over and over again, as this flat rate tax approach is studied.

Both the Joint Committee on Taxation (JCT) and the Congressional Budget Office (CBO) have given us some examples of the possible redistributional effects of a single rate, flat rate tax. CBO estimates that the flat rate tax would create a substantial redistribution of the tax burden. A single person with an adjusted gross income (AGI) of $15,000 would pay 14 percent more under the Hall–Rabushka plan than under the 1984 law as it presently exists. Four-person families with adjusted gross incomes of $25,000, $35,000, and $45,000, and typical itemized deductions, would pay, respectively, 43 percent, 22 percent, and 11 percent more in tax. In contrast, taxpayers with very high incomes would enjoy substantial tax cuts. Indeed, those with adjusted gross incomes between $100,000 and $200,000 would receive tax cuts of about 45 percent. Those with incomes over $1 million would have their taxes cut by about 85 percent. I think this tells us that the regressivity problem would have to be addressed.

Another question concerning the fairness of the Hall-Rabushka proposal involves the taxation of fringe benefits. As I understand the proposal, employers would not be able to deduct fringe benefits for their workers. This raises the question of what fringe benefits that are part of doing business would be deductible. The business lunch? The hunting lodge? If those things were deductible as a part of doing business, and fringe benefits to workers were not deductible, the issue of fairness would be an impediment to implementation of the Hall-Rabushka plan.

Second, I think we must consider transitional problems. The transitional problems of moving to a new tax system are enormous, and also involve the question of fairness. Some companies would receive either windfall gains or significant losses. For example, a firm whose income fluctuates cyclically, which is presently caught up in the economic doldrums and may be unprofitable in the foreseeable future, would get little benefit from expensing of new investment under a flat rate system. We estimate, in investment credits alone, these firms could lose as much as $10 billion in credits. Transitional problems would create an impediment to a quick implementation of any kind of a flat rate tax approach.

Third, I am concerned about the revenue estimates we have seen for the Hall-Rabushka plan. As I understand the Hall-Rabushka plan, if federal spending could be held to the level proposed in the President's budget for fiscal year 1983, then a 19 percent tax rate would balance the federal budget by 1985. CBO clearly does not agree with such revenue estimates and states that the estimates may be overstated by as much as $100 billion per year. Revenue estimates would be another question that would be raised if and when Congress gets into this issue.

The final point I would like to make concerns international trade. I think everyone who looks ahead into the next century recognizes that if the United States is going to maintain a viable, growing economy that accommodates our hopes and aspirations for the future, we have to become more export-minded. We must become competitive in the international market. We must find some mechanism to either change our rules under the General Agreement on Tariffs and Trade (GATT), with regard to the rebatable value added tax that most of the European countries and Japan use, or we must find something to compete with that system. The question is whether the Hall-Rabushka plan, or any income-based tax, is the right approach to take if we are going to become more aggressive in international trade. If that is the case, and if we do not change the GATT regulations, perhaps we might concentrate more on a consumption-oriented tax with a rebatable feature for exports, rather than an income-based tax.

I do believe that the proposal presented—while pure in form and obviously in need of a great deal of compromise and changes if it is to pass the political test of both Houses of Congress—offers a great move forward in spelling out how this one form, and other basic forms of tax reform, could be implemented in the United States.

COSTS AND BENEFITS OF ADOPTING A FLAT RATE TAX

John S. Nolan

The following comments on the Hall-Rabushka flat or simplified income tax proposal point up, to some extent, the practical differences between a broad-based tax, whether imposed on income or consumption, and the hybrid tax presently known as the U.S. income tax. The latter tax is imposed on a base considerably narrowed by efforts to seek equity, achieve social objectives, and affect investment decisions. The present U.S. income tax is neither an income tax nor a consumption tax in a pure sense; it has elements of both systems.

It is equally true, however, that the Hall-Rabushka proposal is neither fish nor fowl. Losses on the business form cannot be applied to reduce compensation income; the proposal, therefore, is not truly a personal consumption tax. In a sense, compensation received is *deemed* to have been consumed. This hybrid character in and of itself creates complexities not acknowledged by the proponents.

Thus, the owner of a closely held business is, as a practical matter, at liberty to withdraw earnings from the business either as compensation or as dividends, as he sees fit. If he chooses to reinvest earnings in investment assets, he may avoid the Hall-Rabushka compensation tax simply by taking no compensation income. This might be avoided by deeming the existence of compensation income equal to the value of his services, but that would create an extraordinary administrative complexity. In the absence of such treatment, however, there will be substantial differences in treatment from persons realizing compensation income who have no such control over the nominal source of their income.

The proposal otherwise severely underestimates the transitional difficulties and social effects of the change from our present system of taxation. It also overestimates its simplification and fairness benefits.

Thus, the elimination of personal interest and real estate tax deductions would heavily burden low- and middle-income families who purchased their existing homes partly in reliance on the tax savings from these deductions. Many of these persons are paying tax currently at an effective rate below 19 percent; thus, they will not realize an offsetting benefit in lower rates. Higher income groups can largely avoid this effect by selling investment assets and repaying their mortgages; the proposal does not attempt to tax the returns from owner-occupied housing. This would create a new inequity in the tax system.

The treatment of gain on the sale of a residence under the proposal is not entirely clear. The returns from such an asset will not have been taxed, but the gain will likely be more attributable to inflation than to value added by any production or services. Thus, presumably the gain would not be taxed, but it seems doubtful that this would be regarded as "fair" where very large gains are realized by the wealthy.

By eliminating the charitable contribution deduction, the proposal threatens the existence of a wide range of social institutions and could create new and costly responsibilities for the government. These institutions include churches, private educational organizations, hospitals, museums, charities such as the Red Cross and Salvation Army, extensive scientific and research activities, and many others. All of these institutions, including churches, provide a wide range of support to the poor, the disadvantaged, and others, and they are uniquely efficient in doing so. Repeal of the incentive to give voluntarily for their support will severely reduce their activities and will either force the government to provide their support, with resulting enormous problems of selection and inefficiency, or require the government directly to take over their activities, at even greater loss of efficiency. This has major budget implications.

Denial of a deduction for state income tax will result in double taxation of the same income and create severe pressures to reduce state income tax rates, possibly pushing up real estate and sales taxes, with substantial distributional effects. The denial of any deduction for state income, property, and sales taxes would represent the withdrawal of substantial revenue aid to the states. Is this realistic? Increased revenue sharing would become necessary, and this would push up the necessary tax rate that the proposal assumes.

Denial of any deduction for extraordinary medical expenses presents similar difficulties. A deduction for such costs in an income tax system is probably justified as a matter of theory—they clearly represent reduced ability to pay. If such a deduction is to be denied, it would become infinitely more important that we have much more widespread health insurance, but the proposal to deny employer deductions for the cost of employer-provided health insurance would reduce the likelihood of doing so through employment relationships. The result could well be to create pressures for government-provided or funded medical and hospital services with all the emotional debates that would bring.

The treatment of fringe benefits will present extraordinary difficulties. The proposal would not tax an employee at the time the employer makes pension contributions on his behalf but only when the employee receives the pension. Will the employer get a deduction for his pension contribution at the time it is made to the pension trust? If so, given that dividends and interest would no longer be taxable, the existing federal subsidy for private pension plans would largely be preserved. If the employer does not get a deduction making his pension contribution, he will have no incentive to fund the pension, creating new risks for employees. Since employer contributions to the social security trust fund will presumably continue to be deductible, pressures will develop to abandon the private pension in favor of increased social security benefits and taxes.

In the case of other fringe benefits, administrative difficulties will still arise. The Hall-Rabushka proposal denies a deduction to businesses for the cost of such fringes. But what is done as to fringes accruing to employees of tax-exempt organizations, including governments? Elimination of the deduction for cost of group life insurance, disability insurance, and health insurance for employees of businesses will result in employers substituting cash wages in lieu of these in-kind benefits, since there are substantial administrative costs in providing such benefits. This would have significant economic and social effects, requiring employees or the government to make new provisions in cases of employee death, disability, or illness.

On the business tax side, there are obvious major transitional difficulties in going to a system that allows complete first-year write-off of depreciable assets and deduction of the cost of all purchases without requiring capitalization of inventory costs. It would be too difficult to explain to taxpayers why the unrecovered cost of *existing* plant and equipment and inventories should not be allowed as deductions in some fashion. I think deductions would be allowed for these accounts. These deductions, combined with current deduction of new plant and equipment costs and raw material purchases, would result in no business tax for many businesses for a substantial period of time.

The proposal for dealing with international transactions by taxing only domestic operations is sound in theory but would be immensely difficult in practice. In today's complex world, it is very frequently the case that the production and sale of goods and services cross international lines in multiple degrees. Products are partially fabricated in the United States and completed abroad for sale abroad, or upon reentry to the United States, for sale in the United States, and vice versa. The same occurs with respect to the costs of providing services, that is, engineering for a complex communications system for a Middle Eastern country will be partly accomplished in the United States and partly abroad. The concept of attempting to value exports and imports at the border of partially completed goods or services boggles the mind. Our existing extreme difficulties in determining arm's-length prices on intercompany transactions, or in using formula apportionment methods to allocate income, would be multiplied beyond comprehension.

Further, there can be no assurance that foreign governments would follow suit and implement a worldwide system of apportionment based on this concept. What is to be done if a foreign government taxes the entire income (selling price less cost of goods sold) upon a sale within its borders when most of the costs have been incurred in the United States? A foreign tax credit would be necessary, and much of the sought-after simplification in this area would be lost.

Having made the foregoing criticisms, I do not wish to be interpreted as opposed to the concept. I personally support the critical need for a tax on a comprehensive base in the United States. The question whether it should be more in the mold of an income tax or a consumption tax is a fundamental matter involving a balancing of economic efficiency and fairness considerations. I favor a consumption tax. The question whether it should be a flat or progressive tax (in either an income tax or consumption tax system) is a separate question that largely involves considerations of fairness versus administrability.

AN OPPORTUNITY FOR TAX REFORM

Bob Packwood

Looking down the road to 1985, 1986, 1987 and 1988, I can see an opportunity for great tax reform. Congress is eventually going to say that we must enact major changes in the tax Code. I think the possibility exists, driven by the large projected deficits, that Congress may move toward some kind of a consumption tax, such as an energy tax tied to cost or BTU content.

We have reached the stage on the revenue side that we can no longer raise great quantities of money either by closing loopholes or by taxing the rich. I do not intend to demean one or two billion dollars. Either sum is a lot of money, but to raise $10, $20, or $30 billion by picking up $300 million here and $500 million there would be difficult. We closed many loopholes and tightened compliance rules in 1982, and I question whether Congress will try to raise substantial additional revenues in the same fashion soon. Also, taxing the rich does not raise massive tax revenues because there are not enough rich people. I asked the Joint Taxation Committee (JTC) to calculate how much money could be raised if we confiscated 100 percent of all income over $100,000. I do not mean 100 percent of all taxable incomes over $100,000, but rather 100 percent of all incomes over $100,000. The JTC calculated that $60 billion could be raised. And that amount could only be raised once, because no one would make over $100,000 the second year. Taxing the rich would not eliminate the deficit problem for one year, let alone for future years.

One tax reform that people talk about is the flat tax. Every time somebody in the audience says, "What do you think of the flat tax?", I ask the individual to define the term. Does it refer to a flat tax with no deductions? Or does it mean a progressive flat tax? And what about deductions, credits, or exclusions? Most people who ask about the flat tax think it would lower their total tax bill. We should not fool ourselves. Current and projected deficits do not allow massive general tax cuts. Many look wide-eyed at the flat tax and think it would lower my taxes and raise your taxes. Indeed, that may be what happens; future tax rates depend on what measure is proposed, and which tax bracket a person is in when asking the question.

At the moment we use the tax Code for a great many things in addition to collecting money. We use the Code for incentives to accomplish what we regard as legitimate social purposes. To the extent the government chooses to encourage activities beyond the marketplace, there are two ways to do it. One is the tax incentive, and the other is a government program supported by appropriated funds and run by the government bureaucracy. As an example, consider housing. The mortgage interest and taxes deduction exists. Imagine that deduction null and void. If you still wanted to encourage housing beyond the marketplace, you could create a program, I assume run by the Department of Housing and Urban Development. Individuals wanting to buy a house or build a house would go to the local HUD office and apply for a grant. They would fill out a form, making sure to have enough bathrooms per square foot, or whatever the regulations might be. They may or may not get the grant; and they may or may not get it for several months. Now, multiply that through a variety of other incentives that we have in the tax Code, such as charitable contributions, Individual Retirement Accounts (IRAs), solar energy, municipal bonds, and capital gains. If you are willing to get rid of all the tax incentives and to suffer a government-administered program instead of the tax incentive, then your suggestion has merit.

If we are going to compete in this world, then I think we are going to have to compete on a reasonably comparable basis, and we are going to have to move toward lower taxes on capital. All of our European trading partners have higher rates of taxation relative to their gross national product; yet they have lower rates of taxation on income and capital, especially interest, dividends, and capital gains. They also have higher rates of taxation on consumption. The Japanese have a lower overall level of taxation than do we, but business provides a great many fringe benefits that otherwise would be provided by government. The Japanese tax consumption much more heavily than we do, and they tax income and capital more lightly than we do.

One type of consumption tax being discussed seriously is a per barrel oil fee. Congress may eventually turn to this or a broader energy tax to cut the deficit. Discussions in the media and the press abound. There is a fairly broad base of interest in academia. Some are also talking about an energy tax that does not discriminate among the various forms of energy.

Those who grasp the fact that we need to encourage savings, investment, and capital formation to create jobs and preserve our trade position must seize the opportunity. I cannot guarantee that major tax reforms will be enacted, but the opportunity exists. I think Congress has an opportunity to achieve reforms that have eluded us in the past.

Chapter 13

International Tax Issues: Aspects of Basic Income Tax Reform

Thomas Horst and Gary Hufbauer [1]

INTRODUCTION AND SUMMARY

This paper evaluates the international aspects of various proposals for basic tax reform. The two essential features of most proposals for basic tax reform, whether for a value added tax or for some type of flat income tax, are: (1) They would eliminate the present double taxation of income earned by corporations and distributed as a dividend to its shareholders, and (2) they would eliminate most or all of the special exemptions, deductions, and credits that characterize the present U.S. tax system.

Our focus is how those alternative tax proposals would apply to "international" income: income derived by a U.S. citizen or resident (individual, corporate, and so forth) from selling goods or providing services to foreign residents, as well as that derived by foreign residents from providing goods and services to U.S. residents. Here, as elsewhere, we seek to trace the general contours, not the detailed workings, of the tax system.

Part I of this paper reviews the international aspects of the present U.S. tax system. Presently the United States has three separate jurisdictional bases for taxing income: *source* (that is, if the activity or the asset generating income is located within the United States); *residence* (if the person earning the income resides or, for corporations, is incorporated in the United States); and, *citizenship*, (for individuals who are not U.S. residents). Unlike many foreign countries, the United States does not impose a value added tax, federal sales tax or other broadly applicable tax on the value of goods *consumed* in the United States. Part I also includes a cursory review of the international aspects of tax systems in the United States, Canada, the United Kingdom, West Germany, France, and Japan.

Part II reviews the essential features of alternative proposals for basic reform of the U.S. tax system. Proposals are classified according to the basic principle guiding their application to international income: (1) those that would tax the income of U.S. residents but not foreign residents ("residence based tax systems"); (2) those that would tax the income arising from the production of goods and services in the United States but not income arising from foreign production ("location-of-production" tax systems); and (3) those that would tax income derived from the production (domestic or foreign) of goods and services consumed in the United States ("location-of-consumption" tax systems). The third type of tax system includes taxes that are structured as either income or value added taxes but which, through their treatment of savings and investment and by their "border tax adjustments," are the economic equivalent of a consumption tax.

Part III analyzes the three types of proposals in terms of their economic costs, their tax equity implications, and their possible tax revenue consequences. We conclude that tax systems based on location of *production* probably have higher economic costs than tax systems based on either residence or the location of consumption. Because capital, technology, and certain specialized labor services are mobile internationally, taxes are more likely to induce production to shift from the United States to a foreign country than to induce individuals to emigrate or to shift the location of consumption. Thus, to meet any total tax revenue requirement, taxes based on the location of production must be imposed at higher rates and cause greater economic distortions than taxes based on the residence of individuals or the location of their consumption.

Tax systems based solely on *residence* have two serious flaws, each of which is probably fatal: (1) The exemption from U.S. tax of U.S.-source income earned by foreign residents would appear grossly inequitable to many Americans; and (2) the ending of "deferral" of U.S. taxation of income earned by foreign subsidiaries and the U.S. credit for foreign income taxes would be strenuously opposed by those with significant foreign investments and would wreak havoc with present international rules (embodied in U.S. tax treaties) for eliminating the double taxation of international income.

The international ramifications of a tax system based on the location of *consumption*, which from our perspective would appear to be the most attractive of the three alternatives, hinge on whether the tax is structured as an income tax or a value added tax. Although the two taxes can be structured so as to be economically equivalent, the present General Agreement on Tariffs and Trade (GATT) rules permit "border tax adjustments" for value added taxes but not for income taxes. If our international trade relations are not to be further strained, the United States would either have to convince other countries that the present GATT distinction between value added and income taxes makes little sense or would have to adopt a value added or federal sales tax, rather than an economically equivalent income tax.

I. PRESENT U.S. LAW ON THE TAXATION OF INTERNATIONAL INCOME

A. Foreign Individuals and Corporations

In general terms, the present U.S. tax system claims jurisdiction to tax based on three separate criteria. Income is taxed: (1) if it is derived from a U.S. *source*; (2) if it is derived by an individual, corporation, or other entity that is considered a U.S. *resident*; or (3) if it is derived by a U.S. *citizen*, even though that citizen resides in a foreign country.

The delineation of U.S. *source* jurisdiction is particularly important to individuals who are neither U.S. residents nor U.S. citizens and to foreign corporations and other foreign entities. Under U.S. statutory law, such foreigners are taxable with respect to: (1) their U.S.-source "passive income," namely dividends, interest, rents, royalties, and similar types of income, and (2) their income that is effectively connected with a U.S. trade or business. "Passive income" cannot be offset by any expenses, and U.S. tax must be withheld and paid at a statutory rate of 30 percent (in the absence of a lower treaty rate). By contrast, business income may, broadly speaking, be offset by the same deductions, is taxed at the same rates, and qualifies for the same credits as comparable business income earned by a U.S. individual or corporation.

If the foreigner resides in a country with which the United States has a bilateral tax treaty, the rate of withholding tax on U.S.-source passive income may be substantially reduced or, in the case of interest and royalties, even eliminated altogether. Further, tax treaties often eliminate the U.S. withholding tax on dividends and interest paid by foreign corporations that earn more than 50 percent of their gross income from a U.S. trade or business. (Thus, to avoid the withholding tax, a foreigner may use a foreign subsidiary, perhaps incorporated for that sole purpose, to conduct its U.S. business.)

In addition, under bilateral treaties, U.S. taxation of business income is restricted to income "attributable to" a "permanent establishment" in the United States. In some instances, the tax treaty standards allow a resident of a treaty country to avoid the income tax to which that resident would be subject under U.S. statutory law.

Several types of income received by foreigners are exempt from tax under present statutory law. No U.S. tax applies to interest paid on U.S. bank deposits, savings and loan accounts, and insurance company obligations, or to U.S.-source interest in the form of original issue discount on indebtedness with an original maturity of six months or less. Similarly, the income of foreign governments and international organizations of which the United States is a member (for example, the World Bank, the International Monetary Fund) is exempt from U.S. tax unless attributable to certain commercial activities. Similarly, U.S.-source capital gains of foreign persons are, in general, taxable only if effectively connected with a U.S. trade or business or if they arise on the sale or other disposition of an interest in U.S. real property.

B. Foreign Income of U.S. Residents and Corporations

In general, individuals who are U.S. residents and corporations that are chartered under U.S. state or federal law are subject to U.S. tax on their worldwide income. A dollar-for-dollar credit against the U.S. tax is allowed for income taxes paid to foreign governments. The foreign tax credit may not exceed, however, the U.S. tax attributable to foreign-source income.

U.S. tax treatment of foreign-source income differs from that of U.S.-source income in several respects. The following rules are observed in calculating the U.S. tax:

- The Investment Tax Credit (ITC) and the Accelerated Cost Recovery System (ACRS) depreciation allowances cannot be claimed for property used predominantly outside the United States;
- Certain energy credits and the credit for research expenses are restricted to U.S. investments or outlays;
- Percentage depletion, if allowed, is at a lower rate for certain mineral deposits located outside the United States (e.g., nickel, gold, silver, copper, and iron ore) than for similar deposits inside the

United States, and is never allowed with respect to oil and gas wells outside the United States. The amount of foreign tax available for credit may also be reduced when percentage depletion is used in calculating U.S. taxable income;

- Only the first $400,000 of foreign mining exploration expenditures may be expensed; and

- An overall foreign source loss may be offset against domestic-source taxable income in a given year, but that amount is subject to "recapture" through the recharacterization of a comparable amount of foreign-source taxable income as domestic-source taxable income in future years.

Special provisions apply to U.S. corporations that qualify as Domestic International Sales Corporations (DISCs). In general, a DISC must derive at least 95 percent of its gross receipts from qualified export receipts and invest at least 95 percent of its assets in qualified export assets. A DISC itself is exempt from U.S. tax but is deemed to distribute a portion of its income to its shareholders which are taxed on such amounts. The portion of a DISC's income deemed distributed includes: (1) income that, by applying a formula, is attributed to base-period exports; (2) certain other typically small amounts; and (3) 57.5 percent of any remaining net income. The allocation of taxable income between a U.S. corporation and an affiliated DISC is governed by special transfer pricing rules.

Special rules also apply to possessions corporations, which are U.S. corporations deriving at least 80 percent of their gross income from Puerto Rico (or other qualifying U.S. territory), and at least 50 percent (increasing to 65 percent by 1985) from the active conduct of a trade or business therein. The possessions corporation's active business income plus its qualified possessions-source investment income are effectively exempt from U.S. tax, as are dividends received by a U.S. parent corporation from a wholly owned possessions corporation. Safe-haven rules are available for allocating total income, which often includes income from intangibles, between a possessions corporation and its shareholder(s).

A U.S.-owned subsidiary chartered under *foreign* law and deriving its income entirely outside the United States pays no U.S. tax. Its U.S. shareholders would, however, be taxed on dividends received from the foreign corporation. If a U.S. corporation owns 10 percent or more of the voting shares in a foreign corporation, the U.S. corporation may claim a U.S. tax credit for foreign income taxes paid by the subsidiary on the profits out of which a dividend has been paid.

To limit tax avoidance by U.S. individuals and corporations through the use of foreign corporations, present U.S. law, *inter alia*:

- Requires gain to be recognized by a U.S. shareholder on the contribution of certain types of property (for example, patents protecting goods to be sold or used in the United States) to a foreign corporation;

- Requires transactions between foreign corporations and related U.S. persons to be at arm's-length terms;

- Requires U.S. shareholders of a controlled foreign corporation (CFC) to pay tax on the Subpart F income (generally passive income and certain types of business income such as export sales income) earned by that corporation and on certain investments in U.S. property (for example, a loan to an affiliated U.S. corporation); and

- Taxes certain distributions made upon the liquidation of a foreign corporation.

Finally, the earnings and profits of a foreign subsidiary are computed without the benefits of either percentage depletion or the accelerated depreciation deductions allowed under the ACRS.

C. U.S. Citizens Who Are Foreign Residents

The United States taxes U.S. citizens even though they may have become bona fide residents of a foreign country. In 1982, U.S. citizens who were either bona fide foreign residents or who had lived outside of the United States for eleven out of twelve months could exclude from their U.S. taxable income their foreign earned income plus a portion of their housing costs. For 1982, the foreign earned income exclusion cannot exceed $75,000. The maximum exclusion rises in annual increments of $5,000 until it reaches $95,000 in 1986. Dividends, interest, and other nonearned income do not qualify for this exclusion, nor does income earned from U.S. sources (for example, a pension or deferred compensation).

D. Comparison with Foreign Tax Systems

Virtually every country in the world taxes business income that, under its law, is attributable to a domestic branch or other permanent establishment of a foreign corporation or other taxpayer and applies a withholding tax to dividends, interest (with certain exceptions), rents, royalties, and so forth, paid by domestic residents to foreigners. Virtually no other country taxes the income of its nonresident citizens; however, other countries may have stringent cri-

Table 13-1. Essential Features of Taxation of Foreign Income by the United States, Canada, the United Kingdom, West Germany, France, and Japan.

Feature:	Country:					
	United States	Canada	United Kingdom	West Germany	France	Japan
Federal tax rate applied to foreign source income	46%	46%	52%	56%	50%	40%
Foreign income of domestic branch	Taxable	Taxable	Taxable	Taxable	Taxable	Taxable
Income of foreign branch	Taxable	Taxable	Taxable	Taxable	Exempt	Taxable
Dividend from foreign subsidiary	Taxable	Exempt by treaty	Taxable	Exempt by treaty	Exempt	Taxable
Special export incentive	DISC	None	None	None	None	None
Base company sales income of tax haven subsidiary	Taxable	Exempt	Exempt	Taxable	Exempt	Taxable?
Foreign tax credit	Yes	Yes	Yes	Yes	By treaty only	Yes
Foreign tax credit limitation method	Overall	Per country	Per source	Per country	Per country	Overall
Interest, R&D, G&A expense reduce foreign tax credit limitation	Yes	No	No	No	No	No

teria for determining which of its citizens are eligible to claim foreign residency.

Table 13-1 summarizes the tax systems of the United States, Canada, the United Kingdom, West Germany, France, and Japan as they apply to foreign income of domestic taxpayers. That table shows that all six countries tax foreign income attributable to a domestic branch of a domestic taxpayer. France exempts from tax the income attributable to a foreign branch and dividends received from a foreign subsidiary. Canada and West Germany tax the income attributable to a foreign branch, but by treaty exempt dividends received from a foreign subsidiary. The United Kingdom and Japan, like the United States, tax both types of income.

In general, all countries concede that foreign countries have the primary right to tax income arising within their boundaries. That is to say, no country asserts that a taxpayer's country of residence has the primary jurisdiction to tax such income. International double taxation of foreign income earned by domestic taxpayers is generally eliminated by a foreign tax credit. Japan and the United States generally calculate the foreign tax credit limitation on an overall basis; Canada, West Germany, and France (which allows a foreign tax credit only for the taxes of a country with which it has a tax treaty) apply a per country limitation; the United Kingdom applies the limitation separately with respect to each source of income. More significantly, the United States is the only country that requires various overhead expenses to be allocated against foreign source income, a practice that reduces the maximum foreign tax credit that can be claimed.

France, West Germany, and the United Kingdom all impose value added taxes, the standard or normal rates of which range from 13.0 percent to 17.7 percent. Canada imposes a federal sales tax at a rate of 9 percent. Japan, like the United States, has several selective excise taxes but no federal sales or value added tax.

II. REFORM OF THE PRESENT U.S. TAX SYSTEM

Most proposals for sweeping reform of the present U.S. tax system, however much they may differ in other respects, tend to have two features in common. First, they would eliminate the present double taxation of income earned by corporations and paid out to shareholders. Whether the relief would be provided to the corporation paying the dividend or to the shareholder receiving it, the ultimate objective is to eradicate the discrimination inherent in a classical tax system against doing business in corporate form. Second, the reform proposals would eliminate most or all special exemptions, artificial deductions, and tax credits. Consequently, the amount of the tax would vary either proportionately (for example, a flat tax) or progressively with the amount of income subject to tax.

This second feature of reform—the general elimination of preferential tax treatment for various types of income or expense—highlights a tax system's basic jurisdictional rules: what persons and what income are subject to tax. From an international perspective, there are at least three clearcut alternatives for delineating a nation's tax jurisdiction: (1) taxation based exclusively on *residence*; (2) taxation based exclusively on the *location of production*; and (3) taxation based exclusively on the *location of consumption* of final goods and services.

A. Residence Based Tax Systems

Blueprints for Basic Tax Reform, a 1977 report of the U.S. Treasury Department, proposed two alternatives, including an income tax based exclusively on *residence*. Under the Treasury study proposal, after a period of time when other countries would be urged to join in a multilateral move to the residence principle, the United States would:

- Eliminate all U.S. taxes on U.S.-source income derived directly or indirectly (for example, through holding shares in a U.S. corporation) by a foreign resident;

- Eliminate the U.S. credit for income taxes paid directly or by a foreign subsidiary to a foreign government. Foreign income taxes would, however, be deductible in computing taxable income; and

- Tax currently the share of earnings retained by U.S.-controlled subsidiaries.

Under a pure residence-based income tax, the special provisions for possessions corporations and for DISCs would be eliminated. The United States would also presumably give up its right to tax income earned by U.S. citizens who were bona fide residents of foreign countries. In addition, the United States would tax in full the foreign-earned income of U.S. citizens who were working outside the United States, but who were not bona fide foreign residents. Table 13-2 provides an item-by-item comparison of a residence-based tax with the present system and with the production-based and consumption-based taxes described below.

Table 13-2. Comparison of Present U.S. Tax System with Income Tax Systems Based Solely on Residence of Individual, Location of Production, or Location of Consumption.

	Present Law	Residence Location	Production Location	Consumption Location
Income of U.S. Residents				
Income of foreign branch	Yes	Yes	No	No
Retained earnings of foreign subsidiary	Yes	Yes	No	No
Subpart F income	No	Yes	No	No
Other income	Yes	Yes	No	No
Dividends from foreign subsidiary	Yes	Yes	No	No
Portfolio dividends from foreign corporation	Yes	Yes	No	No
Foreign-source interest, rents, royalties, etc.	Yes	Yes	No	No
Foreign-source capital gain	Yes	Yes	No	No
Qualifying income of a possessions corporation	No	Yes	No	No
Tax-deferred income of a DISC	No	Yes	Yes	No
Export receipts in excess of above item	Yes	Yes	Yes	No
Income of Foreign Residents				
Income of U.S. branch	Yes	No	Yes	Yes
Income of foreign-controlled U.S. subsidiary	Yes	No	Yes	Yes
Dividends from U.S. corporation	Yes	No	No	No
U.S.-source interest				
Bank deposits, savings accounts, etc.	No	No	Yes	Yes
Original issue discount	No	No	Yes	Yes
Other Interest	Yes	No	Yes	Yes
U.S.-source rents, royalties, etc.	Yes	No	Yes	Yes
U.S.-source capital gains				
Effectively connected with U.S. business	Yes	No	Yes	Yes
Real estate	Yes	No	Yes	Yes
Other capital gains	No	No	Yes	Yes

U.S.-source earned income	Yes	No	Yes	Yes
Income of foreign governments and international organizations				
Noncommercial	No	No	Yes	Yes
Commercial	Yes	No	Yes	Yes
Receipts from exports to the United States	No	No	No	Yes
Income of Foreign Resident U.S. Citizens				
Foreign-source earned income	No	No	No	No
U.S.-source earned income	Yes	No	Yes	Yes
Foreign-source nonearned income	Yes	No	No	No
U.S.-source nonearned income	Yes	No	Yes	Yes

Note: The United States would tax U.S.-source income paid to foreigners under the location of consumption principle because the goods and services produced with the use of borrowed capital and other factors supplied from abroad are generally consumed in the United States. To the extent those goods and services are exported, the appropriate adjustment is made by tax remission at the border. However, dividends paid by a U.S. corporation to a foreign resident are not taxed because, with basic tax reform, the double taxation of corporate income is eliminated.

B. Production-Based Tax Systems

Income tax systems based largely or exclusively on the *location of production* or other income generating activity are commonly referred to as territorial income taxes. The essential feature of territorial taxation is that all income generated by economic activity within the country is subject to tax regardless of whether the persons to whom the income ultimately accrues are domestic or foreign residents. U.S.-source dividends paid to foreign residents would not be taxed (as part of the broadly applicable provisions eliminating the double taxation of corporate dividends), but the underlying profits from a U.S. business would be taxed. So too would all forms of U.S.-source interest and all U.S.-source income earned by foreign governments and international organizations. The U.S.-source income of U.S. citizens who were bona fide residents of foreign countries would be taxed; foreign-source income, earned or nonearned, would be exempt.

The reverse side of a territorial income tax system is that income of U.S. residents attributable to foreign production—from personal services, a foreign business conducted through a foreign branch or subsidiary, or foreign-source passive investment income—would not be taxed by the United States. Income attributable to a possessions corporation would be exempt from tax, but income of a DISC would be taxable unless that income were actually attributable to a foreign activity of the DISC.

C. Consumption Based Taxation

Robert E. Hall and Alvin Rabushka have recently sketched a proposal for a simple flat rate tax.[2] With respect to international transactions, Hall and Rabushka originally recommended that gross export receipts, not just export profits, be excluded from taxable income, but that a deduction be allowed for the U.S. expenses of earning such income. (Under their revised formulation, Hall and Rabushka would have the tax apply to income attributable to U.S. production for export.[3]) Conversely, the flat rate tax would have been applied to the total value of goods and services purchased from foreign residents. The original Hall-Rabushka proposal would thus assure that only goods and services consumed in the United States would be taxed by the United States.

The original Hall-Rabushka proposal to allow exporters to exclude the full amount of gross export receipts from income, and yet to deduct export expenses from gross receipts from domestic sales, may appear to be an outrageous subsidy to exports. Before deciding that issue, it may be useful to review briefly the General Agreement on Tariffs and Trade (GATT) rules with respect to border tax adjustments as they have been applied to value added taxes and income taxes.

In general terms, a value added tax is imposed on gross receipts from sales minus gross purchases of materials. Value added equals the total incomes of labor, capital, land, and so forth, from production. Under present GATT rules, a value added tax may be converted from a tax on production to a tax on consumption by: (1) allowing producers to claim a value added tax credit for taxes imposed on capital equipment, (2) imposing value added taxes on the full value of imports, and (3) rebating value added taxes on the full value of exports. The application of taxes to imports coupled with rebating such taxes on exports is referred to as "border tax adjustments." These adjustments are similar to those allowed for sales taxes and excise taxes, which may also be applied to imports, and rebated on exports.

It should be noted that the economic literature on border tax adjustments has long pointed to the equivalence of origin principle taxation (that is, taxation based on location of production) and destination principle taxation (that is, taxation based on location of consumption) for generally applicable production or consumption taxes, such as the taxes sought to be imposed by proponents of basic tax reform.[4] In theory, a country gains no permanent economic advantage by taxing only those goods and services consumed domestically rather than goods and services produced domestically. If taxes are rebated on exports and imposed on imports, domestic producers will be able to pass on the tax in the form of higher prices on goods and services sold for local consumption. Competing imports will be higher priced by the amount of the tax, while exports can be sold abroad at lower tax-free prices. Under these circumstances, domestic prices will rise, or the value of the country's currency will depreciate, by the rate of the tax in order to make home sales equally attractive as export sales.[5] In short, border tax adjustments may be significant in gaining political support for a value added tax, but, according to economic theory, such adjustments have no more than a transitory economic effect. Conversely, if border tax adjustments are an important ingredient for securing popular approval for basic tax reform, there should be no international objection to their use.

Under the GATT rules, however, border tax adjustments allowed for value added taxes cannot be made with respect to income taxes. The original Hall-Rabushka proposal would, therefore, be flatly GATT illegal. If the Hall-Rabushka tax had provided for comprehensive withholding on wages, rents, interest, and so forth, and prompt payment of taxes on profits, the amount of withholding and income tax paid by a producer under the original Hall-Rabushka proposal would be based on that producer's value added. Value added equals the total income, wages and salaries, profits, and so forth, generated by production. Thus, a flat rate tax on value added is the economic equivalent of a flat rate tax on income derived from production. Yet the GATT rules for the two types of tax are quite different.

Whether the original Hall-Rabushka proposal should be considered a disguised value added tax, or a value added tax should be considered as a disguised flat rate income tax, is a question of legal form, not economic substance. If the border tax adjustments are GATT legal for value added taxes, U.S. exporters justifiably wonder why those adjustments are GATT illegal for economically equivalent income taxes. Flat rate tax proposals throw into high relief the lack of economic substance to the present GATT rules.

III. ANALYSIS OF ALTERNATIVE TAX JURISDICTION PRINCIPLES

A. Economic Efficiency Considerations

Simple accounting identities indicate that a residence-based income tax is related to a location-of-production tax and a location-of-consumption tax in the following way:

(Total income of U.S. residents)

= (Total income from production of goods and services in the United States)

+ (Foreign source income of U.S. residents)

− (U.S. source income of foreign residents)

= (Total consumption by U.S. residents)

+ (Total Savings by U.S. Residents)

Thus, the choice between a tax system applicable to all income of U.S. residents versus a tax system applicable to all income generated by production in the United States can be stated as follows: Starting from a residence principle, would it be desirable to allow U.S. residents to exclude income earned outside the United States *and* to tax foreign residents on U.S. source income?

From a purely economic standpoint, an income tax based solely on the location of production is probably the least attractive of the three alternative jurisdiction principles. Why? Because the location of production is more sensitive to tax considerations than are an individual's decisions about where to reside or where to consume. As international trade and investment statistics attest, capital, technology, and certain specialized labor services are increasingly mobile internationally; raw materials, components, and finished goods are increasingly produced in one country and consumed in another. Taxing income if and only if it arises from production in the United States creates a tax incentive to U.S.-owned capital, technology, and other relatively footloose factor services to locate outside the United States. It also creates a corresponding disincentive for foreign capital and technology to seek a U.S. location. To be sure, taxes may also affect where some individuals reside or the location of the consumption of some goods and services. By comparison, however, the location of production decisions are *more* sensitive to tax differentials than an individual's residence and consumption decisions. Thus, a tax based solely on the location of production is apt to result in higher tax rates and greater economic distortions than would taxes raising comparable total revenues, but based on either residence or consumption.

The choice between a uniform tax on U.S. residents' total income versus their total consumption is more difficult to resolve on the basis of international economic considerations. With certain exceptions (international travel services), the location of an individual's consumption is determined by his place of residence. The economic choice, in efficiency and growth terms, between residence-based and consumption-based tax systems turns not on international distinctions but on whether it is preferable, in general, to tax income or consumption. The economic considerations that weigh in favor of consumption taxes and against income taxes are described in other conference papers and need not be explored here.

B. Tax Equity Considerations

Tax equity concepts usually call upon a country to apply the same tax rate to a given amount of total economic income of an individual or household, wherever or however that income may be earned. In a world with open borders, this goal is difficult to achieve. The United States, for example, is in no position to assure unilaterally or multilaterally that its own residents or citizens will bear the same income tax burden as foreigners with similar incomes. The Congress, however, is not prepared to accept its impotence in achieving tax equity on an international scale. Compromises that achieve a semblance of equity are much preferred to open abandonment of the goal. The dilemma was illustrated by the recent debate over changing the U.S. taxation of the foreign earned income of U.S. citizens working outside the United States.[6]

Tax equity considerations would appear to weigh heavily against the adoption of an income tax based on residence only. The spectre of foreign individuals and corporations deriving tax-free U.S.-source income—not only from passive U.S. investments but also from a U.S. business, when U.S. residents are subject to tax on such income—may be more than most U.S. voters could accept. Tax equity considerations could also be invoked against a tax restricted to income derived from U.S. production. Why should a U.S. resident's income be tax free when derived from foreign sources, when otherwise comparable income from a U.S.-source is subject to tax? Although Congress might be willing to contemplate some form of U.S. tax exemption for foreign *business* income earned by U.S. taxpayers, an exemption for foreign-source dividends, interest, rents, royalties, and other *passive* income received by U.S. residents would be unpalatable.

C. Tax Revenue Considerations

The potential tax revenue consequences of sweeping changes in the U.S. income tax are shown in Table 13-3. The data in Table 13-3 are extremely rough and take no account of the adjustments that U.S. or foreign taxpayers would make in response to significant changes in U.S. taxation of international income. The tax revenue figures simply represent 20 percent of the associated income levels. Nevertheless, Table 13-3, together with the Table 13-2, which summarizes present U.S. law and its alternatives, suggests some important conclusions:

- The United States presently exempts from taxation significant amounts of U.S.-source income of foreign residents. Interest income, which is exempt by virtue of the present tax provisions applicable to bank deposits, original issue discounts, and foreign governments and international organizations, apparently amounted to more than $40 billion in 1981. Taxing such income might, however, result in offsetting reductions in U.S. interest income and a much smaller gain in U.S. tax receipts than a static revenue analysis would imply. Also, the economic analysis above would suggest that—given the high elasticity in the foreign supply of, and foreign demand for, debt capital—even a modest tax could sharply curtail capital flows to and from the United States; and

- U.S. payments for the import of goods and for services other than those specifically enumerated in Table 13-3 exceed U.S. receipts

Table 13-3. Estimates of Foreign Income of U.S. Residents, U.S. Income of Foreign Residents, and Income of U.S. Citizens Who Are Foreign Residents, by Type of Income, 1981.[a]

	Estimated Income	20 Percent Tax Revenue
	(billions of dollars)	
Income of U.S. Residents		
Income of foreign branch	9.3[c]	1.9[c]
Retained earnings of foreign subsidiary		
Subpart F income	2.5[c]	0.5[c]
Other income	10.5[b]	2.1[b]
Dividends from foreign subsidiary	9.5[c]	1.9[c]
Portfolio dividends from foreign corporation	0.5[b]	0.1[b]
Foreign-source interest, rents, royalties, etc., and foreign-source capital gain	65.0[b]	13.0[b]
Foreign-source earned income	2.4[b]	0.5[b]
Qualifying income of a possessions corporation	3.0	0.6
Tax-deferred income of a DISC	2.5	0.5
Gross export receipts in excess of above item	270.8	54.2
Income of Foreign Residents		
Income of U.S. branch	0.8	0.2
Income of foreign-controlled U.S. subsidiary	5.9	1.2
Dividends from U.S. corporation	3.8	0.8
U.S.-source interest		
Bank deposits, savings accounts, etc.	13.0	2.6
Original issue discount	8.7	1.8
Other Interest	2.0	0.4
U.S.-source rents, royalties, etc. and U.S.-source capital gains	5.3	1.1
U.S.-source earned income	0.5	0.1
Income of foreign governments and international organizations		
Noncommercial	20.5	4.1
Commercial	.0	.0
Receipts from exports to the United States	303.0	60.6
Income of Foreign Resident U.S. Citizens	5.0[b]	1.0[b]

[a] Estimated income amounts are net of foreign taxes and are derived primarily from U.S. balance of payments statistics published by the U.S. Bureau of Economic Analysis, from various U.S. Treasury Department reports, and from unpublished sources. The 20 percent tax revenue column is simply an arithmetic derivation from the estimated income column. Depending on the jurisdiction principle chosen, some of the revenue amounts would not be collected and some would be refunds.

[b] Income believed to be subject to foreign income tax, which if creditable would offset U.S. tax of 20 percent.

[c] Income believed to be subject to foreign income tax, which if creditable would offset U.S. tax of 40 to 50 percent.

for comparable exports by over $30 billion. Thus, border tax adjustments in income taxes, similar to those presently allowed for sales and value added taxes, could result in a substantial revenue gain for the U.S. Treasury.

IV. INTERNATIONAL RAMIFICATIONS OF DIFFERENT TAX JURISDICTION PRINCIPLES

The present system reflects more than fifty years of intricate accommodations in international trade and tax rules. Any basic change in tax jurisdiction principles would necessarily disturb some of these rules.

A. Taxation Based Solely on Residence

An approach based on residence jurisdiction would have the most jarring effect on the present system of international tax rules. As the 1976 Treasury study noted, the U.S. foreign tax credit, which is the cornerstone of present statutory law and guaranteed in all tax treaties, would be scrapped. The income of U.S.-controlled foreign subsidiaries would be taxed currently (deferral would be ended). Taking these steps unilaterally, would, however, cause our foreign commercial relations to suffer. If the residence principle were adopted multilaterally, international double taxation would be avoided by source-country exemption. But it requires a suspension of disbelief to imagine that the United States could sell this approach in Canada, Western Europe, or Japan.

B. Location of Production

Taxation limited to income from U.S. production would cause the least trauma to the existing network of international taxation. For the most part, the change would merely require the United States to surrender tax jurisdiction over the foreign income of its own residents, which would only require a change in U.S. statutory law. However, the United States would also impose a tax on some types of income earned by foreigners that are now exempt by treaty (for example, interest or capital gains). This option would require a renegotiation of some treaties.

C. Location of Consumption

The location of consumption approach, if made in the form of an income tax, rather than a value added tax, would violate present GATT rules. Under those rules, direct taxes cannot be rebated on exports, nor can a tax, in lieu of direct taxation, be imposed on imports. The United States considered making a major attack on these rules in the Tokyo Round, but withdrew from the charge in the face of President Carter's disenchantment with the DISC and the strength of foreign opposition. The United States could, however, take up the battle again. If the GATT rules were changed, it is reasonable to suppose that other countries would also exempt their exports from direct taxation (including social security taxes) and impose such taxes on their imports. Alternatively, the U.S. tax could be structured as a flat rate, value added or sales tax.

NOTES TO CHAPTER 13

1. The views expressed in this paper are those of the authors and not those of the organizations with which they are affiliated.

2. Robert E. Hall and Alvin Rabushka, "A Simple Income Tax with Low Marginal Rates," (Stanford University: Hoover Institution, July 1982).

3. Robert E. Hall and Alvin Rabushka, *Low Tax, Simple Tax, Flat Tax*, (New York: McGraw-Hill Book Company, 1982).

4. George N. Carlson, *Value Added Tax: European Experience and Lessons for the United States*, (Washington, D.C.: Office of Tax Analysis, U.S. Treasury Department, October 1980).

5. See G.N. Carlson, G.C. Hufbauer, and M.B. Krauss, "Destination Principle Border Tax Adjustments for the Corporate Income and Social Security Taxes: An Analysis of Sectorial Effects" (National Tax Association—Tax Institute of America, Proceedings of the 69th Annual Conference, 1976).

6. Significantly, the substantial increase in the exclusion for foreign earned income voted by the U.S. Congress in 1981 appears to have been motivated more by a desire to keep U.S. production competitive in foreign export markets than by any doubt that citizenship *per se* provides an appropriate basis for taxation.

Discussants:

THE OUTLOOK FOR INTERNATIONAL TRADE

William E. Brock

The fundamental purpose of trade is to create jobs and improve our standard of living. The purpose of trade policy, then, should be to take steps that will lead to improvement of our national well-being. The alternatives to increased international trade are simply unacceptable, and yet many people, here and elsewhere around the world, talk about enacting policies that would lead to a substantial reduction in the scope of international business.

For quite a while, we traded very little with the rest of the world. The world's largest common market and largest free trade zone was established in our Constitution within the continental United States, as a fundamental law of the land. For the better part of this century it has been easier for us to sell in Dubuque or Des Moines than it has been to sell in Madrid or Osaka. Even so, we have not done badly. World trade has exploded because the United States took the lead in structuring an international trading system by which nations can do business with one another. The system has stimulated world growth in the trade in goods area; that system did not apply in agriculture, and it applied very little in services. The people of the United States have profited greatly from that process. World trade now totals $2 trillion annually. The United States enjoys five million jobs resulting directly from exports and several million others that are created indirectly. Most importantly, we can look forward to the prospect of doing a lot more trading in the future.

It is indeed strange that this country accounts for only about 10 percent of the world's trade. Despite a few areas where we seem to have dropped out of international competition because of governmental, business, management, or labor problems, we are, by any measure, the most competitive, productive people in the history of mankind. Our so-called principal competitors at the moment, the Japanese, did their own analysis of the relative competitiveness of our two countries. They studied the productivity of Japan and the United States across the whole span of economic activity. Using themselves as the base point, they came to the conclusion that we were 57 percent more productive than they. If we are all that good, why are we not doing more business in Japan?

First, if we are not going to protect ourselves into stagflation, then we are going to have to compete internationally. If we are going to compete, particularly in manufacturing, we must improve our productivity growth even more. If we are going to increase our productivity growth, we must do a better job on the creative side with research, development, and the application of new technology. In order to improve in these areas, we must have a change in tax policy. We must have more incentives for the formation of capital. If we are to maintain this country's competitive posture in manufacturing, which I believe is essential, then we need high levels of capital formation. We must increase the physical plant and equipment with which an individual can create something of value.

Second, we need to look at our skill base. We need to ask ourselves whether we have adequately trained the labor force. I am not talking about only grammar school and high school. Education is a life long process. It is a fact that 90 percent of the workforce for 1990 is in the entire workforce today. We have gone through the baby boom. The new workers in the labor force are acquiring skills, and they are going to be more productive in the 1990s. This offers us an enormous competitive advantage; the countries that are now experiencing population explosions will have more difficulty in competing later. Our workers will be competitive if the job skills that they have acquired today are related to the jobs that they will hold tomorrow. I believe we need to evaluate the training we are providing for a flexible labor force that can adapt as the economy changes.

Despite this good news, serious questions remain to be answered. Are we really forming enough capital? Are we facing the question of deficits? Are we creating the correct tax mix between consumption taxes, payroll taxes, earnings taxes, and corporate taxes? We must evaluate the accelerated cost recovery system and the incentives provided by the research and development tax credit. We must question whether we have enough incentives to provide for individual and collective savings that generate the funds necessary to provide the resources with which we can compete.

We have the opportunity to use the trade debate, including the questions of protectionism and competitiveness, as a framework for evaluating our economy and our economic policies. We need to consider whether we can do better. I think the Economic Recovery Tax

Act of 1981 was a good beginning. The shift in our depreciation schedules and the research and development credits were efforts to address part of the trade problem.

In the final analysis, we are not just talking about tax structures or capital formation; we are talking about what kind of country America will be ten years hence, or, more importantly, what kind of country America will be for our children to inherit. If we can take the opportunity that the trade debate affords us to rethink our mix of economic policies, then I think we can have a future that is brighter than anything we have seen in the last 200 years. There is no limit to our ability to compete. There is no system ever devised by man more efficient in motivating people, challenging people, and achieving results than what we call the free enterprise system, or the competitive marketplace. Nothing comes close to it. Really, the test is up to us.

TAX POLICY AND INTERNATIONAL CAPITAL FLOWS

C.E. Hussey II and Stuart M. Berkson

I. Introduction

The arguments for and against the alternative jurisdictional bases (residence, location of production, and location of consumption) for taxing income have been clearly presented in "International Aspects of Basic Income Tax Reform" by Gary Hufbauer and Thomas Horst in this volume. They conclude that a "location of consumption" jurisdictional basis for the imposition of a tax, whether it be an income tax or a value added tax, is the best of the three alternatives. Under the location of consumption jurisdiction for taxation, the interest income received by foreigners from U.S. firms would be subject to tax, including the withholding tax provision is our current tax system.

We would like to propose an exception to the tax treatment of interest paid to foreigners that the location of consumption tax systems would mandate and that, in fact, our current tax Code requires. In an era of huge federal deficits, significant reductions in social programs, and an almost desperate search for increased federal tax revenue, it is becoming increasingly important that all avenues for international finance be open to domestic and international business in order to promote economic growth. Our objection to the uniform application of the location of consumption tax principle is based on the fear that it would seriously interfere with U.S. firms' access to international capital markets. The discussion which follows focuses on U.S. firms' use of Netherlands Antilles finance companies for Eurobond financing.

The initial inquiry will concern how Netherlands Antilles finance companies came into existence and why they have evolved into a multibillion dollar industry. Current challenges to the system will then be considered, along with the ramification of an untimely demise of Netherlands Antilles finance subsidiaries. Finally, current proposals will be examined with an interim solution suggested, which would accommodate both federal tax policy and the financial needs of U.S. corporations.

II. The Impetus for Netherlands Antilles Finance Companies

The impetus for use of Netherlands Antilles finance companies can be summarized in a short phrase: U.S. companies have required and continue to require large amounts of dollar borrowings at the lowest possible cost. Prior to the 1960s, American businesses were generally able to find sufficient dollars locally to satisfy all of their financing demands. As the 1960s progressed, however, U.S. borrowing needs continued to expand, and the U.S. balance of payments position began to slide into the red. American companies, thus, began to look abroad for funds.

Although U.S. companies have always had the ability to issue debt instruments in the U.S. market to foreign purchasers, this alternative was not particularly attractive for two reasons. First, any sales in the U.S. marketplace would have been subject to all the same federal securities law requirements as an issue sold to domestic purchasers. Although extending the protection of our securities laws to foreigners may be laudable, this protection carries with it cumbersome and time-consuming procedures which decrease the attractiveness of the issues to borrowers.

The more crucial barrier to large-scale sales of U.S. debt instruments to foreigners was the U.S. withholding tax on interest payments mandated by the Internal Revenue Code. The presence of a withholding tax meant that a foreign bondholder would either earn a lower yield or demand a higher interest rate to compensate for the tax. Although many investors might have been covered by a U.S. tax treaty with their country of residence, administrative considerations decreased the utility of these treaties. For treaty provisions to apply, each bondholder would have been required annually to provide the withholding agent (the issuer) with sufficient information to determine that a reduced treaty rate applied. The cost to the issuer of administering such a system would have been prohibitive.

III. The Workings of Netherlands Antilles Finance Companies

Netherlands Antilles finance companies, commonly known as N.V.s,[1] came into widespread use for a single reason: Pursuant to a 1948 protocol, the Netherlands-U.S. income tax treaty was extended to cover the Netherlands Antilles. The Netherlands Antilles is not a country which would be expected to become a major finance center. It is not a particularly convenient location, its language (Dutch) can lead to some impediments, and its communication facilities are not extraordinary. What it does offer, via Article VIII of the treaty, is a means of channeling interest payments made by U.S. borrowers to a foreign lender at a zero withholding rate, irrespective of the lender's country of residence. A modifying protocol to the treaty effective September 28, 1964, generally limited the benefits of Article VIII to Antilles companies subject to Netherlands Antilles profit tax at normal rates; interest remittance to Antilles companies taxed at the preferential holding or investment company rates were subject to full U.S. withholding tax. Thus, a *quid pro quo* to the use of a finance N.V. to avoid U.S. withholding tax is the payment of Antilles tax at normal rates of between 30 to 34 percent. Interest paid by an N.V. was, in turn, exempt from U.S. tax under Article XII of Netherlands Antilles treaty, thereby permitting a complete absence of U.S. withholding tax on payments from the ultimate U.S. borrower and the ultimate European lender.

Although at first glance the Netherlands Antilles tax burden appears equal to or in excess of the U.S. withholding tax, it is actually much less. The base for computation of the U.S. withholding tax is the gross amount of the interest payment; Netherlands Antilles profit tax, however, is imposed on net income earned by the Antilles company. In computing net income, the N.V. is entitled to deduct interest payments made to outside lenders, which generally reduce the total effective tax rate on the interest payments to approximately 7 percent. Moreover, whatever income tax the N.V. is required to pay to the Antilles will be creditable against U.S. income tax, assuming the U.S. parent corporation has sufficient foreign source income and a tax liability against which the credit can be taken. Thus, the transaction can be completed by the U.S. company without the payment of additional income tax. Moreover, foreign purchasers of the bonds remain completely free of withholding tax, a position required for marketability.[2]

Given these beneficial aspects of using an Antilles company along with the ease of creating and administering an N.V., it is easy to see why this mechanism has become so popular. For example, during

1981, U.S. companies raised $6.2 billion through dollar denominated Eurobonds, representing 11 percent of the dollar denominated bonds issued by these companies. Total Eurobond obligations of U.S. companies have been estimated at between $30 to $50 billion.[3]

It is easy to understand why the Treasury is not entirely pleased with the status quo. First, the U.S. government effectively provides the Antilles government with a subsidy estimated at $50 million per year, in the form of income taxes paid to the Antilles by finance N.V.s and claimed as a foreign tax credit by their U.S. parents. Second, the Antilles tax agreement permits the type of treaty shopping that the United States is anxiously trying to stop. As drafted, the Antilles treaty benefits apply to any Antilles company, even if it is simply a shell, wholly owned by non-Antilles shareholders. In essence, therefore, the Antilles treaty is a treaty between the United States and investors from any nation that wish to establish an N.V., even if those investors are residents of nations with less favorable tax treaties in effect with the United States. Finally, the Internal Revenue Service suspects that many U.S. citizens and residents are utilizing the shield of anonymity provided by N.V.s to hide otherwise taxable income.

IV. Challenges to Treaty Benefits

To minimize the perceived abuses of the treaty, the United States has begun challenges in two areas. First, the United States commenced discussions with the government of the Netherlands Antilles aimed at renegotiating the provisions of the agreement that permit treaty shopping. In particular, the United States would like to impose Article 16 of the Treasury's Model Income Tax Treaty, which essentially would limit treaty benefits to corporations that are owned by local residents. This measure would effectively eliminate the flow of Eurobonds through the Netherlands Antilles, since the islands' 245,000 residents would not be able to absorb even a fraction of 1 percent of the issues floated annually. The Treasury's serious intent in pursuing this change is evidenced by the United States' recent unilateral termination of the British Virgin Islands Treaty after that nation refused to include an anti-treaty shopping provision.

A second challenge to the U.S. firms' continued access to financing through the Netherlands Antilles has been advanced by the Internal Revenue Service Houston office, which in an audit of Texas International Airlines' 1979 tax return, attempted to impose a 30 percent withholding tax on interest payments made by TIA to its Netherlands Antilles finance subsidiary in conjunction with issues sold during 1978 and 1979. The amount of the proposed deficiency is approximately $1.2 million. The basis for the Service's position appears to be that the N.V. was a sham entity, the existence of which should be ignored. As a result, the U.S. parent/guarantor is characterized as the bond issuer and payor of interest to the bondholders. In the absence of the N.V. intermediary between the U.S. parent and the bondholders, all interest payments made by TIA became subject to U.S. withholding tax. Of particular concern to U.S. issuers are the statements of Texas International officials that indicate that the N.V. in question was structured and managed no differently from hundreds of other finance N.V.s.

V. The Impact of Terminating Treaty Protection

Although a unilateral termination of the treaty by the United States or a widespread attack on finance N.V.s would end the abuses associated with the treaty, both actions would have a much more far reaching impact. First, there would be a tremendous reduction in the future access of U.S. borrowers to foreign capital markets.

A second and even more significant consequence would face issuers of existing securities. Most bonds issued by finance N.V.s have been issued with the stipulation that the interest rate specified and owed the holder is net of any withholding or other tax. Thus, to the extent that the issuer wished to keep the issue outstanding, it would be required to absorb the full 30 percent withholding tax. Alternatively, the issuer could exercise the right contained in most issues permitting it to call the bonds (usually at no penalty) if a withholding tax were imposed on the payments of interest by the N.V. or by the U.S. borrower to the N.V.

Although an early call would eliminate any future withholding obligations, reliance on this as a safety valve would be ill advised because of the many grave consequences that would accompany it. Billions of dollars of Eurobonds would immediately have to be refinanced through domestic markets. Even if there were sufficient domestic capital to absorb new issues of this magnitude, the sheer volume of new issues would drive up interest rates and borrowing costs. Since it is unlikely that a refinancing of this scale could be completed without foreign capital, interest rates would be pushed even higher as foreign investors would demand a greater return to compensate for withholding taxes. For many borrowers, current market rates would be significantly above the costs of their older issues, which were marketed when rates were dramatically lower. Some issuers might be completely excluded from the market, because their financial condition would not support the same level of debt as at the time of original issue of the Eurobonds. Such an exclusion would create difficult problems for other creditors, since a company's inability to refinance could trigger a default. Since most loan and debt arrangements contain extensive cross default provisions, a call on Eurobonds could theoretically bring down the company.

Neither of these challenges would provide a satisfactory solution to the problems associated with use of Netherlands Antilles finance companies. Any satisfactory alternative should have two characteristics. Initially, it should cause a minimum disruption to the U.S. financial system. It should leave open the access of foreign capital to U.S. borrowers. It should also confront and address the abuses of the treaty arrangement. Both of the following proposals possess these characteristics.

VI. Proposals

A. **Elimination of 30 Percent Withholding Tax.** One alternative would be elimination of the 30 percent withholding tax on interest payments under Section 871 and 881. Representatives Barber Conable and Sam Gibbons introduced such a proposal on September 29, 1981, in H.R. 4618. This bill would have eliminated withholding tax on certain payments to nonresident aliens by U.S. companies. The Treasury Department supported the measure for the following reasons. First, it recognized that by utilizing cumbersome structures, a U.S. borrower could usually tap foreign capital on a tax-free basis. Thus, rather than terminating a tax, elimination of withholding would simply "reduce the cost of borrowing from foreigners, including the costs associated with the use of a foreign finance affiliate."[4] Moreover, elimination of withholding would result in a net revenue gain for the United States. This *gain* would occur because the reduction in foreign tax credits claimed by U.S. companies for taxes paid by N.V.s to the Antilles would more than offset the $20 million of lost withholding revenue.

In theory, elimination of the 30 percent withholding tax is the preferable alternative. The measure would eliminate the incentive to treaty shop, enhance U.S. tax revenues, and reduce current inefficiencies. In practice, however, there is little chance that such elimination of the withholding tax will ever be implemented. Beginning July 1, 1983, interest payable to U.S. persons is subject to a withholding tax of 10 percent. Many are strongly opposed to this tax, and a number of bills are expected in the Ninety-eighth Congress to repeal the tax. Given the recent passage of a domestic withholding tax in the Tax Equity and Fiscal Responsibility Act of 1982, it would be politically difficult for Congress to support the abolition of a longstanding withholding tax on remittances to foreigners that are not otherwise subject to U.S. tax.

B. Modification of Treasury Model and the Antilles Treaty. Given the small chance that the withholding tax can be eliminated, the next best solution would be to retain some of the benefits of the Antilles treaty while reducing the potential for abuse. This could be accomplished by inserting Article 16 of the Treasury model into the Antilles treaty and adding an exception that retains treaty benefits for certain issuers of debt securities. The exception would cover issuers that currently have outstanding, or have had outstanding within the prior two-year period, debt of at least $15 million U.S. dollars.[5] This change would be beneficial because it would be a clear indication from the U.S. government that Eurobond financing can continue. Furthermore, the $15 million minimum debt level would lead to a reduction in the abusive use of the treaty. Although the $15 million figure is arbitrary, it represents an approximate minimum principal amount that a U.S. company could sell efficiently on the Eurobond market. Investments below that amount are generally made by small groups of individuals that either may be covered by a tax treaty or represent the type of treaty-shopping the Treasury would like to prevent.

To some extent, this proposal favors the giant corporate borrower over small U.S. entities that borrow funds from a limited group of foreign investors. Some of these investors may be able to qualify under other treaties, for example, in the interest swap transactions under the U.S.-German tax treaty. Moreover, small U.S. borrowers tend to be able to borrow domestically at a comparable total cost, after all of the expenses of administering an N.V. are considered. Finally, the arbitrariness of the $15 million figure represents a policy decision based on a balancing of the three alternatives: leaving the status quo untouched so that abuses continue unchecked; minimizing abuses through the proposal; or totally eliminating these abuses by terminating the treaty but in the process cutting off U.S. access to foreign capital. The second alternative is the most rational, since it allows the majority of current American borrowing to continue at a greatly reduced rate of abuse.

The best solution—elimination of U.S. withholding on interest paid to foreigners—is unfortunately the least realistic solution, politically. Rather than leaving this loophole completely open, we suggest a second-best proposal, one that would be more easily implemented.

In an area as crucial as the access of U.S. companies to international capital, second-best is better than no solution at all. Second-best is also superior to the present uncertainty.

NOTES

1. N.V. is an abbreviation for "naamloze vennootschap," or "nameless company." An N.V. is a Dutch equivalent to an incorporated entity in the U.S. N.V.s have been utilized by many for direct investment into the U.S. as opposed to simply acting as issuers of Eurobonds.

2. The Netherlands Antilles (as well as the United States) imposes no withholding or income tax on remittance of interest payments to nonresidents by an N.V.

3. *Daily Report for Executives* no. 169 (BNA) G-6 (Sept. 1, 1982).

4. Letter from John E. Chapoton, Treasury Assistant Secretary for Tax Policy, to Representative Sam Gibbons (May 21, 1982), reprinted in *Tax Notes*, June 7, 1982, p. 859.

5. Reference to prior years is necessary because in the final years of some large serial bond issues the principal amount of debt in any single year could dip below $15 million.

POLITICAL AND ECONOMIC COMPLEXITY IN INTERNATIONAL TAX ISSUES

Daniel Patrick Moynihan

Thomas Horst and Gary Hufbauer's paper illuminates, in part directly and in part obliquely, two basic difficulties we in Congress face in making tax policy. First, the United States can no longer approach questions of tax policy—or for that matter, any other dimension of economic policy—as if ours were effectively a closed economy. We cannot do so, at least, if we hope to achieve predicted results. For some two decades following the Second World War, America's preeminent position in the world economy, and the economic arrangements established immediately following the war, enabled our policymakers to attend essentially only to domestic factors. In 1952, our gross national product accounted for more than 60 percent of all the goods and services produced by all the developed nations of the world. In this context, and especially given the arrangements of the Bretton Woods agreement, other nations found themselves in a fundamentally reactive position to the movements of our domestic economy and the decisions of our economic policymakers. Today,

I need hardly add, we account for barely 40 percent of world GNP, and Bretton Woods is a receding memory.

In those simpler times—times simpler at least for American policymakers—we could construct tax policy with little regard to any adverse impact on world capital flows. The United States was the preeminent source and market for capital. To say it bluntly, little else mattered, at least with regard to the ability of any other nation to affect adversely our own economic life to any significant degree. This paper tells us, as do the daily newspapers in less elegant terms, that those days are now past. We are part of a world economy in which the independent responses of foreign markets affect our economic life to nearly the same degree as we affect them. At the very least, enough to matter.

This makes the process of writing intelligent tax law a much more complicated and problematic affair. We must now take into account effects distant in place, medium, language, and time, from our own acts, and effects the precise nature of which are less well-known. We can no longer rely on models based on a few, or a few dozen, variables. As we can no longer assume that economic policy decisions made in Washington are the only ones that count for us, we must also accept the fact that by our decisions we can no longer set the parameters for those made elsewhere. Such are the general facts of the world economy of which U.S. tax policy must take into account.

One common response to the increasing complexity of economic life is to overlay complicated issues with simple formulae. This is perhaps a natural response. We all need some basis, whatever it may be, for deciding how to proceed, for if we cannot comprehend, then we cannot act in any deliberate way. As the policy world grows more complicated, we may be compelled to simplify in our drive to secure a grasp on it. We have seen too much of this of late. Moreover, the impulse to simplify as a prelude to action is reinforced by those among us who, regardless of the complexities apparent to most of us, really do view the world in simple terms.

This turn of mind has long been an intellectual predilection of the political extremes. Those so disposed come to know the world in vivid black-and-white terms and therefore insist that the complex patterns of the nation's or world's economic life be made to conform to their ideological prescriptions. Their policies, then, correspond in an unmediated fashion to one or the other side of their inevitable dichotomies.

Thus, we in Congress found ourselves considering policies based on the view and the deep conviction that our economy is essentially a homogenous entity. There are few distinctions and only a few simple complications that matter. In such a simple world, some insisted, one sweeping policy prescription could alter every part in a predictable way.

What utter nonsense. And what enormous costs it entailed for the economy. We are suffering today through just such a sequence of consequences. The nation was told that reducing all tax rates by the same percentage, again and again, for three years, would represent optimal personal tax reform. No matter that informed observers viewed the economy as a seriously complex organism. Such a view, it was insisted, was merely the rationale for failed policies of the past. This time one rule would suffice: 10 percent cuts in tax rates, again and again and again, and a drastic revision of depreciation schedules. That done, the economy would once more be right. And in an economy with simple factors and simple actors, this policy would carry no fiscal costs. The reductions, you see, would provide just the incentives required to increase production, so these precise lower rates would increase tax revenues, whatever the context.

The issue here is not merely whether tax rates should have been reduced in 1981. They should have been. More to the point, greater incentives for investment were certainly needed. The issue is the implicit view of the economic world and the corresponding attitudes toward tax policymaking. The issue is whether the simple approach of reducing all tax rates by the same percentage, done thrice, made any economic sense and whether a theory that generated such a course could reliably predict the consequences.

In this context, I take some special note of Thomas Horst and Gary Hufbauer's view of the implications for international income of a pure flat tax scheme. A pure flat tax would eliminate all the credits, exemptions, and deductions from the tax Code; it would eliminate all the provisions devised, ably or not, to take account of the complexities of everyday economic life. As tax rates should have been reduced in 1981, so some tax expenditures should be eliminated or reformed. However, these changes should be made on a case-by-case basis, in light of the fact that these provisions recognize that economic problems facing different sectors are distinct and deeply complicated, requiring the most careful responses in the tax law.

One such provision that would fall before the simple dictate of a pure flat tax is Section 936 of the Internal Revenue Code, tax treatment for corporations in U.S. possessions. This provision encourages American corporations to establish factories in Puerto Rico by exempting profits earned there from the corporate income tax. Section 936 has been part of the tax Code since 1921, and there is little argument that it has been fundamental to the economic development of the commonwealth of Puerto Rico. I have seen responsible estimates that fully half of all manufacturing jobs in Puerto Rico can be traced to the Section 936 exemption. Corporations using this tax credit generate about 35 percent of the island's entire gross national product (GNP). However, last July the Senate Finance Committee moved to abolish this provision. I recall the circumstances in which the Senate Finance Committee voted repeal of Section 936. Chairman Robert Dole, having reached agreement with the majority members of the Committee, presented the proposal to the full Committee at 9:24 A.M. on the morning of June 30, 1982; the full measure was adopted 16.5 hours later, at 1:53 A.M. the following morning.

No hearings had been held to investigate the complex consequences of such a move. There had been no consultations with the minority. When, in the course of our long session, we came to the Section 936 provision, I protested against its repeal with such force as I could. We could not alter this provision, I argued, without the most serious inquiry into its economic consequences and without close consultation with the government of Puerto Rico. I asked that the repeal provision be stricken, but my motion lost on a voice vote. In the end, the Commiteee approved the bill. Where most actions by the Finance Committee are unanimous or nearly so, or at any event are adopted by a bipartisan majority, in this case the vote was nine to eleven, with all minority members opposed. I think it is fair to say we were as much opposed to the procedures that had been followed as to the substance; we were as much opposed to the attitude that tax law can be rewritten with attention to little else but the immediate effect on the deficit, as to the particular means selected to reduce that deficit. It comes to much the same thing. Had the Finance Committee followed its usual procedures, I cannot imagine that we would have dealt so casually with a matter of such utter consequence to the economy and people of Puerto Rico. The procedures are designed precisely to weigh the complex results of proposed changes in tax law, as against single note prescriptions.

I believe this because in the end Congress did realize it was on the verge of doing immense harm to the economy of Puerto Rico, with very small potential return to the Treasury. When the Finance Committee bill came to the floor of the Senate, I raised the question of Section 936 once again. This time, I found Senator Dole, the distinguished chairman of the Committee, much more responsive. He declined to drop the provision (a tactical decision based on the judgment that if he dropped one provision, the majority coalition supporting the entire bill would begin to unravel, and the whole bill could be lost). He did say, however, "Mr. President, I have assured the Senator from New York . . . that we are going to do the best we can for Puerto Rico in conference." In the meantime, a delegation from the government of Puerto Rico had successfully concluded protracted negotiations with the Treasury Department to revise Section 936, in ways which would protect the economy of Puerto Rico. The conference committee was offered and accepted this agreement, one based on the view that changing the tax law is a complicated affair with complex consequences that go far beyond any one note concern, including even the deficit. We do our nation little good if we reduce the deficit at the cost of undermining the basis in the tax Code for long-term investment and growth.

Our government can do both: reduce the deficit and pursue tax policies to encourage economic investment and growth. Indeed, the most powerful instrument available for reducing the budget deficit is greater economic growth, which government can help generate through the reasoned coordination of tax, spending, and monetary policies. This task is surely a profoundly complicated and complex one, which will continue to require the intelligence and dedication of all those involved in and out of government.

PRIORITIES FOR THE REFORM OF INTERNATIONAL TAX POLICY

John G. Wilkins

The paper prepared by Thomas Horst and Gary Hufbauer is a most interesting and provocative economic study but one that, from my perspective, lacks a few critical links required to relate the conclusions to the theoretical framework.

Although the Treasury Department has argued that a uniform tax structure is the correct model for tax reform, Horst and Hufbauer's inverse association of tax rates to the elasticities of price with respect to supply and demand would achieve a more economically efficient tax structure, that is, one that would distort to a lesser degree the free market allocation of resources that would take place in a tax-free world. A good example of such a nondistorting tax would be one on insulin. For those that demand it, the price elasticity is presumably close to zero over a wide range of prices, so that a hefty tax on insulin would not affect the allocation of resources going into the production of insulin and other nontaxed goods. Another less provocative example would be a salt tax. Still another example would be a simple head tax. As the authors concede, adherence to the inverse elasticity principal leads to a complicated set of tax rates that could be set only by econometric studies, which we all know tend to yield as many answers to a given question as there are economists attempting to provide the answer. So, while theory suggests the most efficient tax is one based on the inverse elasticity principal, there are other objectives of tax reform, such as simplicity and equity. For example, is it fair to tax diabetics more highly than, say, cigarette smokers? When all these objectives are given reasonable weight, a uniform tax looks pretty good.

Nevertheless, the authors suggest that the inverse elasticity principal may be the appropriate criterion for determining taxes on "international income." They define international income as income from exports as well as income from imports. Later they state that "an economic case can be made for taxing 'international' income at lower rates (or exempting it altogether) than the rates applicable to 'domestic' income." This is because the data "suggest" that both the foreign supply of imports into the United States and the foreign demand for U.S. export goods and services have become more elastic. The conclusion apparently reached is that of three possible tax approaches—taxation on the basis of (1) residence, (2) location of production, or (3) location of consumption (defined as source basis taxation with an exemption for export income)—the authors prefer option (3). Taxing on the basis of where goods and services are consumed is preferred, in part, because it would raise revenue. (We have net imports, and the tax would apply to imports and not to exports.)

Given this summary, let me raise some critical questions that, in my view, are not adequately answered in the course of the Horst-Hufbauer paper. First, I concede that a consumption based model tax would, in its pure form, lead to the same conclusion reached in this paper. Imports generally would be taxed. Exports generally would not.

Where, however, is the evidence that elasticities on international income are high? The authors state that the trends "suggest" they are higher than they used to be, but how relevant is this fact? Does not preferential tax treatment require that the elasticities that apply to "international income" be higher somehow than those that apply to domestic income?

Also, since international income is defined as encompassing both imports and exports, what leads us to the conclusion that only imports should get a tax break? One can begin with the assumption that a uniform consumption tax is the correct answer and, therefore, exports will be exempt; however, the inverse of this argument does not hold. If one begins with the assumption that "international income" deserves a tax break one does not necessarily reach the conclusion that a consumption tax is the correct answer.

Last, as part of the support for tax treatment based on location of consumption, the authors draw upon the revenue argument. We should not give much weight to this point, since revenue considerations ought not be the criterion for establishing structural provisions under basic tax reform. Once the revamped structure is in place, tax rates would be calibrated to raise current revenues with the expectation that economic efficiencies gained in the restructuring would give rise to still higher future revenues. Moreover, the authors conclude that any revenue gains from border tax adjustments would be transitory, because exchange rates would adjust to eliminate those gains.

In summary, I found Thomas Horst and Gary Hufbauer's analysis and statements provocative. Further, I suspect the authors have arrived at reasonable conclusions. I do not, however, think the authors have established a sufficiently solid analytical basis for reaching those conclusions. Consequently, the Treasury Department will be very interested in any further work on these issues by the authors.

Index

Ability to pay principle, 188-190, 266-267, 273, 274. *See also* Equity principle
"Ability-to-pay" income/consumption concept, 250-251
Accelerated Cost Recovery System (ACRS), 47-91
  compared to expensing, 62-63, 64-69, 78
  and foreign-source income, 328, 330
  and neutrality, 89, 90-91, 103-104, 178-179
  and TEFRA, 48, 49, 64, 65, 69-70, 78, 103-104
Accounting methods for consumption tax, 238, 240, 242-243
Accounting rules and the tax base, 246-251
Accounting standards and depreciation, 48, 49-51
Accrual income tax, 241
Accumulated wealth and the consumption tax, 259-260
Accumulation, taxation of, 282-285
Accretion concept of income, 246, 268, 278-282
Administration
  and capital recovery allowances, 63
  of consumption tax, 274, 283-284
  and economic depreciation, 58-59
  and the individual tax system, 231
  and particularization, 61

  of the value added tax, 189, 193-194, 195, 221, 223
  See also Measurement; Simplicity
Advisory Commission on Intergovernmental Relations surveys, 190-191, 218, 267
American Council for Capital Formation: Center for Policy Research, 3, 13, 21, 23, 35, 158
Archer amendment, 156
Armstrong amendment, 156
Asset depreciation range, 62, 63, 69, 85
Asset revaluations, 260
Auten, Gerald, 149, 150, 155, 157
Averaging
  of capital gains, 131, 139, 146n18
  and consumption tax, 240-241

Balance of payments
  and interest rates, 39
  and value added tax, 186-187, 197-198, 214-215
  See also Export volume
Ballhaus, William, 150
Banks, taxation of, 302
Benefit principle, 188-190, 206n17
Bequests
  under a consumption tax, 108, 113, 232-233, 245nc, 250-251
  and income tax base, 268, 269, 279

361

362 Index

Bipartisanship, 10, 262
Blueprints for Basic Tax Reform, 107, 108, 333
Boren, David, 261
Boskin, Michael, 112-120 *passim*
Border tax adjustments
  and flat rate tax, 336-338, 340-342
  and value added tax, 187, 197, 203, 205n15, 327
Bracket creep, 15, 268, 288, 298-299
Bradford, David, 253-264 *passim*
Bradley, Bill, 156, 286, 313
Brennan, Geoffrey
  The Power to Tax, 315
Bretton Woods agreement, 353-354
British Virgin Islands Treaty, 349
Buchanan, James
  The Power to Tax, 315
Budget, balanced, 316
Budget deficits, 4, 6-7, 103, 181
  and capital formation, 23, 33-34, 98-99, 117-118
  and economic growth, 35-43
  and flat rate tax, 306-308, 316
  and savings, 273
  and value added tax, 188
Business assets, personal use of, 303
Business expenses, allocation of necessary, 313
Business tax, 299-303, 304-305, 321-322

Canada, 156, 331-332
Capital allocation, efficiency of, 60, 77-78, 94. *See also* Economic efficiency
Capital formation, 15-19, 25-26, 28-29
  and budget deficits, 23, 33-34, 98-99, 117-118
  and capital recovery provisions, 48, 59-61
  and economic growth, 23, 109
  and employment, 150-153
  and international competitiveness, 345
  and technological progress, 117
Capital gains
  bunching of, 131-134, 139
  and consumption tax, 30, 140, 313
  and flat rate tax. *See* Flat rate tax
  of foreign individuals, 328
  nominal and real, 130-131
  preferential treatment of, 121, 139, 271-272
  unrealized, and income tax base, 269, 280-282
  See also Long-term capital gains

Capital gains tax, 122-130, 138-140, 152-153
  and comprehensive income tax, 271-272
  effect of, on savings, 96-97, 124-125
  and equity, 122, 139, 140
  and indexing, 139, 154-157
  and inflation, 130-131, 272, 313
  in Japan, 324
  and 1978/1981 tax cut, 135-138, 149-150, 154-155, 157-159
Capital recovery, 47, 48, 52-61, 63, 64, 66-67, 70-71
  first-year, and flat rate tax, 300-301, 303, 321-322
Carter, Jimmy, 8, 158, 268, 286, 343
Cash-flow accounting, 284
Cash flow tax, 78, 243-246
Chafee, John H., 114
Chapoton, John, 311
Children, shift of property income to, 294-295
Citizenship as jurisdictional principle, 325, 327, 330-332, 336
Commissions and policymaking, 10
Compensation tax, 299, 303-304, 305, 319-321
Comprehensive Income Tax, 243-246, 265-295
Comprehensive, Integrated Personal and Corporate Consumption Tax, 106, 108-109, 110, 112-114, 119-120
Conable, Barber, 351
Congress, 8-10
  and capital gains tax, 123-124
  and consumption tax, 119
  and personal income tax, 275
  tax policymaking in, 89, 317, 323, 324, 353-357
Connally, John, 3, 5, 7
Conservative lock on Presidency, 9
Consumption
  as part of accretion, 281
  definition of, 246-251
  as tax base, 31, 78, 109, 113, 229-251, 274-275, 282-285
Consumption tax, 23, 29-32, 95, 168, 172, 176, 234-243, 255-256, 261
  and capital gains, 30, 140, 313
  and comprehensive income tax, 282-285
  and equity, 234-235, 258-260, 262
  and neutrality, 99-100, 106, 107-108
  political prospects for, 119-120, 254-255, 262

transition to, 107-109, 110, 114, 262
See also "Location of consumption" tax system
Cost of capital, 60, 65, 69-70, 79-82
Cost of earnings, 248-249, 268
Cost of funds, 79, 87
Cranston, Alan, 158
Credibility and new taxes, 4
Credits, income tax, 19-20. *See also* Foreign tax credit; Investment Tax Credit
Credit method of value added tax computation, 202-203, 210n72
Cultural factors and saving, 116-117
Cyclical deficits, 37-38

Deadweight losses, 99, 122, 284
Debt creation, 253-256
Debt financing, 79, 163, 168-169, 179, 180-181
Decay rates, 83, 84, 85
Declining balance method, 63-64
Deductibility of losses, 125, 126
Deduction method for consumption tax, 238, 242-243
Deductions, 16, 268-269, 280
  for charitable contributions, 290-291, 320
  for consumer interest, 290
  and consumption tax, 31
  elimination of, 325, 333
  and flat rate tax, 303, 304, 312
  for interest, 300, 302, 303
  itemized, repeal of, 290-291
  for medical expenses, 312, 321. *See also* Health care expenditures
  for mortgage interest, 280
  for rent, 280
  for state taxes, 290, 320-321
Deferral
  of tax on accrued gains, 138, 280-281
  of tax on foreign subsidiaries, 326
Democratic Party, 6, 8-9
Depreciation rules, 27-29, 47-61, 63, 85, 216, 345-346. *See also* Accelerated Cost Recovery System; Expensing
Designated capital cost recovery periods, 61
Discount rate, 74
Domestic International Sales Corporations, 329, 333, 336, 343
Double taxation
  of capital gains, 135
  of corporate income, 325, 332, 342

Earned income, 274, 275, 284-285
Economic depreciation
  administrative problems of, 58-59
  determination of, 72-76
  tax neutrality of, 51-52, 55-57, 76n2, 78, 178-179
Economic efficiency
  and consumption tax, 235-236
  as goal of a tax system, 14, 19, 230-231, 257
  and taxation of international income, 338-339, 357
  See also Capital allocation, efficiency of
Economic growth, 13, 23-24, 93-94
  and budget deficits, 35-43
  and depreciation rules, 48, 59-61
  and neutrality, 60-61, 109-110
  and tax incentives, 77
  and value added tax, 196, 201
Economic Recovery Tax Act of 1981 (ERTA), Accelerated Cost Recovery System of, 49, 61, 62, 64, 69-70
  capital recovery provisions of, 180
  cost of capital under, 69-70, 79-82
  depreciation schedules of, 85, 345-346
  and expensing, 168
  and indexing, 287
  IRA provisions of, 114-115
  and investment, 26-29, 77, 102, 103-106
  and marginal tax rates, 15, 103-104, 124
  and marginal tax rates on capital gains, 124, 136-138, 150
  and net interest exclusion, 294
Economic Report of the President, 1982, 103
Educational expenses and tax base, 191-192
Efficiency, business, 220
Elections, 1982, 9-10
Employee benefits, tax treatment of, 291-293
Employee expenses, deductibility of, 312
Employer-paid health insurance premiums, 291-293, 321
Employment and taxation, 14, 150-153, 158-159
Energy tax, 324
Entitlements spending, 181
Equity financing, 79
Equity principle, 47, 49, 71, 105, 172, 286-287

364 Index

and consumption tax, 106-107,
  233-235, 258-260, 262
and corporate income tax, 172
and international income, 339-340
and value added tax, 194-195, 219
See also Capital gains tax, Fairness,
  Horizontal equity, Progressivity,
  Regressivity, Vertical equity
Eurobond financing, 347, 349,
  350-351, 352
Exchange rates, 198
Excise taxes, 175-176
  on employee benefits, 291, 295n1
  in Japan, 332
  and present revenue needs, 226
Exclusions
  of foreign earned income, 330, 339,
    343n6
  of long-term capital gains, 123-124
  of net interest, 294
Exemptions
  from consumption tax, 255
  from value added tax, 203-204, 216
Expenditure tax. *See* Consumption tax
Expensing
  and Accelerated Cost Recovery
    System, 62-69, 103-104
  and corporate income tax, 162,
    168-169, 178-179, 180
  requirements of, 70-71, 90
  and tax neutrality, 47, 54-55, 57,
    78
Export volume, 220-221, 225,
  318-319. *See also* Balance of
  payments

Fairness, 13, 15-16, 19, 230
  of capital gains tax, 159
  of consumption tax, 32, 261-262
  and economic efficiency, 257
  See also Equity principle
Fair Tax Act of 1983, 313
Farm debt, 253-254
Federalist Papers, The, 5
Feldstein, Martin, 129, 316
Financial investments and consumption tax, 78
Flat rate tax, 16, 297-324, 336-338
  and capital gains, 139-140, 156-157,
    302
  and consumption tax, 31, 226, 235,
    241-242
  international aspects of, 304-305,
    318-319, 336-338, 355
  redistributive effects of, 273,
    311-312, 317-318, 320
  See also Budget deficits; Political
    dynamics; Tax base; Transition
Food, taxation of, 191, 194

Foreign capital, 24, 118, 339, 340.
  See also International movement
  of capital
Foreign earned income exclusion, 330,
  339, 343n6
Foreign individuals and corporations,
  327-342 *passim*
Foreign residents, 330-342 *passim*
Foreign-source income, 331-342
  passim
Foreign subsidiaries, 329-330, 333,
  336, 342
Foreign tax credit, 172, 326, 328,
  329, 332, 333, 342
France, 24, 25-26, 331-332
Friedman, Milton, 314
Fringe benefits, taxation of, 293, 318,
  321
Fullerton, Don, 216

General Agreement on Tarriffs and
  Trade, 327, 336-338, 342-343
General equilibrium incidence analysis,
  164-167
General Theory (Keynes), 257
Gephardt, Richard, 156, 286, 313
Gibbons, Sam, 114, 351
Goode, Richard, 278-295 *passim*
Government sector spending,
  101-102, 199, 286, 315-316
Greenspan Commission, 10
Guideline lives, 61, 62

Hall, Robert E., 80, 82, 216
  Flat rate tax proposal, 273, 274,
    311-324 *passim*, 336-338
Hansen, Clifford, 149, 158
Harberger, Arnold, 171, 177, 178,
  179, 180, 198
Hart, Gary, 261
Hatsopoulos, George, 77
Hayek, Frederick, 314
Health care expenditures, 191, 194,
  207n35. *See also* Deductions, for
  medical expenses; Employer-paid
  health insurance premiums
Hobbes, Thomas, 258, 283
Holmes, Oliver Wendell, 257
Horizontal equity, 13, 14, 49, 122,
  139, 140, 234-235. *See also*
  Equity principle
Horst, Thomas, 353, 355, 357, 359
Housing, owner-occupied
  as investment, 136, 141-144
  in tax base, 191, 269, 279-280
Hufbauer, Gary, 346, 353, 355, 357,
  359
Hybrid tax, 319

Income
 definition of, 231-232, 246-251
 real and nominal, 313
 as tax base, 229-251
Income-based value added tax, 207n30
Income tax, corporate, 13, 17-19, 86, 161-168
 and consumption tax, 241-242
 elimination of, 104, 168-169, 171-172, 177-179, 180-181
 incidence of, 164-168, 198, 209n60
 integration of, with personal income tax, 108, 169, 313
 and rate of investment, 27-29, 172-176
 replacement of, by business tax, 299, 309
 replacement of, by value added tax, 185, 198, 209n61, 216, 223
 See also Comprehensive Income Tax
Income tax, individual, 27, 265-269, 297
 and consumption tax, 32
 and economic growth, 13, 266
 equity in, 14-16
 integration of, with corporate income tax, 108, 169
 public opinion of, 190-191, 267-268
 replacement of, by compensation tax, 299, 309
 See also Comprehensive Income Tax
Indexed government programs, 38
Indexed security investment plan, 156
Indexing, 62-63, 287-288, 313
 of capital gains, 139, 156-157
India, expenditure tax in, 274
Individual Retirement Accounts (IRAs)
 and consumption tax, 107-108, 120, 261
 and rate of savings, 26, 105, 114-115
Individual tax base, 229-231, 241-242
Inflation, 86-87, 267-268
 and bracket creep. *See* Bracket creep
 and budget, 36-39, 42
 and capital gains tax, 130-131, 272
 and capital recovery, 300-301
 and effective tax rate, 27-29, 32, 102, 130-131
 and indexing. *See* Indexing
 and measurement of income, 238-240, 313
 and value added tax, 20, 296-297, 221
Inflation premium, 239-240

Integration, 95, 108, 112-113, 169, 313
Integration of international capital, 166
Interest deductions, 300, 302, 303
Interest income, 301-302, 346-353
Interest elasticity, 100-101
Interest rates
 and budget deficits, 39-43, 104
 and corporate investment, 77-78
 and flat rate tax, 309
 and foreign investment, 118
 inflation premium in, 239-240
International capital markets, U.S. access to, 346, 350-353
International movement of capital, 165-166, 177, 339. *See also* Foreign capital
International trade, 304-305, 318-319, 344-345. *See also* Border tax adjustments
International transactions, 325-359
 and flat rate tax, 304-305, 318-319, 322, 336-338, 355
 and tax policymaking, 353-355
 and value added tax, 319, 327, 337-338
Internal Revenue Service, 61
Inventory appreciation, 80, 88n3
Inventory obsolescence, 88n2
Inverse elasticity principle, 357-358
Investment, 4, 15-16, 18, 59, 94-95
 and budget deficits, 39-40
 and capital gains tax, 101, 125
 and consumption tax, 255
 and ERTA, 28-29, 77-78
 and marginal tax rates, 103-104
 rates of national, 23-25, 33
 and rate of return, 100-101
 and technological progress, 97-98
 See also Savings
Investment allocation, 129-130, 136, 141-144, 241. *See also* Neutrality
Investment Tax Credit, 62, 64-69, 83-85, 90-91, 162-163
 and Accelerated Cost Recovery System, 48, 64
 elimination of, 168, 178-179, 180
 and expensing, 71
 and foreign-source income, 328
 and inflation, 28
 and TEFRA, 85

Japan, 344-345
 and foreign-source income, 331-332
 rate of national investment in, 24, 25-26, 254
 taxation of capital in, 324
Jorgenson, D.W., 80, 82

Kaldor, Nicholas, 236-237
Keogh plan, 26-27, 261
Keynes, John Maynard
   General Theory, 257
Keynesian policies, 14, 25-26

Laffer Curve, 135, 138
Legislation, tax, 23, 150, 156. *See also* Congress; Economic Recovery Tax Act of 1981; Fair Tax Act of 1983; Tax Equity and Fiscal Responsibility Act of 1982; Tax Reform Act of 1969; Tax Revenue Act of 1978; Ullman bill (Tax Restructuring Act of 1980)
Lifetime wealth, 234-235
Loans, 30
"Location of consumption" tax system, 326, 327, 333-342 *passim*, 346, 358-359
"Location of production" tax system, 326, 333-342 *passim*
Lock-in effects, 126-130, 136, 140, 145n12, 145n16, 272
Long, Russell B., 316
Long-term capital gains, 123, 127, 136-138, 155, 271
Long-term debt
Loopholes, tax, 13, 14, 162, 226, 257, 314-315, 323. *See also* Tax shelters

Managerial era in politics, 6
Market price of capital, 60, 74-76
Marriage penalty, 299
McClung, Nelson, 144
McLure, Charles, 214-227 *passim*
McKinley, William, 5
Measurement, 236-240, 279-280, 313
Mill, John Stuart, 283
Minarik, Joseph, 129, 131
Minimum tax, 123-124, 127
Model Income Tax Treaty, 349, 352
Monetary policy, 40-43
Money supply, 41
Moore, Henson, 114
Municipal bond interest exemption, 278

Netherlands Antilles finance companies, 346-353
Net interest exclusion, 294
Neumark Commission, 185
Neutrality
   and consumption tax, 99-100, 106, 107-108
   and corporate income tax, 162-164, 171-172
   among diverse capital types, 55-59, 89-90, 168-169, 266-267, 270-271
   and economic depreciation, 51-52, 55-57, 76n2, 78, 178-179
   and economic growth, 60-61, 109-110
   as goal of tax policy, 47, 48-49, 60, 89, 95, 99-100, 103, 104, 149-150
   and particularization, 51
   between savings and consumption, 52-55, 59, 78, 106
   and true expensing, 70, 78, 103, 104, 162, 168-169
   and value added tax, 189-190, 193-194, 195-196, 201, 219-220
   See also Accelerated Cost Recovery System; Investment allocation
Nixon, Richard, 61-62, 185-186
Nondeductible contributions to IRAs, 115, 120

Open capital market, incidence in, 165-168
Optimal saving rate, 96-97
Optimal tax theory, 233

Particularization, 51, 58, 61, 75, 76
Parties, political, 7
Pechman, Joseph A., 270
Passive income, 327, 330, 340
Payroll taxes, 230, 299
   neutrality of, 195, 208n49, 208n51
Percentage depletion, 328-329, 330
Personal allowances, 306, 309
Personal Income Taxation (Simon), 278
Petroleum industry, 173-176
"Placed in service" constraints, 70
Political dynamics, 4-5, 298, 317
   of capital income tax, 89
   of comprehensive income tax, 275-276, 286, 288
   of consumption tax, 119-120, 254-255, 262
   of deductions, 16
   of flat rate tax, 314-316
   of integration, 112-113
   of repeal of corporate income tax, 172
   of value added tax, 19, 216-217, 222-225
Political climate, change in, 4-11
Possessions corporations, 33, 329, 336, 355-357

Power to Tax, The (Brennan and Buchanan), 315
Pratt, Stanley, 159
Prepayment method, 140, 238, 240, 242-243
Presidency, 8-9
Press, 18, 21
Prices
  effect of value added tax imposition on, 196-197, 209n55-56
  performance of, 39
  stability of, 14, 42
Productivity, 4, 17-18, 36-37, 119
  and capital formation, 23-24, 117
  cultural factors and, 116-117
  in U.S. and Japan, 344-345
Progressivity, 14-16, 188-189, 206n16, 266
  in capital gains tax, 122, 126
  in comprehensive income tax, 269-270
  in consumption tax, 30-31, 107, 119, 258-260
  effect of, on high risk investment, 126
  and tax base, 191
  in value added tax, 194-195, 201, 219
  See also Vertical equity
Proportional taxes on capital gains, 125, 126
Prorating of capital gains, 139, 146n22, 150
Public opinion on taxes, 190-191, 218, 267-268
Puerto Rico, 329, 355-357

Qualified accounts method, 140, 242-243, 246nG-H

Rabushka, Alvin, flat rate tax proposal of, 273, 274, 311-324 *passim*, 336-339
Rate of return, 25, 27, 173
  and consumption tax, 275
  and corporate income tax, 164-165
  effect of, on savings and investment, 96, 100-101, 124-125, 145n2, 235
  and 1981 tax rate reduction, 105
Rayburn, Sam, 10
Reagan, Ronald, 26-29, 257
Realism in depreciation rules, 47-48
Recession, 37-38
Reconstruction Finance Corporation, 181
Redistribution of income, 14. *See also* Flat rate tax

Refundable deductions, 90
Regressivity
  of capital gains tax, 122
  of consumption tax, 106-107
  of corporate taxes, 17
  of value added tax, 19-20, 185, 201, 224
  See also Equity principle; Flat rate tax; Progressivity; Vertical equity
Repair and maintenance policies, 73
Republican Party, 6, 8-9
Reserve ratio test, 61-62
Residence as jurisdictional principle, 325, 327, 328-330
Residence-based tax system, 326, 333-335, 338-340, 342
Ricardo, David, 117
Risk-taking and capital gains taxes, 125-126
Rollovers, tax-deferred treatment of, 150

Safe-harbor leasing provisions, 69, 70, 78, 90
Safe-haven rules, 329
Sales growth and capital formation, 150-153
Sales tax, 187, 196, 199-200, 219, 225
Salvage value, 73
Savings, 4, 15-16, 39, 94-97, 100-102, 253
  and comprehensive income tax, 270-273
  and consumption tax, 31-32, 95, 109, 256, 259, 260, 274, 275
  cultural factors and rate of, 116-117
  and ERTA, 26-27, 29, 103-106
  low rate of U.S., 23-26, 94-96, 254
  and neutrality, 48, 52-55, 59, 78, 106
  and productivity, 117, 119
  and rate of return, 96, 100-101, 124-125, 145n2, 235, 259
  and tax base, 232-236, 242-243
  and tax rates, 26-27, 105
  See also Investment, Neutrality
Scholz, John Karl, 270
Schumpeter, Joseph, 116
Simons, Henry, 282
  Personal Income Taxation, 278
Simplicity, 95, 122, 140, 223, 286-288
Skill base, 345
Slemrod, Joel, 129
Social security, 10, 208n51
Source as jurisdictional principle, 325, 327-328

Sri Lanka, expenditure tax in, 274
Standard-of-living income/consumption concept, 251
State taxation and value added tax, 199-200, 222, 223-224
Steiger, William, 158
Straight-line method, 63, 64
Structural deficits, 37, 38, 39, 40-43
Substantially closed economy, 164-168
Sun Belt, political power of, 7-8, 9-10
Supply-side economics, 14
Surtax, 226, 262-264

Tax base, 95, 287, 297
  broadening of, 113, 261, 262, 289-295
  comprehensive, 322
  of comprehensive income tax, 268-269, 283, 289-295
  of consumption tax, 31, 78, 109, 113. *See also* Consumption, as tax base
  definition of, 246
  of flat rate tax, 298, 300, 304, 306
  of value added tax, 191-193
Tax burdens, distribution of
  with consumption tax, 31, 254, 261-262
  with flat rate tax, 273, 311-312, 317-318, 320
  with value added tax, 195, 208n46, 215
Tax Equity and Fiscal Responsibility Act of 1982, 28, 91, 276, 287
  and Accelerated Cost Recovery System, 48, 49, 64-65, 69-70, 78, 103-104
  and cost of capital, 69-70, 79-82
  and expensing, 168
  and petroleum industry, 175
  and savings and investment, 102, 103-106
  and witholding tax, 351-352
Tax evasion, 298
Tax expenditures and consumption taxes, 284
Tax incentives, 77, 324
Tax losses, 303
Tax rates
  and capital gains, 122, 123-124, 135-136, 138-140, 141-144
  in comprehensive income tax, 269-271, 289
  differential, and value added tax, 193-194, 195, 208n50, 215
  and ERTA, 124

effect of Accelerated Cost Recovery System on, 103-105
  in flat rate tax, 300, 306-308
  and inflation, 27-29, 32, 102, 130-131
  and international location of business, 305
  and investment, 127
  reduction of, as tax reform, 261, 262, 287, 289, 309-310, 355
  and Tax Revenue Act of 1978, 123-124, 135-136
  See also Progressivity; Regressivity
Tax reform, approaches to, 13, 20-21, 256, 261-262, 325
Tax Reform Act of 1969, 62
Tax Revenue Act of 1978
  effect of, on capital gains tax, 123-124, 149, 157-159
  and taxation of unemployment benefits, 293-294
Tax revenues, 298
  from capital gains tax, 139
  from flat rate tax, 301, 303-304, 309, 315-316, 318
  and 1978/1981 reductions, 16, 135-138
  and taxation of international income, 340-342, 359
  from value added tax, 203, 215-216, 221-222, 226
Tax shelters, 14, 32, 259, 281, 282, 298. *See also* Loopholes, tax
Tax straddles, 139, 155
Tax treaties, 327-328, 347, 349-353
Tax unit organization, 122
Technical analysis and cultural factors, 116-117
Technological progress and rate of investment, 97-98, 117
10-5-3 proposal, 61, 62
Territorial income taxes. *See* "Location of production" tax system
Texas International Airlines, 349-350
Time series model, 136-138, 141-144
Tokyo Round, 343
Transition
  to comprehensive income tax, 275
  to consumption tax, 107-109, 110, 114, 262
  to flat rate tax, 309, 318, 320
  to value added tax, 200-201
Trigger for tax changes, 262-264
Ture, Norman, 77, 78, 89, 90
Turnover tax, 187, 200, 203

Ullman, Al, 186, 222, 316
Ullman bill (Tax Restructuring Act of 1980), 191, 215, 218, 223

Uncertainty and investment decisions, 256
Unemployment benefits, 37-38, 293-294
Uniformity in treatment of income, 311-314, 357-359
United Kingdom, 24, 25-26, 256, 331-332
"Useful life" concept, 61, 62, 63, 73-74

Value, conventional and true, 281-282, 284
Value added tax, 13, 16, 19-20, 185-227, 332
  and consumption tax, 30
  and flat rate tax, 274
  and international trade, 319, 327, 337-338
  political history of, 7, 185-186, 218-219
  and sales tax, 187, 196, 199-200, 219, 225
Venture capital, 126, 135, 149, 158-159
Vertical equity, 13, 14-16
  and capital gains tax, 122, 139, 140
  and consumption tax, 234-235, 258-260
  and corporate income tax, 49
  and value added tax, 189-190
  See also Equity principle; Progressivity; Regressivity
Vertical integration, 187, 203

Wage levels, 166-168, 259
Walker, Charls, 3, 7
Washington Post, 8
West Germany
  national investment in, 24, 25-26, 254
  value added tax in, 199-200, 332
Wetzler, James, 159
Windfall gains and losses, 89-90, 107, 175, 260
Witholding tax on interest, 327, 347-353
World economy, U.S. place in, 353-354

Yitzhaki, Shlomo, 129

Zero rating and value added tax, 203-204, 216

About the Editors

Charls E. Walker is voluntary chairman of the American Council for Capital Formation, the ACCF: Center for Policy Research, and Charls E. Walker Associates, Inc., a Washington-based consulting firm. Dr. Walker served as Deputy Secretary of the Treasury in the first Nixon Administration, and, from 1959-1961, he was assistant and principal economic adviser to Secretary of the Treasury Robert B. Anderson. Dr. Walker holds the Alexander Hamilton Award, the highest honor granted by the Treasury Department.

Mark A. Bloomfield is executive director of the American Council for Capital Formation and President of the ACCF: Center for Policy Research. He served as secretary of President Reagan's Transition Task Force on Tax Policy. Mr. Bloomfield is a member of the Carlton Tax Group and the advisory board of the *Washington Tax Review*.

The American Council for Capital Formation: Center for Policy Research was established in 1977 to educate the public, especially opinion leaders, on the role of capital formation in the economy. To achieve its objectives, the ACCF: Center for Policy Research sponsors original research on the determinants of economic growth, underwrites conferences and seminars on tax and budget policies, and assists in the development of alternative economic policies conducive to economic growth. In January 1983, the Center sponsored a conference on tax policy; *New Directions in Federal Tax Policy for the 1980s* is a collection of the papers prepared for the symposium.

The American Council for Capital Formation: Center for Policy Research is a nonprofit, tax exempt organization under section 501 (c) (3) of the Internal Revenue Code. Its programs are supported by grants from corporations, trade associations, foundations, and individuals; such grants are tax deductible as charitable contributions. The Center for Policy Research is the education and research affiliate of the American Council for Capital Formation (ACCF), a Washington-based organization that advocates pro-capital formation policies to the Executive Branch, the Legislative Branch, the press and opinion leaders.

List of Participants

Henry Aaron is professor of economics at the University of Maryland and a senior fellow at The Brookings Institution. Professor Aaron served as Assistant Secretary for Planning and Evaluation at the U.S. Department of Health, Education, and Welfare from 1977 to 1978. He was senior staff economist, Council of Economic Advisers, from 1966 to 1967.

William D. Andrews is professor of law at Harvard University. He was special assistant to the Deputy Assistant Secretary of Defense for Military Assistance Programs from 1957 to 1958. Professor Andrews was reporter for Subchapter C in the American Law Institute Federal Income Tax Project from 1974 to 1982.

Alan J. Auerbach is associate professor of economics at Harvard University, currently on leave at Yale University as visiting professor of economics. He serves as associate editor of the *Journal of Public Economics* and on the board of directors of The Taxpayer's Committee.

Gerald E. Auten is associate professor of economics at Bowling Green State University. During 1978 and 1979, Dr. Auten was a Brookings economic policy fellow in the Office of Tax Analysis of the U.S. Treasury Department. He recently completed a study on capital gains taxation for the U.S. Treasury Department.

J. Gregory Ballentine is Deputy Assistant Secretary (Tax Analysis) at the U.S. Treasury Department. Dr. Ballentine is on leave as professor of economics from the University of Florida. He was coeditor of the *Public Finance Quarterly*. He has also served as a consultant to the General Accounting Office.

Stuart M. Berkson is an associate in the Chicago law firm of McDermott, Will & Emery. Mr. Berkson is a member of the Chicago Bar Association. He has served as an editor of the *Harvard Law Review*.

David L. Boren (Democrat, Oklahoma) is a member of the Senate Finance Committee, a ranking member of its Subcommittee on Estate and Gift Taxation, and serves on its Subcommittees on Social Security and Income Maintenance Programs and on International Trade. Senator Boren is also a member of the Senate Committees on Agriculture, Nutrition, and Forestry, and on Small Business. The Governor of Oklahoma from 1975 to 1978, Senator Boren is serving his first term in the U.S. Senate.

Michael J. Boskin is professor of economics at Stanford University. He is also director of the National Bureau of Economic Research Social Insurance Program. Professor Boskin was a member of several of President Reagan's economic policy task forces. He is a member of the board of directors of the American Council for Capital Formation and the ACCF: Center for Policy Research.

David F. Bradford is professor of economics and public affairs at the Woodrow Wilson School of Public and International Affairs at Princeton University. Professor Bradford served as Deputy Assistant Secretary (Tax Analysis) at the U.S. Treasury Department from 1975 to 1976. He was awarded the U.S. Treasury Department exceptional service award in 1976.

William E. Brock is the U.S. Trade Representative. Ambassador Brock is the President's chief trade adviser and international trade negotiator, and he chairs the Cabinet-level Trade Policy Committee. He served in the U.S. Senate from 1971 to 1977, representing the state of Tennessee and in the U.S. House of Representatives from 1963 to 1971.

James M. Buchanan is university distinguished professor and general director of the Center for the Study of Public Choice at George Mason University. He serves on the Advisory Council of the Institute of Economic Affairs (London).

Horace W. Busby is president of Horace W. Busby and Associates and the author of "The Busby Papers." Mr. Busby served as both special assistant to the President and secretary to the Cabinet in the Johnson Administration.

Edwin S. Cohen is a partner in the Washington law firm of Covington & Burling. He is also Joseph M. Hartfield Professor of Law at the University of Virginia. He was Under Secretary of the Treasury from 1972 to 1973 and Assistant Secretary of the Treasury (Tax Policy) at the U.S. Treasury Department from 1969 to 1972.

Barber B. Conable, Jr. (Republican, New York) is the senior Republican member of the House Committee on Ways and Means. Representative Conable also serves on the Congressional Joint Committee on Taxation and the Ethics Committee. He recently served on President Reagan's task force on private sector initiatives and the National Commission on Social Security Reform. Representative Conable is serving his tenth term in Congress representing the thirtieth Congressional district of New York.

John B. Connally is a senior partner in the Houston law firm of Vinson & Elkins. Governor Connally served as Secretary of the Treasury from 1971 to 1972. He served three terms as Governor of Texas from 1963 to 1969. Governor Connally also was Secretary of the Navy in 1961. Governor Connally is a member of the board of directors of the American Council for Capital Formation.

Alan Cranston (Democrat, California) is Senate Democratic Whip. He serves on the Senate Banking Committee, is the ranking Democratic member on its Subcommittees on Financial Institutions and Rural Housing and serves on its Subcommittees on Economic Policy and on Housing and Urban Affairs. Senator Cranston serves on the Senate Foreign Relations Committee and is the ranking Democratic member on the Senate Veterans' Affairs Committee. He is also a member of the Democratic Steering Committee and the Democratic Policy Committee. Senator Cranston is serving his third term representing the state of California.

Robert F. Dee is chairman of the board of SmithKline Beckman Corporation. Mr. Dee is a director of the National Association of Manufacturers, The World Affairs Council, and The Heritage Foundation. He is a member of The Business Council, The Conference Board, and the Finance Committee of the Joint Council on Economic Education.

Martin Feldstein is chairman of the Council of Economic Advisers. He is on leave from Harvard University, where he has been a professor of economics since 1969. Prior to his appointment to the Council of Economic Advisers, Dr. Feldstein was president of the National Bureau of Economic Research.

William Fellner is Sterling Professor of Economics Emeritus, Yale University, and a resident scholar at the American Enterprise Institute. He is also project director and contributor to the AEI annual publication, *Contemporary Economic Problems*. Dr. Fellner was a member of the Council of Economic Advisers from 1973 to 1975. He has also served as a consultant to the Congressional Budget Office.

Richard Goode is a guest scholar at The Brookings Institution and a professorial lecturer at the School of Advanced International Studies at The Johns Hopkins University. Dr. Goode served as an economist at the U.S. Treasury Department from 1945 to 1947 and as a fiscal analyst in the U.S. Bureau of the Budget from 1941 to 1945.

Robert E. Hall is professor of economics and senior fellow at the Hoover Institution, Stanford University. Professor Hall is also director of the Research Program on Economic Fluctuations of the National Bureau of Economic Research.

Arnold C. Harberger is Gustavus F. and Ann M. Swift Distinguished Service Professor of Economics at the University of Chicago. Professor Harberger served as a consultant to the Council of Economic Advisers from 1969 to 1974 and to the U.S. Treasury Department since 1962.

George N. Hatsopoulos is president and chairman of the board of Thermo Electron Corporation. He is a senior lecturer at the Massachusetts Institute of Technology and a member of the Board of the Federal Reserve Bank of Boston. Dr. Hatsopoulos is a member of the American Business Conference.

Frederic W. Hickman is a partner in the Chicago law firm of Hopkins & Sutter. Mr. Hickman served as Assistant Secretary (Tax Policy) at the U.S. Treasury Department from 1972 to 1975. He is the former chairman of the American Bar Association Committee on Depreciation and a member of the American Enterprise Institute Technical Advisory Committee on Taxation.

Thomas Horst is the managing partner of Taxecon Associates. From 1977 to 1981, he was director of the International Tax Staff at the U.S. Treasury Department. Dr. Horst has taught economics at Harvard University and the Fletcher School of Tufts University.

Gary Hufbauer is a senior fellow at the Institute for International Economics and a partner in the Washington law firm of Chapman, Duff and Paul. Mr. Hufbauer served as Deputy Assistant Secretary (International Trade and Investment Policy) at the U.S. Treasury Department from 1977 to 1980. From 1980 to 1982 he was the deputy director of the International Law Institute at Georgetown University.

C. E. Hussey II is a partner in the Chicago law firm of McDermott, Will & Emery. Mr. Hussey is a member of the Chicago and American Bar Associations. He also is a member of The Chicago Committee and director of various domestic and foreign corporations.

James R. Jones (Democrat, Oklahoma) is chairman of the House Committee on the Budget. He is a senior member of the House Ways and Means Committee and its Subcommittee on Trade. He is also a member of the House Democratic Steering and Policy Committee. Representative Jones is serving his sixth term in Congress representing the first Congressional district of Oklahoma.

Charles E. McLure, Jr. is a senior fellow at the Hoover Institution, Stanford University. Prior to joining the Hoover Institution in 1981, Dr. McLure was vice president of the National Bureau of Economic Research. He served as senior economist on the staff of the Council of Economic Advisers and as a consultant to the U.S. Treasury and Labor Departments.

Tor Meloe is chief economist for Texaco, Inc. Dr. Meloe has held positions as an economist in the U.S. Departments of Commerce and Labor. Dr. Meloe is a member of the Forecasters' Club of New York and the Economics Advisory Council of the Graduate School of Business at Columbia University.

W. Henson Moore (Republican, Louisiana) is a member of the House Ways and Means Committee, serves on its Subcommittees on Select Revenue Measures, on Health, and on Public Assistance and Unemployment Compensation. Representative Moore is also a member of the Republican Policy Committee and the Republican Executive Committee. He is serving his fifth term in Congress representing the sixth Congressional district of Louisiana.

Daniel Patrick Moynihan (Democrat, New York) is a member of the Senate Finance Committee and serves on its Subcommittees on Economic Growth, Employment and Revenue Sharing, on International Trade, and on Social Security and Income Maintenance. He also serves on the Senate Budget Committee and the Environment and Public Works Committee. He is vice-chairman of the Select Committee on Intelligence. He is a member of the Democratic Policy Committee and served on the National Commission on Social Security Reform. Senator Moynihan has served in the Cabinet or the subcabinet of Presidents Kennedy, Johnson, Nixon, and Ford. First elected in 1976, he is serving his second term in the Senate representing the state of New York.

John S. Nolan is a member of the Washington law firm of Miller & Chevalier, Chartered. He served as Deputy Assistant Secretary (Tax Policy) at the U.S. Treasury Department from 1969 to 1971. Mr. Nolan was awarded the Alexander Hamilton Award, the Treasury Department's highest honor, in 1971. He served on the advisory group to the Commissioner of Internal Revenue from 1967 to 1968 and as chairman of the American Bar Association's Section on Taxation during 1981 and 1982. Mr. Nolan is a member of the board of directors of the American Council for Capital Formation.

Bob Packwood (Republican, Oregon) is chairman of the Senate Committee on Commerce, Science and Transporation. He is a member of the Senate Finance Committee, chairs its Subcommittee on Taxation and Debt Management, and is a member of its Subcommittees on Health and on Savings, Pensions and Investment Policy. Senator Packwood is also a member of the Senate Small Business Commitee. He is serving his third term representing the state of Oregon.

Joseph A. Pechman is director of economic studies at The Brookings Institution. In the past few years, he has served as editor and contributor to the annual series, *Setting National Priorities*, published by The Brookings Institution. From 1954 to 1956, Dr. Pechman was an economist with the Council of Economic Advisers and from 1956 to 1960 he was associated with the Committee for Economic Development.

Perry D. Quick is vice president for economic and social policy at the Roosevelt Center for American Policy Studies. Dr. Quick has served as a senior staff economist at the Federal Reserve and at the Council of Economic Advisers. He has also been a financial and economic consultant to several federal agencies. Prior to joining the Roosevelt Center, Dr. Quick helped Senator Gary Hart develop his "Economic Strategy for the 80s."

Alvin Rabushka is a senior fellow at the Hoover Institution, Stanford University. He served on President Reagan's tax policy task force. He is also co-editor of the Hoover Institution's project, *The United States in the 1980s*. Along with Professor Robert E. Hall, of Stanford, he has developed a proposal for a flat rate tax system.

Steven R. Resnick is senior investment strategist at Merrill Lynch, Pierce, Fenner & Smith, Inc. Prior to joining Merrill Lynch he was an insurance analyst and financial consultant.

Donald V. Seibert is chairman of the board and chief executive officer of J.C. Penney Company, Inc. He is presently serving as chairman of the American Retail Federation. Mr. Seibert is a director of the New York Chamber of Commerce and Industry, the Committee for Economic Development, and the National Retail Merchants Association. He is a member of the President's National Productivity Advisory Committee, The Business Roundtable, The Business Council, and The Economic Club of New York.

James M. Shannon (Democrat, Massachusetts) is a member of the House Ways and Means Committee and its Subcommittees on Social Security and on Health. Representative Shannon is serving his third term representing the fifth Congressional district of Massachusetts.

Lawrence H. Summers is the domestic policy economist at the Council of Economic Advisers. He is currently on leave as professor of economics at Harvard University. Dr. Summers is a member of the Brookings Panel on Economic Activity and is a research associate of the National Bureau of Economic Research. He has served as a consultant to the U.S. Departments of Labor and Treasury.

Emil M. Sunley is director of tax analysis in the National Affairs Office of Deloitte Haskins & Sells. From 1977 to 1981, he served as Deputy Assistant Secretary (Tax Policy) at the U.S. Treasury Department. He has also served as associate director of the Office of Tax Analysis, U.S. Treasury. Mr. Sunley was a senior fellow in economic studies at The Brookings Institution from 1975 to 1977.

List of Participants

Steven D. Symms (Republican, Idaho) is a member of the Senate Finance Committee and chairs its Subcommittee on Estate and Gift Taxation. He is also a member of the Senate Committees on the Budget and on the Environment and Public Works and is a member of the Congressional Joint Economic Committee. Senator Symms, who earlier served four terms in the House of Representatives, is serving his first term in the Senate representing the state of Idaho.

Norman B. Ture is an economic consultant and chairman of the board of the Institute for Research on the Economics of Taxation (IRET). He served as Under Secretary of the Treasury for Tax and Economic Affairs from 1981 to 1982. He has also served on task forces on taxation for Presidents Kennedy and Nixon. Dr. Ture is a member of the board of directors of the American Council for Capital Formation and the ACCF: Center for Policy Research.

Al Ullman is president of Ullman Consultants, Inc. He served as chairman of the House Ways and Means Committee from 1975 to 1981 and as chairman of the House Committee on the Budget from 1974 to 1975. Mr. Ullman was a member of the U.S. House of Representatives from 1957 to 1981, representing the second Congressional district of Oregon. He is a member of the board of directors of the American Council for Capital Formation and the ACCF: Center for Policy Research.

Paul A. Volcker is chairman of the Board of Governors of the Federal Reserve System. He was designated chairman on August 6, 1979. As chairman of the Board of Governors, Mr. Volcker also serves as chairman of the Federal Open Market Committee, the Federal Reserve System's principal monetary policymaking body. Mr. Volcker was president and chief executive officer of the Federal Reserve Bank of New York from 1975 to 1979. He also served as Under Secretary of the Treasury for Monetary Affairs from 1969 to 1974.

James W. Wetzler is deputy chief of staff of the Congressional Joint Committee on Taxation. Prior to his present position, Dr. Wetzler was chief economist at the Congressional Joint Committee on Taxation.

John G. Wilkins is director of the Office of Tax Analysis, the economics branch of the U.S. Treasury Department's tax policy staff. Prior to his current position, Mr. Wilkins was in charge of the Treasury Department's revenue estimating operations.

Ed Zschau (Republican, California) is a member of the House Foreign Affairs Committee and of the Executive Committee of the House Committee on Committees. He is also chairman of the Republican task force on high technology. Representative Zschau was founder and chairman of System Industries. He is a former member of the board of directors of the American Council for Capital Formation and the American Electronics Association. He is serving his first term representing the twelfth Congressional district of California.